EMPLOYMENT LAW

IN A NUTSHELL

THIRD EDITION

By

ROBERT N. COVINGTON

Professor of Law

Vanderbilt University

WEST®

A Thomson Reuters business

Mat # 40760215

Nutshell Series, In a Nutshell and the Nutshell Logo are trademarks registered in the U.S. Patent and Trademark Office.

COPYRIGHT © 1995 WEST PUBLISHING CO.
© West, a Thomson business, 2002
© 2009 Thomson Reuters

    610 Opperman Drive
    St. Paul, MN 55123
    1–800–313–9378

Printed in the United States of America

ISBN: 978–0–314–19540–1

PREFACE

When Kurt Decker and I launched the first edition of this short book in 1995, we identified our audience as including three groups:

- Readers with little, if any, prior knowledge of employment law, seeking an overview of the field.
- Students in employment law courses in undergraduate, business or law schools who are looking for an introduction and study aid.
- More sophisticated readers whose usual subject matter interests lie outside employment law, but who find themselves working with a problem in the area and want a springboard from which to do further research.

For the benefit of that third group, the book includes a relatively larger number of case citations than usual for a Nutshell, though I have attempted to be more restrained in this edition when addressing issues on which there are many state-to-state variations.

We have been aided by many over the course of three editions. Patrick Paul, now of the Arizona bar, Erich Rhynhart, now corporate counsel in Boston, Mary Ann Miranda, and others who have provided truly valuable research assistance. The librarians at the Alyne Queener Massey Law Library have been helpful as always. That there are not far more errors in spelling and the like is largely due to the efforts of an extraordinary secretary, Janis Stewart.

This edition contains relatively less new material than the second, because the pace of change since 2002 has been somewhat slower than in earlier decades. In part this reflects the realities of politics at the federal level, both the deregulatory stance of the White House and the number of years of divided government in which the ability of the Congress to override vetoes was limited. In part, however, it is probably a reflection of the fact that many earlier changes were of the sort that take a while to digest. The "at will" doctrine changes, for example, were hard to categorize for a time; now most of the states are refining those changes in an incremental way. The language of many of the discrimination statutes was general in nature, and the courts have had some difficulty in discerning just what the Congress had in mind about some matters. Thus we get amendments, such as the Lilly Ledbetter Fair Pay Act, intended to overturn the interpretation the Supreme Court gave some of that general language.

I continue very much to miss the continued collaboration of Kurt Decker, whose untimely death during preparation of the second edition brought that to a close. I hope he would approve of the changes in organization and content in this edition.

Robert N. Covington

Nashville
May 2009

*

This Book Is Dedicated To
Paula and Hilary
Proverbs 31:29

And To The Memory Of
Kurt H. Decker
1946–2000

*

OUTLINE

X

Page

OUTLINE

TABLE OF CASES

References are to Pages

TABLE OF CASES

TABLE OF CASES

TABLE OF CASES

TABLE OF CASES

TABLE OF CASES

TABLE OF CASES

TABLE OF CASES

TABLE OF CASES

EMPLOYMENT LAW

IN A NUTSHELL

THIRD EDITION

*

CHAPTER 1

THE DEVELOPING LAW
OF EMPLOYMENT

A. INTRODUCTION

The financial crisis of 2008 has reminded us once again of the central role employment plays in our economy. High unemployment rates mean lower consumer spending and saving, both essential to a healthy nation. Employee and employer ought to want each other to prosper, it would seem. After all, if the employer's business does well, employees can often expect to share in that good fortune. Employers who find themselves with a disgruntled and unhappy workforce soon realize that productivity is down, and labor costs up. In practice, however, conflict between employee and employer is a constant feature of our economic system and social structure. A prospering business firm is likely to want to expand; to get the capital it needs for that, the firm may well try to trim its labor costs, perhaps by lay-offs accompanied by the use of temporary workers working at a lower rate of pay. In the current era, a large number of American employers continue to move production, and thus good jobs, to other countries where wage rates are much lower than in the United States. "Employment law" is the body of legal rules that seek to deal with this

1

ongoing set of conflicts. Statutes and court decisions reflect a constantly shifting balance between employee and employer making employment law one of the most dynamic—and also most political—of all legal areas. Historically, employment law has been a maze of statutes, common-law doctrines, contract-established rules, and administrative agency findings. Sometimes the decision makers act in harmony, sometimes not. Even within a narrow area, such as defamation or the right of privacy, legislators, courts, administrative agencies and arbitrators often do not all see things the same way.

The employment relationship is more than an income source. In our society, self-worth, dignity, satisfaction, and accomplishment are achieved largely by one's employment responsibilities, performance, and rewards. Because of this, employees regularly seek to have a voice in determining their wages, hours, and terms and conditions of employment. Employees have often achieved these objectives through unionization and collective bargaining. In recent decades, however, the unionized portion of the workforce has been shrinking, and there has been a growing emphasis on legal protection of individual employee rights.

American law regulates the employment relationship in various ways. The most common methods involve individual employment contracts, the application of constitutional, tort, and contract doctrines, and a range of statutory regulation on such issues as the right to organize and negotiate collective bargaining agreements, protection from discrimination, wages and hours, pensions and benefits, and health and safety.

To introduce "employment law" to readers in a way that will give some notion of its breadth and complexity, this Chapter first discusses the nature of the employment relationship and then provides a brief overview of the principal types of legal regulation.

B. THE EMPLOYMENT RELATIONSHIP

Employee and employer relationships are among the basic building blocks of our economic and societal structure, affecting most people over the greater part of their lives. Employment is the means by which society's goods and services are provided and through which individuals obtain part of their identity, including the ability or inability to successfully meet life's daily economic responsibilities of food, shelter, and clothing.

Employers often invest heavily in their employees. They spend considerable money selecting and training them. Rational employers are eager to retain good employees so they can capitalize on their skills and knowledge to operate a profitable business. Through employment's economic rewards, individuals obtain assets for fulfilling current and future gratifications ranging from basic living requirement needs to nonessential luxuries.

Employment also serves social purposes. The workplace is a place to meet people, converse, and form friendships. Likewise, the type of employment undertaken may confer social status on employee and family.

Employment loss can be a considerable hardship having disastrous consequences. Fifty years ago, one observer wrote:

> We have become a nation of employees. We are dependent upon others for our means of livelihood, and most of our people have become completely dependent upon wages. If they lose their jobs they lose every resource, except for the relief supplied by the various forms of social security. Such dependence of the mass of the people upon others for all of their income is something new in the world. *For our generation, the substance of life is in another man's hands.*

F. TANNENBAUM, A PHILOSOPHY OF LABOR 9 (1951) (emphasis in original).

Outside marriage, probably no other relationship shapes our daily affairs so completely. Two centuries ago, Blackstone described the three great relations in private life as:

1. That of master and servant, which is founded in convenience, whereby a man is directed to call in the assistance of others, where his own skill and labor will not be sufficient to answer the cares incumbent upon him;

2. That of husband and wife; and

3. That of parent and child.

W. BLACKSTONE, COMMENTARIES 410 (1765).

Not only is employment a fundamental societal relationship, it is also a complex one, made so in part by pervasive government regulation. One reason for this extensive regulation is that employment subjects one person to another's control to a substantial extent. Consider, for example, an employee's privacy right. When entering into an employment relationship, little employee choice exists in providing sensitive, often detailed information about one's personal life. This information may reveal the employee's innermost beliefs, interests, and actions. If not handled sensitively, these disclosures may result in incorrect evaluations that affect an employee's hiring, promotions, standing, and reputation at and outside the workplace.

C. LEGAL REGIMES GOVERNING THE EMPLOYMENT RELATIONSHIP

"Employment law" is a complex of federal and state controls. For the most part, employment law is essentially "new" law, even though much of it is based on principles that have been evolving for centuries. It is far from being stable and unchanging. Solutions to employment law issues are no more static than is employment itself. The pressure of economic, political, social, and personal interests on the ever-developing pattern of employment law cannot be over-emphasized. See Nelles, *Commonwealth v. Hunt*, 32 COLUM. L. REV. 1128 (1932). Historically, the law's treatment of the employment relationship has combined status-based rules, rules that fix the obligations of employer and employee to another as a matter of law, with rights and duties the parties have set for themselves by contract.

Four principal types of legal rules are regularly applied in cases arising out of the employment relationship. One is a large body of statutes. These often authorize action of various sorts by administrative agencies, whose rules, regulations and decisions form a second body of employment law. Third are common law tort and contract doctrines developed by the courts, sometimes incorporated into legislative mandates or modified by them. Finally, there are state and federal constitutional provisions that define employee and employer rights, principally those of government employees.

In addition, much of the control over employment matters is found in sources many would not think of as law at all: individual employment contracts and collective (union-management) bargaining agreements. These often provide for interpretation and enforcement by private arbitrators, and only limited judicial review is available. This private ordering can be of immense importance, particularly since the Supreme Court decided to permit arbitrators to make binding decisions on statutory rights. *14 Penn Plaza LLC v. Pyett,* 129 S.Ct. 1456 (2009); *Gilmer v. Interstate/Johnson Lane Corp.,* 500 U.S. 20 (1991).

1. Statutory Regulation

The scope of statutory regulation of the employment relationship has increased markedly throughout the past century. (See section E of this chapter.) A work of this size can only hint at the number of technical problems involved in these varied laws, particularly those at the state level.

One can divide statutory regulation into two broad categories: (1) statutes governing collective action by employees; and (2) statutes imposing rights and duties on employers and employees without regard to whether a union is involved. The two principal federal statutes that address collective rights are the National Labor Relations Act [29 U.S.C.A. §§ 151–169], as amended by the Labor Management Relations Act, applicable to most private employments; and the Railway Labor Act [45 U.S.C.A. §§ 161–163], which regulates the railroad and airline industries' union-management relations. A third statute, the Labor–Management Reporting and Disclosures Act [19 U.S.C.A. §§ 401–531] regulates certain internal union affairs, and a variety of less frequently used statutes address matters of kickbacks and apprenticeship. Finally, there are statutes regulating collective rights of federal civilian employees. See, e.g., 39 U.S.C.A. §§ 1001–1011 (Postal Reorganization Act).

State statutes governing collective rights in private employment have only a limited scope of application, because the NLRA and LMRA coverage is broad and state regulation of union-management relations is often preempted by the federal statutes. For example, in *Lingle v. Norge Division of Magic Chef, Inc.*, 486 U.S. 399 (1988), the court held that an employee's state tort remedy for wrongful discharge is preempted by federal law if, but only if, the employee's claim requires a collective bargaining agreement's interpretation. Many states do, however, have "little Wagner Acts," and most have enacted statutes governing state and local government employee collective bargaining rights. See, e.g., Pa. Stat. Ann. tit. 43, §§ 211.1–211.11 (private sector collective bargaining rights); Pa. Stat. Ann. tit. 43, §§ 1101.101–1101.2301 (public sector collective bargaining rights).

This Nutshell's chapters are primarily devoted to statutes, common law doctrines, and constitutional provisions that regulate the employment relationship directly, without regard to the presence or absence of a union. Individual rights and collective rights are inevitably bound up together, though, and thus there are occasional references to collective bargaining and one chapter that discusses a few fundamental rights of individuals guaranteed by NLRA and LMRA. In general, this Nutshell is organized by the employee interest affected, rather than by chronology or by statute. For example, regulation of child worker safety is treated in the chapter on physical safety rather than in the chapter on wage and hour legislation, even though the principal federal child labor statute is a section of the Fair Labor Standards Act (FLSA) [29 U.S.C.A.

§§ 201–219], which is primarily a regulation of minimum wages and maximum hours.

2. Common Law

a. *Tort*

(i) Overview: "Intentional" and "Negligent" Wrongdoing

The body of doctrines lumped together under the heading of "tort law" is so varied that there is no very helpful definition of the term "tort." One common thread linking these legal principles together is that each person possesses interests that the law should protect. When one of these interests is intruded upon, the intruder is held liable to pay damages to the person whose interest has been harmed, unless the intrusion was justified or excusable. The simplest example is the tort of battery, i.e., an offensive touching of one person by another. The interest protected is a basic one: the integrity of one's body. Intrusions that can lead to liability take many forms: blows struck by a fist, gunshots, poisoning, and many others. Possible justifications include self-defense.

Battery is an example of what are known as "intentional" torts, i.e., harms that flow from intended actions that carry the risk of the damage that has been done. Other frequently litigated intentional torts are assault, trespass, defamation, false arrest, intentional infliction of emotional distress, interference with contractual relationships, and invasion of privacy. All of these torts may occur in the employment context. The usual burden of proof that must be met to recover for one of these torts is that the alleged wrongdoer acted intentionally in a way that directly caused the type of harm for which tort law awards damages. The precise nature of the burden varies, however, according to which type of tort is involved.

The other principal type of tort is negligence. The concept of negligence was well summarized by the Tennessee Supreme Court in *Lindsey v. Miami Development Corp.*, 689 S.W.2d 856 (Tenn.1985):

> It is axiomatic that three elements are necessary for the existence of a cause of action for negligence: (1) a duty of care owed by the defendant to the plaintiff; (2) a breach of that duty by the defendant; and (3) an injury to the plaintiff which was proximately caused by the defendant's breach of a duty.

At one time, negligence actions by employees against employers for physical injury were fairly common, but most of those claims are now pursued under workers' compensation statutes.

(ii) Illustrations of Work–Related Torts

Later chapters of this book will spell out doctrines about specific torts in greater detail. Here, we provide a few brief illustrations to give a general sense of the variety of interests protected.

Invasion of Privacy.—An employee's reasonable expectation of privacy at work is limited, but at times employer "snooping" goes too far.

For example, in *Sowards v. Norbar, Inc.*, 78 Ohio App.3d 545, 605 N.E.2d 468 (Ohio App.1992), a trucking company violated an over-the-road driver's right to privacy by searching the employee's motel room without prior consent for a missing permit book. The employee used it as a private refuge during a layover, he possessed the key, no business was transacted there, and the public was not invited. This tort action is discussed further in Chapter 3.

Defamation.—The law of defamation involves harm to a person's character, fame, or reputation by false and malicious statements.

In *Bolton v. Minnesota Department of Human Services*, 527 N.W.2d 149 (Minn.Ct.App.1995), an employer, after terminating an employee, accompanied the employee to his office, stayed while he packed his personal belongings in full view of other employees, and escorted him out of the main door. The employer actions were sufficient to support a defamation claim because "defamatory language" may include gestures or actions conveying a statement that an employee was dishonest and was not to be trusted. This tort action is discussed further in Chapter 3.

False Imprisonment.—False imprisonment consists of the unwarranted detention of a person for any length of time where the person is deprived of personal liberty to leave and is aware that he or she cannot leave.

A jury imposed liability on a security-services owner who joined a security guard in detaining and interrogating a grocery clerk suspected of theft from a market. *Buckel v. Rodrigues,* 133 Or.App. 399, 891 P.2d 16 (Or.App.1995). In the room, the guard positioned himself between the clerk and the only door and told her that he would decide whether she would go to jail that evening. The clerk was allowed to receive only one telephone call. The owner acquiesced in the clerk's restraint and continued the interrogation started by the guard over a three-hour period.

Intentional Infliction of Emotional Distress.—A plaintiff worker seeking recovery for the intentional infliction of emotional distress must prove: First, the employer's conduct was extreme and outrageous. Second, the employer acted with intent to cause emotional distress or with substantial certainty that distress would result from its conduct. Third, severe emotional distress resulted from the employer's conduct. An Oregon case illustrates contrasting judicial notions of "outrageousness." An employer ordered a worker to drop his pants and expose himself to fellow workers. The trial court dismissed the mental distress claim, the appellate court reversed, and the state supreme court reinstated the trial court's judgment. *Madani v. Kendall Ford,* 312 Or. 198, 205–06, 818 P.2d 930, 934 (1991).

Fraudulent Misrepresentation.—This tort occurs when an employer fraudulently makes a misrepresentation of fact, opinion, intention, or law for the purpose of inducing the employee to act upon it.

For example, an employer promised to purchase an employee's home in Illinois if he accepted a position in California. When the employee attempted to enforce the promise after assuming the California position, he was terminated. Recovery was permitted because the employee could not properly evaluate his alternatives based on the employer's fraudulent representation. *Palmer v. Beverly Enterprises*, 823 F.2d 1105 (7th Cir.1987).

Intentional Interference with Contractual Relations.—For a claimant to succeed, she must show: (a) a prospective or existing contractual relationship exists between the claimant and a third party; (b) the defendant acted for the purpose of causing the specific type of harm to the claimant; (c) the defendant's act was unprivileged; and (d) actual harm resulted to the claimant. See RESTATEMENT (SECOND) OF TORTS §§ 766–767 (1979).

To be liable, the defendant must act with knowledge of the prospective or existing contract and for the purpose of interfering with it. This tort requires only an intention to interfere with claimant's prospective or existing contractual relationship and not malevolent employer spite.

For example, a former employer intentionally interfered with a former employee's contract by sending three letters to a competitor that had hired the employee. *Collincini v. Honeywell*, 411 Pa.Super. 166, 601 A.2d 292 (Pa.Super.1991). The former employer's letters threatened legal action if the competitor did not instruct the employee to stop soliciting contract renewals from the former employer's customers. These letters induced the new employer to terminate the employee even though the employee had not signed a noncompetition agreement protecting proprietary information and trade secrets with the former employer. In finding for the former employee, the court found that the former employer never contacted the employee before sending the letters to the new employer and that the alleged proprietary information and trade secrets were unclassified information available on the open market.

Malicious Prosecution.—To prevail in a malicious prosecution action, one must plead and prove that: (a) the adversary initiated the underlying action; (b) the proceeding did not terminate in the adversary's favor; (c) the adversary lacked probable cause to bring the action; (d) the adversary brought the action with "malice;" and (e) the proceeding caused a compensable harm. *Chauncey v. Niems,* 182 Cal. App.3d 967, 973, 227 Cal.Rptr. 718, 722 (Cal.App. 1986). Either an employee or an employer may use this theory of recovery, but malicious prosecution is a disfavored action and courts construe the requirements strictly. If a claimant succeeds, substantial damages can be recovered.

In *Wainauskis v. Howard Johnson Co.,* 339 Pa.Super. 266, 488 A.2d 1117 (Pa.Super.1985), the employer's security manager accused the employee of theft of deposits, even though she had not worked on the date one of the thefts had occurred. She had also previously informed the manager of her discovery of a deposit bag hidden in a linen closet. The security manager did not inquire into her employment history, personal background, or interview other persons who were in possession of the safe's combination prior to terminating her and instituting criminal proceedings. The criminal proceedings against the employee were dismissed. A $100,000 judgment against an employer was sustained for malicious prosecution.

Abuse of Process.—Related to malicious prosecution is an action for abuse of process, another theory of recovery that may be used by either employee or employer. Historically, litigants have found abuse of process easier to establish than malicious prosecution because "it evolved as a 'catch-all' category to cover improper uses of the judicial machinery that did not fit within the earlier established, but narrowly circumscribed, action of malicious prosecution." See *Twyford v. Twyford,* 63 Cal.App.3d 916, 923, 134 Cal.Rptr. 145, 148 (Cal. App.1976). To recover, one must plead two essential elements: (a) that the defendant entertained an ulterior motive in using the process; and (b) that a willful act was committed in the use of the process not proper in the regular conduct of the proceeding. The process must be used for some purpose other than that for which the process was designed. See *Friedman v. Stadum*, 171 Cal.App.3d 775, 779, 217 Cal.Rptr. 585, 588 (Cal.App.1985).

For example, a corporation was found liable for the acts of its employees in planting evidence and falsely accusing a former employee of a crime. *But-*

ler v. Flo–Ron Vending Co., 383 Pa.Super. 633, 557 A.2d 730 (Pa.Super.1989). Those employees, who were sons of the firm's owner, planted a ring in the former employee's truck and falsely reported to the police that he had stolen property from the employer.

Blacklisting.—"Blacklisting" involves preventing or attempting to prevent one from obtaining employment. It shares characteristics both with defamation and with intentional interference with contractual relations. Indeed, the author regards it not as a separate wrong itself, but simply a species of one of those other torts. It is not an easy case for a plaintiff to make out. For one thing, to sustain a blacklist action, the employee must establish malice. Also, courts have recognized that in order to encourage exchanges of information it is necessary to afford employers a fair amount of latitude in what they say to one another. A qualified privilege exists for employers to discuss matters of mutual concern.

Giving a "bad" reference for a former employee is a classic illustration. If a former employee proves his former employer gave out false information about him, he has laid a foundation for recovery. But if the former employer's challenged statements consist of evaluations of an employee's overall "suitability," is that "information" or just "opinion?" *Austin v. Torrington Co.*, 810 F.2d 416 (4th Cir.1987), cert. denied, 484 U.S. 977 (1987).

b. Contracts

It is typical to define employment as "a relationship in which one person performs services for another under a contract of hire." To determine whether there is a contract of hire, one seeks to discover whether the three "elements" of a contract are present. These elements are offer, acceptance, and consideration. The usual "offer" is found in the employer's express or implied promise to pay for services. "Acceptance" may be either the act of working or a promise to perform. "Consideration" is provided by wages and by the benefit flowing from the services.

Binding employer commitments may be made in a variety of ways, ranging from detailed formal negotiations to a hasty "You're hired." Employment handbooks and policies may also create these binding employer commitments. An employer may also seek to protect its competitive interests by having the employee enter into restrictive covenants. These covenants may: (a) curtail the employee's future employment possibilities; (b) restrict the employee's use and disclosure of the employer's information, inventions, and trade secrets; and (c) prevent a former or current employee from dealing with the employer's customers or clients. In the United States, one major contract doctrine has been that the employment agreement is presumed to be "terminable at will," i.e., that the employment relationship can be ended by either the employee or the employer at any time, for any or no reason, with or without notice. Each of these is discussed further in Chapter 2.

A number of judges and scholars have argued that it is an appropriate function of the legal system to assist the "weaker party." In the employment context this usually means assisting the employee. These observations raise additional questions, particularly:

1. In what ways should employment be treated as a special kind of contract, different from the typical "bargain and sale" sort of contract? and

2. How far should a court go in providing such "assistance"?

The contract doctrines peculiarly important to employment law include:

- rules to determine when a contract has been formed

- doctrines that flesh out incomplete contracts by supplying default terms

- doctrines that determine when to use a particular remedy, such as damages or an injunction.

3. Constitutional Provisions

The federal constitution allocates power among the branches of the federal government and between state and federal governments. It also limits the powers of both federal and state governments to act, by forbidding unreasonable searches and seizures, for example. U.S. Const. amend. IV. It does not regulate the relations of citizens to one another with the exception of the Thirteenth Amendment abolishing slavery. Id. amend. XIII. Even though slavery was a private relationship, this provision may fairly be thought of as a check on the governmental enforcement of property rights in human beings.

The direct impact of the federal constitution on the employment relation is generally limited to employers and employees in the public sector unless some form of state action is involved.

Neither the federal nor a state or local government can use its power as an employer to take away an employee's constitutional rights. Constitutional rights are particularly important to government employee privacy and with respect to rights of free speech and association. In *O'Connor v. Ortega*, 480 U.S. 709 (1987), the unauthorized search of a public employee's desk was found unconstitutional. In *Rutan v. Republican Party*, 497 U.S. 62 (1990), the Court held that basing hiring, promotions, transfers, and recalls on support for a political party impermissibly infringed on first amendment rights of low-level public employees unless party affiliation was an appropriate requirement for effective performance of the position involved. The equal protection guarantee of the Fourteenth Amendment has been important as a ban on invidious racial discrimination by government employers.

The indirect impact of federal constitutional concepts on the private sector has been substantial. Notions of due process, for example, have been reshaped by labor arbitrators into implied limitations on private sector employer power to discipline. In *Cameron Iron Works, Inc.*, 25 Lab. Arb. (BNA) (1955) (Boles, Arb.), a due process/just cause requirement was considered to be implied in a collective bargaining agreement for employee terminations.

Doctrines of preemption developed under the supremacy clause have had important effects in several areas. It is, however, important to remember that the specific employee and employer rights in the private sector will be grounded in some source other than the United States Constitution.

The same is generally true of state constitutions, but not always. A few provisions of state constitutions directly regulate private relationships. One example that has attracted recent attention is a provision in the California constitution concerning privacy. In *Luck v. Southern Pac. Transp. Co.*, 218 Cal.App.3d 1, 267 Cal.Rptr. 618 (Cal.App.1990), cert. denied, 498 U.S. 939 (1990), a private employer's random alcohol and drug testing program was held to violate privacy rights guaranteed by that Constitution where the employee's job duties did not relate to a safety risk that the employer sought to protect.

D. IDENTIFYING RESPONSIBLE PARTIES: WHO ARE "EMPLOYEES" AND "EMPLOYERS"?

Many of the protections afforded workers by the statutes and common law doctrines discussed apply only if those workers are "employees;" the duties are owed only by "employers." The typical statute defines those terms, but these definitions are often couched in general terms, providing courts and administering agencies with little concrete guidance about how to work out the details. A large number of other relationships can resemble employment, such as partnerships in which one partner does most of the decision-making while others do most of the work. To complicate matters further, it is not uncommon for more than one person or entity to be the "employer" of a given individual at the same time. The following sections explore some of these problems, concentrating on two of the most important concepts used in determining which duties are owed a worker by whom: independent contractorship and the concept of joint employment (with special emphasis on the borrowed servant doctrine).

1. Independent Contractors

When the bedroom needs to be repainted, or the attic cleaned out, or the leaves raked, one faces a choice: Do it in person, or hire someone else to do it, or at least to help with the task. Deciding to get help is not the end of the choosing, however. One may get Eddie, the teenager next door, to come help with the leaf-raking at $5 an hour for seven or eight hours, so that the job takes only a day instead of a whole weekend. Or the homeowner may call Gerry's Lawn Care Service to do the whole job for a flat fee of $85; Gerry's sends Susan Small out to do the job. Finally, the homeowner may hire Ike Evans, the local jack-of-all-trades, who stops by to say he needs a little work and would love to clean up the lawn for, say, $50.

In this illustration, Eddie is almost certainly an employee of the homeowner, while Gerry's Lawn Care Service is very likely an independent contractor as to the homeowner, and an employer of Susan. The job to be done remains the same in each case, but the protections afforded the worker performing the task and the homeowner's level of responsibility are likely to be significantly different.

Suppose the leaf raker fails to pay close enough attention, trips over the rake and suffers a back sprain. If the leaf raker is Eddie, odds are that his medical bills are his own responsibility and that he is entitled to no compensation for disability; in most states he would be excluded from workers' compensation coverage as a "casual employee" or the homeowner would be excluded from the definition of "employer." Susan, on the other hand, is much more likely to be covered by workers' compensation, social security, and a host of other statutes as an employee of Gerry's Lawn Care Service. The homeowner pays for these protections indirectly, as part of the fee of the lawn care service. But what of Ike Evans? Is he more like Eddie, an employee of the homeowner who may or may not be excluded from workers' compensation depending on what the particular statute has to say about "domestic" and "casual" workers, or is he an independent contractor so that there is no possibility of workers' compensation coverage at all? The question can be a vexing one with respect to social security, since if Ike is an employee, the cash payment by the homeowner may involve enough dollars to trigger the obligation to pay social security taxes, and possibly withhold sums for income tax. If Ike is an independent contractor, on the other hand, the responsibility for dealing with social security taxes, and thus for seeing to it that he is eligible for disability benefits, is his alone.

Determining whether a given relationship is employment or independent contractorship is often challenging. A number of approaches have been used in recent years to determine the proper characterization. The dominant test is one that began to be used in cases in which tort victims sought application of the doctrine of respondeat superior, so that they could seek damages from a wealthier "master" (employer) rather than an impoverished "servant" (employee). This test emphasizes the extent of control exercised over the performance of work, and is often called the "control test." An often-quoted formulation of this test appears in section 220 of the RESTATEMENT (SECOND) OF AGENCY:

In determining whether one acting for another is a servant or an independent contractor, the following matters of fact, among others, are considered:

(a) the extent of control which, by the agreement, the master may exercise over the details of the work;

(b) whether or not the one employed is engaged in a distinct occupation or business;

(c) the kind of occupation, with reference to whether, in the locality, the work is usually done under the direction of the employer or by a specialist without supervision;

(d) the skill required in the particular occupation;

(e) whether the employer or the workman supplies the instrumentalities, tools, and the place of work for the person doing the work;

(f) the length of time for which the person is employed;

(g) the method of payment, whether by the time or by the job;

(h) whether or not the work is a part of the regular business of the employer;

(i) whether or not the parties believe they are creating the relation of master and servant; and

(j) whether the principal is or is not in business.

RESTATEMENT (SECOND) OF AGENCY § 220 (Copyright 1958 by the American Law Institute. Reproduced with permission. All rights reserved.). When the Congress (or a state legislature) does not define "employee" with specificity, it is this sort of multi-factor approach that is generally used to determine the nature of the relationship. *Nationwide Mutual Ins. Co. v. Darden*, 503 U.S. 318 (1992); *Community for Creative Non–Violence v. Reid*, 490 U.S. 730 (1989).

Courts differ about how heavily to weigh particular factors. The most "traditional" approach is one that attaches primary importance to the first factor listed in the RESTATEMENT: control over the details of performance, emphasizing the right to give particularized orders or directions. See, e.g., *Jones v. Atteberry*, 77 Ill.App.3d 463, 33 Ill.Dec. 28, 396 N.E.2d 104 (Ill.App.1979). During recent decades there has been a constant trend toward paying greater attention to the "economic realities" of the situation, trying to determine whether the alleged employer has the power over the person claimed to be its employee that the worker ought not to be regarded as a truly independent economic entity. In a famous case interpreting the National Labor Relations Act (NLRA), for example, the Supreme Court approved a National Labor Relations Board (NLRB) opinion holding that street corner news vendors were "employees" of a newspaper publishing company because they lacked any real power to direct their own business destinies and thus needed the opportunity to band together as a group to bargain with the publisher. *NLRB v. Hearst Publications*, 322 U.S. 111 (1944). Three years later, the Congress overruled that decision, requiring the Board to return to a test that would pay greater attention to traditional control factors. Despite that, the move away from a mechanical application of the control test toward a flexible one that gives great weight to economic realities has continued. See, e.g., *United States v. Silk*, 331 U.S. 704 (1947).

One approach that has won a number of adherents in the workers' compensation arena is the "relative nature of the work test" advocated by Professor Larson in a treatise on workers' compensation law. As the name implies, this test emphasizes factors (b) and (h) in the RESTATEMENT version of the control test, asking whether the worker has in fact become an integral part of the alleged employer's business.

2. Joint Employment

Lending employees is an old and familiar practice. In rural areas of nineteenth-century America, many a farmer whose crops had not yet ripened would go with hired hands (and family, as well) to help a neighbor harvest ahead of rain and rot, often expecting the favor to be returned. This neighborly lending continues every day in all sorts of businesses, but most of the lending and borrowing of employees in the closing decade of the twentieth century is done on a commercial basis.

A modern-day large farmer in need of harvest help is less likely to turn to nearby friends, and more likely to call in a labor contractor who will bring a migrant harvest crew to the scene. In countless factories and offices, the "leasing" of workers is a common practice. The typical arrangement is for the business in need of help to pay the labor contractor, and for the labor contractor to pay the individual worker. Who, then, is the "employer"? The answer is likely to depend on why the question is being asked. If the purpose is to determine liability for paying the minimum wage, the answer will often be that both the labor contractor and the firm using the contractor's services are liable. Under the Fair Labor Standards Act (FLSA), the definition of "employer" includes "any person acting directly or indirectly in the interest of an employer" and this expansive language has led courts to find simultaneous liability in a number of situations. See, e.g., *Hodgson v. Griffin and Brand of McAllen, Inc.*, 471 F.2d 235 (5th Cir.1973).

The answer to "Who is the employer?" does not always answer the question "Who is responsible?" The Family and Medical Leave Act (FMLA) covers only those employers that employ 50 or more workers during 20 or more weeks of the year. 29 U.S.C.A. §§ 2631–2636. The regulations state that "an employer who jointly employs 15 workers from a leasing or temporary help agency and 40 permanent workers is covered" by the act. 29 C.F.R. § 825.106(d). In the next paragraph, however, the regulation states that "only the primary employer is responsible for * * * providing leave, maintenance of health benefits, and job restoration. * * * For employees of * * * leasing agencies, for example, the placement agency would most commonly be the primary employer." Sometimes, however, a leasing employer may control the worker in question so completely and for such a long term that the leasing agency ceases to be an "employer" under the Act. *Astrowsky v. First Portland Mortgage Corporation*, 887 F.Supp. 332 (D.Me.1995).

The FMLA, like many other statutes, protects only workers who have been "employees" of the "employer" for a specified period of time. The time spent as an employee in a joint employment context "counts" toward that time. *Miller v. Defiance Metal Products*, 989 F.Supp. 945 (N.D.Ohio 1997).

In addition to the language and purpose of the particular statute and regulations involved, the court or agency confronted with this may turn to the principles developed under the general title of "borrowed servant." The need for this doctrine would arise at common law when an injured person sought to recover damages for injuries caused by a worker's negligence and the court needed to determine which one(s) of various possible defendants to treat as the employer for the purposes of respondeat superior. The testing questions used to determine whether a worker is a borrowed employee can be very detailed. The Fifth Circuit has developed a nine question framework for this analysis:

(1) Who has control over the employee and the work he is performing, beyond mere suggestion of details or cooperation?

(2) Whose work is being performed?

(3) Was there an agreement, understanding, or meeting of the minds between the original and the borrowing employer?

(4) Did the employee acquiesce in the new work situation?

(5) Did the original employer terminate his relationship with the employee?

(6) Who furnished tools and place for performance?

(7) Was the new employment over a considerable length of time?

(8) Who had the right to discharge the employee?

(9) Who had the obligation to pay the employee?

Ruiz v. Shell Oil Co., 413 F.2d 310 (5th Cir.1969).

Particularly troublesome fact patterns in which to decide whether a duty owed to an employee is shared by two or more entities are parent-subsidiary cases, and those involving sister companies, firms controlled by the same entrepreneurial group. In the case of parent and subsidiary, special attention must be paid to the extent of the subsidiary's real independence in setting its own labor and employment policies. If the subsidiary can make only the most trivial decisions about hiring, termination, and working conditions, there is a good chance that the parent will be responsible for compliance with many of the statutes. How elusive a proper resolution of these questions can be is well illustrated by *Local 217, Hotel & Restaurant Employees v. MHM, Inc.*, 976 F.2d 805 (2d Cir.1992), a case involving responsibility for giving notice of the closing of a hotel. The majority of the court of appeals panel decided that the subsidiary constituted the "employer" for the purposes of the Workers' Adjustment and Retraining Notification Act (WARN), but both the trial court and a concurring judge at the appellate level concluded that the parent was the WARN employer, although recognizing that for National Labor Relations Act purposes the employer was the subsidiary.

Only one of the federal statutes discussed in other Chapters has attempted to resolve the joint employer problem presented by sister companies in a detailed fashion, the Fair Labor Standards Act (FLSA). The "enterprise" coverage language in the FLSA permits treatment of commonly controlled establishments as a single employing unit. 29 U.S.C.A. § 203(r), (s). Under other statutes, the courts and administering agencies have applied similar notions under an "alter ego" concept. This approach has frequently been used by the National Labor Relations Board (NLRB), which looks at such indicia as "substantially identical management, business purpose, operation, equipment, customers and supervision." *Advance Electric*, 268 NLRB 1001 (1984); see also *South Prairie Construction Co. v. Local No. 627, Operating Engineers*, 425 U.S. 800 (1976) (determination of single employer status not determinative of single bargaining unit issue).

3. Successorship

When a new owner purchases an entire going business and continues its operations, or when two firms merge to form a new enterprise, civil liability for the violations of the rights of employees of the "old" business will usually attach to the new entity. In such cases, it is sensible to think of the "new" entity as an "alter ego" of the old. Extending liability to employees to the surviving business is consistent with the way the law treats other creditors, as the Supreme Court noted in *John Wiley & Sons, Inc. v. Livingston*, 376 U.S. 543 (1964). There are, of course, limits to this concept. Some statutes, such as WARN, contain provisions that fix liability for violations on certain dates solely on one entity or the other. See 29 U.S.C.A. § 2101(b)(1). If the "new" entity is not the result of merger or the purchase of a going business, it is not likely to be considered an "alter ego" of the old, and if so liability will depend upon a number of factors. As important as any is awareness on the part of a purchaser of the possibility that past violations may have occurred. See, e.g., *Golden State Bottling Co. v. NLRB*, 414 U.S. 168 (1973). Courts are also likely to consider the extent of business continuity and whether the former employer still survives as a possible defendant. See, e.g., *Wheeler v. Snyder Buick, Inc.*, 794 F.2d 1228 (7th Cir.1986) (Title VII).

4.   Undocumented Aliens

For what purposes are alien workers to be treated as employees? Clearly those who are legally admitted are to be treated essentially as any other employee. Persons who enter the country and take jobs without proper documents, however, pose problems. The Supreme Court has held that they are not entitled to certain back pay remedies under the

National Labor Relations Act. Most states grant undocumented workers at least some protection under their workers compensation acts, but not all states do so, and it is possible that the wording of a few such statutes will entitle such persons to medical benefits, but not income replacement benefits. The problem is an ongoing one, and awaits reform of immigration law at the federal level.

E. THE PACE OF CHANGE

Any reader of this Nutshell needs to be aware that labor and employment law is constantly changing in content and emphasis. The volume of labor and employment law has increased markedly during the past six decades, so that those who practice it often remark about how little of what they do in 2009 would have been done by lawyers a generation earlier. The pace of change is not constant, of course. Since the 1980s, the United States has often experienced "divided government," with one major party controlling the White House, another the Congress. This tends to slow the rate at which new programs can be formulated. Moreover, certain types of change can be accomplished without formal changes in the legal structure. If, for example, one does not favor aggressive regulation of wage payment, it is possible to reduce the significance of the FLSA simply by hiring fewer investigators for the Wage and Hour Division of the Department of Labor. Overall, however, the period since the end of the Second World War has been an active one in employment law. A brief listing of major developments makes this clear:

1947: Taft–Hartley Act, amending the National Labor Relations Act in major ways, expanding the size of the National Labor Relations Board and creating an independent General Counsel's office

1949: Fair Labor Standards Act amendments, changing rules and coverage

1959: The first common law abusive termination case decided, in California

1959: Landrum–Griffin Act, regulating labor organization practices and amending the National Labor Relations Act significantly; substantial enforcement powers given to the Secretary of Labor

1961: Fair Labor Standards Act amendments, vastly increasing the scope of coverage of the federal wage and hour law

1963: Equal Pay Act, outlawing gender discrimination in pay for equal work

1964: Title VII of the Civil Rights Act makes employment discrimination unlawful under federal law; the Equal Employment Opportunity Commission created

1965: Service Contract Act, regulating wages of federal service contractors

1967: Age Discrimination in Employment Act, protecting persons 40 and above from discrimination

1969: Federal Mine Safety and Health Act, revamping a major federal inspection program

1970: Occupational Safety and Health Act, the first broad federal workplace safety law; standard-setting and enforcement powers given to the Secretary of Labor; Occupational Safety & Health Review Commission created

1972: Longshore and Harbor Workers' Compensation Amendments, making substantial changes in this federal scheme by redefining the basis of coverage, raising benefit levels, and limiting access by longshore workers to remedies under general maritime law

1973: Release of the Report of the National Commission on State Workers' Compensation laws, prompting a period of major change in those laws

1974: Privacy Act, regulating release of personal data in files maintained by the federal government

1975: Employee Retirement Income Security Act, the first major federal regulation of pension and welfare plans; enforcement activity divided between Treasury and Labor departments

1975: Indiana decision in the *Frampton* case, launching a major series of state court decisions on wrongful termination

1978: Civil Service Reform Act, regulating collective bargaining by federal employees

1988: Workers Adjustment and Restraining Notification Act, requiring notice of plant closures and major layoffs

1988: Drug Free Workplace Act, requiring employers to develop substance abuse programs

1988: Employee Polygraph Protection Act, limiting employer use of "lie detectors" and similar devices

1990: Americans with Disabilities Act, prohibiting discrimination against qualified individuals with disabilities

1991: Civil Rights Act of 1991, overruling several Supreme Court decisions and expanding remedies

1993: Family and Medical Leave Act, requiring employers to grant up to 12 weeks of unpaid leave to most employees for disability or dependent care

1999: Ticket To Work and Work Incentives Improvement Act, amending the Vocational Rehabilitation Act of 1973 and seeking to coordinate programs to get beneficiaries under Social Security Disability Insurance and other programs back into jobs

2006: Pension Protection Act, amending funding rules, changing the time period in which underfunding must be corrected, limiting some conditions that could be imposed by employers on their stock contributions to pension funds, requiring "defined contribution" plans to meet tighter diversification standards, permitting specified types of advice to be given to employees about their investment choices.

2008: ADA Amendments Act, overruling a series of Supreme Court decisions that had denied protection to a significant number of persons with medical conditions that affected their ability to obtain and hold jobs.

2008: Genetic Information Nondiscrimination Act, limiting the extent to which employers, employment agencies, and labor organizations can obtain and use genetic information about the individual employee and his or her family members.

2009: Lilly Ledbetter Fair Pay Act, amending Title VII of the Civil Rights Act to permit a broader range of claimants to challenge discrimination in compensation practices.

As this highly selective listing indicates, much has been happening, in courts, legislatures, and regulatory bodies.

The demands on those who study and practice labor and employment law have increased as well. The 1952 edition of United States Code (the official edition) included a Title 29 (Labor) that occupied 58 pages and ended with section 262; by 1970, its 149 pages concluded with section 678; the 1988 edition version of Title 29 was 578 pages in length. The 712 pages of the 2000 edition go through section 3058. Case law growth has been similar.

The implications of this for the teaching and studying of labor and employment law are sobering. It is clear that no current graduate from law school can hope to have the proportionate mastery of basic doctrine that he or she could have reasonably sought in 1949 or 1969, or even 1999. The fledgling labor practitioner must face up to leaving law school with a staggering amount of basic learning still to be done. The challenge for teachers of the subject is to make ever more difficult choices about what to teach and what to leave out. Trying to "cover everything" is not only impossible, attempting to do it is likely to lead to treatment of individual subjects that is so superficial that it is useless.

CHAPTER 2

FORMING AND TERMINATING THE EMPLOYMENT RELATIONSHIP

A. INTRODUCTION

For each of us, the work we do helps to establish our identity within society. Given how important employment is, it may be surprising that both hiring and firing may be done very informally. As Chapter 1 said, a simple "You're hired" may well be enough to create an employment contract. At other times—hiring the basketball coach at a major university, for instance—there may be lengthy negotiations and a complex written memorial must be signed before employment begins. Firing can be just as easy, or as complex. Studies indicate that few workers realize that the typical working relationship is so fragile that it can be unilaterally terminated by our employer, without cause, and that we have no recourse to challenge the action. Absent an agreement to the contrary, both employee and employer can generally terminate the employment relationship at any time, for any or no reason, with or without notice.

Termination has been called the "capital punishment" of the workplace. Being terminated may

37

label one as a failure or unfit for employment. Because disputes over whether a contract of employment has been formed occur so often in the context of a dispute over firing, this chapter will focus first on the circumstances under which employees can be terminated and what statutes and common law rules are available to assist employees when a loss of work occurs. The doctrines that govern forming and modifying the employment contract will be discussed below, as they affect the outcome of cases involving the legality of discharge.

B.   AT–WILL EMPLOYMENT

1.   The Traditional Concept

Historically, the law that governs the employment relationship has limited an employee's ability to challenge an employer's unfair, adverse, or damaging practices, including arbitrary firing. It has generally denied any redress to an employee who is arbitrarily treated, unless that employee is represented by a union or has rights under an explicit employment contract. The general rule has been that absent a statutory or contractual restriction, an employee or employer can terminate the employment relationship at any time, for any or no reason, with or without notice.

The mutual promises by employer to pay and by employee to serve may be terminated by notice, or by lapse of time or "supervening events." See

RESTATEMENT (SECOND) OF AGENCY § 422 (1958).

The body of common law we inherited from Great Britain could easily have led to a very different set of doctrines. Employee and employer rights within the United States trace their beginnings to England's Statute of Laborers, a law enacted in response to the extreme labor shortage that resulted from the Black Death in the mid–14th century. It provided that a "general hiring" of labor for an unfixed term was presumed to be for a year and that a "master" could not "put away his servant" except for "reasonable cause." W. BLACKSTONE, COMMENTARIES 425 (1765). After its repeal, English courts continued to apply the statute's spirit by presuming that a "general hiring" was intended to serve as an employment contract for one year. If the employment continued for longer than one year, it could be terminated only at the end of an additional year. See *Beeston v. Collyer*, 130 Eng.Rep. 786 (C.P.1827). This one year presumption embodied the reality of the agrarian society as well as the slightly paternalistic notions of "master and servant." It prevented the harshness of hiring laborers for the harvest season and then "putting them away" for the winter without any food or shelter, as Blackstone alluded. The one year presumption, however, could be rebutted by proof of an agreement for a different term or none at all. The evidence might consist of an explicit understanding as to the employment term, or it could arise from the custom in the trade, the frequency of wage payments, or the length of notice required to terminate.

The American at will employment doctrine has been viewed both as a departure from and as part of this English heritage. Early American courts adopted the English approach. As late as the 1890s some American courts seemed ready to presume that certain types of employment are ordinarily for a term, such as a month or a year. See *Adams v. Fitzpatrick*, 125 N.Y. 124, 26 N.E. 143 (N.Y.1891).

The presumption that employment is terminable "at will" was, however, already taking hold by mid century. In *Blaisdell v. Lewis*, 32 Me. 515 (Me. 1851), the plaintiff had agreed to perform work at daily wages in the community of Hallowell, but was never called to duty. He sued and won a jury verdict, but the defendant's exceptions were sustained. The court's entire opinion was as follows:

An infirmity in this contract is, that it fixed no time during which the plaintiff's services should be rendered to the defendant. Suppose the plaintiff had gone to Hallowell, and tendered his services, there was nothing to prevent the defendant from discharging him at the end of a single day. In such a contract there is no value.

In the same year (1851), in *De Briar v. Minturn*, 1 Cal. 450 (Cal.1851), the California Supreme Court ruled against a barkeeper who had been terminated from his job and ejected from his room at the defendant's inn. The court noted that he "was not hired for any definite period." In *Hathaway v. Bennett*, 10 N.Y. 108 (N.Y.1854), the New York Court of Appeals ruled that a newspaper deliverer's contract for an indefinite period could be terminated "at pleasure" by the defendant. In 1871, the Wisconsin Supreme Court ruled in *Prentiss v. Ledyard*, 28 Wis. 131 (Wis.1871), a breach of contract action, that "[e]ither party, however, was at liberty to terminate the service at any time, no definite period for which the service was to continue having been agreed upon." In 1874, Illinois reached the same result in *Orr v. Ward*, 73 Ill. 318 (Ill.1874), in which an employee was denied recovery because the contract "contain[ed] no undertaking * * * for a definite period." In 1872, California enacted the first at will statute in its original California Civil Code.

In 1877, the first edition of H. G. Wood's treatise on the master-servant relationship articulated what seemingly became America's at will employment doctrine. Wood wrote that:

With us the rule is inflexible that a general or indefinite hiring is prima facie a hiring at will, and if the servant seeks to make it out a yearly hiring, the burden is upon him to establish it by proof. A hiring at so much a day, week, month, or year, no time being specified, is an indefinite hiring, and no presumption attaches that it was for a day even, but only at the rate fixed for whatever time the party may serve. H. WOOD, MASTER AND SERVANT § 134 (3d ed. 1886).

Although Wood's "Rule" has been challenged and in certain instances negated, it became a primary basis for what constitutes at will employment today. Virtually every state eventually accepted his formulation of the at will rule. The Court of Appeals of Maryland called Wood an "authority of great repute" when it adopted the at will doctrine in *McCullough Iron Co. v. Carpenter*, 67 Md. 554, 11 A. 176 (Md.1887), and New York's highest court noted in *Martin v. New York Life Insurance Co.*, 148 N.Y. 117, 42 N.E. 416 (N.Y.1895), that the at will doctrine was "correctly stated by Mr. Wood."

Why choose to presume that employment is at will? Several reasons have been suggested. American courts may have believed that Wood's Rule would facilitate economic development during the industrial revolution of the 1800's by promoting the prevalent ideology of *laissez faire* and freedom of contract. Wood's rule also offered administrative advantages. It was simple and consistent. It settled conflict among the lower courts and spared judges and juries from undertaking complicated factual analyses. Most importantly, the at will doctrine fit the times.

Within this framework, Wood's Rule seemed equitable. It provided the employer the flexibility to control the workplace through the unchallengeable power to terminate the employment relationship at will. In turn, the employee retained the freedom to resign if more favorable employment presented itself or if working conditions became intolerable. The at will employment relationship has been codified in several jurisdictions. See, e.g., West's Ann. Cal. Labor Code § 2922.

For a time, the at will doctrine even assumed constitutional proportions. In *Adair v. United States*, 208 U.S. 161 (1908), the U.S. Supreme Court ruled that a federal statute prohibiting the termination of certain employees for union membership was "an invasion of the personal liberty, as well as the right of property" protected by the Fifth Amendment. Justice Harlan's opinion endorsed the at will doctrine as follows:

> In the absence, however, of a valid contract between the parties controlling their conduct towards each other and fixing a period of service, it cannot be, we repeat, that an employer is under any legal obligation, against his will, to retain an employee in his personal service any more than an employee can be compelled, against his will, to remain in the personal service of another * * *. [The employee] was at liberty to quit the service without assigning any reason for his leaving. And the defendant was at liberty, in his discretion, to discharge [the employee] from service without giving any reason for so doing. Id. at 175–176.

Whatever its philosophic basis, the concept that employment is at will continues to exert a powerful influence on American law. Three specific rules that flow from this concept are particularly important:

- *First*, if an employer fires an at will employee, for any reason whatever, there is no tort liability, since an at will contract is of no real value. Until recently, courts consistently upheld the legality of arbitrary terminations and denied damage claims even where the termination reasons were based upon false information, mistake, malice, or where the employer did not follow its own published disciplinary and appeal procedures.

- *Second,* since employment is presumed to be at will, any person who seeks damages for breach of an employment contract must establish by a preponderance of the evidence that the contract is for a defined term.

- *Third*, provisions in an employment contract that relate to its duration but are indefinite, such as "permanent" or "lifetime" are interpreted to mean "at will" unless additional consideration beyond performance of services has been given.

For just over fifty years now, a number of American courts have begun to reformulate the ways in which these rules govern the employment relationship. We turn to these recent developments next.

2. Judicial Modifications

a. *The Public Policy Exception*

The majority of states now recognize an employee cause of action (usually in tort, but in a couple of states in contract) for a termination that infringes on a specific public policy interest. This exception to at will employment embodies a principle that employees whose acts enhance or promote clearly expressed public policies should be protected.

The public policy exception was the first major modification of an at will rule, and it is the most widely accepted. The effect of the exception is to protect employees' interests in job security when continued employment is threatened not by an employer's genuine dissatisfaction with job performance or some other legitimate business need but because the employee: (1) has refused to act in an unlawful manner, (2) has attempted to perform a statutorily prescribed duty, (3) has exercised a right that the law specifically confers on the employee, or (4) has reported unlawful or improper employer conduct ("whistleblowing").

Balanced against these interests of employees and society are employers' important and legitimate interests in being able to terminate at will employees when they decide that it is best for their business. Courts recognize that running a business is hard work, and that managers must often act quickly, with little time for reflection. Thus they are often reluctant to question employer decisions, and they have not been eager to adopt a rule that allows a tort action for damages whenever a jury determines, long after the fact, that an employee's termination was "wrongful." The recognition and expansion of the public policy exception has involved the balancing of these conflicting interests.

Although the principle seems straightforward, the term "public policy" remains ill defined. Some early cases indicated that public policy is "a prohibition for the good of the community against whatever contravenes good morals or any established interests of society." *Petermann v. International Brotherhood of Teamsters*, 174 Cal.App.2d 184, 344 P.2d 25 (Cal.App.1959). Other courts described it more broadly, to ban conduct "motivated by bad faith or malice based on retaliation." *Monge v. Beebe Rubber Co.*, 114 N.H. 130, 316 A.2d 549 (N.H.1974). More recently, the majority opinion in *Palmateer v. International Harvester Co.*, 85 Ill.2d 124, 52 Ill.Dec. 13, 421 N.E.2d 876 (Ill.1981) defined public policy as that which:

> * * * concerns what is right and just and what affects the citizens of the State collectively. It is to be found in the State's Constitution and laws and, when they are silent, in its judicial decisions. * * * A matter must strike at the heart of a citizen's social rights, duties and responsibilities before the tort claim will be allowed.

Two dissenting justices found this too broad.

In reading opinions involving "public policy" challenges to terminations, therefore, one should look first at what the court has to say about potential sources of public policy: constitutions, statutes, administrative regulations, common law doctrines, general notions of fairness and justice. Then one can analyze whether it is appropriate to give that particular source a relatively broader or more narrow reading. Specific examples of employee termi-

nations violating some form of recognized public
policy include terminations for:

- Refusing to act improperly:

  Refusing to violate mandated staff-child ratios
  at a day-care center. *Jasper v. H. Nizam, Inc.*,
  2009 WL 151568 (Iowa)

  Declining to drive a truck lacking a required
  inspection certificate *Adams v. George W. Cochran & Co., Inc.*, 597 A.2d 28 (D.C.App.1991).

  Refusing to drive a truck after the worker told
  the employer he did not have the required
  commercial driver's license. *Kempfer v. Automated Finishing*, 211 Wis.2d 100, 564 N.W.2d
  692 (Wis.Sup.Ct.1997).

  Refusing to participate in an illegal price fixing
  scheme. *Tameny v. Atlantic Richfield Co.*, 27
  Cal.3d 167, 164 Cal.Rptr. 839, 610 P.2d 1330
  (Cal.1980).

  Refusing to perform catheterizations that the
  employee was neither trained nor licensed to
  undertake. *O'Sullivan v. Mallon*, 160 N.J.Su-
  per. 416, 390 A.2d 149 (N.J.Super.1978).

- Performing public duties:

  Refusing to seek to be excused from serving on
  a jury. *Nees v. Hocks*, 272 Or. 210, 536 P.2d 512
  (Or.1975).

  Responding to a subpoena. *Hummer v. Evans*,
  129 Idaho 274, 923 P.2d 981 (Idaho 1996);
  Ludwick v. This Minute of Carolina, Inc., 287
  S.C. 219, 337 S.E.2d 213 (S.C.1985).

- Exercising a legally protected privilege or right:

Filing workers' compensation claims. *Frampton v. Central Ind. Gas Co.*, 260 Ind. 249, 297 N.E.2d 425 (Ind.1973).

Refusing to take a lie detector test in a state prohibiting its administration. *Perks v. Firestone Tire & Rubber Co.*, 611 F.2d 1363 (3d Cir.1979).

Filing litigation against the employer. *Tacket v. Delco Remy, Division of General Motors Corp.*, 959 F.2d 650 (7th Cir.1992).

Filing an unemployment compensation claim against the employer during the time period when the employee was temporarily unemployed. *Highhouse v. Avery Transportation*, 443 Pa.Super. 120, 660 A.2d 1374 (Pa.Super.1995).

- "Whistleblowing":

Complaining to the employer about unlawful mislabeling of packaged goods. *Sheets v. Teddy's Frosted Foods, Inc.*, 179 Conn. 471, 427 A.2d 385 (Conn.1980).

Informing her lawyer employer's attorney that the employer had submitted false evidence in a disciplinary proceeding. *Paralegal v. Lawyer*, 783 F.Supp. 230 (E.D.Pa.1992).

Reporting that fellow firefighters had downloaded pornography on fire department computers. *Hufford v. McEnaney*, 249 F.3d 1142 (9th Cir.2001).

One major problem in public policy exception cases is what to do when a fired worker's common law claim has a statutory counterpart. The Fair Labor Standards Act includes an anti retaliation clause, for example, and a majority of courts have therefore held that a worker who claims she was fired for reporting FLSA violations is limited to the statutory remedy and has no common law tort claim. See, e.g., *Morgan v. Future Ford Sales*, 830 F.Supp. 807 (D.Del.1993). At least one federal district court disagrees. *Fitzwater v. Namco Am. Inc.*, 130 Lab.Cas. (CCH) ¶ 33,233 (N.D.Cal.1994). There is also disagreement about the pre-emptive effect of the federal False Claims Act. See the discussion in *Palladino ex rel. U.S. v. VNA of Southern New Jersey, Inc.*, 68 F.Supp.2d 455 (D.N.J. 1999). The Supreme Court has held that ERISA precludes state law wrongful termination actions if the plaintiff's claim requires referring to an employee benefit plan covered by the statute. *Ingersoll–Rand Co. v. McClendon*, 498 U.S. 133 (1990).

Both the FLSA and ERISA provide civil remedies for persons filed in violation of their protections. Some statutes provide only fines or administrative remedies. Courts differ about whether common law remedies are precluded by such limited remedy enactments. A Wisconsin case involving nurses who were fired for reporting nursing home shortcomings, as required by a statute, is a good illustration. The Wisconsin Court of Appeals held that the fines provided by the statute were an exclusive remedy; no private right of action was implied, and any existing common law remedy was cut off. The Wisconsin Supreme Court reversed, reasoning that "a criminal penalty is no remedy to the terminated employee." *Hausman v. St. Croix Care Center*, 207 Wis.2d 400, 558 N.W.2d 893 (Wis.App.1996), rev'd by 214 Wis.2d 655, 571 N.W.2d 393 (Wis.1997). In *Charvat v. Eastern Ohio Regional Wastewater Authority*, 246 F.3d 607 (6th Cir.2001), the court held that a First Amendment claim for wrongful retaliation brought under 42 U.S.C.A. § 1983 was not precluded by the whistleblower provision of the Clean Water Act. The court emphasized that the latter statute provides only administrative remedies. Holding that a public sector employee is confined to a statutory remedy usually means the claim must be pursued through administrative channels before going into court. Federal employees must generally pursue whistleblower discrimination claims before the Merit System Protection Board. 5 U.S.C.A. §§ 2121, 2302(b)(8).

b. *Contract Analysis: Establishing What the Parties Have Promised*

Employees and employers daily enter into employment contracts with each other in highly informal ways. These employment contracts may be oral or written, indefinite or for a specified term, detailed or simple.

(i) *Employment Contracts*

Employment contracts are often referred to as "relational contracts," agreements that establish what the parties usually expect to be an ongoing relationship. Other relational contracts include partnership agreements, most insurance contracts, and the membership agreements of labor organizations. In recent years, courts have become increasingly aware of how difficult it is to apply to these contracts the "traditional" doctrines of contract law. Those doctrines are largely based on a "bargain and exchange" model—like the purchase of a stereo—that may not always resemble the circumstances of employment. Trying to decide just when traditional contract principles should be modified in the employment context is not easy, either in theory or in the deciding of concrete cases. For the present, the soundest course to follow in analyzing an employment contract problem is to begin with a relatively mechanical "traditional" contract law approach. Having done so, one can then more easily decide whether the results are sufficiently odd so that some doctrine modification is required. According to the traditions of contract law, then, employment contracts, like all contracts, involve the elements of "offer," "acceptance," and "consideration." Unless all three of these elements are present, there is no employment contract.

Employment contracts are formed when one party (the offeror) extends an offer that is accepted by the other party (the offeree). The offer must contain the employment contract's essential terms and conditions. To form the contract, the offeror and offeree must agree to the same terms and conditions at the same time, i.e., "mutual assent" must occur.

After the offer has been made, the offeree has the power to create a binding employment contract by accepting it. Depending on what sort of response the offer calls for, acceptance may be either a promise to work or actual performance of the requested duties. For the offer and acceptance to become a final employment contract, "consideration" must be present, i.e., something of value must be provided for it. The employee's work or promise to work will generally be adequate consideration for an employer's promise to pay a certain wage, bonus, pension plan, fringe benefit, etc. Similarly, an employer's promise to pay a salary will be adequate consideration for the employee's promise to work, to assign inventions to the employer, or not to compete with the employer.

When a written memorial of an employment contract states the contract's duration, it is relatively easy to determine liability under breach of contract principles. Often, however, no written memorial of the employment contract exists or if it exists it says nothing about duration. In either case, the employment is presumed to be at will; employment can be terminated by either the employee or employer at any time, for any or no reason, with or without notice. RESTATEMENT (SECOND) OF AGENCY § 442 (1958). It is in fact rare for all the terms of an employment relationship to be set out in a single integrated memorial. Particularly when a worker has stayed with the same firm for a long time, the obligations of employer and employee to one another are likely to be in part unwritten, and the written record will comprise not one document, but rather a series of applications, letters, benefit certificates, manuals, and so on. Because of this, the parol evidence rule is unlikely to be important in most employment contract cases. See *McLain v. Great Am. Ins. Co.*, 208 Cal.App.3d 1476, 256 Cal. Rptr. 863 (Cal.App.1989).

To overcome the at will employment presumption, the party seeking damages for breach must establish:

1. A promise was made to employ or to work for a particular time period or to terminate the employment only for certain reasons or through certain procedures.

2. The promise is enforceable, because consideration was given (or through a doctrine that avoids the requirement of consideration).

3. Breach of the promise.

4. (In the case of a contract for more than a year), that the contract does not violate the Statute of Frauds.

(ii) Handbooks and Employment Policy Documents

A promise may be contained in a written or oral statement made directly to the employee. In a number of states, courts are willing to find these promises in statements contained in handbooks or other employment policy statements. The likelihood of this depends in part on the size of the firm. Small employers can usually operate without formal books

of rules. For larger employers, individualized decision making becomes impractical. Increased size
multiplies the number of employment decisions that
must be made beyond one person's ability to make
them. A system of rules becomes necessary for
orderly and efficient administration of the workforce.

Handbooks and employment policy manuals create this order. They often include:

1. Rules of expected employee behavior;

2. Disciplinary or termination procedures to be
    used if those rules are violated;

3. Compensation and hours of work; and

4. Benefit items, such as overtime, lay off, recall,
    health care insurance, pensions, leaves of ab-
    sence, holidays, vacations, etc.

A handbook is often the only way an employer
communicates this information to its workers. No
two employers' handbooks and employment policies
are exactly alike. They reflect the employer's particular operational and management style. They are
commonly intended to create a closer relationship
between an employer and its employees.

Employer oral promises of continued employment
can support a binding commitment by themselves,
if proved, but spoken words are more readily given
effect when supported by a handbook statement
providing that employment would be terminated
only for cause or only after exhaustion of certain
procedures.

Few handbooks are written in language that is clearly promissory, few are the result of true bargaining, and, therefore, for many years courts shied from giving them much significance for enforcement of their terms and condition. Now, however, it is widely recognized that statements made in handbooks and employment policy manuals may create binding employer commitments. Often, provisions in handbooks are used as supporting evidence, to clarify other documents or statements. For example, in *Ritchie v. Michigan Consol. Gas Co.*, 163 Mich.App. 358, 413 N.W.2d 796 (Mich.App.1987), representations by a manager and supervisor that an employee would be employed for her 20–year mortgage's duration and as long as the employer was in business, along with a handbook that listed discipline causes, were sufficient to raise a question of whether the employment was actually at will. In *Toussaint v. Blue Cross & Blue Shield of Michigan*, 408 Mich. 579, 292 N.W.2d 880 (Mich.1980), an employee was told at the time of hiring that he would be employed as long as he did his job. This promise was supported by language in the handbook stating that it was the employer's policy to terminate for "just cause" only. These oral and written promises were found to be enforceable as an express or implied agreement that set forth legitimate employee expectations based on the employer's representations. In *Terrio v. Millinocket Community Hospital*, 379 A.2d 135 (Me.1977), a supervisor's assurance that the employee was secure in her job "for the rest of her life," made in "the context of her long service in a position of substantial responsibility * * * provided the critical evidentiary support for her contract claim." That assurance was interpreted to constitute a promise of employment to age 65 in light of provisions in the employer's Personnel Policy and Retirement Plan, documents the employee had been given. In *Schipani v. Ford Motor Co.*, 102 Mich.App. 606, 302 N.W.2d 307 (Mich.App.1981), the court denied summary judgment to an employer on the grounds that oral agreements combined with a personnel manual, policies, and employment practice could be sufficient to constitute an employment contract to age 65, despite a signed written contract stating that employment was terminable at will.

There are also occasional cases in which the discharged employee relies entirely upon a handbook as the source of an employer promise of employment that is not at will. In such a case, the employee must convince the court that the language of the handbook is clear enough to create a reasonable expectation of longer term work, and that the employee was in fact aware of that promissory language and relied upon it by commencing or continuing to work. See *Duldulao v. St. Mary of Nazareth Hospital Center*, 115 Ill.2d 482, 106 Ill.Dec. 8, 505 N.E.2d 314 (Ill.1987).

Once made, how long does the employer's promise remain binding? One common analysis is that the handbook or employment policy is an offer, communicated by distributing the handbook to workers. See *Arie v. Intertherm, Inc.*, 648 S.W.2d

142 (Mo.App.1983). At will employees accept the new offer and provide consideration by continuing their employment. See *Pine River State Bank v. Mettille*, 333 N.W.2d 622 (Minn.1983). The resulting contract is a "unilateral" contract, since the duties to be performed are concentrated on one side, the employer's. Characterizing handbooks and employment policy manuals as unilateral employment offers has led many courts to conclude that the employer may unilaterally augment, modify, or even withdraw them. When an employer distributes a new handbook or manual, the employer makes a new offer of employment to the at will employee. This new offer is limited to the new handbook's or employment policy's contents and becomes effective on the date it is distributed. Where these are withdrawn, the new offer becomes effective on the date that the employer notifies the employee of the withdrawal. *Elliott v. Board of Trustees of Montgomery County Community College*, 104 Md.App. 93, 655 A.2d 46 (Md.App.1995). Other courts have rejected this approach, however, when the promise made in the "old" handbook but left out of the new was one on which an employee might reasonably rely in deciding whether to accept or stay with a job. *Torosyan v. Boehringer Ingelheim Pharmaceuticals, Inc.*, 234 Conn. 1, 662 A.2d 89 (Conn.1995) held that an employer that had promised it would terminate employees "for cause" in its handbook could not unilaterally convert an employee's status back to an at-will relationship by mere issuance of a second handbook. It would be improper to infer that the

employee consented to the new terms simply because he or she continued to work, since the only alternative would be to resign, thus giving up the job security the employer had previously promised. See also *Thompson v. Kings Entertainment Co.*, 674 F.Supp. 1194 (E.D.Va.1987). In *Demasse v. ITT Corp.*, 194 Ariz. 500, 984 P.2d 1138 (Ariz.1999), the employer's handbooks had contained statements that an employee would not be laid off ahead of less senior employees. The employer then issued a new handbook omitting that statement and soon laid off workers without regard to seniority. The Arizona Supreme Court reasoned that the promise to lay off in reverse order of seniority was one on which employees could rely, since it was definite in its terms and appeared in a handbook that contained no disclaimers. Therefore, no change in the policy could be made without an offer of additional consideration. Illinois has joined this group. *Doyle v. Holy Cross Hospital*, 186 Ill.2d 104, 237 Ill.Dec. 100, 708 N.E.2d 1140 (Ill.1999). A sharply divided California Supreme Court has taken an intermediate position, holding that an employment policy pledging long term job security to a firm's managers could be modified, provided (a) that the policy was of "indefinite duration," (b) that the policy was in effect for a "reasonable time," (c) that "reasonable notice" was given of the change, and (d) that no "vested benefits" were affected by the change. *Asmus v. Pacific Bell*, 23 Cal.4th 1, 96 Cal.Rptr.2d 179, 999 P.2d 71 (Cal.2000).

To counter this trend toward finding promises in these documents, many employers have begun inserting disclaimers in handbooks and in job application forms, seeking to preserve the at will employment relationship. In *Novosel v. Sears, Roebuck & Co.*, 495 F.Supp. 344 (E.D.Mich.1980), the court gave effect to a disclaimer that was included on an employment application that the employee had signed some 12 years before the challenged termination.

Not all courts are so ready to hold that disclaimers defeat an employee's claim. Some readily find disclaimers to be unclear or ambiguous, so that a jury must determine their meaning. See, e.g., *Jones v. Central Peninsula General Hospital*, 779 P.2d 783 (Alaska 1989). One reason for requiring a disclaimer to be clear and conspicuous is the perception that it is "unfair to allow an employer to distribute a policy manual that makes the workforce believe that certain promises have been made and then to allow the employer to renege.... " *Woolley v. Hoffmann–La Roche, Inc.*, 99 N.J. 284, 491 A.2d 1257 (N.J.1985) modified, 101 N.J. 10, 499 A.2d 515 (N.J.1985). Courts sometimes insist that a disclaimer be prominent, perhaps by setting it out in bold type. See, e.g., *Durtsche v. American Colloid Co.*, 958 F.2d 1007 (10th Cir.1992); *Jimenez v. Colorado Interstate Gas Co.*, 690 F.Supp. 977 (D.Wyo.1988). It is likely that the employer will bear the burden of proof to show the disclaimer was in fact communicated to the employee before the employment commences or continues. See, e.g., *Montgomery v. Asso-*

ciation of American Railroads, 741 F.Supp. 1313 (N.D.Ill.1990).

Sometimes a discharged employee seeks to rely on employer documents that she was not aware of before (or even during) employment. Many employers provide their supervisory or management personnel with confidential policy manuals and oral guidelines to assist in hiring, disciplining, and terminating employees. The typical employee never sees these or knows of their details. Personnel guidelines set forth in supervisory manuals are often used offensively against the employer in litigation. Arbitrators have referred to such documents in judging whether a discharge was "arbitrary or capricious" under a collective agreement. See *Father Flanagan's Boys Home v. Boys Town Education Assoc.*, 165 L.R.R.M. 2760 (D.Neb.2000). Courts have reasoned that these supervisory manuals are evidence of the usual practices of the employer and that the typical employment contract therefore includes these provisions as implied terms. The extensive opinion in *Morriss v. Coleman Co., Inc.*, 241 Kan. 501, 738 P.2d 841 (Kan.1987) develops this idea in modifying earlier precedent that refused to give weight to these documents since their terms were not bargained for.

Manuals intended solely for management use may be relevant to issues other than whether employment is at will, of course. In the trial of a charge that the employer terminated an employee for whistleblowing, for example, proof that the employer did or did not follow its usual pre termination procedures could be very important. See *Griffin v. Erickson*, 277 Ark. 433, 642 S.W.2d 308 (Ark.1982).

c. *The Duty of Good Faith and Fair Dealing*

In many states, all relational contracts are interpreted to impose an implied duty of good faith and fair dealing on the parties. In the ordinary situation this means simply that the parties are expected to perform their contractual obligations in a straightforward way, without evasions or taking unfair advantage. See RESTATEMENT (SECOND) OF CONTRACTS § 205. If a contract provides for payment for services upon "completion satisfactory to" a party, for example, that party is obliged not to withhold approval unreasonably or arbitrarily. However, because an at will employment is terminable "for no reason," some jurisdictions have held that there is no independent cause of action for the breach of the "good faith" requirement. See, e.g., *LaScola v. US Sprint Communications*, 946 F.2d 559 (7th Cir.1991). Others hold the doctrine does apply, at least if the employer's breach can be characterized as deceitful or fraudulent in some sense. *E.I. DuPont de Nemours & Co. v. Pressman*, 679 A.2d 436 (Del.1996).

A few courts have taken the position that the duty of good faith and fair dealing in employment contracts goes much further. Before its wrongful termination statute was enacted, for example, the courts of Montana held that tort damages, including punitive damages, were available to an employee who had a reasonable expectation of ongoing employment and who was unreasonably discharged. See, e.g., *Stark v. Circle K Corp.*, 230 Mont. 468, 751 P.2d 162 (Mont.1988). Most states have either rejected the notion that there is an independent duty of good faith and fair dealing that goes beyond the employment contract itself (see, e.g., *Thompson v. St. Regis Paper Co.*, 102 Wash.2d 219, 685 P.2d 1081 (Wash.1984)), or have limited recovery for breach of the duty to contract damages. See *Foley v. Interactive Data Corp.*, 47 Cal.3d 654, 254 Cal.Rptr. 211, 765 P.2d 373 (Cal.1988).

3. Statutory Modifications

a. Current Protections

Statutory bans on improperly motivated terminations pre date by several decades the judicial changes to at will doctrines discussed in the prior section. Since 1935, the National Labor Relations Act (NLRA) has forbidden employers to terminate employees because of their support for a union, for example. 29 U.S.C.A. § 158(a)(3). Title VII of the Civil Rights Act of 1964 prohibits any termination based upon discrimination involving race, color, religion, sex, or national origin. 42 U.S.C.A. § 2000e–2(a). Other federal statutes restricting employee termination include: Age Discrimination in Employment Act of 1967 (ADEA), 29 U.S.C.A. §§ 621–634; Occupational Safety and Health Act of 1970 (OSHA), 29 U.S.C.A. §§ 651–678; Vietnam Era Veterans Readjustment Assistance Act, 38 U.S.C.A. §§ 2021(a)(A)(i), 2021(a)(B), 2021(b)(1), 2024; Fair Labor Standards Act (FLSA), 29 U.S.C.A. §§ 201–

219; Vocational Rehabilitation Act of 1973, 29 U.S.C.A. §§ 701–796; Americans with Disabilities Act, 42 U.S.C.A. §§ 12101–12213; Employee Retirement Income Security Act of 1974 (ERISA), 29 U.S.C.A. §§ 1140–41; Family and Medical Leave Act, 29 U.S.C.A. § 2615; Energy Reorganization Act of 1974, 42 U.S.C.A. § 5851; Clean Air Act, 42 U.S.C.A. § 7622; Federal Water Pollution Control Act, 33 U.S.C.A. § 1367; Railroad Safety Act, 45 U.S.C.A. §§ 441(a), 441(b)(1); Consumer Credit Protection Act, 15 U.S.C.A. § 1674(a); Judiciary and Judicial Procedure Act, 28 U.S.C.A. § 1875.

State statutes contain similar limitations. See, e.g., Pa. Stat. Ann. tit. 43 §§ 951–963 (Pennsylvania Human Relations Act regarding termination for discrimination involving race, color, religion, sex, national origin, or disability).

The ability of trial courts and administrative agencies to apply these statutes with reasonable consistency may well have made it easier to persuade appellate judges to consider adopting doctrines such as the "public policy exception" discussed earlier in this Chapter.

The availability of federal statutory claims may pose preemption problems for some terminated workers who seek relief under state law. In *San Diego Building Trades Council v. Garmon (Garmon II)*, 359 U.S. 236 (1959), the Supreme Court held that a state may not provide a remedy for conduct arguably protected by Section 7 or prohibited by Section 8 of the NLRA (subject to two exceptions, one for matters of "merely peripheral concern" to the NLRA, the other for matters deeply rooted in local responsibility). The Court has also held that where state involvement would interfere with the "free play of economic forces," which the NLRA deliberately did not regulate, state regulation is prohibited. See *Lodge 76, Int'l Ass'n of Machinists v. Wisconsin Employment Relations Comm'n*, 427 U.S. 132 (1976). Some federal statutes address the issue of preemption explicitly (see, e.g., OSHA, 29 U.S.C.A. §§ 657, 667; ERISA, 29 U.S.C.A. § 1144(a)), but often the issue of whether state law is preempted is left to the courts to determine.

Under both the Railway Labor Act and Section 301 of the Taft–Hartley Act, there is also a strong federal policy favoring the resolution of labor disputes by the use of arbitration. Therefore, an employee subject to Taft–Hartley whose wrongful termination claim requires interpretation of a collective bargaining agreement will be required to pursue that claim through the agreement's grievance and arbitration system, and will be denied access to the courts. *Allis–Chalmers Corp. v. Lueck*, 471 U.S. 202 (1985). If, on the other hand, a plaintiff can make out a wrongful termination claim without relying on any bargaining agreement provision to establish liability, then there is no preemption. See *Lingle v. Norge Division of Magic Chef, Inc.*, 486 U.S. 399 (1988) (Taft–Hartley Act); *Hawaiian Airlines, Inc. v. Norris*, 512 U.S. 246 (1994) (RLA).

b. Possible Future Modifications

Pressure may be gradually developing for a comprehensive statutory treatment of wrongful employee terminations. A good argument can be made that the piecemeal protection provided by federal and state anti discrimination laws, workplace safety statutes, workers' compensation laws, etc. already restrain arbitrary terminations to the extent that a general statute would not be a significant added burden on employers. Many commentators have argued that the newly developed doctrines have too many gaps, vary too much from state to state, and are difficult for trial courts to apply. A statutory solution, if well drafted, could deal with many of the uncertainties, such as whether "whistleblowing" that is limited to intra company protests ought to be protected. The statute could bring logic and order to an area of the law that is confused.

Counter arguments can be made, however. To enact a comprehensive statute less than fifty years since the assault on the at will concept started would deny the ever flexible common law process the chance to produce the level of refined detailed doctrine of which it is capable. Moreover, what some view as a random patchwork of statutes limiting the power to terminate on particular grounds seems to others a well balanced mosaic of laws that provide remedies for wrongful terminations that reflect careful legislative judgment about the nature and seriousness of the wrong done. It would be wrong to equate a termination caused by deeply held racism with one arising from an out of control argument over a World Series bet.

Which arguments will prevail? Statutory action occurs when political power favors change. Action is generally determined by the strength and intensity of groups that have similar interests on a particular subject. Usually public discussion and debate precedes statutory action while interest groups develop their positions and move an issue into more prominence. Legislation protecting against wrongful termination throughout the United States is still in the early stages of evolution.

Employers have generally opposed statutory action that would restrict their employment practices or impose liability for their adverse action against employees. Some courts' action in modifying at will employment may change employers' minds. The language of some of these court decisions is very general in nature, and many seem very open ended with respect to remedies. This may cause employers to support wrongful termination legislation that provides orderly review procedures and limits remedies.

Historically, unions have advanced employee rights legislation. They also educate workers about the limits on the legal protections against wrongful discharge available to non union employees. In supporting wrongful termination legislation, unions may further their image as the group that is primarily concerned with fair and equitable employment rights. Some unionists have argued, however, that organized labor ought not to support wrongful termination statutes, since protection against abusive termination is a major "selling point" for union organizers.

Whatever the reason, no general federal wrongful termination legislation exists. Piecemeal state legislation has been adopted in Puerto Rico, P.R. LAWS ANN. tit. 29, § 185a, South Dakota, S.D. CODIFIED LAWS ANN. §§ 60–1 to 60–4, and the Virgin Islands, V.I. CODE ANN. tit. 24, §§ 76–79. Montana is the only state that has adopted a comprehensive wrongful termination statute. MONT. CODE ANN. §§ 39–2–902 to 39–2–914.

The Montana situation illustrates the interaction between judicial and legislative change. In 1982, the Montana Supreme Court indicated it was ready to consider awarding tort damages for breach of an implied duty of good faith and fair dealing owed by employers. Over the next few years, several substantial damage judgments were awarded for this tort. Montana employers, previously indifferent or opposed to legislation on the subject, became vigorous supporters of a comprehensive statute. The end result was a law that bars termination of non probationary employees, other than "for cause," but severely limits the amount of damages that can be awarded. MONT. CODE ANN. §§ 39–2–902 to 39–2–914. Employees who are wrongfully terminated may be awarded lost wages and fringe benefits for up to four years, as well as punitive damages where there is evidence that the employer "engaged in actual fraud or actual malice" in the termination.

In the summer of 1991, the National Conference of Commissioners on Uniform State Laws approved a "Model Employment Termination Act" for consideration by state legislatures. NATIONAL CONFERENCE OF COMMISSIONERS ON UNIFORM STATE LAWS, MODEL EMPLOYMENT TERMINATION ACT. Under this proposal, a terminated "at will" employee who has worked for a covered employer a year or more, including at least 520 hours during the 26 weeks prior to his or her termination, is entitled to a remedy against that employer unless: (a) the employer can demonstrate that the termination was for cause, or (b) the employer and employee had agreed to "waive the requirement of good cause for termination" in an agreement that provides for severance pay that amounts to "at least one month's pay for each period of employment totaling one year * * *" up to a maximum of 30 months. The drafters state a clear preference for resolving these disputes through an arbitration system set up in Sections 5 and 6 of the statute, but they have also drafted alternative provisions for enforcement by an administrative agency or by the courts. The remedy provided to an employee found to have been terminated without cause is either: (a) reinstatement (with full or partial backpay); or (b) a lump sum severance pay award of up to 36 months. Attorney's fees and costs are also recoverable. The arbitrator may not award any sum for pain or suffering, nor award punitive damages. The statute explicitly states that it does not preempt any other statutory claim for wrongful termination or any claim under a collective bargaining agreement. Sums obtained in other proceedings, however, are to be credited against any amount awarded under the Model Act.

The proposal has yet to be adopted The proposal was fiercely debated during drafting, and the last minute decision to designate it a "model" rather than a "uniform" act is additional evidence of the controversial nature of its provisions. The various associations of attorneys who regularly represent plaintiffs in tort actions are vigorously opposed and may be expected to lobby hard against the act in various state legislatures. Their point of attack is likely to be the limits on employer liability. Those limits on damages are extraordinary in their stringency, totally eliminating punitive damages and cutting off liability for the various common law causes of action that are "associated torts" with wrongful termination. Even the Montana statute enacted with strong employer support does not cut off punitive damages entirely, but makes them available only in the case of actual fraud or actual malice in the termination of the employee.

If the Model Act were to be enacted in roughly its present form, one impact would likely be a change in which employees are the primary beneficiaries of legal limits on wrongful termination. To date, the "ideal" plaintiff in a wrongful termination case has been an executive level employee with a number of years of service. Such an individual is going to be entitled to relatively high special damages, since the actual wage loss is going to be high and there is a good argument for "front pay" damages: sums assessed because the wrongfully terminated worker is unlikely to be able to find a similar job in the future, given the employee's age and relatively high earnings experience. This sort of plaintiff is also likely to have a sympathetic case for other types of damages, those for mental distress or defamation, for example, and also for punitive damages. The prospect of potential high damage awards makes it relatively easy for this type of plaintiff to obtain counsel on a contingency basis. With the limits on damages in the Model Act, the attractiveness of these cases to counsel is reduced although not eliminated, since substantial damages may well be available under associated statutory theories. Thus, the principal beneficiary of the Model Act would likely be the "rank and file" worker who receives a more generous severance pay because of an agreement entered into with an employer that wishes to avoid liability under the statute.

A somewhat similar controversy, though not about a statute, is going on now within the American Law Institute, which is debating whether to adopt a *Restatement* on some topics of employment law. Since so much employment law is statutory, the field would not seem a likely one for "restating," but apparently the internal politics of the ALI have reached a point such that some document is fairly likely to emerge. Given the background and the division within the community of employment scholars on the subject, whether any such *Restate-*

ment will have significant impact on the courts is open to question.

C. WHAT IS "GOOD CAUSE" FOR TERMINATION?

Whenever a fired worker claims her discharge was unlawful, whether under a statute or a common law doctrine, an employer may escape liability by demonstrating that the sole reason for the discharge was "good cause." Defining "good cause" for termination is a formidable task. The myriad reasons why an employer may be justified in terminating an employee are so numerous and so context dependent that no short one sentence definition of good cause (in some statutes simply "cause") is possible. The drafters of the Model Employment Termination Act have attempted it (one sentence, but certainly not short) that is probably as inclusive as any. Their provision states:

"Good cause" means (i) a reasonable basis related to an individual employee for termination of the employee's employment in view of relevant factors and circumstances which may include the employee's duties, responsibilities, conduct on the job or otherwise, job performance and employment record, or (ii) the exercise of business judgment in good faith by the employer, including setting its economic or institutional goals and determining methods to reach those goals, organizing or reorganizing operations, discontinuing, consolidating, or divesting operations or positions or parts of operations or positions, determining the size of its workforce and the nature of the positions filled by its workforce, and determining and changing standards of performance for positions. NATIONAL CONFERENCE OF COMMISSIONERS ON UNIFORM STATE LAWS, MODEL EMPLOYMENT TERMINATION ACT § 1(4) (August 8, 1991).

The burden of proof of good cause is usually borne by the employer. This is either because an agreement or statute places the burden there directly, or because a terminated employee (or representative) has already carried the burden of producing evidence that the employee was terminated for a forbidden reason, such as age, race, or refusal to perform an unlawful act.

Inadequate job performance. In these cases, the first difficulty is deciding what constitutes adequate performance. Some job performances can be measured quite readily—number of words typed per minute, for example—but measuring the performance of a circus clown or a tenure track faculty member can be demanding indeed. Claims of poor performance are more credible if the employer can show that the employee was counseled about poor performance and failed to improve, or that similar performance by others has led to discharge. See *Wilking v. County of Ramsey*, 153 F.3d 869 (8th Cir.1998). If, on the other hand, poor performance is first mentioned late in the termination procedure, the claim is less likely to be believed. See *Carlton v. Mystic Transportation, Inc.*, 202 F.3d 129 (2d Cir.

2000), cert. denied, 530 U.S. 1261. The manner in which performance is evaluated is also a source of controversy. Courts are understandably skeptical of highly subjective evaluation systems.

Job related misconduct. Two types of employee misconduct may justify termination. One is conduct that is so offensive that reasonable persons would agree it cannot be tolerated in a work environment, conduct such as assaulting a fellow worker with intent to harm her in the absence of provocation. In that sort of case, the employer need only show that the terminated worker engaged in these serious acts. See, e.g., *Taylor v. Procter & Gamble Dover Wipes*, 184 F.Supp.2d 402 (D.Del.2002). Violations of rules present different issues. The use of profanity may not be viewed as highly desirable conduct by society in general, but it is not regarded as intolerable, and will not constitute good cause for termination unless it is inappropriate in the special context of the job or unless it violates a rule that the employer has issued. For this rule to be given effect, the employer must be able to demonstrate that it was understandable and also that it was communicated to the employee. See, e.g., *Martin v. Parrish*, 805 F.2d 583 (5th Cir.1986). Even then, the employee may be able to prevail by demonstrating that the rule has not been consistently enforced. *Pearson v. Metro–North Commuter Railroad*, 57 F.E.P.Cases (BNA) 1589 (S.D.N.Y.1990).

Off the job conduct. While all courts would agree that an employer is entitled to a wide range of discretion in making rules to govern the conduct of work and the workplace, there is little consensus as yet about the propriety of rules about off duty conduct. Many courts are willing to entertain challenges to the reasonableness of rules attempting to prevent such conduct as off the job smoking or consensual sexual conduct. Nonetheless, many of these rules exist, and some are surely enforceable. A religious publisher might well be able to terminate its editor in chief for engaging in highly publicized extramarital affairs and not be liable for breach of a contract of employment for a term of years. It is much less likely the same employer would be held justified in terminating a loading dock employee named as co respondent in his neighbor's divorce proceeding.

Business needs. When an employer defends a termination as "for cause" because of business needs, such as eliminating a product line, there is a major difference between contract and tort theory cases. In the case of the tort of wrongful termination this defense, once established by adequate proof, will ordinarily entitle the employer to escape liability entirely. In contract cases, however, it is necessary for the court to determine first whether the contract has put the risk of business changes entirely on the employer's shoulders. If, for example, a corporation attracts an executive by a promise of a five year contract at a high salary, the usual interpretation would be that the executive is entitled to the full five years of compensation even if the business does not succeed and has to close down. On the other hand, a handbook pledge of continued employment unless there is "good cause" for termination would very likely be read so that decreasing demand for the employer's product would be included in that "good cause." Since many employment contracts do not specify who bears what business risks, the question of whether the employer's duty to pay is absolute or qualified by an implied exception for business conditions must be made on the basis of the totality of the circumstances.

In tort cases and in those contract cases in which changes in business needs explicitly or impliedly excuse the employer from further performance, the range of business needs that can be good cause for termination is broad. This surely reflects a desire not to burden managements with the need to justify in detail in court proceedings why, short of bankruptcy, they decided to take such steps as: (1) eliminating a product or service, *Telesphere International, Inc. v. Scollin*, 489 So.2d 1152 (Fla.App. 1986); (2) ceasing operations, *Friske v. Jasinski Builders, Inc.*, 156 Mich.App. 468, 402 N.W.2d 42 (Mich.App.1986); or (3) consolidating operations, *Nixon v. Celotex Corp.*, 693 F.Supp. 547 (W.D.Mich. 1988). In each of these instances, the change in operations is one that reduces the scope of the employer's business, and thus of its opportunity to make a profit. It is reasonable to assume these decisions are not made lightly. Other restructurings do not involve that loss of profit opportunity, such as a general reduction in force without a noticeable change in the size of the business. In some of these cases, a few courts have been willing to give terminated employees a chance to show that the proffered reason for a general reduction—improved efficiency, or a generalized need to reduce costs—is simply a pretext for a wrongful termination. It is also important to remember that a generalized reduction in force does not by itself explain why a specific employee was selected to be one of those eliminated. *Ewers v. Stroh Brewery Co.*, 178 Mich. App. 371, 443 N.W.2d 504 (Mich.App.1989); *Harlan v. Sohio Petroleum*, 677 F.Supp. 1021 (N.D.Cal. 1988).

After acquired evidence. A lively debate has gone on in recent years about the effect of evidence of employee misconduct that might justify termination, but that is not discovered by the employer until after the actual termination has taken place. This has been addressed by the Supreme Court under the Age Discrimination in Employment Act (ADEA). In *McKennon v. Nashville Banner*, 513 U.S. 352 (1995), the Court ruled, in an action for wrongful termination brought under the ADEA, that a federal court should admit evidence of employee misconduct uncovered after the termination, but not as a bar to liability. This evidence is relevant for more limited purposes, such as deciding what might constitute an appropriate remedy. In particular, the Court's opinion indicates reinstatement is not an appropriate remedy if the employer proves the after discovered misconduct was such that it would have led the employer to terminate the worker in the first place.

This debate still continues in other areas of employment law. Some courts have been willing to accept evidence that an employee falsified an employment application, for instance, as a complete defense to a wrongful termination charge. Others have held that this evidence is admissible, but is relevant only to the issue of what remedy should be given. Such a court might, for example, find a termination to have been wrongful and award modest damages but refuse to grant reinstatement. Another group of courts, and many arbitrators, have regarded after acquired evidence as irrelevant. In their view, what matters in deciding whether a termination was proper or not was what the employer knew at the time of the termination that is being challenged. See *United Paperworkers Union v. Misco, Inc.*, 484 U.S. 29 (1987).

D. "CONSTRUCTIVE" TERMINATIONS AND QUITS

On occasion an employer may seek to get rid of a troublesome employee not by saying, "You're fired!" but by making the conditions of work so unpleasant that the employee will feel compelled to leave the workplace "voluntarily." The courts and administrative agencies that apply the doctrines discussed in this Nutshell have long since recognized that this departure is not truly voluntary, and have held that an employer that has acted in this fashion is to be treated as having terminated the worker. A college that relieved a faculty member of teaching responsibilities and assigned her instead to preparing a revision of a handbook and other largely clerical duties associated with grant applications was found to have constructively terminated her. *Lincoln v. University System of Georgia Board of Regents*, 697 F.2d 928 (11th Cir.1983). The burden of proof that conditions have reached a level that compels leaving is a heavy one. Being demoted or passed over for an expected promotion is by itself rarely thought so humiliating as to constitute a termination, even though one continues to work with persons who are aware of the adverse action. See, e.g., *Jurgens v. EEOC*, 903 F.2d 386 (5th Cir.1990).

The "flip" side of constructive termination is the concept of the "constructive voluntary quit," most often employed in unemployment compensation proceedings. An employee that for several days neither shows up for work on schedule nor calls in to notify the employer of the absence may reasonably be thought by the employer to have lost interest in the job. Since terminating the employee might at times lead to liability for severance pay or some other benefit, the employer may instead argue that the worker's actions are so totally inconsistent with employee status that it is proper to treat the case as one of resigning rather than of termination. *Midwest Metallurgical Laboratory, Inc. and Molders, Local 120*, 79 Lab.Arb. 21 (1982) (Jason, Arb.).

E. WORKER ADJUSTMENT AND RETRAINING NOTIFICATION ACT

1. Scope

The Worker Adjustment and Retraining Notification Act (WARN), enacted in 1988, requires business enterprises that employ 100 or more employees to provide affected employees, or their bargaining representatives, and certain state and local government entities, 60 days advance written notice before "plant closings" or "mass layoffs." 29 U.S.C.A. §§ 2101–2109.

WARN is enforced exclusively by actions brought by employees or by local governments in the United States district courts. A union that represents employees entitled to WARN Act notification has standing to sue on their behalf. *United Food and Commercial Workers Local 751 v. Brown Group*, 517 U.S. 544 (1996). The Secretary of Labor is authorized to issue regulations for its implementation. 29 U.S.C.A. § 2107; see 20 C.F.R. pt. 639.

WARN states that the Act and its remedies are not intended to alter or affect any other contractual or statutory remedies, except that the notification period required under the Act runs concurrently with any period of notification required under a contract or statute. This means that in addition to compliance with WARN, Massachusetts, Connecticut, and Maine employers, for example, must comply with applicable provisions of their respective state plant closing statutes. WARN contains no statute of limitations, but the Supreme Court in *North Star Steel Co. v. Thomas*, 515 U.S. 29 (1995) determined that courts presented with WARN Act cases should borrow the limitations period from the most analogous state statute.

2. Coverage

An "employer" is a "business enterprise" that employs at least 100 persons, other than part time employees, or that employs at least 500 employees who in the aggregate work at least 4,000 hours in a week exclusive of overtime. Use of the phrase "business enterprise" has been held to exclude from the "employer" category individual managers and executives, even including owners of employing corporation unless it is appropriate to "pierce the corporate veil." *Wallace v. Detroit Coke Corp.*, 818 F.Supp. 192 (E.D.Mich.1993); *Carpenters District Council v. Dillard Department Stores, Inc.*, 778 F.Supp. 297 (E.D.La.1991), aff'd in part, 15 F.3d 1275 (5th Cir. 1994). Liability has been imposed on the parent of a wholly owned subsidiary on the ground that the effective control of labor policy decisions rested with the parent so that it was the "alter ego" of the employing unit. *Local 397, IUE v. Midwest Fasteners, Inc.*, 779 F.Supp. 788 (D.N.J.1992). When government, rather than the employer, makes the effective decision to shut down, the employer is not liable for failure to give the proper notice. *Deveraturda v. Globe Aviation Security Services*, 454 F.3d 1043 (9th Cir. 2006).

"Plant shutdown" and "mass layoff" are terms of art that are carefully defined in the statute. "Plant closing" means the shutdown of a site, or of one or more facilities or operating units at a single site, that results in an "employment loss" for 50 or more employees. 29 U.S.C.A. § 2102(a)(2). It does not matter that the employer expects to reopen the site, facility or operating unit in seven months after renovation, only that it is totally shut down. "Mass layoff" refers to a situation in which there is an "employment loss" during any 30–day period at a single site for either: (1) 33 per cent of the employees at that site, if they number 50 or more, or (2) 500 or more employees. 29 U.S.C.A. § 2101(a)(3). Such a layoff may be part of a plan to phase out a plant, but be treated under the statute as a layoff rather than as a closing until the final shutdown phase. The definition of "employment loss" adds to the technical nature of these provisions: "(A) an employment termination, other than a discharge for cause, voluntary departure, or retirement, (B) a layoff exceeding 6 months, or (C) a reduction in hours of work of more than 50 per cent during each month of any 6–month period." An individual does not suffer an employment loss, however, if the closing or layoff is the result of a consolidation or relocation and the employer offers the employee a suitable job at a different site that will begin within 6 months, provided either that (1) the new site is within a reasonable commuting distance, or (2) the employee accepts the offer. 29 U.S.C.A. § 2101 (a)(6), (b)(2). To further complicate matters, a special aggregation section provides that if employment losses occur within a 90–day period at a site that do not constitute "plant closings" or "mass layoffs" when considered alone because the numbers of affected involved are too small, these events may be combined to determine whether the aggregate numbers meet the Act's numerical requirements, "unless the employer demonstrates that the employment losses are the result of separate and distinct actions and causes * * *." 29 U.S.C.A. § 2102(d).

An "affected employee" is one who may reasonably be expected to experience an employment loss as a result of a plant closing or mass layoff. Part time employees—those employed for an average of fewer than 20 hours a week or who have been employed for fewer than 6 of the 12 months preceding the date of a required notice—are not included in the counts that determine whether there is a plant closing or mass layoff. A part time worker may, however, be an "affected employee" and thus entitled to notification. In similar fashion, employees at sites other than the location of the closing or layoff are not counted for determining whether notification is required, but may be entitled to notice if it is clear they will suffer an employment loss because of the shutdown. Laid off employees may be affected employees, according to the regulations, but only so long as they have a reasonable expectation of recall. *Damron v. Rob Fork Mining Corp.*, 945 F.2d 121 (6th Cir.1991) (no reasonable expectation after an 8–year layoff).

3. Content and Timing of Notification

The statute itself says very little about what the notification should contain. The Department of Labor's regulations provide the needed detail. Those regulations list different items of information depending on the identity of the person or entity being notified. These differences reflect the drafters' understanding of why the notice is to be given. For instance, a notice sent to an individual employee is to include a statement about bumping rights, so that the worker can make judgments about whether to exercise such rights or whether he or she is in danger of being bumped by another person. No such requirement exists in the case of the notice to be sent to the chief official of a union. Instead, that notice must include information about affected job classifications and the names of employees in each. Presumably the labor organization is fully aware of whatever bumping rights exist, because of its role in bargaining on behalf of employees subject to those rights. The unrepresented individual is not. Perhaps the most controversial regulation is that defining the precision that should be achieved in identifying the probable date of termination or layoff: no more than a 14–day span. An employer's argument that the best it could be expected do in a notice to a union was to project the likely gross numbers of layoffs by calendar quarters over a year was rejected in *OCAW Local 7–515 v. American Home Products Corp.*, 790 F.Supp. 1441 (N.D.Ind.1992).

The general requirement of the statute is that notice be given 60 calendar days prior to the closing or layoff. This makes fixing the date of either event critical, and as discussed above, there are two "aggregation periods" that must be taken into account: the 30–day period used to determine whether a sufficient number of employees have been terminated or laid off in a single facility or unit at a site, and the special 90–day rule to be applied when these employment effects occur in different facilities and units. Moreover, in the lay off situation it is possible that the employer is not entirely sure at the commencement of the layoff whether it will last 6 months or longer. Whether the uncertainties that arise from these factors will lead employers to gamble on whether notification is required remains to be seen. The regulations seek to make that gamble unattractive, by discouraging the use of "rolling" notification, under which an employer is constantly telling employees they are in danger of being fired or laid off, and by providing concrete illustrations in many sections of the regulations that will reduce the level of uncertainty.

The statute provides for a shorter than 60–day notification period in three circumstances: (1) An employer seeking an infusion of capital or new business in order to keep the business going may give shorter notice if that employer reasonably and in good faith believed that giving notice for the full 60 days would have lessened the chance of getting the required capital or business. (2) An employer may give shortened notice if the closing or layoff is the result of "business circumstances that were not reasonably foreseeable" at the beginning of the 60–day period. (3) No notification is required if the closing or layoff is the result of a natural disaster such as a flood, earthquake, or drought. In any of these three situations, the employer is to give "as much notice as is practicable." 29 U.S.C.A. § 2102(b). Each of these is likely to give rise to substantial litigation, especially when a factor that is not a valid reason for short notice under the statute, such as unreasonable optimism that "things will turn around and get better," is combined with a true unforeseeable circumstance, such as an unpredictable drop in the prices of the employer's products. See, e.g., *Chestnut v. Stone Forest Industries, Inc.*, 817 F.Supp. 932 (N.D.Fla.1993). Ordinarily, cancellation of a major contract will probably be an unforeseeable circumstance. *Gross v. Hale–Halsell Co.*, 554 F.3d 870 (10th Cir. 2009). In *IAM District Lodge 776 v. General Dynamics Corp.*, 821 F.Supp. 1306 (E.D.Mo.1993), however, the court held that the employer should have been able to forecast that its failure to meet schedules and its cost overruns were likely going to cause loss of a major defense project.

4. Exemptions

The statute contains two principal exemptions. It does not apply to a plant closing or layoff at a temporary facility, or as the result of completing a particular project, provided that the affected employees were hired with the understanding that their jobs would be temporary. Nor does it apply in the case of a strike or lockout, unless intended as a means of evading the requirements of WARN.

5. Good Faith Defense

An employer that has violated the statute may nonetheless escape all or much of its liability by proving "to the satisfaction of the court that the act or omission that violated this chapter was in good faith and that the employer had reasonable grounds for believing that the act or omission was not a violation of this chapter * * *." 29 U.S.C.A. § 2104 (a)(4). "Subjective" good faith is not enough; the employer must have objective reasons for its belief. *Castro v. Chicago Housing Authority*, 360 F.3d 721 (7th Cir. 2004); *Saxion v. Titan–C Manufacturing, Inc.*, 86 F.3d 553 (6th Cir.1996). Giving notice in a fashion that arguably meets the requirements of the regulations according to one possible (though incorrect) reading of those requirements is action in good faith. See *OCAW Local 7–515 v. American Home Products Corp.*, 790 F.Supp. 1441 (N.D.Ind.1992). Not giving notice to laid off employees because of reasonable misunderstanding as to whether they were entitled to notice has also been found to be in good faith. *Kildea v. Electro–Wire Products, Inc.*, 144 F.3d 400 (6th Cir.1998). Delaying notice because of a highly unlikely possibility that a shutdown may not occur is not. *Jones v. Kayser–Roth Hosiery, Inc.*, 748 F.Supp. 1276 (E.D.Tenn.1990).

6. Liability

An employer that violates the act may be required to pay: (1) a civil penalty of up to $500 for each day of violation, payable to the appropriate unit of local government that was not notified; (2) back pay to each aggrieved employee for each day of violation; (3) at the court's discretion, costs including attorney's fees. The civil penalty due a unit of local government may be avoided if the employer pays all sums due each affected employee within three weeks from the date the employer orders the layoff or closing. The back pay due to each employee is to be computed by using either that employee's average rate of pay during the three previous years, or the final rate of pay being received at the time of the employment loss. It also includes benefits (as defined in ERISA) except that the medical benefits due are not the amount of premium contributions that would be ordinarily made, but rather the "cost of medical expenses incurred during the employment loss which would have been covered * * * if the employment loss had not occurred." The circuit courts have divided over whether the penalty is due for each calendar day of violation, even though the employee might not have been expected to work all those days, or for each workday. Most use the workday approach. See the discussion of the split in *Burns v. Stone Forest Industries*, 147 F.3d 1182 (9th Cir.1998). An employer is entitled to credits against the amounts due for such items as wages actually paid for any day during the time of violation, other payments made to the affected employee voluntarily and without condition for that period, and contributions to benefit plans for the relevant period. Defined benefit pension liabilities may be met by crediting each affected employee with the appropriate additional amount of service. 29 U.S.C.A. § 2104.

F. POST–TERMINATION OBLIGATIONS OF EMPLOYEES: DUTIES OF LOYALTY AND RESTRICTIVE COVENANTS

Whether the employment contract documents say so or not, the employee owes the employer a duty of loyalty that includes, among other things:

- a duty not to appropriate or disclose the employer's trade secrets;

- a duty not to take for one's self business opportunities that, under ordinary business practice, would be thought to belong to the employer; and

- a duty not to compete with the employer while an employee.

The first two, particularly the duty to protect trade secrets, extend beyond the employment term, the third usually does not. All are subject to negotiation (they are, in current contract law jargon, "default" terms). The scope of each is murky and varies from state to state. In order to clarify the extent of each, these are often the subject of specific written memorials, familiarly known as "restrictive covenants." Since one function of these covenants is usually to limit the activities of employees shortly before and after termination, we consider them here.

1. Trade Secrets and Other Confidential Information

Agreements not to reveal trade secrets have been enforced in the United States since at least 1868. *Peabody v. Norfolk*, 98 Mass. 452 (Mass.1868). One can argue for an even earlier date. See *Vickery v. Welch*, 36 Mass. 523 (Mass.1837). A trade secret is an employer's secret plan, device, process, tool, mechanism, or component of a unique nature. It may "consist of any formula, pattern, device, or information compilation that is used in an employer's business and that gives the employer an opportunity to gain an advantage over competitors who do not know or use it." RESTATEMENT OF TORTS § 757, comment (b) (1939). The RESTATEMENT comment elaborates on the variety of trade secrets. They include "a formula for a chemical compound, a process of manufacturing, treating, or preserving materials, a pattern for a machine or other device," or a customer list. A trade secret may relate to the production of goods; the sale of goods (discount codes); or a way of carrying on a business function (a computer bookkeeping program). The Uniform Trade Secrets Act, first issued in 1979, has been adopted in roughly forty states, but often with modifications.

The general knowledge and skill one acquires during employment by a firm is not a "trade secret." Neither is information commonly known in an industry or acquired by an employee from another source. *GTI Corp. v. Calhoon*, 309 F.Supp. 762 (S.D.Ohio 1969). The employer must take steps to maintain the "secrecy," such as insisting on employee and customer agreements to maintain confidentiality, or protection will be lost. *Rockwell Graphic Systems, Inc. v. DEV Industries, Inc.*, 925 F.2d 174 (7th Cir.1991).

It is not necessary that a process or machine be patentable to be a trade secret. The law protecting trade secrets is for the most part state law, and it is not preempted by federal law unless the two conflict. *Kewanee Oil Co. v. Bicron Corp.*, 416 U.S. 470 (1974); *Bonito Boats, Inc. v. Thunder Craft Boats, Inc.*, 489 U.S. 141 (1989).

Generally, if someone outside the employer's business learns innocently of a trade secret, that person will be able to use it unless prevented by a patent or copyright. See, e.g., *Underwater Storage, Inc. v. United States Rubber Co.*, 371 F.2d 950 (D.C.Cir.1966), cert. denied, 386 U.S. 911 (1967). If, however, a third party outside the employer's business obtains the trade secret from a former employee and knows that employee disclosed the information in breach of a restrictive covenant, the third party as well as the employee will be liable to the former employer. See, e.g., *A.H. Emery Co. v. Marcan Prods. Corp.*, 268 F.Supp. 289 (S.D.N.Y.1967), aff'd, 389 F.2d 11 (2d Cir.), cert. denied, 393 U.S. 835 (1968).

Because just what information is a trade secret is hard to define, employers routinely take steps to designate information as "confidential" and to exact promises from employees to protect this confidentiality. American courts have recognized that being able to entrust confidential information to workers is important to running a business, and have therefore enforced these agreements, provided they meet a general "reasonableness" standard, at least for so long as the employment relation continues. Once employment is terminated, some courts have concluded that the only confidential information that is protected is trade secrets. See *Hickory Specialties, Inc. v. Forest Flavors International, Inc.*, 12 F.Supp.2d 760 (M.D.Tenn.1998). Others appear, at least, to allow an employer to protect confidential information other than trade secrets from disclosure by former employees. See *McCombs v. McClelland*, 223 Or. 475, 354 P.2d 311 (Or.1960).

Business information entitled to protection may include:

1. A manufacturing process, provided that the process is not readily available to a competitor (see Phillips v. Frey, 20 F.3d 623 (5th Cir.1994));

2. Customer information, if their identities or their requirements are not generally known in the marketplace (see, e.g., Arnold's Ice Cream Co. v. Carlson, 330 F.Supp. 1185 (E.D.N.Y.1971)); or

3. Sales techniques and marketing approaches, when truly unique or confidential (see U.S. Reinsurance Corp. v. Humphreys, 205 A.D.2d 187, 618 N.Y.S.2d 270 (App.Div.1994)).

To be entitled to protection, the information must in fact be confidential. In determining whether confidential information entitled to protection is involved, a court will consider both:

1. The availability of the information in the marketplace and

2. The manner in which the employer itself treats the information; does the employer treat it as confidential and take the necessary means to protect it?

If the employer acts as if the information is not confidential, it will not be protected. See, e.g., *Capsonic Group, Inc. v. Plas–Met Corp.*, 46 Ill.App.3d 436, 5 Ill.Dec. 41, 361 N.E.2d 41 (Ill.App.1977). Likewise, it will not be protected if the employer discloses the information to third parties without conditions. See, e.g., *John D. Park & Sons Co. v. Hartman*, 153 Fed. 24 (6th Cir.1907), cert. dismissed, 212 U.S. 588 (1908). However, if the employer treats the information in a confidential manner by restricting access, the likelihood it will be held to be protected is increased. In one Alabama case, the court held it was for a jury to determine whether a firm had failed to keep information secret because it had put the papers containing the data into regular trash containers without shredding it. *Soap Co. v. Ecolab, Inc.*, 646 So.2d 1366 (Ala.1994).

2. Restrictive Covenants

By and large American law seeks to foster competition and an open market. Despite that, employee agreements not to compete during and after employment are regularly enforced by American courts, if they meet certain standards.

It is easy enough to understand this obligation during the employment term. For an employee to form a competing company and siphon off business from his employer has at least a whiff of thieving about it. See *American Federal Group, Ltd. v. Rothenberg*, 136 F.3d 897 (2d Cir.1998); *AGA Aktiebolag v. ABA Optical Corp.*, 441 F.Supp. 747 (E.D.N.Y. 1977). But even during employment, there can be exceptional cases. Suppose Frank's Foods is desperate for a manager for its upscale restaurant in Anytown. It approaches Al Adams, co owner with his wife of Chez Paris, in Bigtown, a community 30 miles away, and he takes the job. Mr. Adams continues to aid his wife in the Chez Paris business, even though the parties never discussed this and there is some modest overlap in the customer base. Surely when Frank's Foods hired Mr. Adams, knowing his situation, it did not contemplate he would cease all activity at Chez Paris. If it did, we would expect that firm to say so. But may Mr. Adams talk freely with his wife about interesting dishes available at his new place of employment? The question is not all that easy to answer. In an era when computers make some forms of moonlighting easier than ever, questions like this will likely tax attorneys—and in rare cases the courts—more often.

There is substantially more case law on non competition agreements with respect to former employees. Because of the general principles favoring competition, a former employee is free to compete with her former employer except when doing so requires the use of a trade secret or other protected information, or breaches an enforceable covenant. Such covenants are rarely, if ever, implied. See *American Federal Group, Ltd. v. Rothenberg*, 136 F.3d 897 (2d Cir.1998). For restrictive covenants to be enforceable, they must be:

- Designed to protect a legitimate employer interest;

- Supported by consideration; and

- Reasonable in scope.

a. Protection of "Legitimate Business Interests"

One of the most common issues in cases involving restrictive covenants is whether the covenant in question was designed to protect a legitimate interest. Such interests include:

- Near permanent relationships with clients. *Outsource International, Inc. v. Barton*, 192 F.3d 662 (7th Cir.1999); *Rapp Ins. Agency, Inc. v. Baldree*, 231 Ill.App.3d 1038, 173 Ill.Dec. 962, 597 N.E.2d 936 (Ill.App.1992).

- Trade secrets and other confidential information. *Ackerman v. Kimball Int'l, Inc.*, 634

N.E.2d 778 (Ind.App.1994) (customer and supplier lists); *SI Handling Sys., Inc. v. Heisley*, 753 F.2d 1244 (3d Cir.1985) (detailed evaluation of protected and unprotected categories of information).

• Good will. *Garber Bros. v. Evlek*, 122 F.Supp.2d 375 (E.D.N.Y.2000); *Thomas W. Briggs Co. v. Mason*, 217 Ky. 269, 289 S.W. 295 (Ky.1926).

Employers may not use restrictive covenants merely because they think they are a good idea, to intimidate employees, or to discourage employees from looking for employment elsewhere. If the covenant is for a purpose such as eliminating competition or maintaining a proprietary interest in one's customers, the covenant will not be enforced. See, e.g., *Statesville Medical Group v. Dickey,* 106 N.C.App. 669, 418 S.E.2d 256 (N.C.1992).

b.   *Consideration for Restrictive Covenants*

Since a covenant not to compete is a contract, consideration for the promise is critical. To be valid, the covenant must be given in exchange for something, either some benefit to the employee or some detriment to the employer. See, e.g., *Davis & Warde, Inc. v. Tripodi*, 420 Pa.Super. 450, 616 A.2d 1384 (1992). There need not be a separate consideration for each provision in an employment contract. If there is consideration for the contract, there is consideration for each provision within it, including the covenants. See, e.g., *Sarnoff v. American Home Prods. Corp.*, 798 F.2d 1075 (7th Cir.1986).

Generally, commencing employment is sufficient consideration to support a restrictive covenant. See, e.g., *Ruffing v. 84 Lumber Co.*, 410 Pa.Super. 459, 600 A.2d 545 (Pa.Super.1991). However, entering into a covenant during employment creates special problems. Consideration must still exist to support the covenant. For many courts, continued employment is not sufficient unless a change has occurred. See, e.g., *Bilec v. Auburn & Assoc., Inc. Pension Trust*, 403 Pa.Super. 176, 588 A.2d 538 (Pa.Super.1991). Examples of consideration that will support a covenant entered into during employment include:

- Additional compensation; see, e.g., *Hollingsworth Solderless Terminal Co. v. Turley*, 622 F.2d 1324 (9th Cir.1980);

- A new employment benefit; see, e.g., *Wainwright's Travel Service, Inc. v. Schmolk*, 347 Pa.Super. 199, 500 A.2d 476 (Pa.Super.1985);

- Greater responsibility; see, e.g., *Davis & Warde, Inc. v. Tripodi* (Pa.Super.1992);

- A new position; see, e.g., *Hollingsworth Solderless Terminal Co. v. Turley* (9th Cir.1980); or

- Changing the employee's status from at will employment to employment for a term. *Kramer v. Robec, Inc.*, 824 F.Supp. 508 (E.D.Pa.1992).

c. *Scope*

Most of the cases dealing with whether a restrictive covenant is "overbroad" address one or more of three factors:

- geographic limits imposed by the covenant;
- time limits imposed by the covenant; and
- activity limits imposed by the covenant.

There is a major difference in how courts treat the "scope" issue as compared to the "legitimate business interest" or "consideration" issues. If a covenant does not protect a legitimate interest, or if no consideration was given for the employee's pledge not to compete, then the covenant simply is void and will not be enforced. If, on the other hand, there is a legitimate interest to be protected, and if consideration was given, but the covenant is found to be too broad, a court has an option. It may decide to issue an injunction enforcing only that portion of the covenant that the court finds to be reasonable. In *John Roane, Inc. v. Tweed*, 89 A.2d 548 (Del. 1952), an employee of an insurance adjusting company agreed not to compete with the employer for a period of five years within a fifty mile radius of the employer's home base in Wilmington, Delaware. The court decided that the covenant should be enforced, but reduced the geographic restriction to the immediate Wilmington area, so that the former employee could compete in the Philadelphia market, and cut the time limit by a year. Other courts are reluctant to "reform" or "red-line" a covenant and then enforce it. See *Crowe v. Manpower Temporary Services*, 256 Ga. 239, 347 S.E.2d 560 (Ga.1986).

Deciding whether a restriction is reasonable or overbroad involves a balancing of many factors. Three questions are particularly important:

1. Is the restriction greater than necessary to protect the employer's legitimate business interests?

2. Is the restriction oppressive to the employee, by making it unduly difficult for the employee to get work that fits her skills and experience?

3. Is the restriction injurious to the general public? See, e.g., *Hamer Holding Group, Inc. v. Elmore*, 202 Ill.App.3d 994, 560 N.E.2d 907, 148 Ill.Dec. 310 (Ill.App.1990).

A restriction's reasonableness depends on the scope of the employer's business and the nature of the employee's position. If the employer does not do business in a large part of the geographic area covered by the covenant, then the covenant is probably overbroad. *John Roane, Inc. v. Tweed*, 89 A.2d 548 (Del.1952). If the employer does business in an area, but the employee has not represented the employer in that area, then the question becomes one of what interest the covenant protects. If it protects "good will" then forbidding the former employee to compete in that area probably goes too far, since that former employee would not be associated with the employer in the minds of customers. *Crowe v. Manpower Temporary Services*, 256 Ga. 239, 347 S.E.2d 560 (Ga.1986). If the purpose is to prevent the former employee from using the employer's confidential information and trade secrets, on the other hand, a broader geographic limitation is probably proper. *Orkin Exterminating Co. v. Mills*, 218 Ga. 340, 127 S.E.2d 796 (Ga.1962).

Deciding how long is a reasonable restriction on competition is also difficult. One factor is how long it might take the employer to train a new worker to be an effective competitor with the former employee. *Curtis 1000, Inc. v. Youngblade*, 878 F.Supp. 1224 (N.D.Iowa 1995).

Restricting a former employee from working at all for a competitor probably goes too far in most cases; a restriction preventing the former employee from using or revealing trade secrets or from soliciting former customers is more likely to be acceptable. *Blue Ridge Anesthesia and Critical Care, Inc. v. Gidick*, 239 Va. 369, 389 S.E.2d 467 (Va.1990).

During the last few years, the American Medical Association and other specialty medical groups have issued position statements indicating that restrictive covenants should be little used in the employment agreements of physicians, because of the potential impact on health care. Courts have taken note of this, but are not agreeing on the extent to which these pronouncements should affect decisions. See, e.g., *Murfreesboro Medical Clinic, P.A. v. Udom,* 166 S.W.3d 674 (Tenn. 2005) (physicians covenants not to compete void except as specifically permitted by statute); *The Community Hospital Group,Inc. v. More,* 183 N.J. 36, 869 A.2d 884 (2005) (covenant enforced as reformed by court); *Mohanty v. St. John Heart Clinic,* 225 Ill.2d 52, 310

Ill.Dec. 274, 866 N.E.2d 85 (2006) (AMA statement given little weight).

G.   UNEMPLOYMENT COMPENSATION

1.   General Structure

The Federal Unemployment Compensation Act is designed to provide unemployment compensation to employees who become unemployed through no fault of their own. 42 U.S.C.A. §§ 501–504, 1101–1105. The unemployment insurance system in the United States had its origin during the Great Depression of the 1930's when high unemployment occurred. The system's principal objectives are:

1.   To enhance employment opportunities through a network of employment service offices throughout the nation where job seekers and job openings can be matched efficiently;

2.   To stabilize employment by encouraging employers to retain employees during short periods of economic downturns through the experience rating features of state statutes; 29 U.S.C.A. § 469; and

3.   To minimize the economic loss of unemployment by paying benefits to the unemployed. 26 U.S.C.A. § 496.

Unemployment compensation is a joint federal-state program. The federal statute imposes a tax on payrolls. That tax rate is reduced, however, to less than one percent if the employer is covered by a state unemployment compensation law that meets standards set out in the federal statute. These standards address both substantive matters, such as what should be the conditions of eligibility for benefits, and the procedures by which benefits are to be paid. The typical tax rates paid under state law are lower than five percent for most employers, thus creating a substantial incentive for states to participate. An argument that this type of incentive is an unconstitutional coercion of the states by the federal government was rejected in *Chas. C. Steward Machine Co. v. Davis*, 301 U.S. 548 (1937). This federal state sharing of responsibility has generally worked fairly smoothly, but it has made it necessary to work out a number of multi state agreements to handle certain administrative problems.

2. Eligibility for Benefits

To qualify for benefits, an applicant must show that he or she:

1. has earned a minimum amount of wages in a job covered by the unemployment compensation tax system during the period prior to becoming unemployed;

2. is currently out of work;

3. is able and available to work; and

4. has registered at an appropriate government operated employment service office, from which the applicant may be referred to prospective employers.

Benefits paid under this system are chargeable against the employer's individual reserve account into which have been deposited state unemployment taxes attributable to individuals in the employer's employ.

Employer payroll taxes that finance unemployment compensation are established at rates that are lower for employers that experience relatively few benefit claims from former or laid off employees. Experience ratings, determining the amount of tax the employer pays, are based on maintaining separate accounts for each employer's contributions and for the benefits paid based on employment with that employer.

Benefits are paid weekly, based on past earnings, and are subject to a weekly maximum based on an index of average wages received by those employed. The maximum number of weeks of benefits has usually been 26, but during economic downturns this has sometimes been lengthened.

3. Disqualification

All unemployment compensation statutes contain "disqualification" provisions of various sorts. The severity of these varies from a brief postponement of eligibility for benefits to making a person ineligible for up to a year. See, e.g., Tenn. Code Ann. § 50–7–303(7) (fraudulent claims).

Voluntary Quit. Employees are not entitled to unemployment compensation benefits for a voluntary resignation. See *Putnam v. Department of Employment Security*, 103 N.H. 495, 175 A.2d 519 (N.H.1961). The wording of this disqualification varies from state to state. Some disqualify if the individual leaves a job without "good cause;" others deny benefits if the employee left a job without good cause "connected with" or "attributable to" the work. Omitting the work connection requirement permits a slightly wider range of consideration of "personal" causes for leaving a job. See, e.g., two cases in each of which a claimant took a job at a considerable distance from home with the intention of seeing how intolerable the travel and absence from family would prove. Each found the situation involved far too many complications and quit. Benefits were denied under an "attributable to the work" statute (*Lyons v. Appeal Bd. of Mich. Employment Security Comm'n*, 363 Mich. 201, 108 N.W.2d 849 (Mich.1961)) but were allowed under a statute without the phrase (*In re Baida's Claim*, 4 App.Div.2d 910, 167 N.Y.S.2d 145 (N.Y.App.Div. 1957)).

Persons who quit for reasons of conscience have also caused difficulties. The applicant for benefits in *Thomas v. Review Board of the Indiana Employment Security Division*, 450 U.S. 707 (1981) quit because his job required him to produce parts for a military tank, a task that violated his religious convictions. The Supreme Court held that to deny him unemployment benefits would violate the free exercise clause of the First Amendment.

Misconduct. Disqualification may also occur where employment was terminated for misconduct. For example, in *Jones v. Review Board*, 583 N.E.2d 196 (Ind.App.1991), failure to comply with a reasonable order constituted willful misconduct. It is important not to equate "misconduct" with "good cause" for termination. An employee's marginal competence, inexperience, or poor quality of output may well justify termination, but at the same time not be "misconduct" that would disqualify for unemployment benefits. See, e.g., *Fidelity Electric Co. v. Unemployment Compensation Board of Review*, 41 Pa.Cmwlth. 631, 399 A.2d 1183 (Pa.Cmwlth. 1979), in which the court found that the employer had not proved that the applicant was terminated because of chronic absenteeism and tardiness, but because his work was not very good. The court awarded benefits, stating "claimant's inability to measure up to employer's standards is not a bar" to benefits. Poor performance or recurrent acts of negligence can, however, be evidence of a calculated indifference to one's work that would count as misconduct. See, e.g., *Cullison v. Commonwealth, Unemployment Compensation Board of Review*, 66 Pa.Cmwlth. 416, 444 A.2d 1330 (Pa.Cmwlth.1982).

Deciding when off duty activity away from the workplace may be treated as disqualifying misconduct has proved troublesome. In *Best Lock Corp. v. Review Board*, 572 N.E.2d 520 (Ind.App.1991), the applicant for benefits was terminated for violating a rule forbidding the use of tobacco, alcohol, or drugs at any time or any place. The applicant admitted drinking off duty at a bar. The court upheld an agency determination that the applicant was not disqualified, on the ground that the rule was not reasonably related to the employer's business interests. The opinion distinguished an earlier Wisconsin ruling, *Gregory v. Anderson*, 14 Wis.2d 130, 109

N.W.2d 675 (Wis.1961), disqualifying an employee who violated an off duty no drinking rule, because that rule made it possible for the employer to maintain the insurance it needed on its fleet of trucks. This emphasis on the relationship between rule and the interests of the business would lead one to think that an employer whose business is drug rehabilitation may surely characterize off duty use of drugs as misconduct, and no doubt that is usually the case. In *Employment Division, Department of Human Resources v. Smith*, 485 U.S. 660 (Smith I, 1988), 494 U.S. 872 (Smith II, 1990), however, the issue was complicated by the facts that the drug in question was peyote, the employee/users were members of the Native American Church, and the ingestion of the drug occurred in a ceremony of that church. The claimants argued that to disqualify them from benefits would be an unconstitutional interference with their right to free exercise of religion under the First Amendment. The Court ultimately upheld the disqualification. Five justices did so on the ground that there is no First Amendment violation when the burden placed on religious practice is only an incidental effect of a "valid and neutral law of general applicability" that does not attempt to regulate religious beliefs or teaching. Four justices rejected that rationale, but one, Justice O'Connor, would nonetheless uphold disqualification on the basis of the strength of the state's interest in controlling the use of drugs. What the claimants lost in the Court, they won, for a time, in the Congress. The Religious Freedom Restoration Act of 1993 provides, in part:

Government may substantially burden a person's exercise of religion only if it demonstrates that application of the burden to the person;

> (1) is in furtherance of a compelling governmental interest; and

> (2) is the least restrictive means of furthering that compelling governmental interest.

42 U.S.C.A. § 2000bb–1(b).

In *City of Boerne v. Flores*, 521 U.S. 507 (1997), however, the Court held the statute to be unconstitutional. The dissenting opinions in *Flores* suggest that the correctness of *Smith II* is open to question, but no case presenting that precise issue has reached the court again.

Refusing Employment. Refusal of suitable reemployment also disqualifies an employee for benefits. The problem, obviously, is to decide just what job offers are, in fact, suitable. The federal statute places three major limits on the drafters of state plans in what is called the "labor standards" provision of the statute, Int. Rev. Code § 3304(a)(5):

> (5) compensation shall not be denied in such State to any otherwise eligible individual for refusing to accept new work under any of the following conditions:

> > (A) if the position offered is vacant due directly to a strike, lockout, or other labor dispute;

> > (B) if the wages, hours, or other conditions of the work offered are substantially less fa-

vorable to the individual than those prevailing for similar work in the locality;

(C) if as a condition of being employed the
individual would be required to join a company union or to resign from or refrain
from joining any bona fide labor organization.

Beyond these fairly straightforward guidelines,
however, lie dragons. The applicant's age, education, and experience obviously matter, but how
much? Other factors include degree of risk to an
employee's safety and health; the employee's past
earnings; distance of the job offered from the employee's residence; likelihood of finding more suitable work in the locality; and the length of unemployment. Some states also provide that a position
of the same type as that most recently held is to be
considered suitable. The decisional law reflects the
individualistic nature of these criteria, so that refusal of work 60 miles distant was held not to disqualify in *Pittsburgh Pipe & Coupling Co. v. Board of
Review*, 401 Pa. 501, 165 A.2d 374 (Pa.1960), while
work 126 miles from home was held suitable in
Crowley v. Appeal Board, 1B CCH Unemp.Ins.Rep.
¶ 1965 (Cal.Super.1954).

In *Sherbert v. Verner*, 374 U.S. 398 (1963), the
Supreme Court held that a state wrongly disqualified a claimant who refused an otherwise suitable
job that would require her to work on her religion's
sabbath. Cutting off benefits would interfere with
her free exercise rights, the Court held, while pay-

ing benefits limited both in amount and duration to an individual does not constitute establishing that person's religion.

Labor Disputes. Most states also disqualify at least some claimants whose joblessness is the result of a labor dispute. Some statutes draw a distinction between job loss due to a lockout and that due to a strike: A striking worker is disqualified for benefits and the employer's account is not charged, but a locked out worker is eligible for benefits and, therefore, the employer's experience rating may suffer. The breadth of these labor dispute disqualifications varies greatly, reflecting different judgments about what constitutes official "neutrality" in a strike situation. Because of experience rating, an employer whose workers receive substantial amounts of unemployment compensation benefits will eventually have to pay higher payroll taxes. This puts added pressure on an employer to settle a strike. A striker who goes a long period without pay and also without benefits is also going to feel greater pressure to settle than if benefits were paid during the strike. How to strike a fair balance has thus far evaded consensus. One version of this disqualification deprives employees of benefits whenever the claimant's unemployment is "due to" a labor dispute (other than a lockout). This very broad version can have the effect of depriving employees of benefits even though they belong to a different bargaining unit from the striking workers and have no personal stake in the outcome of the strike at all. Some states restrict the disqualification to workers who are either strikers themselves or are members of the same class or group of workers as those on strike. Others apply the disqualification only if there is a "stoppage of work" that has been caused by the labor dispute, reasoning that the pressure felt by an employer to settle is much reduced if the employer is able to continue production of goods or services. At least one state has added a time element, allowing strikers and locked out workers to receive benefits after being out of work for eight weeks. The Supreme Court has upheld state laws that run the full gamut, against challenges based on a mix of preemption, due process, and equal protection theories. See *Ohio Bureau of Employment Services v. Hodory*, 431 U.S. 471 (1977) (disqualification if unemployment caused by any "labor dispute other than a lockout" by most recent employer; upheld); *New York Telephone Co. v. New York State Dep't of Labor*, 440 U.S. 519 (1979) (benefits available to strikers after eight weeks; upheld).

Integration with Other Programs. Benefit coordination provisions in these statutes typically provide that benefits may be lost or reduced because payments are being received from other sources, including worker's compensation, severance pay, pay in lieu of termination or layoff notice, or employer financed retirement benefits. See Int. Rev. Code § 3304(a)(15).

4. Procedure

An informal administrative process is used in making the initial eligibility determination. The employer is informed of the claim and may contest it. In making statements regarding a former employee's eligibility for benefits as part of the administrative and judicial process, the employer has an absolute privilege to communicate defamatory information regardless of how false and libelous they are. See *Milliner v. Enck*, 709 A.2d 417 (Pa.Super.1998). Appeals from the eligibility decision are heard by an administrative hearing officer. In most states the hearing officer's decision is appealed to an administrative commission or board. The final administrative decision is appealed to a state court, usually a lower level court but in a few states an appellate court.

The characteristics of an unemployment insurance "hearing" may not measure up to normal perceptions of what takes place at evidentiary presentations. Generally, these hearings are quite informal and brief. To take an extreme example, in *Small v. Jacklin Seed Co.*, 109 Idaho 541, 709 P.2d 114 (Idaho 1985), the unemployment claimant asserted that she quit because of a supervisor's sexual harassment. The hearing consisted of a recorded telephone conference call in which questions were posed by the Appeals Examiner. The claimant appealed from an adverse decision to the Industrial Commission which affirmed based on its review of the transcript of that telephone call. The court reversed and remanded because two exhibits mailed to the agency had not been included in the case record. The court did not question the propriety of this sort of hearing, though it did observe: "The commissioners may well want to consider a new hearing to obtain an accurate record * * * considering the apparent inadequacies of the telephone conference record presently before the Court."

Often employees or employers attempt to use the results of unemployment compensation proceedings to sustain or defend actions in other administrative or judicial proceedings. Administrative decisions of unemployment compensation boards of review are not considered collateral estoppel or res judicata in other legal proceedings. See *Pinkerton v. Jeld–Wen, Inc.*, 588 N.W.2d 679 (Iowa 1998) (no res judicata); *Rue v. K–Mart Corp.*, 552 Pa. 13, 713 A.2d 82 (Pa.1998) (no collateral estoppel).

All states have entered into agreements that permit workers who have moved from one state to another to file for benefits in their new residence, and to combine their qualifying work experience in multiple states. These are reviewed periodically by the Interstate Conference of Employment Security Agencies.

CHAPTER 3

EMPLOYEE DIGNITY, PRIVACY AND REPUTATION

A. INTRODUCTION

Privacy and reputation are highly valued by most people. We value them for personal reasons; many of us feel psychological needs to establish and maintain identity and self-esteem, for example. We value them also for practical reasons; a poor reputation makes it hard to get a decent job and keep it. This Chapter reviews how the law treats these interests in the context of work, through common law tort principles, and also through statutory and constitutional protections.

In approaching these issues, it often helps to think in terms of two basic "privacies." One is "informational privacy": the interest in controlling how information about a worker is collected, maintained, used and disclosed. The other is "behavioral privacy": the interest in participating in activities free from employer regulation or surveillance both at the workplace and beyond.

When thinking about informational privacy, "privacy" and "confidentiality" are similar but distinct. "Privacy" concerns what information may lawfully be collected and maintained about an individual.

"Confidentiality" involves employer representations to those from whom it collects information that unauthorized uses or disclosures will not be made. An employer's disclosure of either "private" or "confidential" information may result in liability, unless the employer's action was protected by a legally recognized privilege.

B. COMMON LAW TORT PRINCIPLES

The common law has protected the interest in reputation for several centuries by imposing liability for defamation. Recognition of a right of privacy has only emerged more recently. Defamation consists of the publication of an untrue statement that holds a person up to ridicule, hatred, contempt, or opprobrium. Communicating negative performance evaluations or reasons for termination may create employer liability, for example. See *Biggins v. Hanson*, 252 Cal.App.2d 16, 59 Cal.Rptr. 897 (Cal.App. 1967).

As a legal concept in the United States the right of privacy is generally traced to a law review article by Samuel D. Warren and Louis D. Brandeis. Warren & Brandeis, *The Right to Privacy*, 4 HARV. L. REV. 193 (1890). That article attempted to weave various strands of common law into a single privacy theme embodying Judge Thomas Cooley's phrase, a "right to be let alone." Id. at 195. See also T. COOLEY, A TREATISE ON THE LAW OF TORTS 29 (1888). Even though no prior case law explicitly supported a privacy right's existence, Warren and Brandeis maintained that a reasoned development of common law principles and society's changing circumstances supported it. They maintained that this innovation was needed due to the newly developed methods of invading private and domestic life through photography and newspapers that were emerging at the end of the 19th century. Today, a not dissimilar technological development is occurring through the use of personal computers, voice mail, electronic mail, and the internet, making privacy all the more difficult to achieve.

Warren and Brandeis recognized that a privacy right ought not be unlimited. Their proposed rules included several limits on its scope, including:

- The right does not prohibit publication of a matter of public or general interest;
- The right does not prohibit communications privileged under libel and slander law;
- There is probably no redress for oral invasions absent special damages;
- The right terminates upon the subject's own publication or consent.

They also, however, urged that liability should be imposed despite facts that would constitute defenses to other torts. Thus:

- Truth should not be a defense; and
- The absence of "malice" should not be a defense.

Since George Orwell raised the specter of "Big Brother" with his book *1984*, computer technology, court decisions, government intrusion, and the employer's desire to know more about the individuals they employ have eroded the employee's sense that his/her life is a private matter.

1. Defamation: An Overview

Defamation is subdivided into the torts of libel and slander. Libel essentially involves a writing while slander concerns speech.

The critical findings that justify imposing liability for defamation are (1) an "unprivileged publication to another" of (2) a statement that is false and defamatory and (3) fault with respect to publication. In some instances, a plaintiff must also prove that the statement has caused a special harm. RESTATEMENT (SECOND) OF TORTS § 558(b).

a. *Publication*

Proving that an employer, or the employer's agent, communicated a defamatory statement to a single other person is usually enough to establish "publication." Id. § 557. In some contexts, many courts do not treat communication from one person to another within the same employment relationship as a "publication," at least where a clear "need to know" exists. See *Munsell v. Ideal Food Stores*, 208 Kan. 909, 494 P.2d 1063 (Kan.1972).

A troubling issue that divides American courts is whether a repetition of a defaming statement by the one defamed is a "publication." This "compelled publication doctrine" is critically important in the context of a termination, for example, when the only person to hear the original defamatory statement is the terminated employee, who is told on the notice of termination that the reason is his or her serious misconduct. In *Lewis v. Equitable Life Assurance Soc'y*, 361 N.W.2d 875 (Minn.App.1985), aff'd in part, 389 N.W.2d 876 (Minn.1986), plaintiffs were asked by prospective employers why they had been terminated by the defendant. They repeated the employer's reason, "gross insubordination." Liability was found on the basis of these publications, since the injured plaintiffs were under "strong compulsion to republish" and the defendant was aware that this sort of repetition was almost certain to occur. See also *Churchey v. Adolph Coors Co.*, 759 P.2d 1336 (Colo.1988). Other courts have rejected this approach, fearing that liability would be unfairly imposed too easily. *Starr v. Pearle Vision*, 54 F.3d 1548 (10th Cir.1995).

b. Privileged Communications

A "privilege" to act without being held liable for one's action even though the same act would usually result in liability is a familiar concept. Hitting another person with the intention of knocking the person out is usually a battery; doing so in self-defense or because one is in a boxing match may be privileged. Privileges can be subdivided into two broad categories "absolute" and "conditional."

As one would expect, absolute privileges are rare. There is one, however, that crops up occasionally in defamation cases. Statements, written or oral, made by judges, attorneys, witnesses, parties, or jurors during judicial proceedings are absolutely privileged from slander or defamation actions, even if the statements were made with malice. Pleadings become part of the judicial proceeding upon filing. Conduct that otherwise would be actionable escapes liability because an interest that is entitled to protection—vindication of legally protected rights— is being furthered through litigation even at the expense of uncompensated harm to another's reputation. The potential harm that may result is mitigated by the formal requirements of notice and hearing, the trial judge's control, and the availability of false swearing and perjury actions. *Rainier's Dairies v. Raritan Valley Farms*, 19 N.J. 552, 117 A.2d 889 (N.J.1955); *Twelker v. Shannon & Wilson, Inc.*, 88 Wash.2d 473, 564 P.2d 1131 (Wash. 1977). The privilege is a narrow one, however. Republishing the same allegations outside the litigation process may well be risky. Employers who distribute court documents about terminated employees to those not part of the judicial process prior to their official filing lose this privilege and may be subject to defamation liability. *Citizens State Bank v. Libertelli*, 215 N.J.Super. 190, 521 A.2d 867 (N.J.Super.1987).Whether the absolute privilege should extent to quasi-judicial proceedings, such as the arbitration of grievances, is questionable. See *Gintert v. WCI Steel, Inc.*, 2007 WL 4376178 (Ohio App. 2007).

An employer has a conditional privilege to communicate employee information for legitimate business purposes. RESTATEMENT (SECOND) OF TORTS § 600

(1977). Employers are protected under this "privilege" to defame in certain circumstances. Id. §§ 593–605A. This privilege can be lost by communicating information known to be false or by acting in reckless disregard concerning its truth or falsity. It can be lost if the person communicating defamatory material does not act for the purpose of furthering the interest that the privilege protects. This may occur where an employer discloses adverse information more broadly than is necessary for legitimate employment purposes. See *Sias v. General Motors Corp.*, 372 Mich. 542, 127 N.W.2d 357 (Mich. 1964). Negligent communications can also forfeit this privilege. See *Banas v. Matthews Int'l Corp.*, 348 Pa.Super. 464, 502 A.2d 637 (Pa.Super.1985).

It is ironic that systems of "progressive discipline" and employee appeals against supervisor action, systems that have developed out of a concern for individual rights, may occasionally increase the chances for actionable defamation to occur. In *Agriss v. Roadway Exp., Inc.*, 334 Pa.Super. 295, 483 A.2d 456 (Pa.Super.1984), for example, the plaintiff had been employed by Roadway Express as a truck driver. Before beginning a scheduled vacation, Agriss was handed a "warning letter." The employer refused to withdraw the warning and Agriss filed a grievance under the collective bargaining agreement. As part of this grievance procedure, the warning letter and Agriss's protest were forwarded to the union business agent. The procedure also provided for the warning letter to be distributed to Roadway's manager of labor relations and to Agriss' personnel file. The court held that Roadway had an absolute privilege to publish Agriss's warning letter to parties entitled to receive it. These were Agriss, the union business agent, and Roadway management personnel. The copy of the warning letter sent to Agriss' employee personnel file also was covered by the privilege. This formed the "protective circle" within which this defamatory communication could be published without incurring employer defamation liability. However, when Agriss returned from a vacation in Hawaii, he was greeted with comments and questions about the warning from several drivers and also heard this discussed indiscriminately over the citizens band radio. Only a handful of possible employer sources could have originated the unprivileged publication. Therefore, Agriss was entitled to attempt to establish his defamation claim, using circumstantial evidence.

Employer representations to the media regarding employees may also be privileged where they involve matters of public interest. In *Palmisano v. Allina Health Systems, Inc.*, 190 F.3d 881 (8th Cir. 1999), a hospital responded to media inquires on a subject of public interest on a proper occasion. The employer's statement identified a vice president by name, position, and described the disciplinary action taken after an internal investigation. Serious billing improprieties had taken place. The vice president knew or should have known about them. Among the improprieties was overbilling patients for psychological testing services, potentially in violation of Medicare–Medicaid billing rules.

c. *Defamatory Character*

A statement that one is a thief or a prostitute is so likely to be regarded as degrading that no special proof of its defamatory nature is needed. Other statements are not so clearly defaming on their face, and in these cases a plaintiff must prove the defamatory potential ("innuendo") of the words. In *Clampitt v. American University,* 957 A.2d 23 (D.C. 2008), the court concluded that a jury would find the way in which university officials described the reasons for firing an administrator could be taken to concede the truth of charges made against her in the press shortly before her discharge.

In *Raffensberger v. Moran*, 336 Pa.Super. 97, 485 A.2d 447 (Pa.Super.1984), Joe Moran, a "relay manager" for Roadway Express, Inc., sent a telex message to terminals in seven states implying that drivers were "breakdown artists." Moran's telex message was found to be capable of a defamatory meaning. It was susceptible to an interpretation that the drivers were contriving equipment failures and exploiting minor malfunctions dishonestly to obtain additional compensation and injure Roadway by causing unnecessary expense. A driver with this reputation, a jury might find, could be held in low esteem by owners and drivers alike, could be subjected to ridicule by drivers and terminal managers, and could experience increased difficulty in obtaining future work.

d. Employer Fault

The plaintiff must demonstrate that the defendant was at fault to recover. In some cases, the degree of fault that must be proved is simple negligence; a botched investigation led the employer to believe an employee was stealing when a proper investigation would have shown the thief was another person. In other cases, a plaintiff may be required to prove more serious fault. If the plaintiff is a public figure, or if the defendant is a "media defendant," for example, the plaintiff may be required to convince the court that the defendant acted with "malice," i.e., with knowledge of falsity or with reckless disregard for its truth or falsity. See *Gertz v. Robert Welch, Inc.*, 418 U.S. 323 (1974); *Dun & Bradstreet, Inc. v. Greenmoss Builders, Inc.*, 472 U.S. 749 (1985). Proof of "malice" was necessary in *Raffensberger*, for example, because the defamatory statements were made in the context of a labor dispute. (*Linn v. United Plant Guard Workers*, 383 U.S. 53 (1966) held that state libel law is not preempted by the National Labor Relations Act (NLRA), but that the state law must be modified to include a proof-of-malice requirement when the statement occurred in the context of activity subject to the NLRA.) The manager, Moran, developed his list of 30 "breakdown artists" by examining employer records showing the frequency of breakdowns experienced by the drivers. Moran denied that he had a malicious intent, but conceded that his purpose was to encourage improved performance, and also that the records did not reveal and he did not know the reasons for the breakdowns. Under these circumstances, a jury could find that Moran's statement that the drivers were dishonestly contriving breakdowns was made recklessly without regard for the truth. Thus a jury trial was granted.

Litigation continues to confirm that defamation remains a significant concern. Employer violations have been found in:

1. Falsely accusing an employee of having AIDS and terminating the employee. *Little v. Bryce*, 733 S.W.2d 937 (Tex.App.1987).

2. A supervisor's statement to other employees that a female employee had given him a venereal disease, characterizing her as a whore, and searching her personal belongings. *Lewis v. Oregon Beauty Supply Co.*, 302 Or. 616, 733 P.2d 430 (Or.1987).

3. Failing to verify that an employee was actually stealing before disseminating information that the employee had been terminated for theft. *Mendez v. M.S. Walker, Inc.*, 26 Mass. App. 431, 528 N.E.2d 891 (Mass.App.1988).

4. Firing an employee for poor performance without a proper investigation of the performance claims against the employee. *Keenan v. Computer Associates International, Inc.*, 13 F.3d 1266 (8th Cir.1994).

5. Treating an employee as if he were dishonest—without ever using the term—where the

employer's supervisor, after firing the employee, accompanied him to his office, stayed while he packed his personal belongings in full view of other employees, and escorted him out the main door. *Bolton v. Minnesota Department of Human Services*, 527 N.W.2d 149 (Minn.App.1995).

6. Crediting co-employees' statements accusing a sales manager of selling company sales incentive items at a yard sale that resulted in his termination where the employer did not allow the manager to explain and did not look at the employer's records to determine whether the manager reported his activities on the day of the yard sale. *Gibson v. Philip Morris, Inc.*, 292 Ill.App.3d 267, 226 Ill.Dec. 383, 685 N.E.2d 638 (Ill.App.1997).

Nonetheless, the privilege defenses often stand up, even when the charges made are clearly defaming, provided the employer keeps the number of persons involved to a minimum. See, e.g., *Saxonis v. City of Lynn*, 62 Mass.App.Ct. 916, 817 N.E.2d 793 (Mass. App. 2004).

2. Defamation in the Context of Reference Checks

Most job applicants will present employment histories to their prospective employers, either on resumes or through answers given to questions on application forms. For a prospective employer not to check these may well be negligent conduct, particularly if the position in question involves risks to the

person or property of others. The duty to hire with
care exists because the employer is best placed to
know that nature of the risks associated with the
job. Hiring a person who the employer knows is just
completing a prison term for second degree murder
and assigning that person to unsupervised security
duties is so risky that liability flows almost as a
matter of course. See *Henley v. Prince George's
County*, 305 Md. 320, 503 A.2d 1333 (Md.1986). The
crew of a ship are required to work together for
sustained periods; a job applicant with a history of
brawling poses an obvious danger in that setting. If
hired, such a person may make the vessel unseaworthy. See *Miles v. Apex Marine Corp.*, 498 U.S. 19
(1990). The same potential for liability may occasionally arise for the person providing a reference.
Palmer v. Shearson Lehman Hutton, Inc., 622 So.2d
1085 (Fla.App.1993) held that a brokerage firm
could be liable for failing to inform a regulatory
agency of the real reason for termination of a broker. The former employer listed "voluntary quit" as
the reason for termination, rather than stating he
may have engaged in questionable transactions.
Had the firm been forthright, questions would have
been raised when the individual sought to re-regis-
ter with the agency at the time he was hired by
another brokerage company.

Both the prospective employer that checks references and former employers that supply information are, however, also subject to potential liability
if the exchange of information illegally harms the
applicant. This liability may arise under several

common law principles, including defamation, but also the right of privacy, and interference with prospective economic advantage. Some states have enacted statutes to modify the common law.

The potential for defaming a former employee by giving a bad reference is obvious. Each of the elements of the plaintiff's burden of proof can give rise to tricky issues. As discussed above, states vary as to whether the "publication" element of a defamation case can be made out by proving "compelled self publication." In a state that recognizes that doctrine, an employer is not protected from liability by a policy under which it will release only information as to whether and when a former employee was in its service. What constitutes a defamatory reference is at times a question. An arguably neutral statement that an employee was terminated "for cause" may be actionable because a likely inference would be that the worker was incompetent. *Carney v. Memorial Hospital*, 64 N.Y.2d 770, 485 N.Y.S.2d 984, 475 N.E.2d 451 (N.Y.1985). Stating that a former in-house attorney "suddenly resigned" might suggest to a prospective employer that the attorney had left under a cloud of suspicion and scandal. *Klages v. Sperry Corp.*, 118 L.R.R.M. 2463 (E.D.Pa.1984).

A defendant former employer in a defamation action may assert a defense of qualified privilege. Because checking references is responsible conduct that may protect public interests as well as legitimate interests of the prospective employer, the giving of a reference is protected if done in good faith without malice or reckless disregard for the truth. See *Kass v. Great Coastal Express*, 152 N.J. 353, 704 A.2d 1293 (1998); *Dalton v. Herbruck Egg Sales Corp.*, 164 Mich.App. 543, 417 N.W.2d 496 (1987); *Lewis v. Equitable Life Assurance Society of United States*, 361 N.W.2d 875 (Minn.App.1985), aff'd in part, 389 N.W.2d 876 (Minn.1986).

Statutes dealing with references have become more common. The California and Iowa codes address the problem in much the same way. West's Ann. Calif. Labor Code §§ 1050–1053; Iowa Code Ann. §§ 730.1–730.3. Each statute makes it a misdemeanor for an employer to furnish untruthful information about a former employee. Violation of the statute may lead to imposing treble damages. Furnishing a truthful statement of the reason for termination in response to a request is privileged. The California statute provides, however, that a statement that is not in response to a request or that is accompanied by marks or symbols that convey information contrary to the statement is prima facie evidence of a violation. Cal. Labor Code § 1053. These statutes are often known as "anti-blacklisting" laws. Whether "blacklisting" is a common law tort, either as a form of defamation or as a separate category of wrong, is a matter of state-to-state variation. In some jurisdictions a plaintiff can recover only by proving malice. See *Austin v. Torrington Co.*, 810 F.2d 416 (4th Cir.1987), cert. denied, 484 U.S. 977.

In an attempt to reduce potential liability, many employers have adopted a policy under which they require an employee who wants a reference to execute a release form, stating that the employee will not hold the reference giver liability for what the reference document says. Sometimes, such a release may not be sufficient to protect the employer. In *McQuirk v. Donnelley*, 189 F.3d 793 (9th Cir.1999), a job reference release was found to be unenforceable, because it attempted to shield the employer from liability for intentional torts. California's statute provided that all contracts that "exempt anyone from responsibility for his own ... willful injury to ... another ... are against the policy of the law." Cal. Civ. Code § 1668. Consequently, California employers cannot contract for more than the qualified privilege granted to them in the statute discussed earlier.

3. Invasion of Privacy

From the moment an individual first enters an employer's property to apply for a job, many privacy rights are relinquished. As an employment condition, employees will be asked to disclose personal facts about their background and may be required to submit to continuing employer scrutiny that may or may not be job-related. Current or prospective employees may confront a physical examination, polygraph examination, psychological evaluation, or even an antibody test for Human Immunodeficiency Virus (HIV). Physical intrusion may also occur through locker searches or frisking employees as they leave the workplace. Some employers operate video cameras in work areas and in employee restrooms; others use software programs designed to monitor performance of video display terminal operators.

In recent years, many legislatures and courts have found reasons to limit employer intrusion into private areas. These enactments and decisions seek to control the use of irrelevant, inaccurate, or incomplete facts to make employment decisions; and to regulate disclosure of employment information to third parties. They focus mainly on five areas:

1. Speech—what one says or is said about someone;

2. Beliefs—what one privately or publicly thinks;

3. Personal information—identifying information, credentials, performance data, medical information, and the like

4. Association—with whom one shares similar interests; and

5. Lifestyle—how one lives.

One major problem in setting appropriate limits on employer inquiries is deciding what data is job-related. Employers have a legitimate need to know certain things about their employees, including their abilities, honesty, and prior employment histories. Keeping track of employee performance seems generally reasonable, depending on how it is done. Some employers want to know much more, and assert that everything about an employee is relevant to employment, that it is necessary to examine the "whole person" to determine whether employment suitability exists. Such an employer may want to know things as whether the employee smokes marijuana at home, is a homosexual, or socializes with the "wrong" kind of people.

When employers disclose employment information to third parties other interests are implicated. Statements made to an employer's clients or in reference letters may cause embarrassment, may subject an employee to ridicule, or may have even more direct economic impact, by limiting future employment prospects.

Courts and commentators have recognized four types of tortious invasions of privacy, for which damages may be recovered:

1. Intrusion upon seclusion;

2. Appropriation of name or likeness;

3. Publicity given to private life; and

4. Publicity placing a person in a false light.

See RESTATEMENT (SECOND) OF TORTS §§ 652B, 652C, 652D, 652E (1977).

The first type, *intrusion*, involves invading an area where a reasonable privacy expectation exists. Liability does not depend on whether the employer publicizes the information it has collected. In *Love v. Southern Bell Telephone & Telegraph Co.*, 263 So.2d 460 (La.App.1972), use of a locksmith by an employer to force entry into an employee's trailer home after the employee failed to report for work violated the employee's privacy expectation. The intrusion does not have to be physical. In *Awbrey v. Great Atlantic & Pacific Tea Co.*, 505 F.Supp. 604 (N.D.Ga.1980), liability was imposed for wiretapping.

American courts have demonstrated a variety of attitudes about the level of privacy an employee can reasonably expect in different areas of their lives. A terminated female employee recovered damages in *Phillips v. Smalley Maintenance Serv., Inc.*, 711 F.2d 1524 (11th Cir.1983), because her employer interrogated her about her sexual relationship with her husband. In *Mares v. ConAgra Poultry Co., Inc.*, 971 F.2d 492 (10th Cir.1992), on the other hand, questions about what medications an employee was currently taking were held acceptable. In *Cort v. Bristol–Myers Co.*, 385 Mass. 300, 431 N.E.2d 908 (Mass.1982), recovery for wrongful discharge was denied when an employee was terminated after refusal to answer personal questions on a questionnaire.

Appropriation of name or likeness occurs when it is done for the appropriator's advantage; it is not necessary that money change hands. In the workplace, it may occur when employers photograph employees for advertising literature. For example, in *Colgate–Palmolive Co. v. Tullos*, 219 F.2d 617 (5th Cir.1955), the employer used a former employee's name for advertising purposes without consent.

Publicity given to a private life involves disclosing employment information (a) that would be highly offensive to a reasonable person and (b) that is not of legitimate public concern. RESTATEMENT (SECOND) OF TORTS § 652D comment a (1977). It is distinguished from defamation because the publicized information need not be false and the publication must be to the public at large. It is different from intrusion in that publicity must exist. In *Bratt v. International Business Machines Corp.*, 392 Mass. 508, 467 N.E.2d 126 (Mass.1984), the court found an employer breached the state's privacy statute if it wrongfully disclosed an employee's medical information.

Publicity placing a person in a false light must involve something that would be objectionable to a reasonable person under the circumstances. RESTATEMENT (SECOND) OF TORTS § 652E (1977). Placing one in a false light is similar to defamation, but the information need not be defamatory. There must be proof of publicity and falsity. In *Anderson v. Low Rent Housing Comm'n*, 304 N.W.2d 239 (Iowa 1981), for example, the jury held that an employer falsely charged that a terminated employee had "antagonized" others and had shown poor judgment. The charges were widely disseminated in the media. A judgment for the plaintiff was upheld.

In an action for invasion of privacy, the same conditional privilege defenses are available to an employer as in a defamation action. RESTATEMENT (SECOND) OF TORTS § 652C (1979). The employer can defend by showing that its conduct is reasonably necessary to its business operation. Consent is also an important employer defense. See *Johnson v.*

Boeing Airplane Co., 175 Kan. 275, 262 P.2d 808 (Kan.1953) (use of employee's photograph).

Despite the uncertainty surrounding the scope of an employee's privacy expectations, recent litigation confirms that invasion of privacy is gaining wider court approval. Employer violations have been found in:

- Employer letters regarding employee activities that were distributed more widely than necessary. *Beaumont v. Brown*, 401 Mich. 80, 257 N.W.2d 522 (Mich.1977), partially overruled in *Bradley v. Saranac Board of Education*, 455 Mich. 285, 565 N.W.2d 650 (Mich.1997) in order to avoid conflict with the Freedom of Information Act.

- Showing photographs of an employee's "unsightly wound" on numerous occasions at plant safety meetings. *Lambert v. Dow Chem. Co.*, 215 So.2d 673 (La.App.1968).

- Reading employee personal mail. *Vernars v. Young*, 539 F.2d 966 (3d Cir.1976).

- Interrogating an employee about dating a competing firm's employee. *Rulon–Miller v. IBM*, 162 Cal.App.3d 241, 208 Cal.Rptr. 524 (Cal. App.1984).

- Harassing an employee for an interracial relationship. *Moffett v. Gene B. Glick Co., Inc.*, 604 F.Supp. 229 (N.D.Ind.1984).

- Improper locker search. *K–Mart Corporation Store No. 7441 v. Trotti*, 677 S.W.2d 632 (Tex.

App.1984), aff'd per curiam, 686 S.W.2d 593
(Tex.1985).

- Improper employee strip search. *Bodewig v. K–
  Mart, Inc.*, 54 Or.App. 480, 635 P.2d 657 (Or.
  App.1981) (under an "outrageous conduct" the-
  ory).

- A supervisor's yelling during a workplace fight
  that the employee's wife had been having sexual relations with certain people. *Keehr v. Consolidated Freightways, Inc.*, 825 F.2d 133 (7th
  Cir.1987).

- Terminating an employee for refusing to identify fellow drug-using employees after confidentiality had been pledged. *Paradis v. United
  Technologies*, 672 F.Supp. 67 (D.Conn.1987).

- Disclosing an employee's mastectomy to numerous co-employees constituted public communication of private facts. *Miller v. Motorola,
  Inc.*, 202 Ill.App.3d 976, 148 Ill.Dec. 303, 560
  N.E.2d 900 (Ill.App.1990).

- Improper search of an over-the-road driver's
  motel room by an employer without the driver's prior consent for a missing permit book
  even though the employer paid for the motel
  room where an expectation of privacy existed in
  the motel room as a private refuge during the
  driver's layover, the room's key was retained by
  the driver, no business was transacted in the
  room, and the public was not invited. *Sowards
  v. Norbar, Inc.*, 78 Ohio App.3d 545, 605 N.E.2d
  468 (Ohio App.1992).

- Singling out an African American store clerk each day to search for stolen items. *Wal–Mart, Inc., et al. v. Stewart*, 990 P.2d 626 (Alaska 1999).

C. STATUTORY PROTECTION

1. Federal Legislation

There is no all-encompassing federal statute protecting privacy and reputation. There are, however, several statutes that recognize these interests in specific contexts.

Federal statutes addressing these interests for private and public sector employees include:

- The Freedom of Information Act (FOIA)
- The Privacy Act of 1974 (Privacy Act)
- The Fair Credit Reporting Act
- The Omnibus Crime Control and Safe Streets Act
- Postal Code provisions on mail tampering
- The Employee Polygraph Protection Act
- The Drug–Free Workplace Act
- The Americans with Disabilities Act (ADA)
- The Health Insurance Portability and Accountability Act of 1996 (HIPPA)
- The Genetic Information Nondiscrimination Act of 2008 (GINA)
- The American Recovery & Reinvestment Act of 2009, Title XIII,(HITECH Act) subtitle D

The first two statutes listed above concern the gathering, maintenance, and dissemination of information by the federal government itself. The others regulate conduct primarily in the private sector. Only two of these statutes focus principally on the employment relationship.

a. Freedom of Information Act

The Freedom of Information Act of 1966 (FOIA), 5 U.S.C.A. § 552, is "broadly conceived" and its basic policy "is in favor of disclosure." *NLRB v. Robbins Tire & Rubber Co.*, 437 U.S. 214 (1978).

The FOIA evolved from three prior statutes. A "housekeeping" statute, originally passed in 1789, gave each department head the authority to "preserve regulations for the government of his department" by setting up filing and record keeping systems. Rev. Stat. § 161, as amended, 5 U.S.C.A. § 301. Some of the rules and practices developed under this statute came under fire from the American Society of Newspaper Editors on the grounds that they made too many records inaccessible. See H. Rep. No. 1461 (1958). As a result, Congress amended the statute in 1958 to provide that it "does not authorize withholding information from the public or limiting the availability of records to the public." In the intervening years, Congress had passed the Administrative Procedures Act (APA) of 1946, one provision of which required that agencies publish information about their organization, powers, procedures, substantive rules, and final opinions or orders in adjudicated decisions. 60 Stat. 238, as amended, 5 U.S.C.A. § 552(a)(1)(2). In 1966, Congress broadened the right of access to information via the FOIA, incorporating the 1789, 1946, and 1958 statutes and building upon them. The FOIA requires that all federal agency documents be publicly disclosed unless exempted. Documents described as "rules of procedure" must be published in the Federal Register. 5 U.S.C.A. § 552(a)(1). Final opinions or orders in adjudicated agency decisions, agency policy statements and interpretations, and staff instructions that "affect a member of the public" must be made available. Id. at § 552(a)(3).

The statute lists nine categories of documents that are exempt from compulsory disclosure. 5 U.S.C.A. § 552(b). The exemptions most relevant to individual employee rights are:

- trade secrets and confidential commercial, or financial material,

- inter-agency or intra-agency memoranda or letters,

- "personnel and medical files or similar files, the disclosure of which would constitute a clearly unwarranted invasion of personal privacy," and

- investigatory records compiled for law enforcement purposes.

Id. at § 552(b)(4)–(7). Determining what is a "clearly unwarranted invasion" of privacy requires a careful balancing of the individual privacy interest against the interest of the public in knowing how the government is doing its job. *U.S. Department of State v. Ray*, 502 U.S. 164 (1991). Although agencies are not required to disclose information that is statutorily exempted, they may elect to divulge material. An individual or firm that seeks to enjoin disclosure therefore must rely not on FOIA but on some other confidentiality statute, such as that discussed in the next subsection. See *Chrysler Corp. v. Brown*, 441 U.S. 281 (1979).

Interpreting the FOIA in the individual employee context poses special problems because its full disclosure policy conflicts with policies underlying other statutes. For example, problems may arise under the National Labor Relations Act when an interested party requests the release of a witness' statement taken in the investigation of an unfair labor practice charge. See *NLRB v. Robbins Tire & Rubber*, 437 U.S. 214 (1978).

b.   Privacy Act of 1974

(i) Basic Analytical Pattern and Integration with FOIA

The Privacy Act of 1974, 5 U.S.C.A. § 552a, regulates information collected, maintained, used, and (potentially) disclosed by federal agencies. It seeks to protect two interests of individual citizens, those (1) in accuracy of recorded personal data and (2) in personal privacy. Since it prohibits disclosure of information, it contrasts sharply with the FOIA, and must be read and analyzed together with that statute.

Consider, for instance, the FOIA exemption just discussed, that allows an agency to withhold from mandatory disclosure information which constitutes "a clearly unwarranted invasion of personal privacy." 5 U.S.C.A. § 552(b)(6). This exemption is permissive; under its language it is for the agency to decide whether to disclose the information or not. The Supreme Court has held that not just the language but also the logic and history of the FOIA evidence an intent to permit an agency to withhold certain information but not to require such withholding. *Chrysler Corp. v. Brown*, 441 U.S. 281 (1979). The Privacy Act plugs this gap; it forbids agency disclosure, without the written consent of the subject, of personal information contained in "record systems" covered by the Act, unless otherwise required by the FOIA. 5 U.S.C.A. § 552a(b)(2). Consequently, the scope of discretion enjoyed by agencies under the FOIA has been significantly restricted by the Privacy Act.

If an individual charges that an agency has violated her privacy rights, the analysis therefore has to go through several steps. First, the court must decide whether the data constituted a "record" under the Privacy Act. If so, then the court must decide whether the challenged disclosure falls within any of the exemptions contained in 5 U.S.C.A. § 552a(b), including that for disclosures *required under section 552 of this title* (the FOIA). This means the court will have to decide whether an agency could have withheld the information because of the exemptions provided by 5 U.S.C.A. § 552(b), including the exemption for disclosures that would be "a clearly unwarranted invasion of privacy."

(ii) "Records" and "Record Systems"

A *"record"* includes any item, collection, or grouping of information that is maintained by an agency. 5 U.S.C.A. § 552a(a)(4). The statutory definition is so broad that it is not very helpful in making concrete decisions. The Supreme Court has not provided a detailed definition either, so that the lower federal courts have had to devise tests on their own. *Bechhoefer v. United States Department of Justice*, 209 F.3d 57 (2d Cir.2000) reviews the varied approaches that have been taken and adopts one similar to that of the Third Circuit: "any personal information 'about an individual that is linked to that individual through an identifying particular.' " Records might relate to an individual's education, financial transactions, medical history, and criminal or employment history. This list, however, is not exclusive. Id. A "system of records" refers to individualized information under agency control that may be retrieved by use of the particular individual's name or some other common identifier such as a social security number. Id. at § 552a(a)(5). A statistical record, as its name suggests, refers to records maintained for statistical research and not otherwise used for determinations about specific individuals. Id. at § 552a(a)(6).

In *Boyd v. Secretary of Navy*, 709 F.2d 684 (11th Cir.1983), a memorandum about a supervisor and employee meeting that was not kept within a system of records was not subject to the Privacy Act. Likewise, in *American Fed'n of Gov't Employees v. NASA*, 482 F.Supp. 281 (S.D.Tex.1980), daily sign-in/sign-out sheets showing when employees left for lunch and finished work were found not to be "records" and could be left in open view. The court held that the Privacy Act was not violated in *Johnson v. United States Dep't of Air Force*, 526 F.Supp. 679 (W.D.Okl.1980), by circulation of a petition by co-employees that claimed an employee was responsible for a "no-reading" policy in the data automation division. The employer did not authorize or participate in circulating the petition and it was not placed in the employee's official personnel file, pay records, or any other employer records.

(iii) Limits on Collecting Information

Agencies have authority to collect information about individuals only if the Constitution, a statute, or executive order explicitly authorizes or directs this. Id. § 552a(e)(4).

In collecting information, the agency must tell the person it asks to supply the data of the purposes for which the records will be used, especially those likely to affect determinations of rights or benefits. Id. § 552a(e)(3). Agencies must publish in the Federal Register a notice regarding their records each year and must also publish where records are maintained. Id. § 552a(e)(4)(A). Where information is not obtained from the individual, the agency must publish the source from which the information was obtained.

(iv) Limits on Disclosure

An agency must make reasonable efforts to notify an individual when a record is made available under legal process. Id. § 552(e)(8). Disclosure accounting is required when the agency complies with a subpoena. Id. § 552a(c)(1).

An individual's name and address may not be sold or rented by an agency unless specifically authorized by law. 5 U.S.C.A. § 552a(n). The FOIA authorizes disclosure of name and address lists, but not if disclosure would be a "clearly unwarranted" privacy invasion. Id. § 552(b)(6). See *Campbell v. U.S. Civil Service Comm'n*, 539 F.2d 58 (10th Cir. 1976); *U.S. Dept. of Defense v. FLRA*, 510 U.S. 487 (1994).

An agency cannot disclose a record to any person or to another agency without the individual's written request or prior written consent, unless the disclosure is exempted. Id. § 552a(b). Disclosure, however, is permitted without the individual's consent when made to agency officers and employees maintaining the record who need it to perform their duties or for other "routine" uses. The agency is not required to make public any record it is not mandated to release. Records traditionally considered public include final orders and opinions of quasi-judicial agencies or press releases.

(v) Rights of Persons Who Are Subjects of Records

Each individual is entitled to: (1) gain access to any record containing information about him or her; (2) request amendment of that record; and (3)

review by the agency of a refusal to amend. Id.
§ 552a(d). The agency must provide a copy of all or
part of the record in a comprehensible format. Access may not be conditioned upon providing a reason or justification. An agency cannot rely on the
FOIA's exemptions to withhold records accessible
under the Privacy Act. Id. § 552. The FOIA's exemptions permitting an agency to withhold information from the public are not applicable to individuals seeking access under the Privacy Act. Id.
§ 552a(d)(1). Another person may accompany the
individual to review the record, but written authorization may be required from the individual to disclose the record in the presence of the accompanying person. Id. § 552a(d)(1). The individual is not
required to furnish reasons for the person accompanying him or her. If access is sought by mail, the
agency may require the individual to provide identifying data of name, date of birth, or other personal
information. The agency cannot deny access because an individual refuses to disclose their Social
Security number. For access to medical and other
sensitive data, the agency may require a signed
notarized statement verifying identity.

A person may request amendment of a record in
person, by telephone, or by mail. The agency must
promptly correct the record if inaccurate, irrelevant, untimely, or incomplete. If the agency refuses
to amend, it must inform the individual of the
reason, the review procedures, and reviewing officer's name and business address. Id. § 552a(d)(2).

An individual may bring a civil action against an agency for Privacy Act violations. Federal courts have jurisdiction whenever an agency:

1. makes a determination not to amend or fails to review such a determination;

2. refuses to comply with an individual request;

3. fails to maintain a record concerning an individual with the accuracy, relevance, timeliness, and completeness necessary to assure fairness in any determination relating to the qualifications, character, rights or opportunities of, or benefits to the individual that may be made on the basis of the record and consequently a determination is made adverse to the individual; or

4. fails to comply with the Privacy Act or any rule promulgated under it that has an adverse effect on an individual.

A court may order an agency to amend its records according to the individual's request or in other ways. Reasonable attorney fees and costs also may be assessed against the United States. The agency may be enjoined from withholding records and ordered to produce them. Where the court determines that the agency acted intentionally or willfully, the United States may be liable to the complainant in an amount equal to the sum of: (1) actual damages sustained by the individual as a result of the refusal or failure, but in no cases less than $1,000; and (2) costs of the action together with reasonable attorney fees, as determined by the court.

These remedies are not exclusive. An individual may also seek judicial review: (1) pursuant to the Administrative Procedure Act, by alleging criminal misconduct; (2) by civil suit directly against the agency or employee where the action was intentional or willful; or (3) for federal employees, by grievance procedures.

The Privacy Act has limited application to private sector employment. It would be violated, for example, if an agency impermissibly disclosed private sector employee information without the individual's consent, or furnished information about the employee that was incorrect. This could occur under many statutes, such as the National Labor Relations Act (NLRA) [29 U.S.C.A. §§ 151–169] or the Occupational Safety and Health Act (OSHA) of 1970 [29 U.S.C.A. §§ 651–678], because these statutes require the NLRB and the Department of Labor to collect substantial amounts of data identified by individual. Public sector employees working for state and local governments are similarly situated.

Federal government employees, however, have additional recourse. The Privacy Act was designed in part to stop internal blacklisting of persons who do not comply with non-job-related agency expectations, such as participation in savings bond drives or charity campaigns and to eliminate listing employee test or performance results. See *Parks v. United States Internal Revenue Serv.*, 618 F.2d 677 (10th Cir.1980).

Federal employee unions are entitled under the Federal Service Labor–Management Relations Act [5 U.S.C.A. §§ 7101–7135] to information about the bargaining unit they represent "to the extent not prohibited by law." 5 U.S.C.A. § 7114(b)(4). In *U.S. Department of Defense v. Federal Labor Relations Authority*, 510 U.S. 487 (1994), the Supreme Court held that the Privacy Act bars granting a union's request for home addresses of agency employees in a unit represented by that union (including the addresses of employees who were not members of the union). The interest of the union in this information was not, the majority opinion reasoned, part of the "core public interest" that the FOIA was designed to further: the ability of the public to know how the government is doing its work. That concept was first established in a non-employment case, *U.S. Department of Justice v. Reporters Committee for Freedom of the Press*, 489 U.S. 749 (1989), and its extension to the labor-management sphere is open to question, as Justice Ginsburg pointed out in her concurring opinion in the more recent case.

The wealth of information now available on electronic databases prompted Congress to amend the Privacy Act in the Computer Matching and Privacy Act of 1988. P.L. No. 100–503. A "matching program" is a computerized comparison of two or more automated systems of "records" or a "system of records" with non-federal records, generally to determine eligibility under federal benefit programs. 5 U.S.C.A. 552a(a)(8). Matches performed to produce aggregate statistical data without any personal identifiers are not considered "matching programs." No record contained in a system of records may be disclosed to a recipient agency or a non-federal agency for use in a computer matching program except pursuant to a written agreement between the source agency and the recipient or non-federal agency. 5 U.S.C.A. § 552a(*o*).

Every agency conducting or participating in a matching program is required to establish a Data Integrity Board (the Board) to oversee and coordinate the agency's implementation of the Privacy Act Amendments. 5 U.S.C.A. § 522a(a)(1).

c. *Fair Credit Reporting Act*

The Fair Credit Reporting Act of 1970 (FCRA), 15 U.S.C.A. §§ 1681–1681t, was enacted to curtail credit agency abuses in reporting information. Prior to the FCRA's passage, credit reports giving information on an individual's financial status, medical history, and even sexual relationships were available to almost anyone that requested the information. This often resulted in embarrassment and humiliation. Reporting inaccurate, incomplete, or obsolete information frequently caused denial of credit, employment, or insurance. The individual was generally unaware that this information was being reported and, even if aware, had limited legal right to require correction of the reports or to remedy the harm.

Under the FCRA, a "consumer report" includes any information communicated by a consumer reporting agency bearing on a consumer's credit capacity, character, or general reputation "which is used or expected to be used or collected in whole or in part" for a statutory purpose. Id. § 1681a(d). An "investigative consumer report" is a consumer report based on information collected via interviews with neighbors, friends, and other associates. Id. § 1681a(e). A "consumer reporting agency" includes an individual or corporation which regularly engages "in the practice of assembling or evaluating consumer credit information" and which provides this information to third parties. Id. § 1681a(f). Firms that employers hire to investigate charges of employee misconduct may be included. Vail Opinion Letter, FTC Staff Letter, April 5, 1999. Not every report concerning employee performance is a consumer report, however, although the line is at times a difficult one to define. See, e.g., *Owner–Operator Independent Drivers Association, Inc. v. USIS Commercial Services, Inc.*, 537 F.3d 1184 (10th Cir. 2008) Merely furnishing information about consumers' accounts to a credit reporting agency does not transform the reporter into a consumer reporting agency. See *Rush v. Macy's New York, Inc.*, 775 F.2d 1554 (11th Cir.1985).

Under the FCRA, a consumer reporting agency may furnish a consumer report only:

1. In response to a court order;

2. In accordance with the consumer's written instructions; or

3. When the consumer-reporting agency has reason to believe that the person requesting the information will use it:

- for a credit transaction involving the consumer;

- for employment purposes;

- for underwriting insurance involving the consumer;

- to determine the consumer's eligibility for a license;

- to assess risks associated with a present credit obligation; or

- to serve a "legitimate business need" in connection with transaction initiated by the consumer or to review a consumer's account.

15 U.S.C.A. § 1681b.

The FCRA is important for this book because employers frequently request consumer reports and use them in making decisions. If an employer decides to fire or not to offer employment wholly or partly because of information in a report, the employer must provide the individual with a copy of the report before taking the adverse action. 15 U.S.C.A. §§ 1681b(3); 1681m(a). The employer in *Mathews v. GEICO*, 23 F.Supp.2d 1160 (S.D.Cal. 1998), failed to notify applicants that they were screened on the basis of consumer credit reports. Punitive damages were assessed against the employer because of its reckless disregard of its responsibilities under the FCRA.

The applicant may request from the credit agency the "nature and substance" of the information maintained. 15 U.S.C.A. at § 1681g(a)(1). The credit agency must disclose the information's sources and all report recipients within the preceding six months. Id. § 1681g(a)(3). If the accuracy of any file item is disputed, that item must be reinvestigated by the credit agency. Id. § 1681i(a). If after reinvestigation, the dispute remains unresolved, a counter statement may be included in subsequent reports. Id. § 1681i(b), (c). When a reinvestigation results in deleting the information or causes a dispute over the reinvestigation's results, the credit agency must, upon request, notify designated prior recipients. Id. § 1681i(d). An individual is entitled to request a copy of the report as often as once a year. (The free report requirement does not apply to one's credit score, however.) Visit AnnualCreditReport.com.

A credit agency's report may not include outdated matters. Id. § 1681c. The FCRA defines these matters to include among other things most information that is more than seven years old when the report is made. Id. § 1681c(a)(6). If an employer requests a more in-depth report that will require neighbors, friends, or others to be interviewed by the credit agency, the subject must first be notified. Id. § 1681d(a)(1).

The FCRA imposes criminal and civil penalties for violations. Administrative enforcement is the responsibility of the Federal Trade Commission "except to the extent that enforcement * * * is specifically committed to some other government agency * * *." 15 U.S.C.A. § 1681s(a). A civil action may be brought by a consumer in any federal or state court. Id. § 1681p. Willful failure to comply with the FCRA subjects the non-complying party to liability for punitive damages, attorneys' fees, and all court costs. 15 U.S.C.A. § 1681n. See *Millstone v. O'Hanlon Reports, Inc.*, 528 F.2d 829 (8th Cir. 1976). Liability for negligent noncompliance is limited to actual damages, attorneys' fees, and costs. 15 U.S.C.A. § 1681o.

A credit agency generally has no liability for reporting accurate and truthful information. For example, in *Goodnough v. Alexander's, Inc.*, 82 Misc.2d 662, 370 N.Y.S.2d 388 (N.Y.Sup.1975), a seventeen-year-old department store clerk was terminated after the employer learned from a credit report that she had been accused of shoplifting at age twelve. This information was less than seven years old and thus not obsolete under the FCRA's standards. The court acknowledged that a better statute might treat information about children differently from information about adults, but given the language of the statute in force, the clerk had no FCRA remedy against the employer. A credit agency must maintain reasonable procedures to assure the information's accuracy and correct inaccurate information. See *Bryant v. TRW, Inc.*, 689 F.2d 72 (6th Cir.1982).

The FCRA also prohibits obtaining information on a consumer from a consumer reporting agency under false pretenses. 15 U.S.C.A. § 1681q. The defendants in *Hansen v. Morgan*, 582 F.2d 1214 (9th Cir.1978), who obtained a political candidate's consumer report not for extending credit, but for political purposes to assist a congressional committee, were found liable. Defendants asserted that the report had been obtained to evaluate the candidate's fitness for employment as a public official, but the court rejected defendants' argument that this constituted an "employment purpose." Likewise, in *Russell v. Shelter Fin. Servs.*, 604 F.Supp. 201 (W.D.Mo.1984), a consumer loan company's request for a consumer report about a former employee could not be justified for "employment purposes" where this report was not sought until after the employee's resignation had been announced. The use of credit reports by attorneys representing adverse parties (who had no credit relationship with the consumer) has also been found wrongful. See *Bakker v. McKinnon*, 152 F.3d 1007 (8th Cir.1998).

d. Omnibus Crime Control and Safe Streets Act and the Electronic Communications Privacy Act

Title III of the Omnibus Crime Control and Safe Streets Act of 1968 (Title III) regulates deliberate interceptions of wire and oral communications that may affect privacy and reputation. 18 U.S.C.A. §§ 2510–20. Much of the statute is devoted to regulating the conduct of police officers, but interceptions by private parties, including employers, are also prohibited. In *Watkins v. L.M. Berry & Co.*, 704 F.2d 577 (11th Cir.1983), an employer violated Title III by listening on an extension telephone to an employee's private conversation. Title III also bans use or disclosure of telephone conversations intercepted in violation of the Act. 18 U.S.C.A. § 2511.

"Intercept" refers to obtaining the contents of any wire, electronic, or oral communications through the use of any electronic, mechanical, or other device. Id. at § 2510(4). For interception of an oral communication to constitute an offense under the act there must be: (1) a willful interception; (2) the oral communication must be uttered by a person exhibiting an expectation that communication would be private; and (3) the communication must have been made under circumstances justifying an expectation of privacy. *United States v. Carroll*, 337 F.Supp. 1260 (D.D.C.1971). No finding of bad faith or malice is required for recovery under the Act.

A violation involving interception, disclosure, or use subjects one to a fine of not more than $10,000, or a term of imprisonment not more than five years, or both, Id. at § 2551(1). Violation also subjects one to a civil cause of action by the person whose communication was unlawfully intercepted, disclosed, or used. Damages that may be recovered include: (1) actual damage but not less than liquidated damages computed at the rate of $100 a day for each day of violation or $10,000, whichever is higher; (2) punitive damages (for a violation that is wanton or malicious); and (3) reasonable attorneys' fees and other litigation costs reasonably incurred. Id. § 2520. The United States may seize, and declare forfeited, any electronic mechanical, or other device used in violation. Id. § 2513.

Employer defenses to Title III violations include implied consent by the employee, *Griggs–Ryan v. Smith*, 904 F.2d 112 (1st Cir.1990) or that the interception occurred in the ordinary course of business. *Briggs v. American Air Filter Co., Inc.*, 630 F.2d 414 (5th Cir.1980). The latter defense is sometimes referred to as the "extension telephone exception" and essentially applies if the employer's interception occurs on a telephone being used in the routine conduct of the employer's business. An employer that prohibits personal calls, for example, may monitor telephone use to determine if that ban is being ignored. *Simmons v. Southwestern Bell Tel. Co.*, 452 F.Supp. 392 (W.D.Okl.1978), aff'd, 611 F.2d 342 (10th Cir.1979). Employers who utilize telephone extensions to intercept employees' telephone calls, however, must limit the scope of their intrusion. Thus, personal calls may be intercepted in the ordinary cause of business to determine their nature, but not their contents. The employer in *Deal v. Spears*, 780 F.Supp. 618 (W.D.Ark.1991), who taped and disseminated an employee's personal telephone conversations prior to firing the employee, violated the Act by not obtaining employee consent or limiting the intrusion on the privacy of the callers. An employer can limit its liability by adopting a policy forbidding violation of the Act, provided it acts promptly to enforce the policy when it is breached. See *Thomas v. Ohio Dept. of Rehabilitation and Correction*, 36 F. Supp. 2d 997, 1005 (S.D.Ohio 1998).

To respond to the growing importance of electronic communications, the Congress amended Title III by enacting the Electronic Communications Privacy Act of 1986 (ECPA). Under the ECPA, electronic mail (E-mail) is specifically protected. 18 U.S.C.A. § 2510(17)(A). The ECPA prohibits the interception of E-mail and provides criminal and civil sanctions for the unauthorized access to E-mail. Id. at §§ 2511(1)(a), 2520, and 2521.

Two types of e-mail systems exist. One is operated by a communications company; the other is the "in-house" system operated by a private concern. In a communications company's e-mail system, individuals transmit messages to each other via terminal lines and routing mechanisms contained in a central computer. A sender types messages into a computer terminal and transmits the messages to an intended recipient via telephone lines owned and operated by an electronic mail company. The computer service company stores the messages in a computer mailbox. The recipient, who subscribes to the same service, can call in to the system and retrieve his or her personal, computer-mail messages. Each user receives a password to access the system. In the public network system, (MCI–Mail, Sprint–Mail, and AT & T Mail, for example), the password prevents unauthorized individuals from accessing a user's files.

The private concern's system, however, is just that: completely private. Such a system needs no connection to a public communications system. The employer, as owner of the system, handles all computer calls within the company and considers these calls its exclusive property. There are several security devices that users within a company can use to ensure privacy. These devices include frequent changes of passwords, encryption of passwords, and multiple-level password entry. Although these security devices operate to secure against unwarranted invasion by other employees and hackers, they do not prevent the employer from gaining access to an employee's files. Because the employer provides the system, these systems generally do not have the security features that a public E-mail network system contains. An employer can ordinarily "call up" all messages stored in its private system without needing the employees' passwords, even those that have been thought to have been deleted. The internal mechanics of the systems do not provide the employee with privacy protection from the employer.

The ECPA protects individuals using electronic mail network systems from unauthorized interception of messages in transmission by employers (or others). 18 U.S.C.A. § 2511(1). However, an employer, as provider of a service may intercept a communication without suffering liability as long as the activity is "a necessary incident to the rendition of his service or to the protection of the rights or property of the provider of that service...." 18 U.S.C.A. § 2511(2)(a)(i). Section 201 of ECPA, 18 U.S.C.A. § 2701, regulates access to stored communications. It forbids access "without authorization [to] a facility through which an electronic communication service is provided...." Since an employer operating its own system regulates the "authorization" for access to that facility, the statute as such does not forbid it from looking at stored material.

See *United States v. Simons*, 29 F.Supp.2d 324 (E.D.Va.1998) aff'd in part, rev'd in part, 206 F.3d 392.

The employer thus enjoys substantial freedom to monitor the substance of its employees' e-mail. The statute nonetheless provides important protections: against unauthorized access by other employees and by individuals outside the business, such as hackers.

Despite its generally favored position under the statute, an employer may still be subject to liability for invasion of the employee's privacy. This depends in large measure on the extent to which an employee has a reasonable expectation of privacy in that e-mail. When one is using a computer furnished by an employer, one generally has only a limited expectation of privacy. *Leventhal v. Knapek*, 266 F.3d 64 (2d Cir.2001). The employee must recognize that the system exists primarily for the convenience of the employer. This does not, however, mean that a worker can never expect a message to be treated as private. In an e-mail system, the system stores messages in a file for later retrieval. The system operates in a manner analogous to an employee's placing a file in a cabinet or papers in a desk drawer for retrieval at a later time. It is at least arguable that e-mail can be considered a form of personal mail. Any correspondence is addressed specifically to an intended recipient. Most individuals hold a reasonable expectation of privacy in their personal mail. Unless an employer notifies all employees that monitoring is taking place, courts may infer that invasion of an individual's e-mail is an invasion of privacy. See *Schowengerdt v. General Dynamics Corp.*, 823 F.2d 1328, 1333 (9th Cir.1987).

To limit the scope of an employee's reasonable expectation of privacy in e-mail, an increasing number of employers announce that the electronic work aids can be monitored and that they are to be used only for employer business and that use for personal communications may be subject to employee discipline up to an including termination. See, e.g., *Conneaut School District,* 104 Lab.Arb.(BNA) 909 (1995) (Talarico, Arb.). The more specific the warning that system security features do not neutralize the employer's ability to access information at any time, the more likely it is to be effective.

The right of privacy based on the First Amendment may provide somewhat greater protection to public sector employees. However, the Fourth Circuit upheld a Virginia statute that restricted state employees' access to sexually explicit material on state-owned or—leased computers, absent the agency head's permission, against such a constitutional attack. *Urofsky v. Gilmore*, 167 F.3d 191 (4th Cir. 1999). A legitimate interest for this regulation existed because the state must retain the right to control the manner in which employees perform their duties at the workplace. The statute regulated the employees' speech only in their capacity as employees and not as private citizens where they retained the right to view this material outside the workplace.

e. Mail Tampering

Federal law prohibits any person from taking mail addressed to another person before it has been delivered with the intent "to obstruct the correspondence, or to pry into the business or secrets of another." 18 U.S.C.A. § 1702. This law is designed to protect the mails and correspondence from theft, embezzlement, obstruction, and prying. To violate this law the wrongdoer must have the specific intent to obstruct correspondence or to pry into the business or secrets of another. *United States v. Ashford*, 530 F.2d 792 (8th Cir.1976). Mail is protected until it is physically delivered to the addressee or an authorized agent. *United States v. Gaber*, 745 F.2d 952 (5th Cir.1984).

For employers and employees, this statute has only limited impact. If an employer were to open mail that is clearly personal, in the employer's hands as a conduit for getting it to the employee, that would be a violation. An analogous case is *United States v. Cochran*, 646 F.Supp. 7 (D.Me. 1985), in which the court found that distribution of mail from a university office to dormitories was a further extension of the mail route. Violations carry a penalty of up to five years in prison and a fine of $2,000. 18 U.S.C.A. § 1708. There is no civil liability. Even absent this statute, opening of employee mail without permission may be a privacy intrusion. See *Vernars v. Young*, 539 F.2d 966 (3d Cir.1976) (unauthorized opening and reading of mail marked "personal").

f. Employee Polygraph Protection Act

The Employee Polygraph Protection Act of 1988 is a Congressional response to the perceived unfairness of refusing to hire an applicant or firing a current worker based solely upon the results of an often unreliable test. 29 U.S.C.A. §§ 2001–2009. Although "polygraph" appears in the title of the statute, its reach is in fact broader, extending also to a "deceptograph, voice stress analyzer, psychological stress evaluator, or any other similar device * * *." 29 U.S.C.A. § 2001(3). The EPPA generally prohibits most private employers from using lie detector examinations either for pre-employment screening or during the course of employment. This statute does not, however, govern the use of paper-and-pencil honesty tests. By its terms it regulates only the use of the polygraph and "any other similar device (whether mechanical or chemical)." 29 U.S.C.A. § 2001(4); see 29 C.F.R. § 801.2(d). (Some state statutes regulating polygraphs apply to them; others do not. See *State by Spannaus v. Century Camera, Inc.*, 309 N.W.2d 735 (Minn.1981), limiting the term "any test purporting to test honesty" to mean a test measuring physiological responses.)

The Act's private sector coverage is broad. It applies to all employers "engaged in or affecting commerce or in the production of goods for commerce." 29 U.S.C.A. § 2002. "Employer" is defined as "any person acting directly or indirectly in the interest of an employer in relationship to an employee or prospective employee." 29 U.S.C.A. § 2001(2). At least two courts have found that a polygraph examiner who decides to test, and under what conditions, may be considered an "employer" subject to the provisions of the EPPA. See *Rubin v. Tourneau, Inc.*, 797 F.Supp. 247 (S.D.N.Y.1992); *James v. Professionals' Detective Agency*, 876 F.Supp. 1013 (N.D.Ill.1995). The test is one of "economic reality." *Fallin v. Mindis Metals, Inc.*, 865 F.Supp. 834 (N.D.Ga.1994).

The Act imposes a number of specific requirements. All employers must post a notice in a "prominent and conspicuous" place that explains the Act. 29 U.S.C.A. § 2003. More importantly, the EPPA precludes employers from: (1) causing any employee or prospective employee to take a lie detector test; (2) using, accepting, or inquiring about the results of such a test; or (3) terminating, disciplining, or discriminating against any employee or prospective employee, on the basis of the results of a test, for refusal or failure to take the test, or for exercising any rights afforded by the Act. 29 U.S.C.A. § 2002.

The EPPA does, however, contain several exemptions. Section 2006(a) excludes from the coverage of the Act all public sector employers, federal, state or local. The Act also permits the federal government to test private sector employees who work for firms that have certain types of government contracts or access to classified information. Section 2006(b). Section 2006(c) allows the federal government to administer a polygraph test to any employees of a contractor of the Federal Bureau of Investigation, "in the performance of any counterintelligence function."

There are also three limited exemptions for private employers. Section 2006(d) provides an exemption for employers who are conducting an "ongoing investigation" involving "economic loss or injury," such as theft, embezzlement or industrial espionage. An employer who has a "reasonable suspicion" that an employee was involved in such an activity may ask that employee to take a polygraph test if the employee had access to the property, and if the employer executes a statement, to be given to the examinee, setting forth: (1) the specific investigated incident or activity "with particularity;" (2) the specific economic loss or injury; (3) the basis of the employer's reasonable suspicion; and (4) that the employee had access. Id. The employer must have a proper basis for its request *before* asking an employee to take a polygraph test. See *Long v. Mango's Tropical Café, Inc.*, 972 F.Supp. 655 (S.D.Fla.1997). An employer may not, for example, request that employees submit to a polygraph test to determine randomly whether or not any thefts have occurred. 29 C.F.R. § 801.12. Nor may an employer claim that an "ongoing investigation" is continuous because things are frequently missing. Id. In addition, no adverse employment action may be taken under this exemption on the basis of a polygraph test or refusal to take one "without additional supporting evidence." 29 U.S.C.A. § 2007(a)(1).

Section 2006(e) allows private employers involved in security services (armored car, security alarm, and security guard employers) to test prospective employees. The exemption applies only if the employer's "primary business" function includes the protection of: (1) "facilities, materials, or operations" that have a "significant impact on the health and safety" of a State (e.g. public utilities) or subdivision, or on the national security or (2) currency, precious commodities, negotiable securities, or proprietary information. Id. § 2006(e)(1)(A), (B).

The final exemption allows private employers to administer a polygraph test in situations involving drug security, drug theft, or drug diversion investigations. 29 U.S.C.A. 2006(f). This exemption applies only to employers authorized to manufacture, distribute, or dispense a controlled substance. Id. § 2006(f)(1). These employers may administer a polygraph test to a prospective employee who "would have direct access" to the manufacture, storage, distribution, or sale of any controlled substance and to a current employee if: (a) the test is administered in connection with an ongoing investigation and (b) the employee has access to the person or property that is subject of the investigation. Id. § 2006(f)(2). As with the security service exemption, an employer may not take adverse employment action without another "bona fide" reason beyond the refusal to take a polygraph test or based "solely" on the results of the test. Id. § 2007(a)(2); 29 C.F.R. § 801.21.

Special procedural limitations apply to the private sector exemptions. Failure to comply results in liability, even if the employee may in fact be guilty. See *Mennen v. Easter Stores*, 951 F.Supp. 838

(N.D.Iowa 1997). Under section 2007(b), the exemptions will not apply unless all of the following requirements are met during all phases of the testing (pretest, actual, or post-test): (1) the examinee may terminate the test at any time; (2) the examinee may not be asked questions in a degrading or unnecessarily intrusive manner; (3) the examinee may not be asked questions dealing with his or her religion; beliefs or opinions regarding racial matters; political beliefs or affiliations, sexual preferences; or beliefs, affiliations, opinions, or lawful activities concerning unions or labor organizations; and (4) in no case shall an examinee be subjected to a test when there is written medical evidence that he or she is suffering from any medical or psychological condition or is undergoing any treatment that might cause abnormal responses during the actual testing phase.

Separate requirements must be met during specific testing phases. In the pretest phase, the prospective examinee must be allowed to review all questions that are to be asked, advised that he or she may stop the test at any time, advised of the right to obtain legal counsel, and informed in writing about the specific characteristics of the tests and instruments being used. Id. § 2007(b)(2)(A)–(C). The examinee must sign a written notice that explains the examinee's rights and remedies, including that the examinee cannot be required to take the test as a condition of employment. Id. § 2007(b)(2)(D). During the testing itself, the examiner is prohibited from asking any question that was not presented in writing for review by the examinee before the test. Id. § 2007(b)(3). Also, no test may be conducted less than 90 minutes in length, unless the examinee voluntarily terminates the test. Id. § 2007(b)(5); 29 C.F.R. § 802.24. In the post-test phase, before an employer may take an adverse employment action based on the test, the examinee must be interviewed regarding the test results, and given a written copy of the opinion, questions used, and charted responses. Id. § 2007(b)(4); 29 C.F.R. § 801.25.

The EPPA also has specific requirements for the examiners. The exemptions for private employers are available only if the examiner meets the requirements in Section 2007(c) concerning licensing and liability coverage. The Act sets standards about the data upon which the examiner is to base his or her conclusions. All records produced relating to the polygraph test must be maintained by the examiner for at least three years after the test has been given. See also 29 C.F.R. §§ 801.26, 801.30. The examiner may not disclose any of the information gathered from the test except to the examinee; the employer who requested the test; a court, governmental agency, arbitrator, or mediator through a court order; or the Secretary of Labor. Id. § 2008(a)(b); 29 C.F.R. § 801.35. Employers are subject to similar detailed record-keeping and disclosure requirements. See id. § 2008(c); 29 C.F.R. § 801.30.

The penalties for violating the EPPA can be substantial. Any employer who is found by the Secretary of Labor to have violated the Act's provisions may be assessed civil penalties up to $10,000 for each violation. 29 U.S.C.A. § 2005(a)(1). In addition, a violating employer is liable to the employee or prospective employee for legal or equitable relief, including employment, reinstatement, promotion, the payment of lost wages and benefits, reasonable costs and attorney's fees. Id. § 2005(c). There is a three-year statute of limitations to bring an action. Id. The Secretary or Solicitor of Labor may also obtain restraining orders and injunctions to enforce compliance with this Act. Id. § 2005(b).

The Act prohibits an employee from waiving his or her rights, unless as part of a written settlement signed by the parties. Id. § 2005(d). This provision does not preclude arbitration of claims as provided in an employment agreement, resulting from a charge by an employee of an employer's alleged violation of the EPPA. See *Saari v. Smith Barney, Harris Upham & Co., Inc.*, 968 F.2d 877 (9th Cir. 1992).

Finally, the EPPA states that any state or local law or collective bargaining agreement that either prohibits detector tests or is more restrictive of their use will not be preempted. 29 U.S.C.A. § 2009. Thus, if a state law prohibits all use of polygraph testing in private employment, then testing pursuant to the limited exemptions or private employment would not be allowed. See 29 C.F.R. § 801.5. This provision does not apply to any of the exemptions having to do with public employers. 29 U.S.C.A. § 2009. *Stehney v. Perry*, 101 F.3d 925 (3d Cir. 1996).

g. *The Drug–Free Workplace Act*

The Drug–Free Workplace Act of 1988 requires an employer (other than an individual) that receives grant funds from a federal agency or is a party to a contract "for the procurement of any property or services of a value of $25,000 or more" with a federal agency to certify to the agency that it will provide a drug-free workplace. 41 U.S.C.A. §§ 701–707. The statute enumerates several steps that the employer is to take as a means of achieving this result. The employer must: (1) publish a statement notifying employees that involvement with controlled substances is prohibited in the workplace, and that specific actions will be taken if this prohibition is violated; (2) give employees a copy of the statement; (3) notify employees in this statement that they must abide by its terms and report drug convictions for violations occurring in the workplace within five days; (4) notify the appropriate federal agency within ten days of receiving a notice of conviction; (5) establish a "drug-free awareness program" to inform employees about the dangers of drug use, about the nature of the employer's anti-drug policy, about available drug counseling or employee assistance programs, and about sanctions the employer may impose for drug violations; (6) impose a sanction on, or require participation in a rehabilitation program by an employee with a drug conviction; and (7) make a "good faith effort to maintain a drug-free workplace." Id. §§ 701(a)(1), 702(a)(1).

The statute imposes a simpler requirement on an individual who enters into a contract with or obtains grant money from a federal agency. The individual must certify that he or she "will not engage in the unlawful manufacture, distribution, dispensation, possession, or use of a controlled substance" in performing the contract or conducting activity with the grant. Id. §§ 701(a)(2), 702(a)(2).

Enforcing the statute is the responsibility of each contracting or granting agency. Sanctions include suspension of payments, termination of the grant or contract, and debarment from eligibility for further contracts or grants for up to five years.

The statute does not apply to contracts performed outside the United States, contracts involving law enforcement undercover operations if application of the Act would be "inappropriate," or to contractors or grantees if application of the Act would be inconsistent with international obligations of the United States. See 48 C.F.R. § 23.501. The statute permits a contracting agency to waive compliance with the Act if imposing sanctions (such as withholding payment or terminating the contract) would "severely disrupt the operation of the agency to the detriment of the Federal Government or the general public." A granting agency may waive sanctions if it finds that "suspension of payments, termination of the grant or suspension or debarment of the grantee would not be in the public interest." 29 U.S.C.A. § 704.

The Drug–Free Workplace Act does not directly require an employer to act in a way that would significantly impair employee privacy. The convictions that employers must require workers to report are, after all, virtually certain to be matters of public record. Nonetheless, employers that seek to construct programs to meet their general obligation to maintain workplaces free from drugs may well be led to consider programs of testing or other sorts of surveillance. If employees challenge these programs, employers may well point to this statute as source of a privilege to act. At least one federal circuit court of appeals has overturned an arbitrator's order to reinstate a terminated drug user in part because of the "public policy" it found manifest in this law. *Gulf Coast Industrial Workers Union v. Exxon Company, U.S.A.*, 991 F.2d 244 (5th Cir. 1993). The opinion's reading of Supreme Court precedent has since been undercut. *Continental Airlines, Inc. v. ALPA*, 555 F.3d 399 (5th Cir. 2009).

h.   Americans With Disabilities Act

After an offer of employment has been made, an employer may require its prospective employees to undergo a medical examination, provided the requirement is uniform. The results of the examination must be kept confidential, with only three limited exceptions: (1) the employer may inform managerial employees who need the data to arrange necessary job restrictions or reasonable accommodations; (2) the employer may provide the information to nursing and safety personnel if a detected disability might require emergency treatment; or (3) the employer may provide the information to government officials investigating compliance with the ADA. 42 U.S.C.A. § 12112(d)(3). Releasing medical information without the employee's consent may create employer liability. See *Cossette v. Minnesota Power & Light*, 188 F.3d 964 (8th Cir.1999).

i. *Health Insurance Portability and Accountability Act of 1996 (HIPPA)*

The Privacy Rule called for by this statute (now 45 C.F.R. Part 160, and subparts A and E of Part 164) was the subject of considerable controversy, and was much reworked in the early days of the administration of the second President Bush. Essentially, the Rule applies only to individually identifiable health information, such as data on a particular person's treatment history or present health condition. It is important to workers and employers because one of the types of entities governed by the Rule is a health plan provided in the work place. The Rule's general effect is to make identifiable information readily available to those engaged in the active treatment of the individual, but to permit that individual to restrict access to the information by others. There are exceptions for a number of purposes, including law enforcement, judicial proceedings, and the administration of workers compensation programs. The Rule is administered by the Office of Civil Rights.

j. *Genetic Information Nondiscrimination Act of 2008. (GINA)*

This statute, 42 U.S.C. Chapter 21F, which takes effect in late 2009, prohibits the nonconsensual collection and transmission of genetic data. The principal provision applicable to employers forbids discrimination based on genetic information in hiring, firing, and other employment activities. 42 U.S.C. § 2000ff–1. It also forbids employers to "request, require or purchase genetic information with respect to an employee or a family member of an employee," but there are a number of exceptions. One is for monitoring performed in compliance with requirements of the Occupational Safety and Health Act or the Federal Mine Safety and Health Act. One OSHA regulation, 29 C.F.R. § 1910.1003(g), for example, requires regular screening of employees whose work involves exposure to certain known carcinogens. Another exception permits the employer to request information in order to comply with the Family and Medical Leave Act. Similar restrictions apply to employment agencies and labor organizations. 42 U.S.C. §§ 2000ff–2, –3. If an employer does obtain genetic information, it is to be kept private. 42 U.S.C. § 2000ff–5. Enforcement of the statute is through the procedures of Title VII of the Civil Rights Act of 1964. Regulations are still in the drafting stage as this book goes to press.

k. *American Recovery & Reinvestment Act of 2009—HITECH Act Title*

The overall purpose of this statute (Pub. L. 111–5)is to stimulate the sluggish economy that met the new Obama administration as it took office in 2009. This portion of the legislation, entitled the Health Information Technology for Economic and Clinical

Health Act (HITECH Act) is designed to create an electronic health record for every American by the year 2014. More than $19 billion is to be invested in that effort. Subtitle of the HITECH Act is devoted to privacy protections that will protect individually identifiable information. Much of the statute calls for modification of regulations issued under HIPPA. Other provisions deal with problems specific to electronic records. Regulations to implement the statute are in the process of formulation at the time this book is going to press.

2. State Legislation

State privacy regulation by statute is widespread, but it is also highly varied in coverage and content, so that this Nutshell can only give a rough sketch. First, there are statutes that deal at the state level with the same sorts of issues that have just been outlined with respect to federal law. Fair Credit Reporting acts are common, for example. See, e.g., West's Ann. Cal. Civ. Code §§ 1785–1786.56; Md. Com. Law Ann. §§ 14–201 to 14–204. Statutes regulating interception of telephone messages are also frequent. See, e.g., Tenn. Code Ann. § 65–21–110. More than half the states had enacted polygraph use regulation before the federal statute took effect. See, e.g., Conn. Gen. Stat. Ann. §§ 31–51(g).

Also common are statutes that protect confidential communications between clients and various professionals, particularly medical professionals, lawyers, and clergy. Employers will only rarely have records relating to employee disclosures to clergy, but disclosures to attorneys may well appear in employer files concerned with litigation in which the employee has been involved, and employer-maintained medical records on employees are very common. State medical records statutes must give way to federal regulation in the case of persons protected by the Americans With Disabilities Act (ADA) if the state law gives less protection to individual rights, but these laws are not preempted if they afford greater protection. 42 U.S.C.A. § 12201(b). More than a dozen states restrict access to arrest records. See, e.g., Pa. Stat. Cons. Ann. tit. 43 §§ 1321–24.

State laws that regulate medical testing are particularly varied. They range from statutes requiring testing of specified groups of workers, such as food service employees (see, e.g., Indiana Code Ann. § 16–1–20–21), to laws that prohibit testing for conditions such as AIDS (see, e.g., Wis. Stat. Ann. § 103.15). Laws requiring testing may not be fully preempted by the ADA, but that statute will control the time when the test is to be administered to protected individuals, requiring the test to be given after the offer of employment has been made. 42 U.S.C.A. § 12112(d)(3). GINA provides that it does not preempt state laws that are more protective of employees. 42 U.S.C. § 2000ff–8.

A slowly growing number of states specifically regulate the confidentiality of employee records in the private sector. Some simply give an employee a right to inspect his or her file. See, e.g., Alaska Stat. § 32.10.403. Others give employees an opportunity to seek to correct records. See, e.g., Ill. Comp. Stat. 820:40/6. A handful of states have statutes dealing with employment references. Some grant a conditional immunity to those who give references in good faith. See, e.g. Alaska Stat. 09.65.160. Illinois requires an employer that discloses an unfavorable personnel action to a third party to notify the affected employee on or before the day of disclosure. Ill. Comp. Stat. 820:40/7. The Seventh Circuit interpreted the statute not to destroy a common law limited privilege for an employer reporting such action truthfully. *Delloma v. Consolidation Coal Co.*, 996 F.2d 168 (7th Cir.1993). Those states that have enacted laws along the lines of the federal Freedom of Information Act ordinarily include provisions protecting the confidentiality of public employee personnel files to some extent. See, e.g., Ark. Code Ann. § 25–19–104 (1987).

A growing number of states have adopted legislation prohibiting an employer from discriminating in the hiring, retention, and termination of employees who use lawful products outside of the workplace (for example, alcohol and tobacco). See, e.g., Conn. Gen. Stat. Ann. § 31–40s; Ind. Code Ann. §§ 22–5–4–1 to 22–5–4–4; Me. Rev. Stat. Ann. tit. 26, § 597.

D.   CONSTITUTIONAL PROTECTIONS

Employee interests in privacy are protected by both federal and state constitutions through provisions such as those prohibiting unreasonable warrantless searches or reprisals for expressions of opinion and those protecting freedom of association. These constitutional limits on employer conduct generally apply only to government agencies, whose activities may be thought of as "state action." Some private sector employers, however, are so intertwined with government that they are also subject to constitutional limitations. Determining when this is true is often difficult. In *Holodnak v. Avco Corp.*, 514 F.2d 285 (2d Cir.1975), cert. denied, 423 U.S. 892, the court applied the first amendment to a defense contractor who operated a facility most of which was owned by the federal government. In *Griffith v. Bell–Whitley Community Action Agency*, 614 F.2d 1102 (6th Cir.1980), on the other hand, the court denied constitutional protection to employees of a private corporation almost all of whose funding came from government sources, and most of whose activities were subject to intense government regulation.

There may also be rare instances in which asserting one's constitutional right to hold individual beliefs can become implicated in charges of tortious wrongful termination. In *Novosel v. Nationwide Ins. Co.*, 721 F.2d 894 (3d Cir.1983), the court remanded for trial a claim that the plaintiff was terminated for refusing to lobby on the employer's behalf. A later decision limited *Novosel*, but stated that its analysis still remains a possible approach. *Borse v. Piece Goods Shop, Inc.*, 963 F.2d 611 (3d Cir.1992). Despite these exceptions, and despite the fact that at least one state constitution has been held to limit private employer conduct directly, it remains the general rule that only public sector employees may rely on constitutional protections.

1. Federal Constitution

A limited constitutional privacy and reputation interest arises from the Constitution's First, Fourth, Fifth, Ninth, and Fourteenth Amendments or from "penumbras" thereof. The most famous illustrative cases did not involve employment. See *Roe v. Wade*, 410 U.S. 959 (1973) (abortion); *Griswold v. Connecticut*, 381 U.S. 479 (1965) (contraceptives). This interest is protected against "state action," not against private actors, and thus the great majority of cases in this subsection involve government employees. That is not always the case, however, since at times a private employer may act as an agent of the government in carrying out, to take just one instance, a drug testing program. An employer would not become an agent of government by simply permitting a routine safety inspection by OSHA officials, surely, but if at the behest of police that employer were to saw an employee's personal padlock from a locker in which the employee had a reasonable expectation of privacy, there found illegal drugs, and voluntarily turned these over to the police, there might well be a violation of rights under the Fourth Amendment. For a discussion of what level of participation may make a private employer an agent of the government, see *Muick v. Glenayre Electronics,* 280 F.3d 741 (7th Cir.2002).

Another general point that needs to be made with respect to constitutional protections is that the fact that an employer may have the privilege to search and employee's desk, or locker, or computer drive does not mean that the employee lacks a "reasonable expectation of privacy" in the work place. See *Mancusi v. DeForte*, 392 U.S. 364 (1968).

a. First Amendment

The First Amendment directly impacts upon a public employee's privacy and reputation interests. The United States Supreme Court has reasoned that freedom of association is a right necessary to the first amendment's specific guarantees because freedom of speech, press, assembly, and petition frequently require group activity. See *NAACP v. Alabama, ex rel. Patterson*, 357 U.S. 449 (1958). Mere membership in an organization absent specific advocacy of illegal conduct is constitutionally protected. See *Brandenburg v. Ohio*, 395 U.S. 444 (1969).

First Amendment individual employee right cases tend to fall into four broad categories:

a. "Patronage" cases, involving employees who have been disciplined, terminated, laid off, demoted, etc. because of their political affiliation or beliefs. See *Rutan v. Republican Party*, 497 U.S. 62 (1990); *Branti v. Finkel*, 445 U.S. 507 (1980); *Elrod v. Burns*, 427 U.S. 347 (1976).

b. "Expressive conduct" cases, where employment status has been adversely affected by engaging in spoken, written, or another form of expression. See *Connick v. Myers*, 461 U.S. 138 (1983); *Waters v. Churchill*, 511 U.S. 661 (1994); *Garcetti v. Ceballos,* 547 U.S. 410 (2006);

c. "Hatch Act" cases, challenging statutes that limit the right of public employees to engage in partisan political activity. See *Broadrick v. Oklahoma*, 413 U.S. 601 (1973).

d. "Nonconformist conduct" cases, in which the employee has suffered adverse employment action because of private conduct the employer regards as immoral or otherwise improper. See *City of San Diego v. Roe*, 543 U.S. 77 (2004).

The first of the major Supreme Court *patronage* cases, *Elrod v. Burns,* arose out of the wholesale termination of Republican employees by a Democrat newly elected as Sheriff; it split the Court sharply. The plurality opinion condemned patronage systems in general as destructive of First Amendment freedom. The concurring opinion was more limited in scope, outlawing only the termination (or threat of termination) of a "nonpolicymaking, nonconfidential government employee * * * upon the sole ground of his political beliefs." The dissent would defer to the judgment of the state legislature that only half the employees in the Sheriff's office were to be protected by a merit system, the remainder serving at the pleasure of the elected official. *Branti v. Finkel* also involved terminations, and simply extended the protection given by *Elrod* to assistant attorneys, thus defining broadly the notion of who is a "nonpolicy making" employee. In *Rutan v. Republican Party*, a five justice majority extended the protection to hirings based solely upon political considerations. In determining whether political affiliation is an appropriate consideration for personnel decisions concerning particular positions, the court must examine: (1) the inherent duties of the position in question and (2) the duties that the new holder of that position will perform, as envisioned by newly elected officials. *Hoard, et al. v. Sizemore*, 198 F.3d 205 (6th Cir.1999). Broad responsibilities that are not well-defined may make it more likely that the position is policymaking and the person is subject to removal for political affiliation.

The First Amendment also protects public employees in speaking out on public issues. This free speech guarantee is not absolute. A public employer's interests in regulating its employees' speech differ from those it possesses in regulating the general public's. See *Arnett v. Kennedy*, 416 U.S. 134 (1974), rehearing denied, 417 U.S. 977 (1974). If employee speech is constitutionally protected, a balance must exist between the employee's interest as a citizen commenting on matters of public concern and the public employer's interests of promoting the safe and efficient delivery of services. A public employer may enforce reasonable restrictions on the time and place for public comment; a firefighter ought not to turn off the hose to denounce the mayor while a house continues to burn. Nonetheless, the right to comment without reprisal is a strong one.

During a private conversation that took place in a county constable's office following an assassination attempt on the President, a clerical employee said: "If they go for him again, I hope they get him." The Court held this was protected speech. *Rankin v. McPherson*, 483 U.S. 378 (1987). The statement plainly dealt with a matter of public concern. It was made in the course of a conversation addressing public policies of the President's administration. Given the minimal law enforcement activity engaged in by the constable's office and the clerical employee's position in the office, the constable's interest in terminating her did not outweigh her rights under the First Amendment.

In *Garcetti v. Ceballos,* 547 U.S. 410 (2006), however, a five-justice majority held that an attorney could be disciplined for statements made by him in the course of carrying out his job. The statements in question were challenges to the way in which a criminal case was being handled, and appeared in a memorandum written by the lawyer in the performance of his work. The majority distinguished *Rankin* on the ground that the speech in that case did not directly involve the performance of the speaker's work.

In *Bickel v. Burkhart*, 632 F.2d 1251 (5th Cir. 1980), complaints by fire officers about not having received a raise were constitutionally protected. In *Roberts v. Civil Service Board of Jackson*, 75 Mich.

App. 654, 255 N.W.2d 724 (Mich.App.1977), a police officer could not be terminated for stating that a marijuana law was too severe.

The police department rules involved in *Haurilak v. Kelley*, 425 F.Supp. 626 (D.Conn.1977) barred employees from seeking the aid of any person outside the department with respect to assignment or promotion and forbid employees to speak critically to persons outside the department. The court held the rule could not be applied to prohibit a police officer from writing letters to an alderman and mayor. The letters were written in respectful terms and no close working relationship existed that criticism could not be tolerated or that they interfered with employer operations. However, profane speech may not be protected. See *Martin v. Parrish*, 805 F.2d 583 (5th Cir.1986).

A state may provide in its public sector labor relations law that a majority union is to function as "exclusive representative" of the bargaining unit, just as is true for the private sector under the NLRA. The exclusivity principle cannot be used to thwart a public employee who, like any other citizen, may wish to express views about governmental decisions different from the union's. *Abood v. Detroit Bd. of Educ.*, 431 U.S. 209 (1977), rehearing denied, 433 U.S. 915 (1977). Union dues may be used in the public sector to express the union's political views. However, they must be assessed in a manner that does not coerce the public employee into financing lobbying on behalf of candidates or positions she does not support. The union must provide a means for such a person to pay dues only for employee representation purposes. A state may constitutionally insist that such political activity expenditure requires affirmative authorization by a member. *Davenport v. Washington Education Association,* 551 U.S. 177 (2007). The Court has also upheld an Idaho statute that permits payroll deductions for general-purpose union dues, but not for dues that would support political activity. *Ysursa v. Pocatello Education Association,* 129 S.Ct. 1093 (2009).

Symbolic acts can be protected speech. Latino police officers' interest in marching in uniform behind their banner for the Latino Officers Association in city parades was protected speech under the First Amendment. *Latino Officers Association, New York, Inc., et al. v. City of New York,* 196 F.3d 458 (2d Cir.1999). Public citizens were more likely to understand the association's message about discrimination and misconduct within the police department if the police officers wore their uniforms. The context of the police officers' conduct included significant publicity that the association had received for positions it had taken on those issues.

A bumper sticker, campaign button, or political poster used to express political opinion is constitutionally protected. *Ferguson Police Officers Ass'n v. City of Ferguson,* 670 S.W.2d 921 (Mo.App.1984). In *Nalley v. Douglas County,* 498 F.Supp. 1228 (N.D.Ga.1980), the court struck down a regulation prohibiting public employees from wearing beards.

The right to engage in outside employment may also be constitutionally protected, but only in limited circumstances. A police officer stated a First Amendment claim where he had been denied the permission to teach a concealed handgun safety course as outside employment. *Edwards v. City of Goldsboro*, 178 F.3d 231 (4th Cir.1999). The court's opinion emphasizes that the content, context, and form of the police officer's speech made it a matter of public concern.

At both the federal and state levels there are statutes limiting the range of partisan political conduct that may be engaged in by government workers. To the extent that these limits apply to on-the-job activity, they can be justified both by the notion that "work time is for work" and by the objective of maintaining official government neutrality as between competing political factions. These statutes have sometimes been struck down, however, when they have sought to remove public workers entirely from political activity. In *McNea v. Garey*, 434 F.Supp. 95 (N.D.Ohio 1976), a police department rule prohibiting police from having "direct or indirect connection" with "political organizations" was voided because it unconstitutionally restricted political associations.

Unless the public employer can demonstrate an overriding interest of vital importance requiring that a person's private conduct and beliefs conform to those of the hiring authority, those cannot be the sole basis for denying public employment to that person. *Branti v. Finkel*, 445 U.S. 507 (1980). Termination was not permitted in *Brantley v. Surles*, 765 F.2d 478 (5th Cir.1985), where a white elementary school cafeteria manager transferred her son from a public high school to a private segregated one. A constitutionally protected interest existed in the education of her son and this conduct did not pose a threat of interracial dissension. Decisions about sexual practices are generally treated as private matters. In *Drake v. Covington County Bd. of Educ.*, 371 F.Supp. 974 (M.D.Ala.1974), cancellation of a teacher's employment for immorality in allegedly becoming pregnant while unmarried violated the teacher's privacy right. The case was more egregious because the employer had obtained information about the pregnancy improperly, from the teacher's physician. Public employers cannot arbitrarily ask an applicant concerning private sex habits. Inquiries can only reasonably elicit information concerning an applicant's private sex life that directly relate to employment suitability. *Richardson v. Hampton*, 345 F.Supp. 600 (D.D.C.1972). First Amendment rights were abridged in *Thorne v. City of El Segundo*, 726 F.2d 459 (9th Cir.1983), when an employee was forced during a polygraph examination to disclose personal sexual information.

Just when "private" affairs become matters of "public" concern can be a difficult issue. The plaintiff in *City of San Diego v. Roe,* 543 U.S. 77 (2004), a San Diego police officer, made video tapes of himself stripping off a police uniform (generic, not a San Diego uniform) and then performing sexually explicit acts. He sold copies of these tapes on adult sites on the internet. His user profile identified him as a person "employed in the field of law enforcement." He also sold items of police equipment using the same name, including official San Diego police uniforms. A senior officer saw one of the ads for police equipment, and this led to discovery of the ads for the tapes. In a *per curiam* opinion, the Court found the plaintiff's discharge did not violate his free speech rights. In *Wilson v. Taylor*, 733 F.2d 1539 (11th Cir.1984), the court awarded damages to a police officer who was discharged for dating the adopted daughter of a convicted felon. However, in *Baron v. Meloni*, 602 F.Supp. 614 (W.D.N.Y.1985), a deputy sheriff's termination for violating an order prohibiting associating with a reputed organized crime figure's wife was held not to violate any constitutional right. Here the employer was actively involved in organized crime investigations and the terminated employee had access to criminal history and investigative files. His conduct limited the employee's assignments and tended to discredit the employer. Likewise, no constitutional right protected police officers in *Fugate v. Phoenix Civil Service Bd.*, 791 F.2d 736 (9th Cir.1986), who were terminated for engaging in open, public, on-duty affairs with prostitutes.

Employers, both elected public officials and private entrepreneurs, also enjoy the privilege of free speech under the First Amendment. At times, this must be balanced against employee rights of freedom of association. An employer is entitled to express anti-union sentiments to its workforce, but

may constitutionally be forbidden either to discriminate against union members or to threaten reprisal
for lawful union activity.

In an intriguing case, a private sector employer
unsuccessfully asserted a right to refrain from
speaking. The court held that employer rights of
free speech are not infringed by a statute providing
that whenever an employee is terminated or voluntarily quits, the employer, upon written request,
must issue a letter to the employee setting forth the
nature and character of employment services rendered. *Rimmer v. Colt Industries Operating Corp.*,
656 F.2d 323 (8th Cir.1981).

b. Fourth Amendment

The Fourth Amendment protects individuals
from unreasonable "searches and seizures." U.S.
Const. amend. IV. Because "searches and seizures"
are possible without physical intrusion—by tapping
into an employer's data bank, for example—the
amendment's protection may at times safeguard a
relatively broad interest in confidentiality of information. The amendment is made applicable to the
states through the fourteenth amendment's Due
Process Clause. *New Jersey v. T.L.O.*, 469 U.S. 325
(1985). *T.L.O.* involved a search of a public school
student's purse, but is often cited in employment
cases. The basic purpose of the amendment is to
protect the individual's privacy and dignity against
unreasonable intrusions by the state and "all of its
creatures." Most Fourth Amendment challenges occur in the context of government investigations into

possible violations of law. More often than not, possible criminal activity is the ultimate target of the search. Its strictures have also been applied to the conduct of government officials in various civil activities, however, such as OSHA inspections.

To determine whether a particular intrusion is reasonable, the individual's Fourth Amendment interests must be weighed against legitimate government interests within the context in which the intrusion occurred. *Katz v. United States*, 389 U.S. 347 (1967). Generally, for a search by an agent of the government to be reasonable, it must be undertaken pursuant to a warrant based on probable cause. *Mincey v. Arizona*, 437 U.S. 385 (1978); *California v. Acevedo*, 500 U.S. 565 (1991). This requirement may be dispensed with when "the burden of obtaining a warrant is likely to frustrate the governmental purpose behind the search" or "where a legitimate government purpose makes the intrusion into privacy reasonable." See *Camara v. Municipal Court*, 387 U.S. 523 (1967); *Security and Law Enforcement Employees v. Carey*, 737 F.2d 187 (2d Cir.1984). It may also be inappropriate in these exceptional circumstances where special needs, beyond the normal law enforcement need, make the warrant and probable cause requirement impracticable. *New Jersey v. T.L.O.*, 469 U.S. 325 (1985). In situations in which no warrant is required, however, the reasonableness of the search may still be challenged. By what standard is reasonableness measured in these cases? Several have been suggested. The most stringent alternative to the warrant/probable cause requirement is the independent probable cause standard, i.e., a warrantless search must still be based on probable cause. *New Jersey v. T.L.O.*, 469 U.S. 325 (1985). Less stringent standards are sometimes applied. The opinions in *Skinner v. Railway Labor Executives' Ass'n*, 489 U.S. 602 (1989) and *National Treasury Employees Union v. Von Raab*, 489 U.S. 656 (1989) reveal a sharp division among the members of the Supreme Court about when a warrantless search is justified, particularly when a search of the person is involved. A majority of the Court appear more ready to find special needs for these searches than would have been true earlier. In *Skinner*, seven justices found warrantless drug testing using urine samples to be justified in the case of workers involved in railroad accidents despite the absence of cause for individualized suspicion. (While most railroad employees are in the private sector, the testing program is mandated by government and is thus state action.) In *NTEU*, only five voted to approve a Customs Service program requiring urinalysis of all applicants for promotion to positions involving interdiction of drugs, carrying firearms, or handling "classified" material. Justice Scalia's dissent in *NTEU* vigorously questioned whether the agency had demonstrated a sufficient need for the program.

Extending the restraints of the Fourth Amendment to government acting in the capacity of employer also enlarges the scope of inquiry into what constitute special needs. What might seem a vague suspicion of theft when proffered as a justification for a search by police in the criminal context may seem more substantial as justification for an inventory control scheme in the employment context. A similar change in the appropriate scope of analysis occurs with regard to analyzing what constitutes a reasonable expectation of privacy.

The constitution protects only that "expectation of privacy that society is prepared to recognize as reasonable." What one willingly exposes to public view is not protected. Most of what employees do at work they expect to be seen by fellow workers and supervisors, since work areas are generally within the employer's overall control. Workplaces are seldom private enclaves free from entry by supervisors, managers, other employees, or business and personal invitees. Instead, they are generally continually entered during the workday for conferences, consultations, and other work-related visits.

Requiring an employer to obtain a warrant whenever the employer entered an employee's office, desk, file cabinet, or locker or a work-related purpose would disrupt the routine conduct of public business and be overly burdensome. Imposing warrant procedures upon supervisors would be unreasonable. Employers could not properly function if every employment decision became a constitutional confrontation. Not everything that passes through an employer's doors, however, can be considered part of the workplace. The employee may bring closed luggage to the office prior to leaving on a trip, a handbag, or a briefcase. Most employees can reasonably expect their cars parked in employer lots to be free from search. In *O'Connor v. Ortega*, 480 U.S. 709 (1987), the Court found that an employee had a reasonable expectation of privacy in a locked desk drawer he had consistently treated as private.

Public employer intrusions on the constitutionally protected privacy interests of public employees for non-investigatory, work-related purposes and for work-related misconduct investigations are therefore to be evaluated according to their reasonableness under all the circumstances, including past practice, employment handbooks, supervisor statements, and the like.

A fair number of cases in which the courts have engaged in this sort of balancing have involved employee lockers. In *United States v. Speights*, 557 F.2d 362 (3d Cir.1977), a record of inspecting lockers that included three or four inspections for cleanliness and at least one inspection for the purpose of finding an illegal weapon over a twelve-year period did not counter a police department employee's reasonable privacy expectation. A conviction for possession of an unlawful weapon (a sawed-off shotgun) was reversed, despite the consent of the employer to the search of its locker room. A different balance was reached in *United States v. Bunkers*, 521 F.2d 1217 (9th Cir.1975), cert. denied, 423 U.S. 989. There a conviction for theft from the mails was upheld even though the necessary evidence was obtained through a search of the defendant postal service employee's locker, a search to which she had not directly consented. Both the Postal Manual and the applicable labor union agreement allowed locker searches upon reasonable suspicion of criminal activity. She was furnished a copy both of the Manual and the agreement.

Another area of growing concern has been to balance employee privacy interests against public employer business interests in deciding how much of the information stored on an employee's computer the employer is entitled to access. See *Leventhal v. Knapek*, 266 F.3d 64 (2d Cir.2001).

Employees can waive this amendment's protections by consenting, without coercion, to a search. A waiver may not be valid where it is overbroad. See *McDonell v. Hunter*, 612 F.Supp. 1122 (S.D.Iowa 1985), aff'd as modified, 809 F.2d 1302 (8th Cir. 1987) (waiver a condition of employment).

c. *Fifth Amendment*

The Fifth Amendment provides: "No person * * * shall be compelled in any criminal case to be a witness against himself * * *." It thus protects privacy by permitting individuals to keep secrets from government officials. As in the case of the Fourth Amendment, applying its restrictions against government acting as employer rather than as law enforcer requires careful analysis. The key to understanding the problem is to recognize *first* that requiring a person to disclose information as a condition for obtaining a job is "compelling" that disclosure, and *second* that no government agency is required to employ or retain in its employ a person who refuses to answer direct questions about his or her own job performance.

From these two principles there flow a number of specific applications. The Supreme Court held in 1967 that if a state employee has been required to answer questions as a condition of keeping a job, those answers cannot be used in a subsequent criminal prosecution of that employee, whether by the state, *Garrity v. New Jersey*, 385 U.S. 493 (1967), or by the federal authorities. *Murphy v. Waterfront Comm'n*, 378 U.S. 52 (1964). (A later case limiting *Murphy* does not stretch to this situation. *United States v. Balsys*, 524 U.S. 666 (1998).) The following year the Court held that it is unconstitutional for the state to require as a condition of employment that a public employee waive the privilege against self-incrimination. A termination for refusal to execute such a waiver is improper. *Gardner v. Broderick*, 392 U.S. 273 (1968). In that opinion, however, the Court made it clear that if a government employee refuses "to answer questions specifically, directly and narrowly relating to the performance of his official duties * * * the privilege against self-incrimination" would not bar termination. An employee who has been asked that sort of focused question cannot insist upon any sort of grant of immunity as a condition of answering. If questioning goes beyond the narrow limits set in *Broderick*, however, there can be no termination for refusal to answer unless adequate immunity is given. *Lefkowitz v. Turley*, 414 U.S. 70 (1973). Under the federal constitution, adequate immunity is what is termed "use" immunity, i.e., immunity from use either of the compelled disclosure or from any evidence to which that disclosure has led. The Fifth Amendment also prohibits evidentiary use of documents obtained in contravention of the Fourth Amendment. *Boyd v. United States*, 116 U.S. 616 (1886).

Private sector employers are not directly restricted by the Fifth Amendment, but a number of arbitrators appointed to decide cases under collective bargaining agreements have developed principles of decision using cases decided under the Fifth Amendment as analogies. They reason that in the industrial setting discharge operates much like a criminal law sanction. See, e.g., *King Co.*, 89 Lab. Arb. (BNA) 681 (1987) (Bard, Arb.) (improper to compel employees to implicate themselves in a crime); *Thrifty Drug Stores Co.*, 50 Lab. Arb. (BNA) 1253 (1968) (Jones, Jr., Arb.) (refusing to accept an employee's confession). It can be argued that the "public policy" limit on a private employer's freedom to terminate an at-will employee should be extended to ban a termination for exercise of a Fifth Amendment privilege. The countervailing public policy—encouraging citizen cooperation in enforcement of the laws—is also strong, however, and thus widespread adoption of such a rule seems unlikely.

d.   Ninth and Fourteenth Amendments

The Ninth Amendment states that certain fundamental rights are retained by the people. U.S. Const. amend. IX. The amendment does not identify these rights, however, and perhaps for that reason this amendment has only infrequently been relied on by the courts. In a handful of cases, however, the

Court has indicated that privacy may be entitled to Ninth Amendment protection. *Griswold v. Connecticut*, 381 U.S. 479 (1965); *Roe v. Wade*, 410 U.S. 959 (1973). In *Duckworth v. Sayad*, 670 S.W.2d 88 (Mo. App.1984), a police officer attending a conference on a university campus was held to be protected by both the Fourth and Ninth Amendments from being terminated for alleged sexual conduct in his dorm room, which was visible only by standing in a particular spot on the balcony outside his room.

The Fourteenth Amendment protects employees in several ways. It imposes on state governments the requirement to use fair procedures in deciding to deprive a person of a benefit such as employment. The amendment has both a substantive as well as procedural content, however. Through it the requirements of the Bill of Rights are made applicable to the states. And on some occasions it has been cited as a source of a right of privacy. For example, in *Eckmann v. Board of Education of Hawthorn*, 636 F.Supp. 1214 (N.D.Ill.1986), the court held that a school teacher has a substantive due process right to conceive and raise a child out of wedlock, and may not be disciplined for doing so.

As with the privacy right protected by other amendments, a balancing of interests is involved. In Pennsylvania, a court ordered a police officer discharged who had arranged for his wife to have an adulterous affair with another officer, while he conducted an affair with his wife's sister. *Fabio v. Civil Serv. Comm'n of Philadelphia*, 489 Pa. 309, 414 A.2d 82 (Pa.1980). The affairs led to rumors, scandal, and a complaint by the officer's father-in-law. Adultery, the court said, is still against public policy. In *Tobin v. Michigan Civil Serv. Comm'n*, 416 Mich. 661, 331 N.W.2d 184 (Mich.1982), the Michigan courts found that a state agency's release to various labor organizations of the names and home addresses of employees in the classified civil service did not violate the employees' constitutional privacy right. It was the government's responsibility and prerogative to balance its employees' interests against the public purpose that was served by this information's release. The decision, obviously, stands in contrast to the Supreme Court's decision under similar federal statutes. *U.S. Dept. of Defense v. FLRA*, 510 U.S. 487 (1994). *Hunter v. City of New York*, 58 A.D.2d 136, 396 N.Y.S.2d 186 (App.Div. 1977), aff'd, 44 N.Y.2d 708, 405 N.Y.S.2d 455, 376 N.E.2d 928 (N.Y.1978) invalidated a municipal ordinance requiring city employees to file financial disclosure forms to the extent that the ordinance permitted any member of the public access to the information and provided no means to protect the employees' privacy. A similar disclosure statute that provided that an employee must be told of any request for access to his or her disclosure form and given an opportunity to present arguments why the access request should be denied was upheld. *Barry v. City of New York*, 712 F.2d 1554 (2d Cir.1983), cert. denied, 464 U.S. 1017 (1983).

2. State Constitutions

In one way or another, most state constitutions protect the individual's right of privacy to some extent. Some explicitly mention "privacy." See, e.g., Alaska Const. art. 1, § 22; West's Ann. Calif. Const. Art. I, § 1; Ill. S.H.A. Const. Art. I, §§ 6, 12; West's RCWA Wash. Const. Art. I, § 7. Others resemble the federal constitution; the term "privacy" is not used but there will be a provision similar to, for example, the Fourth Amendment to the Constitution of the United States. See, e.g., Tenn. Const. Art. 1, § 7; Vernon's Ann. Texas Const. Art. I, § 9.

The Alaska court has reasoned that the inclusion of the term "privacy" in its constitution itself indicates an intention to protect this right more broadly than is done under the federal constitution. *Anchorage Police Department Employees Ass'n v. Municipality of Anchorage*, 24 P.3d 547 (Alaska 2001) (portion of drug testing ordinance held invalid). Illinois courts, on the other hand, have held they will use exactly the same analysis for both state and federal constitutional challenges. *People v. Tisler*, 103 Ill.2d 226, 82 Ill.Dec. 613, 469 N.E.2d 147 (Ill.1984). A state that recognizes a right of privacy grounded in the "penumbra" of its constitution's provisions may also develop doctrines more protective of privacy than the current federal restrictions. In *Texas State Employees Union v. Texas Department of Mental Health*, 746 S.W.2d 203 (Tex.1987), for example, the court struck down entirely a program of polygraph testing of employees providing care to mental patients. The opinion reviews the provisions of the Texas Bill of Rights that lead the court to conclude that a right of privacy is implicit among the " 'general, great, and essential principles of liberty and free government' " established by those provisions. It then states: "This right of privacy should yield only when the government can demonstrate that an intrusion is reasonably warranted for the achievement of a compelling governmental objective that can be achieved by no less intrusive, more reasonable means." (In dicta the court indicates it might possibly approve use of polygraph tests for the uniformed services.) Texas thus adopted a state constitutional law doctrine virtually identical to that announced only shortly before by the Supreme Court of California, a state whose constitution explicitly lists privacy as a protected right. See *Long Beach City Employees Ass'n v. Long Beach*, 41 Cal.3d 937, 227 Cal.Rptr. 90, 719 P.2d 660 (Cal.1986). To the extent that a privacy right grounded in a state constitution is broader in scope than that grounded in the federal constitution, the individual has obviously gained an added safeguard from intrusion. The chance that this may happen means that litigants challenging governmental invasions of privacy may be expected routinely to base their challenges on both state and federal constitutional provisions. That a state constitution based right may be broader than a federal right does not, of course, mean it is absolute. Despite the pattern of very intensive protection afforded by California, for example, the courts there permitted a school district to require a screening x-ray examination for tuberculosis as a condition of employment as a substitute school teacher. *Garrett v. Los Angeles City Unified School Dist.*, 116 Cal.

App.3d 472, 172 Cal.Rptr. 170 (Cal.App.1981). The employer's interest in providing a safe working and learning environment overcame the employee's privacy interest.

As with the federal constitution, most state constitutional provisions protect an individual's right of privacy only against governmental intrusion. The intermediate appellate courts of California have held, however, that Article I, section 1 of that state's constitution, listing privacy as an "inalienable right" also operates on private citizens. The intermediate appellate courts there have often been asked to apply the provision in private sector employment cases. In *Board of Trustees of Leland Stanford Jr. Univ. v. Superior Court of Santa Clara*, 119 Cal.App.3d 516, 174 Cal.Rptr. 160 (Cal.App. 1981), an employee's request for a judicial discovery order that would allow him to review the personnel records of a co-employee was denied in part because this would violate the co-employee's privacy right guaranteed by the state constitution. The employer, as the custodian of private information, could not waive the privacy right of an employee who was constitutionally guaranteed this protection.

Private sector alcohol and drug testing have also been reviewed under California's constitution. *Smith v. Fresno Irrigation District*, 72 Cal.App.4th 147, 84 Cal.Rptr.2d 775 (1999); *Luck v. Southern Pac. Transp. Co.*, 218 Cal.App.3d 1, 267 Cal.Rptr. 618 (1990). Factors the court have considered include whether employees had notice of the testing program, the intrusiveness of the collection process, procedural safeguards, and whether the position involved was safety sensitive.

E. BEHAVIOR REGULATION

An employer clearly has the right to impose reasonable non-discriminatory rules for on-the-job conduct. At times, however, the rules may have an impact employees regard as too invasive, and so they will challenge them, perhaps through a bargaining representative, perhaps in court. Also, there have been a significant number of employer attempts to regulate conduct away from the work, sometimes in an effort to reduce health care costs, sometimes because of concerns over employer image. (The earlier discussion of public sector First Amendment cases partially illustrates the latter.) This section addresses three areas in which the balancing or employer and employee interests has proved troublesome.

1. Smoking

The proportion of Americans who smoke tobacco products has been declining in recent years, and non-smokers have become increasingly insistent that they not be required to eat, shop, and work in places that subject them to second-hand smoke. OSHA developed a proposal for regulating the hazard, but withdrew it in December 2001, over the protest of a number of anti-smoking groups.

Pending any preemptive action at the federal level, state law governs, and continues to display some variety, although the spread of bans on smoking in public places and at work has picked up speed in recent years. Attempts by non-smokers to obtain relief at common law have met mixed results. In *Shimp v. New Jersey Bell Telephone Co.*, 145 N.J.Super. 516, 368 A.2d 408 (N.J.Super.1976), injunctive relief was granted to a non-smoker after the employer had turned down the employee's request for a smoke-free environment. The court took judicial notice of the hazards of second-hand smoke, and held that the employer's decision to allow widespread smoking was a breach of its duty to provide a safe workplace. In *Smith v. Western Electric Co.*, 643 S.W.2d 10 (Mo.App.1982), the court reversed a trial court dismissal of a similar action, and remanded the case with instructions to consider evidence on whether smoking constituted a "recognized hazard" the employer had to eliminate. But in *Gordon v. Raven Systems and Research, Inc.*, 462 A.2d 10 (D.C.App.1983), the District of Columbia Court of Appeals was unwilling to impose a common-law duty on an employer to provide a smoke-free environment for its employees.

A host of smoking statutes have been enacted in the past three decades. First, there are state laws that prohibit smoking in a number of settings, typically including restaurants, bars, and enclosed workplaces. At least twenty-seven states now have such bans in place, with more pending in state legislatures. In those states without statewide bans, there are often local prohibitions on smoking. Massachusetts prohibits hiring police officers or firefighters who smoke at or outside the workplace. Mass. Gen. Laws Ann. ch. 41, § 101(A). This statute was enforced in *Plymouth v. Civil Service Commission*, 426 Mass. 1, 686 N.E.2d 188 (Mass.1997), where a police officer was terminated for smoking in a police cruiser. In some states, the matter has now assumed constitutional proportions. Florida's constitution bans smoking in all enclosed work spaces. Fla. Const. Art X, § 20.

At the opposite extreme are "smokers' rights" laws and statutes. These usually permit employers to ban smoking in the workplace but prohibit discrimination against workers who smoke away from the job. Indiana Stat. 22–5–4–1. Enactments like this may coexist in the same state.

A number of disputes have arisen under state unemployment compensation statutes when employees voluntarily leave their jobs because of their inability to work in a non smoke-free environment. Former employees are entitled to compensation in this instance if the workplace smoke was a "necessitous and compelling" reason for terminating employment, and that the employer was unable to meet its burden of showing that a reasonable accommodation was offered. *Lapham v. Unemployment Comp. Board*, 103 Pa.Cmwlth. 144, 519 A.2d 1101 (Pa.Cmwlth.1987). In *Quinn, Gent, Buseck and Leemhuis, Inc. v. Unemployment Comp. Board*, 147 Pa.Cmwlth. 141, 606 A.2d 1300 (Pa.Cmwlth. 1992), a divided court held that an ex-employee who smoked was not entitled to benefits after quitting work because of a new non-smoking policy. The continuing spread of smoking bans will probably result in few such claims being made in the future.

A restriction on off-duty smoking and drinking was at issue in *Best Lock Corporation v. Review Board*, 572 N.E.2d 520 (Ind.App.1991). There the ban was found to be unreasonable because it was not job-related. In *Best Lock*, a former employee's termination for violating this company policy was held not to be a termination for cause that would deprive the worker of unemployment benefits. The reason for the off-duty smoking ban, the owner's dislike of the smell of tobacco smoke, was found to be an inadequate justification for the restriction. The court held that off-duty restrictions are only allowable if they have a reasonable relationship to the employer's business interest, such as a restriction on alcohol consumption for company truck drivers, so that the employer could obtain auto insurance for his trucks. *Gregory v. Anderson*, 14 Wis.2d 130, 109 N.W.2d 675 (Wis.1961). South Dakota is one of the states that forbids firing employees for off-duty tobacco use. There is, however, an exception if the ban is a "bona fide occupational requirement." In *Wood v. South Dakota Cement Plant*, 588 N.W.2d 227 (S.D.1999), the court found it was not a violation for the employer to fire an assistant kiln operator for smoking. A no-smoking restriction during off-duty hours was a bona fide occupational requirement because a physician had concluded that unless the employee stopped smoking he would be unsuitable for the position.

Workers' compensation statutes have also resulted in controversy. In *Palmer v. Del Webb's High
Sierra*, 108 Nev. 673, 838 P.2d 435 (Nev.1992), the
Nevada court held that illnesses caused by workplace exposure to second-hand smoke were not covered by that state's workers' compensation act. In
*McCarthy v. Department of Social and Health Ser-
vices*, 110 Wash.2d 812, 759 P.2d 351 (Wash.1988),
the court held that the workers' compensation act
was not the exclusive remedy for an employee
whose respiratory problem was not covered by the
act. The employee's tort action for harm from second-hand smoke was allowed to go forward.

Under the federal Vocational Rehabilitation Act
of 1973, at least one court has found unusual sensi-
tivity to tobacco smoke to be a disability. See *Vick-
ers v. Veterans Admin.*, 549 F.Supp. 85 (W.D.Wash.
1982). A "qualified person with a disability" may
not be discriminated against and is entitled to reasonable accommodation. The Americans With Disabilities Act (ADA) may also cover this condition.
See *Harmer v. Virginia Electric & Power Co.*, 831
F.Supp. 1300 (E.D.Va.1993). A worker who suffers
from a medical condition causing difficulty in
breathing may suffer from a "disability" and if that
condition is aggravated by cigarette smoke may
have a claim for reasonable accommodation.

In a unionized workplace, where and when one
can smoke has been held to be a "term or condition" of employment, and is thus subject to collective bargaining. Therefore, union employers cannot
unilaterally change the company's smoking policy

during the life of an existing collective bargaining agreement over union objections. *Commonwealth v. Pennsylvania Labor Relations Board*, 74 Pa. Cmwlth. 1, 459 A.2d 452 (Pa.Cmwlth.1983); Chemtronics, Inc., 236 NLRB 178 (N.L.R.B.1978).

In at least one case, a court has decided a "smoker's rights" case under a state constitution. In *North Miami v. Kurtz*, 653 So.2d 1025 (Fla.1995), cert. denied, 516 U.S. 1043 (1996), a prospective employee was denied a job until she had stopped smoking for a year. She challenged the ordinance that authorized this employment practice on the grounds of the right-of-privacy clause in the Florida Constitution. The state supreme court held the constitutional protection did not extend to her in her capacity as a job applicant.

2. Alcohol and Drug Abuse

Substance abuse by employees remains a source of difficult issues for legislators and judges. One reason these problems are so challenging is society's ambivalence about those who use alcohol and other controlled substances in excess. Some think of substance abusers as helpless victims, others view them as free moral agents who have squandered their opportunities and are responsible for their own woes. Thus, many of the state workers' compensation laws contain language similar to this in the Vermont statute: "Compensation shall not be allowed for an injury caused by an employee's willful intention to injure himself or another or by or during his intoxication * * *." Vermont Stat. Ann.

Tit. 21 § 649. Substance addiction is only rarely compensable under these laws, because of the requirement that a compensable disease be occupational in character. See, e.g., *Pierce v. General Motors Corp.*, 443 Mich. 137, 504 N.W.2d 648 (Mich. 1993).

Alcoholism has not been a compensable disability under the Social Security Act since 1996, when the Congress eliminated benefits for most addictions. A drug addict is not a "qualified individual with a disability" protected by the Americans with Disabilities Act (ADA) unless that person has successfully completed a supervised rehabilitation program, or is currently participating in one. 42 U.S.C.A. § 12114(a), (b). A person who is dependent upon alcohol may, in contrast, be covered by the ADA if the alcohol dependency substantially limits one or more major life activities. A similar distinction exists under section 504 of the Vocational Rehabilitation Act of 1973. Discrimination against a former alcoholic is banned in most agencies of the federal government. 42 U.S.C.A. § 290dd–1(b). Some states interpret their statutes forbidding discrimination against disabled persons to protect alcoholics but require expert proof of the existence of the disease. See *Clowes v. Terminix International, Inc.*, 109 N.J. 575, 538 A.2d 794 (N.J.1988); *Connecticut Gen. Life Ins. Co. v. Department of Indus., Labor and Human Relations*, 86 Wis.2d 393, 273 N.W.2d 206 (Wis. 1979).

Many difficult problems exist in regard to the propriety of testing programs. There are three basic types of alcohol and drug screening. "Pre-employment screening" subjects all or selected applicants to testing, usually as part of a physical examination given prior to a final employment offer. "For cause testing" is conducted when an employer has a reasonable suspicion that an employer is under the controlled substance's influence. "Random testing" involves selecting an appropriate, scientifically determined, random sampling of the employer's workforce to undergo testing.

The most popular screening device is the enzyme multiplied immunoassay technique (EMIT) urinalysis test, which measures the presence of the primary active cannabinoid metabolite. Because the EMIT test is relatively inexpensive, quick, and easy to use, it has become popular. There are drawbacks, however. Urinalysis tests cannot be used: (1) to determine the degree of the drug's effect; or (2) to distinguish between recent drug use outside the workplace and current workplace impairment.

A gas chromatography/mass spectrometry (GCMS) test or a blood test may be used either as an initial test or as a follow-up test. The GCMS reduces the constituent chemicals to their molecular level and identifies the "fingerprint" of a specific drug. They are 99.9 percent accurate in confirming amphetamines, barbiturates, benzo-diazephines (librium and valium), cocaine, marijuana, opiates, PCP, methaqualone, and methadone. Another follow-up test is the radioimmunoassay (RIA) or examination of head hair with a high but not perfect reliability. However, like urinalysis testing, the

GMCS test indicates only that a drug has been used. It does not establish or verify workplace drug usage. Only a blood test can detect workplace drug use. It can yield information specific to current use and exposure degree. Complementary blood tests can be used to eliminate the problems associated with other testing. Thus the test that produces the most accurate and meaningful data is also the most invasive physically.

Controlling workplace alcohol and drug abuse generates concerns over individual employee rights similar to those that arise when an employer searches an employee's person or possessions. Chemically testing an employee's urine, blood, hair, or breath provides the employer with knowledge about employee associations and lifestyles outside the workplace.

Federal constitutional restrictions limit the power of an employer to test its employees only when "state action" is involved. State action is present: (1) when the test is administered by a government entity acting as employer or (2) when a private employer conducts a test because required to do so by government action. *Skinner v. Railway Labor Executives' Association*, 489 U.S. 602 (1989). Tests of breath, urine, or blood are "searches" for Fourth Amendment purposes, and thus must be "reasonable." What constitutes an unreasonable warrantless search depends upon the balance to be struck between the individual's right of privacy and the governmental interest in conducting the search. In *Skinner,* the Supreme Court held that a Federal

Railroad Administration regulation requiring post-accident testing of all operating employees involved was reasonable, despite the lack of a warrant and despite the fact that some employees would be tested in the absence of individual cause for suspecting wrongdoing on their part. The interest of the public in safe operation of the trains and the difficulty of making individual probable cause determinations in the confusion following a train wreck justifies the invasion of personal privacy. In *National Treasury Employees Union v. Von Raab*, 489 U.S. 656 (1989), a majority of the Court found the government has a compelling interest that justifies testing those employees in the Drug Enforcement Administration (DEA) who seek positions in which they would carry firearms. The opinion concedes that the regulation was adopted in the absence of evidence of significant drug use among DEA agents, but found the testing justified by the importance of the program to national security and health, which in turn meant that the government was vitally concerned with the integrity of those who carried out the agency's mission. Another DEA regulation, one applying to employees with access to classified information, was returned to the lower courts to determine whether those who would be tested would in fact be only those workers who would have access to "truly sensitive information."

Applying the *Skinner* and *VonRaab* rationales to random testing programs has not been easy. Challenges to the Navy's civilian employee testing program were first brought soon after its announcement in 1989. See *American Federation of Government Employees v. Cheney*, 754 F.Supp. 1409 (N.D.Cal.1990), aff'd 944 F.2d 503 (9th Cir. 1991). At one point in that litigation, the federal district court held that random testing is appropriate for employees in the classifications of Boilermaker, but not for those in the classification of Sheet Metal Worker. The difference, the court stated, lies in the importance of safety concerns. The sheet metal workers perform their duties in a context in which mistakes likely to cause injury are unlikely to occur (or at least go undetected), while the boilermakers work with equipment in which high pressures build up, so that even momentary lapses could result in explosion and serious harm. The same sort of similar highly detailed analysis of job duties was required for a whole array of job classifications.

State constitutions often contain provisions similar to the Fourth Amendment, and these may operate to limit the power to test public employees. In New York, for example, the Court of Appeals has held that a board of education may not engage in random urine testing of probationary teachers in the absence of "reasonable suspicion" (a lesser standard than "probable cause"), but later held that a random testing program for police officers in a special unit dealing with drug offenses is permissible. Compare *Patchogue–Medford Congress of Teachers v. Board of Education*, 70 N.Y.2d 57, 517 N.Y.S.2d 456, 510 N.E.2d 325 (N.Y.1987) with *Caruso v. Ward*, 72 N.Y.2d 432, 534 N.Y.S.2d 142, 530

N.E.2d 850 (N.Y.1988). In California, panels of the intermediate appellate court have applied a provision of the state constitution protecting the right of privacy to private sector employers. In *Luck v. Southern Pacific Transportation Co.*, 218 Cal. App.3d 1, 267 Cal.Rptr. 618 (Cal.App.1990), cert. denied, 498 U.S. 939 (1990), an employer was held liable because it discharged an employee for refusing to take a random test; the employee's work did not involve significant safety or security risks.

Statutory regulation of drug testing is often more important than are the constitutional limitations. Federal regulation is sparse. The ADA states that "a test to determine the illegal use of drugs shall not be considered a medical examination" subject to the requirements of that act, and goes on to provide that it shall not be construed either to authorize or to prohibit drug testing. 42 U.S.C.A. § 12114(d). The Drug–Free Workplace Act does not require or prohibit testing. 41 U.S.C.A. §§ 701–707. There are, however, regulations with respect to the confidentiality of records of employees who consent to participate in rehabilitation programs. There are also testing programs for specific industries, such as nuclear power. See 10 C.F.R. Part 26. State regulation of the right to test and of testing firms and procedures is more common, although by no means universal. See, e.g., Minn. Stat. Ann. §§ 181.950–181.957. In *Eaton v. Iowa Employment Appeal Board*, 602 N.W.2d 553 (Iowa 1999), the employer argued that a former employee was not eligible for unemployment benefits since he was fired for "misconduct," having failed a drug test. The court held that under the existing Iowa statute, the drug test was improper, and also held that the employer placed illegal reinstatement conditions on the employee's return to work. State laws governing the confidentiality of medical records are very common. The common law principles that protect the right to privacy, discussed in Chapter 3, also may apply.

The manner in which alcohol and drug testing is done by an employer may also create employee claims. Direct visual observation of urination to secure drug testing samples may invade an employee's privacy rights where a reasonable person could find this offensive. In the case of public sector employees, it can therefore be justified only by a "real and compelling governmental interest." See *Wilcher v. Wilmington*, 139 F.3d 366 (3d Cir.1998). The chain of custody in handling these testing samples is often an important issue. See *Mollette v. Kentucky Personnel Board and Kentucky Transportation Cabinet*, 997 S.W.2d 492 (Ky.App.1999). An employer may have to show that its collection site was secure and demonstrate the integrity of the sampling's handling prior to and after testing. If a testing laboratory bungles its handling of a test, it may be liable both under state tort law and, if acting on behalf of a government agency, under 42 U.S.C. § 1983 as well. See *Coleman v. Town of Hempstead*, 30 F.Supp.2d 356 (E.D.N.Y.1999). If an employer has the right to insist upon a test, then a worker's refusal to submit to that test may justify discipline up to and including termination and also the loss of unemployment compensation benefits. See *Crider v. Spectrulite Consortium*, 130 F.3d 1238 (7th Cir.1997) (termination for refusal to take drug test); *Rebel v. Unemployment Compensation Board of Review*, 555 Pa. 114, 723 A.2d 156 (Pa.1998) (denial of unemployment compensation for refusal to take drug test).

In unionized workplaces, the most important regulation of drug testing is likely to be provided by the collective agreement. The National Labor Relations Board has held that testing of current employees is a mandatory subject of bargaining, although testing of employee applicants is not. *Johnson–Bateman Co.*, 295 NLRB 180 (N.L.R.B.1989); *Star Tribune*, 295 NLRB 543 (N.L.R.B.1989). Whether an employee's use of drugs or alcohol justifies discharge is, of course, routine grist for the arbitrator's mill. See *United Paperworkers v. Misco, Inc.*, 484 U.S. 29 (1987).

Rehabilitation programs—often designated "employee assistance programs" when sponsored by an employer—are also the subject of regulation. Although employers are not required to offer such programs, they may be under an obligation to accommodate employees who are participating in such efforts. See, e.g., West's Ann. Cal. Lab. Code §§ 1025–1028.

Once an employer has given an employee the choice of rehabilitation or termination and the employee refuses to undergo rehabilitation, most arbitrators uphold the termination. *Pacific Telephone and Telegraph Company*, 80 Lab.Arb. (BNA) 419 (1983) (Killion, Arb.). Employees may be given a second chance to enter a rehabilitation program. Arbitrators generally uphold terminations when an employee has a post-rehabilitation reoccurrence of alcohol or drug abuse. *Tecumseh Products Co.*, 82 Lab.Arb. (BNA) 420 (1984) (Murphy, Arb.).

3. Human Immunodeficiency Virus (HIV)

The Human Immunodeficiency Virus (HIV) remains a significant employment issue, although the increasing ability to treat HIV conditions has lessened some concerns. The HIV infection attacks the body's immune system, leaving it incapable of defending against other, often fatal illnesses. These "opportunistic" infections include Kaposi's sarcoma (KS) (a rare skin cancer) and pneumocytis carnii pneumonia (PCP) (an uncommon lung ailment). The viral agent may be transmitted through blood or semen during sexual intercourse, blood transfusions, or shared needles used by drug users. It is not thought to be spread by casual contact of the type that typically occurs between co-workers at the workplace.

Individuals infected with HIV differ significantly in symptoms and physical conditions. There are those:

1. Who have been exposed to the virus but exhibit no symptoms;

2. Who develop HIV-related complex and exhibit its symptoms but have not yet developed the full syndrome; and

3. Who have an impaired immune system and
    have contracted an opportunistic infection,
    such as KS or PCP.

Tests have been developed to determine whether
an employee has been exposed to the HIV infection.
These tests detect antibodies to the virus. The most
widely used test is the Enzyme–Linked Immunosor-
bent Assay (EIA). Some tests use blood samples;
other use specially collected oral fluids. A slightly
less accurate test employs urine samples. These
tests raise individual employee rights concerns similar to those that exist for drug testing.

The Center for Disease Control has been issuing
HIV guidelines for the workplace since the mid
1980s. These recommendations reflect the scientific
community's conclusion that the infection is blood
borne and is most likely to be spread by sexual
contact, transfusion with infected blood, or by accidental needle stick injury. These guidelines have
therefore emphasized steps to be taken by health
care employees to manage exposure to blood and
other body fluids. The CDC studies and recommendations were a major source of information for the
Occupational Safety and Health Administration
(OSHA) Bloodborne Pathogen Standard, 29 C.F.R.
§ 1910.1030. That standard addresses risks not just
from AIDS but also from another major bloodborne
disease, Hepatitis B virus (HBV). A challenge to the
standard by a dentists' organization was rejected by
the Seventh Circuit. *American Dental Association v.
Martin*, 984 F.2d 823 (7th Cir.1993), cert. denied,
510 U.S. 859. The OSHA regulation requires an

employer that has employees who experience occupational exposure to HIV or HBV to develop an exposure control plan and update it periodically. The employer must also take precautions to protect employees against exposure to blood and other body fluids, must have adequate hand-washing facilities and encourage their use, must provide disposable gloves and other personal protective equipment, must provide containers for the safe disposal of needles and other "sharps," must communicate the presence of these hazards to employees, and must offer HBV vaccinations to those employees who want them. If an employee has been exposed to infection, through blood contact, for example, the employer must provide a post-exposure evaluation and disclose the results to the affected employee. Medical records are to be kept on employees, but must be kept confidential except insofar as disclosure is required by law. 29 C.F.R. § 1910.1030(h)(1). This confidentiality extends in particular to the results of post-evaluation tests. 29 C.F.R. § 1910.1030(f)(5).

A growing number of states have enacted statutes regulating HIV testing. California prohibits testing a person's blood for HIV without written consent with a very limited exception. West's Ann. Cal. Health & Safety Code § 199.22. Other states permit testing without consent if being HIV negative is a bona fide occupational qualification. See, e.g., Vernon's Ann. Texas Civ. Stat. § 7–4–127. If a test is permitted, there are often limits on test result disclosure. In Florida, for example, these test results may not be used to determine if a person may be insured for disability, health or life insurance, or to screen, determine suitability for or terminate employment. West's Fla. Stat. Ann. § 381.606(5); Wis. Stat. Ann. 631.90. Some states require disclosure to a sexual partner.

The same constitutional privacy considerations that apply to drug testing are relevant to HIV testing. Mandatory blood testing infringes a public sector employee's protected privacy "interest in avoiding disclosure of personal matters." See *Whalen v. Roe*, 429 U.S. 589 (1977); *Glover v. Eastern Nebraska Community Office of Retardation*, 686 F.Supp. 243 (D.Neb.1988), *aff'd*, 867 F.2d 461 (8th Cir.), cert. denied, 493 U.S. 932 (1989).

In *Stepp v. Indiana Employment Sec. Div.*, 521 N.E.2d 350 (Ind.App.1988), a laboratory technician's refusal to perform chemical examinations on body fluids from HIV infected patients was just cause for termination and proper denial of unemployment compensation benefits.

A person who is infected with the HIV virus is likely to be entitled to the protection of the Americans with Disabilities Act (ADA) under the statute's three-pronged definition of "disability." In *Doe v. Kohn Nast & Graf, P.C.*, 866 F.Supp. 190 (E.D.Pa. 1994), an infected attorney stated a cause of action against a law firm for violating the ADA. A worker who has developed AIDS and has contracted a disease such as Kaposi's sarcoma fits the first prong of the ADA's "disability" definition: a person who has "a physical * * * impairment that substantially limits one or more major life activities." 42 U.S.C.A. § 12102(2)(A). A person with AIDS who has suffered an opportunistic disease but has recovered from that disease sufficiently to return to work still fits either the first prong or the second: a person with "a record of such an impairment." Id. § 12102(2)(B). A person who is HIV-positive but as yet shows no symptoms may nonetheless be protected by the third prong as a person who is "regarded as having such an impairment." 42 U.S.C.A. § 12102(C).

Reasonable accommodation for a person who is HIV positive might take a number of forms, such as restructuring job duties so that the person is not subjected to risks of catching opportunistic diseases from customers or other employees. Employers will surely be expected to counter the fear or dislike that may be shown by other employees who are reluctant to work in close contact with an AIDS victim.

The discrimination forbidden by the ADA extends beyond that experienced directly by a person with a disability. The act forbids "denying equal jobs or benefits to a qualified individual because of the known disability of an individual with whom the qualified individual is known to have a relationship or association." 42 U.S.C.A. § 12112(b)(4). This provision is particularly important to gay or lesbian partners of an HIV sufferer. Without it, these persons might find themselves put to a choice between continuing to live with the infected individual or losing a job.

Another likely impact of the ADA will be to eliminate benefit limitations for some disabled workers. As discussed in Chapter 8, the Employment Retirement Income Security Act (ERISA) does not mandate welfare benefits. In consequence, the Fifth Circuit held that it was not unlawful under that statute for an employer that had been made aware that one of its employees was a victim of AIDS to limit the AIDS coverage of its group health plan to a maximum of $5,000, a much lower limit than that for other diseases, so long as the employer's motivation was strictly a desire to limit costs. *McGann v. H & H Music Co.*, 946 F.2d 401 (5th Cir.1991), cert. denied, 506 U.S. 981 (2002). The ADA contains a curiously worded provision concerning benefits that states:

(c) *Insurance.*—Titles I through IV of this Act shall not be construed to prohibit or restrict

  (1) an insurer * * * or any agent or entity that administers benefit plans * * * from underwriting risks, classifying risks, or administering such risks that are based on or not inconsistent with State law; or

  (2) a person * * * from establishing * * * or administering the terms of a bona fide benefit plan that are based on underwriting risks, classifying risks or administering risks that are based on or not inconsistent with State law; or

(3) a person * * * from establishing * * * or administering the terms of a bona fide benefit plan that is not subject to State laws that regulate insurance.

Paragraphs 1, 2, and 3 shall not be used as a subterfuge to evade the purpose of chapters I and III of this chapter.

42 U.S.C.A. § 12201(c).

The underlying purpose of the provision is reasonably clear: Employers should be allowed to provide health care packages, either through insurance or by self-funded plans, that do not cover all the possible diseases of life and all possible treatments. This makes health coverage much more affordable and thus more likely to be provided. But at what point does the "subterfuge" language begin to operate? It seems unlikely a health plan is entitled under this language to cap AIDS related treatment on moral grounds, rather than on actuarial data or other cost concerns. See *Carparts Distribution Center v. Automotive Wholesaler's Association of New England, Inc.*, 987 F.Supp. 77 (D.N.H.1997). But how does one prove that a plan is acting for "wrong reasons"? How important might it be that a $10,000 cap for AIDS coverage is matched by a $10,000 cap on maternity costs? About this provision, as about so many issues discussed in this book, much remains to be decided.

CHAPTER 4

DISCRIMINATION

A. INTRODUCTION

No body of employment law has grown more rapidly in the past forty years than that forbidding employers, unions and others to discriminate on the basis of such "protected characteristics" as age, ethnicity, race, gender, national origin and disability.

Despite the complexity of doctrine that has developed, the basic concept of "discrimination" is simple enough: one person or group of persons is treated differently from another person or group, either because of a personal characteristic, or because of conduct. When people are treated differently because of their conduct, the term "retaliation" is often used instead of discrimination. Much discrimination is benign. Selecting an experienced player as backup for a football team with a second year quarterback seems logical to most of us, even though it may lead the team to pass over some very promising rookies. A law school that experiences a sudden need for a labor and employment law teacher is understandably more likely to look with favor on a person with NLRB experience than one coming from the Securities and Exchange Commission.

Much discrimination, however, is clearly not benign. It is based on stereotyping or bias, with no reasonable basis. The notions that all women are weak or that white males are generally smarter than anyone else in the world have done immense harm to many a job applicant or promotion seeker. Moves to counter these attitudes by means of public law gained speed in the years following the Second World War. This chapter can provide only a brief introduction. Another volume of this Nutshell series is devoted entirely to this subject, as are any number of treatises of varying length.

B. SOURCES OF BANS ON DISCRIMINATION

The provisions of the United States Constitution that are most often called into play as a source for banning government discrimination, in employment or in other practices, are the three amendments added at the close of the Civil War.

- The Thirteenth Amendment prohibits slavery and involuntary servitude.

- The Fourteenth Amendment includes in its first section a "due process" clause and an "equal protection" clause; each is important as a limit on state action. Its fifth section empowers the Congress to enforce the provisions of the Amendment.

- The Fifteenth Amendment forbids denying any individual the right to vote on the basis of race or color.

While the equal protection clause of the Four-teenth Amendment does not on its face apply to the federal government, the notion of equal treatment has become part of the concept of due process under the Fifth Amendment. See *Steele v. Louisville & Nashville R. Co.*, 323 U.S. 192 (1944).

The principal federal statutes forbidding "personal characteristic" discrimination are:

- Title VII of the Civil Rights Act of 1964, Pub. L. 88–352, 78 Stat. 253 (1964), as amended, 42 U.S.C. §§ 2000e to 2000e–17; to which particularly important provisions were added by the Pregnancy Discrimination Act of 1978, Pub. L. 95–555, 92 Stat. 2076 (1978), 42 U.S.C. § 2000e(k), and the Civil Rights Act of 1991, Pub. L. 102–166, 105 Stat. 1074 (1991), codified in scattered sections;

- Reconstruction Era Civil Rights Acts, as amended, 42 U.S.C. §§ 1981–1988 (particularly §§ 1981, 1983, 1985(c));

- Equal Pay Act, Pub. L. 88–38, 77 Stat. 56, 29 U.S.C. § 206(d);

- Age Discrimination in Employment Act of 1967, Pub. L. 90–202, 81 Stat. 602, as amended, 29 U.S.C. §§ 621–634; to which particularly significant language was added by the Older Workers Benefit Protection Act, Pub. L. 101–433, 104 Stat. 978 (1990);

- Americans with Disabilities Act, Pub. L. 101–336, 104 Stat. 327 (1990), 42 U.S.C. §§ 12101–12213;

- Immigration Control and Reform Act of 1986, as amended, 8 U.S.C.A. § 1324b.

- Genetic Information Nondiscrimination Act of 2008, 42 U.S.C., 42 U.S.C. §§ 2000ff—2000ff–11.

In addition, there are special requirements that apply to those who contract with the federal government or receive federal funds:

- Executive Order 11246, 30 Fed. Reg. 12319 (1965), as amended;

- Rehabilitation Act of 1973, Pub. L. 93–112, 87 Stat. 357 (1973), as amended, 29 U.S.C. §§ 705, 791–797b; and

- Title IX of the Education Amendments of 1972, Pub. L. 92–318, 86 Stat. 235, 373–375 (1972), 20 U.S.C. §§ 1681–1688.

Also, section 8(a)(3) of the National Labor Relations Act, 29 U.S.C. § 158(a)(3), bans discrimination on the basis of union membership (or non membership). Union membership is a "personal characteristic" in somewhat the same sense as membership in a particular religious group. The Uniformed Services Employment and Reemployment Rights Act (USERRA), 38 U.S.C.A. §§ 4301–4333, provides reemployment rights to those workers whose military service will require them to be absent from work and prohibits discrimination based on military status.

State constitutions include a wide variety of provisions dealing with equal rights. Some are essentially state versions of the federal due process or equal protection clauses, often more or less significantly reworded. See, e.g., Ark. Const. Art. 2 § 3; Mich. Const., 1963 Art. I § 2; N.Car. Const. Art. I § 19. Some are broadly worded Equal Rights provisions, similar to the Equal Rights Amendment that was proposed for the federal constitution but which failed to be adopted. Some of these are limited to gender. See, e.g., Md. Decl. Of Rights Art. 46; Wash. Const. Art. XXXI § 1; Colo. Const. Art. II § 29. Others have a longer list of protected characteristics (adding race, color, creed, national origin, for example). See, e.g., Alaska Const. Art. I § 3; Fla. Const. Art. I § 2 (includes handicap); N.H. Const. Pt. I Art. 2; Texas Const. Art. I § 3a; Wyo. Const. Art. I § 2. Several states prohibit discrimination in public employment, as part of a constitution based merit system. See, e.g., Colo. Const. Art. XII § 13; La. Const. Art. X §§ 8, 46; Mo. Const. Art. IV § 53. The constitutions of two states, California and Illinois, explicitly ban discrimination in non government employment. See Calif. Const. Art. I § 31 ("A person may not be disqualified from entering ... employment because of sex, race, creed, color, or national or ethnic origin."); Ill. Const. Art. I § 17 ("All persons shall have the right to be free from discrimination on the basis of race, color, creed, national ancestry and sex in the hiring and promotion practices of any employer.... These rights are enforceable without action by the General Assembly....")

Roughly half the states had enacted what were then known as "fair employment practices acts" before the Congress passed the Civil Rights Act of 1964. Since then, these laws have become even more common, so that discrimination based on race, religion, gender and national origin is banned by state statute almost everywhere. Most state statutes track the federal statute both in substance and in procedures, at least to some degree, but a number apply to small employers not subject to Title VII. Many also cover conduct not subject to Title VII. Roughly half the states ban employment discrimination based on marital status. Eleven prohibit at least some forms of employment discrimination on the basis of sexual orientation.

Some municipalities ban discriminatory practices, but the variation in coverage and substance is so great that a short text cannot hope to give much sense of them. One area in which local ordinances are particularly important is in banning discrimination based on sexual orientation. A recent decision upheld the Louisville gay rights ordinance against a claim that it violated the plaintiff employer's right to free exercise of religion, since he would be forbidden to discriminate against current or potential employees he regarded as sinners. *Hyman v. City of Louisville*, 132 F.Supp.2d 528 (W.D.Ky.2001). A Colorado constitutional amendment forbidding local governments to enact ordinances protecting the rights of homosexual persons was held unconstitutional in *Romer v. Evans*, 517 U.S. 620 (1996).

C. FEDERAL CONSTITUTIONAL
PROTECTIONS

The Due Process and Equal Protection clauses operate directly on governments as employers. Therefore, if the federal government or a state or local government chooses to prefer one group over another for hiring or promotion or retention, that government must be able to justify why it does so. How strong must the justification be?

If the right to public employment were a "fundamental" constitutional right, like the right to travel freely from state to state, then denying it would require a "compelling governmental interest." *Shapiro v. Thompson*, 394 U.S. 618 (1969). Public employment is not such a right, however; no one has a claim to a public job simply because she is a citizen. *Massachusetts Board of Retirement v. Murgia*, 427 U.S. 307 (1976).

Even though a "fundamental right" is not involved, however, a government employer that discriminates against members of a "suspect class" must demonstrate that its discrimination is "narrowly tailored" to serve "compelling governmental interests." Otherwise the Equal Protection clause is violated. If the group discriminated against is not a suspect class, however, then the government employer can survive this constitutional challenge simply by showing it had a "rational basis" for its action. Thus, the outcome of such challenges turns largely on what "group" one is talking about. If a racial group is disfavored, then proof of a compel-

ling interest will be required. *Adarand Construc-
tors, Inc. v. Pena*, 515 U.S. 200 (1995). Age discrimination is treated more leniently by the Court, which
found a "rational basis" for a mandatory retirement age for state police officers—the need for a
uniformed force able to respond to a wide variety of
physical challenges—justified the policy. Gender
discrimination cases involve an "intermediate level
of scrutiny," summarized by Justice O'Connor in
Mississippi University for Women v. Hogan, 458
U.S. 718 (1982): "The [government's] burden is met
only by showing at least that the classification
serves 'important governmental objectives and that
the discriminatory means employed' are 'substantially related to the achievement of those objectives.' "

Washington v. Davis, 426 U.S. 229 (1976) held
that a plaintiff can establish a prima facie case of
discrimination under the Equal Protection Clause
(and thus under the Due Process Clause of the Fifth
Amendment) only by showing that the discrimination was intentional. This restriction of liability to
intentional acts was extended by *Personnel Administrator of Massachusetts v. Feeney*, 442 U.S. 256
(1979). In *Feeney*, women plaintiffs challenged a
statute that gave a strong hiring and promotion
advantage to military veterans. The majority opinion acknowledges that the statute provided an advantage to a far greater proportion of males than
females, and that the legislature would surely have
been aware of this. Nonetheless, they held the favoring of males not to be the relevant purpose of

the statute, largely because a substantial number of males, not being veterans, would have been just as disadvantaged as females. One result of *Davis* and *Feeney* is thus to limit the direct impact of the Equal Protection Clause on public employment largely to programs that overtly take race or gender into account. These include affirmative action programs, many of them designed to further the employment opportunities of those whose plight the Fourteenth Amendment was enacted to cure. Some find this ironic. A second result is to make even more important the protections afforded public sector workers and job applicants by Title VII.

In *Cleveland Board of Education v. LaFleur*, 414 U.S. 632 (1974), the Court overturned a school board's requirement that all pregnant teachers take unpaid maternity leave at the end of the fourth month of pregnancy. This rigid date amounted to an "irrebuttable presumption" that all women become incapable of doing a variety of tasks at this point. Since the teacher in question had clear medical proof that she remained able to teach, it was clear that the presumption was not justified in all cases. Since there was no reason to think the school board could not adapt its procedures to identify those teachers not physically qualified to continue teaching, the rule violated the Due Process Clause. Later cases (not involving discrimination) have undermined the presumption analysis in *LaFleur*, however, and plaintiffs now bring this sort of claim under Title VII.

One doctrine that is rooted in constitutional concerns has since taken on broader statutory overtones. In *Steele v. Louisville & Nashville R. Co.*, the Court considered a collective agreement between a railroad and one of its unions. The agreement reserved desirable jobs for white employees. The union had acquired the right of "exclusive representation" of its craft under the Railway Labor Act. Thus the government had acted in a way that deprived a minority (African American workers in this case) of the opportunity to negotiate on their own behalf. Because of that, the Court reasoned, it was necessary to impose on the majority union a "duty of fair representation": a duty to consider fairly the interests of all those workers the union represents. Imposing the duty would eliminate concerns about the constitutionality of the statute. A concurring justice would have addressed the constitutional issue squarely. In later cases, the duty was extended to the National Labor Relations Act, under which unions also achieve "exclusive representative" status. The duty is not limited to fair treatment of racial, ethnic or gender minorities, but extends broadly to the interests of all members of the bargaining unit. *Vaca v. Sipes*, 386 U.S. 171 (1967) (grievance handling).

D. STATUTORY BANS: PROVING DISCRIMINATION UNDER TITLE VII AND THE ADEA

1. Covered Parties

Title VII bans discriminatory practices

- under section 703(a), 42 U.S.C.A. § 2000e–2(a), by employers of 15 or more in at least 20 weeks of the relevant year, including state and local governments; (This means fifteen or more persons in an employment relationship with the employer, not necessarily at work on a given day. *Walters v. Metropolitan Educational Enterprises, Inc.*, 519 U.S. 202 (1997).) The 15–person requirement is not jurisdictional and thus may be waived. *Arbaugh v. Y & H Corporation,* 546 U.S. 500 (2006).

- under section 717(a), 42 U.S.C.A. § 2000–e16(a), by the federal government as an employer;

- under section 703(b), 42 U.S.C. § 2000e–2(b), by employment agencies; and

- under section 703(c), 42 U.S.C. § 2000e–2(c), by labor organizations that either operate hiring halls or have at least 15 members.

The ADEA applies to employers of twenty or more persons in twenty or more weeks of the relevant year. 29 U.S.C.A. § 630(b). (The Immigration and Control Reform Act covers employers of four or more, for discrimination against American citizens or on the basis of national origin. 8 U.S.C.A. §§ 1234a–1234b.)

"Employee" sometimes includes prospective and former employees as well as present employees in order to carry out the purposes of a statute. *Robinson v. Shell Oil Co.*, 519 U.S. 337 (1997) (bad reference given to former employee).

2. Prohibited Conduct

The most common claims are those against employers. These fall into two broad categories:

(a) claims that the employer violated section 703(a)(1) by refusing to hire, discharging, or otherwise discriminating "against any individual with respect to his compensation, terms, conditions, or privileges of employment, because of such individual's race, color, religion, sex, or national origin." 42 U.S.C. § 2000e–2(a)(1).

(b) claims that an employer acted "to limit, segregate, or classify his employees or applicants for employment in any way which would deprive or tend to deprive any individual of employment opportunities ... because of his race, color, religion, sex, or national origin." 42 U.S.C. § 2000e–2(a)(2).

The language of the ADEA prohibiting discrimination because of age is almost identical to that of Title VII. 29 U.S.C.A. § 623. Claims may also be brought against employment agencies and labor organizations, although these are less common.

This language has been interpreted to ban both "disparate treatment" of individuals and groups, and also the adoption of policies or practices that have a "disparate impact" on the protected group. The "disparate impact" theory, which was developed by the courts largely on the basis of the language of section 703(a)(2), was given a more detailed statutory outline in the 1991 Civil Rights Act. 42 U.S.C. § 2000e–2(k). In *Smith v. City of Jackson,* 544 U.S. 228 (2005), The Court resolved a split in the circuits by holding that disparate impact theory is available under the ADEA, although as a practical matter it will be difficult to establish such a case. Indeed, the plaintiffs in that case lost, because they were unable to identify a particular practice that resulted in their being disadvantaged, and also because of the ability of the city to demonstrate that reasonable factors other than age had led to the challenged changes in compensation structure.

While most cases involve obvious sorts of adverse employment actions, such as discharge or refusal to hire or promote, the statutes also ban such conduct as harassment because of a protected characteristic. *Meritor Savings Bank v. Vinson,* 477 U.S. 57 (1986).

a. Disparate Treatment

A disparate treatment claim may allege wrongful treatment of a single individual, or be brought as a class action alleging that the employer has engaged in a pattern or practice of discriminatory treatment. The plaintiff's burden of proof in a disparate treatment case may be carried either by showing "facial" discrimination—when a classified ad calls for "men only," for example, or for "young, energetic applicants"—or through circumstantial evidence. The latter is by far the more common, since an offending employer is rarely likely to publicize its bias. Disparate treatment cases involve intentional discrimination, but one must not confuse "intent" with "malice." One may honestly believe that older workers are not good at sales, or that males are "naturally better" at math than females, or that airline passengers prefer women cabin attendants to men. To act on those stereotypes, however, violates the requirements of civil rights laws.

(i) Individual Claims

The ordering of proof in individual disparate treatment cases has been shaped primarily by three major Supreme Court decisions. Under the decisions in *McDonnell Douglas Corp. v. Green*, 411 U.S. 792 (1973), and *Texas Community Affairs Bd. v. Burdine*, 450 U.S. 248 (1981), a plaintiff makes out a prima facie case of discrimination by proving that (a) she is a member of a protected class, (b) she is qualified for the job (or promotion, or other benefit) in question, and (c) that the job (or other benefit) either remained open or was instead given to a person who is a member of a different class. Once this proof has been made out, the burden of going forward shifts to the employer, who must articulate a legitimate nondiscriminatory reason for not selecting the claimant. If the employer does not do so, the employee prevails. If the employer does so, the claimant may challenge that evidence by proof that the employer's professed reason is in fact a pretext.One way of doing so is by demonstrating that the credentials of the plaintiff are superior to those of the person who in fact was hired or received a promotion. In *Ash v. Tyson Foods, Inc.,* 546 U.S. 454 (2006), the Court rejected an approach suggested by the Eleventh Circuit that the difference in qualifications must be so substantial as to "slap[a person] in the face." In *St. Mary's Honor Center v. Hicks,* 509 U.S. 502 (1993), a narrowly divided Court held that even if the plaintiff succeeds in discrediting the employer's explanation, the employer may still prevail if the trier of fact concludes that the plaintiff has not proven that discriminatory intent was in fact the cause of the adverse action. As the dissent points out, this creates a somewhat peculiar situation, since a charged employer is better off presenting an untruthful explanation of its actions than presenting none at all.

The plaintiff in *O'Connor v. Consolidated Coin Caterers Corporation,* 517 U.S. 308 (1996) was 56. He was replaced by a 40–year old worker. A number of lower federal courts had held that under the ADEA a plaintiff establishes a prima facie case by showing that he was replaced by a significantly younger worker, by analogy to *Burdine.* The circuit court in O'Connor refused to apply this approach since the replacement worker was 40 years old, and thus in the "protected group" under the statute. A unanimous Supreme Court reversed, reasoning that difference in age, not whether one is in the protected group, is the key factor in deciding whether there has been discrimination "because of . . . age."

"Mixed motive" cases.—An employer may at times decide to fire a worker, or not promote her, from a mix of motives, some lawful and some not. Suppose a sole proprietor firmly believes both (a) that women do not make good managers, and also (b) that good customer relations must be maintained by his employees, virtually at any cost. Acting on the first basis would be unlawful under Title VII; acting on the second remains the employer's lawful prerogative. A woman employee seeks promotion to a vacant manager's post, soon after a customer has called in with a complaint about that woman's attitude. The employer gives the manager's post to a male, and the woman files a Title VII action. The plaintiff is able to offer strong "smoking gun" proof of the first motivation; the defendant has documented evidence that the customer complained. Notice that in this case, as in many "mixed motive" cases, it is necessary to consider the possibility of pretext; the plaintiff might show, for example, that the complaining customer is a known sorehead whose complaints are regularly disregarded by the employer. The employer may, however, be able to offer proof that he gives serious consideration to complaints of this sort, from customers just like the one in question. If the trier of fact finds that the proof of business motivation is no more than pretext, then the only question is whether the plaintiff's offer of proof is adequate to permit an inference of unlawful motive. But what if the trier

of fact finds that both motives contributed, what then? In such cases, the approach is a "shifting burdens" analysis. First, the plaintiff must demonstrate by a preponderance of the evidence that the forbidden characteristic was a significant motivating factor. At that point, the burden shifts to the defendant. Under section 8(a)(3) of the NLRA an employer defendant may escape liability entirely by proving by a preponderance of the evidence that even in the absence of the forbidden motive it would have taken the same action (such as a discharge). *NLRB v. Transportation Management Corp.*, 462 U.S. 393 (1983). Prior to 1991, that was also the case under Title VII. *Price Waterhouse v. Hopkins*, 490 U.S. 228 (1989) (gender based denial of promotion to partner). Under Title VII as amended by the 1991 Civil Rights Act, however, the court may still enter declaratory relief and award attorney's fees against the defendant. 42 U.S.C.A. § 2000e–5(g)(2)(B). (That section of the 1991 Act does not refer to the Age Discrimination in Employment Act.) Some lower federal courts for a time imposed a special evidence requirement in these cases, saying that "direct evidence" of discrimination is required, but the Supreme Court rejected that approach for Title VII in *Desert Palace, Inc. v. Costa,* 539 U.S. 90 (2003). That decision has led, in turn, to disagreement among the lower courts as to how to handle summary judgment motions in mixed motive cases. In *White v. Baxter Healthcare Corp.,* 533 F.3d 381 (6th Cir. 2008), the Sixth Circuit rejected approaches taken by the Eighth and Eleventh Circuits, which had applied *Burdine* analysis to decide these motions. This set of problems was further complicated by a closely divided Supreme Court in *Gross v. FBL Financial Services, Inc.*, 129 S.Ct. 2343 (2008). The majority rejected burden shifting in ADEA cases.

(ii) Group Claims

Standing and procedural matters.—Much of the litigation under Title VII has involved claims that an employer engaged in systematic discrimination against a protected class. These claims may be asserted in a "pattern or practice" action, brought under section 706, 42 U.S.C.A. § 2000e–6 by the EEOC (private sector cases) or the Attorney General (public sector cases). It is more common, however, for such claims to be made in a class action by a private plaintiff or plaintiffs. A private plaintiff who seeks to have an action certified as a class action must satisfy the court that she meets the standards set out in Rule 23 of the Federal Rules of Civil Procedure: (1) "[T]he class is so numerous that joinder of all members is impracticable" (numerosity). (2) "[T]here are questions of law or fact common to the class" (commonality). (3) "[T]he claims or defenses of the representative parties are typical of the claims or defenses of the class" (typicality). (4) "[T]the representative parties will fairly and adequately protect the interests of the class" (adequacy).

Just how "numerous" the class must be is at times a difficult question. Since discrimination in employment tends to be an ongoing practice, it is appropriate to argue that a court asked to certify a class should consider the impact of the action on future applicants for jobs or promotions. The Supreme Court has allowed a plaintiff to seek relief for unidentified persons who were discouraged from seeking jobs because of an employer's reputation for discriminating. *International Brotherhood of Teamsters v. United States*, 431 U.S. 324 (1977). Some courts have also considered whether a small class should be certified because the members of the class would be reluctant to sue individually for fear of losing their jobs.

It usually makes sense to address the "typicality" and "commonality" requirements together in a discrimination case, as Justice Stevens noted in *General Telephone Co. of Southwest v. Falcon*, 457 U.S. 147 (1982) (fn. 13). The *Falcon* plaintiff alleged he was wrongfully denied a promotion; he also sought to sue on behalf of applicants for jobs with his employer. The Court acknowledged that plaintiff might have proved that denying him a promotion flowed from a general policy of ethnic discrimination that led the employer to refuse to hire other Mexican–Americans. The district court should not have certified the class, however, simply because that possibility existed, without requiring a specific presentation of what the common issues of law and fact might be, and of just what group of persons he sought to represent.

The "adequacy" analysis in these cases may also overlap with typicality and commonality analysis, but there are additional elements to be considered: possible conflicts of interest, for example, between different ethnic groups, or the competency of counsel.

Whether a class member may "opt out" depends on whether the class was certified under Rule 23(b)(3), in which case opting out is a matter of right, or under 23(b)(1) or (2), in which case allowing a class member to withdraw is left to the discretion of the district court. Most Title VII actions are certified under Rule 23(b)(2) and withdrawal by a class member is not often allowed. Intervention is governed by Rule 24.

The ADEA enforcement provisions include a limitation derived from the Fair Labor Standards Act under which no worker "shall be a party plaintiff ... unless he gives his consent in writing...." 29 U.S.C.A. § 216(b). As a result only "opt in" class actions are available for age discrimination.

Later impact.—If a court decides that the representative plaintiffs in a class action have not proved the existence of systemic discrimination, are individual members of the class barred from suing as individuals? No, the Supreme Court decided in *Cooper v. Federal Reserve Bank of Richmond*, 467 U.S. 867 (1984), but that opinion intimates that some of the holdings in the class action will be relevant to the subsequent individual cases.

One major effect of certification as a class action is to limit later challenges both to settlements made between a defendant and the representative plaintiffs and also to judgment orders. A 1991 amendment to Title VII insulates employment practices that implement settlements and orders from successive challenges by workers who feel they are disfavored by those practices. 42 U.S.C.A. § 2000e–2(n). This provision also applies to actions based on the federal constitution.

Proof.—Just as in the case of individual claims, a plaintiff seeks to prove that a defendant is intentionally discriminating. If the discrimination is not overt, or if the plaintiff wishes to demonstrate that one act of overt discrimination is just the "tip of the iceberg," circumstantial evidence becomes crucial.

For group claims, as in disparate impact cases, the most important proof is often statistical. (Statistical proof may also be important in individual claims, but the *Burdine* presumptions operate in such a fashion that statistics will most often be complementary evidence.) The Supreme Court has stated: "[I]t is ordinarily to be expected that non-discriminatory hiring practices will in time result in a workforce more or less representative of the racial and ethnic composition of the population in the community from which employees are hired ... even though § 703(j) makes clear that Title VII imposes no requirement that a work force mirror the general population. Where gross statistical disparities can be shown, they alone may in a proper cases constitute prima facie proof of a pattern or practice of discrimination." *International Brotherhood of Teamsters v. United States*, 431 U.S. 324, 339 n. 20 (1977).

What is the "community from which employees are hired"? This depends very much on the nature of the occupation involved, particularly the skills required. The community from which a fast food restaurant hires cooks is different from the community out of which it hires servers. Hospitals hire physicians and nurses from very restricted communities indeed, since special schooling and licenses are required. Geography also enters in. Some hiring involves an almost entirely local pool; other hiring stretches out over a region or even the nation. See *Hazelwood School District v. United States*, 433 U.S. 299 (1977). The problem of defining the relevant community can sometimes be sidestepped by using "applicant flow" data; comparing the racial composition of the ultimate workforce with the composition of the group who actually applied for the jobs is also appealing because it reflects the "real world" hiring process. Such data may, however, be suspect because the employer has played a role in shaping who applies for jobs. It may have advertised the jobs only in English language newspapers, for instance, despite the presence of a large Spanish speaking population that might well include qualified workers.

What is a significant statistical disparity? Some have suggested that asking whether members of one group are selected at less than 80% of the rate at which members of the other group are selected is a useful "rule of thumb." A number of courts have toyed with the idea that a difference of two "standard deviations" or more is strong proof of discrimination. The Supreme Court, however, has cautioned against adopting such a mechanical approach. *Watson v. Fort Worth Bank & Trust*, 487 U.S. 977, 994 (1988).

(iii) Harassment

Title VII forbids discrimination "with respect to ... compensation, terms, condition, or privileges of employment." This broad language led the Supreme Court to approve the holdings of the lower federal courts that Title VII forbids not only discriminatory hiring, firing and promotion, but also "creating a working environment heavily charged with ... discrimination." *Meritor Savings Bank v. Vinson*, 477 U.S. 57 (1986). The early cases in the lower courts considered ethnic, racial, and religious discrimination. More recently, the principal focus of these cases has been sexual harassment.

Two types of sexual harassment are actionable. The "quid pro quo" cases involve supervisors who condition continued employment, or promotions, or other perquisites on obtaining sexual favors. If a supervisor carries out such a threat, he has used the power delegated to him by the employer in a way that violates the statute. Employer liability follows directly, particularly in light of the definition of "employer" in Title VII to include the employer's "agent." See *Burlington Industries v. Ellerth*, 524 U.S. 742 (1998).

"Hostile environment" harassment cases may involve supervisor's threats that are not fulfilled, but also may involve other sorts of harassing conduct, whether by supervisors or other employees. Sexual innuendoes, offensive touching, rude gestures, the posting of obscene pictures, and similar acts may all contribute to creating the objectionable environment. How severe and pervasive must the conduct be? In the period after the Supreme Court decided that "hostile environment" liability was appropriate under Title VII, the lower federal courts have sought to devise standards that would make trials more manageable and judgments more consistent. The Sixth Circuit at one time required that the harassment be severe enough to "seriously affect [the plaintiff's] psychological well being" or lead the plaintiff to "suffer injury." The Supreme Court rejected that standard, saying that an abusive environment "that does not seriously affect employees' psychological well being can and often will detract from ... job performance, discourage employees from staying on the job, or keep them from advancing in their careers." *Harris v. Forklift Systems, Inc.*, 510 U.S. 17 (1993). So long as the environment "would reasonably be perceived, and is perceived, as hostile or abusive" that is enough to allow a plaintiff to show that his or her working conditions have been altered. There is in this language, obviously, both an objective requirement that the defendant's conduct be reasonably regarded as abusive, and also a subjective requirement that the plaintiff demonstrate that she was in fact offended or otherwise adversely affected by the conduct.

Racial, ethnic and religious harassment cases are, as the Court recognized in *Meritor*, of the "hostile environment" type.

In *Oncale v. Sundowner Offshore Services, Inc.*, 523 U.S. 75 (1998), the Court held that "harassment can violate Title VII ... when the harasser and the harassed employee are of the same sex." There is no requirement that the harassing conduct be homosexual in nature. The conduct need not be the result of sexual desire, although it must be "because of sex."

An employer's liability for hostile environment harassment may be either direct or vicarious. If an employee complains justifiably to his supervisor that fellow workers are harassing him, and the employer fails to respond adequately, then the employer is negligent. If it is a supervisor who is harassing, then there may be liability unless the employer can demonstrate: "(a) that the employer exercised reasonable care to prevent and correct promptly any sexually harassing behavior, and (b) that the plaintiff employee unreasonably failed to take advantage of any preventive or corrective opportunities provided by the employer or to avoid harm otherwise." *Faragher v. City of Boca Raton*, 524 U.S. 775 (1998).

(iv) Pregnancy

In 1978, Congress added section 701(k), 42 U.S.C.A. § 2000e(k), to Title VII, in response to Supreme Court decisions that had held that employer health plans that excluded coverage for pregnancy did not discriminate "because of sex" or "on the basis of sex." The section provides that those two phrases include "because of or on the basis of pregnancy, childbirth, or related medical conditions; and women affected by pregnancy, childbirth or related medical conditions shall be treated the same for all employment related purposes, including receipt of benefits under fringe benefit programs, as other persons not so affected but similar in their ability or inability to work...."

In *Newport News Shipbuilding and Dry Dock Co. v. EEOC*, 462 U.S. 669 (1983), the Court held that this language means that an employer that provides medical coverage for spouses cannot impose limits on coverage for pregnancy related conditions that are different from the limits it imposes on other conditions. To limit spouse coverage for pregnancy related conditions would discriminate against male employees.

The requirement that "women affected by pregnancy ... be treated the same ... as other persons ... similar in their ability or inability to work" could be read to forbid more favorable treatment as well as less favorable treatment. In *California Federal Savings and Loan Ass'n v. Guerra*, 479 U.S. 272 (1987), the employer challenged a California statute that required employers to provide up to four months unpaid pregnancy leave, but did not impose a similar requirement for other medical conditions. The employer argued that Title VII preempted the state law. A sharply divided Court upheld the California statute. Section 401 of The Family and Medical Leave Act, 29 U.S.C.A. § 2651, enacted in 1993, states that it does not preempt state laws that include more generous leave requirements than those in FMLA. This would seem to support the outcome in *Guerra*.

b. Disparate Impact

The Supreme Court announced the core disparate impact doctrine in its first major Title VII decision, *Griggs v. Duke Power Co.*, 401 U.S. 424 (1971). The employer in *Griggs* had set alternative eligibility requirements for jobs in its operating departments: graduation from high school or satisfactory performance on certain general intelligence tests. The requirement of a high school diploma would screen out far more African Americans than whites. The Court accepted findings by the lower courts that the employer acted without an intent to discriminate. Nonetheless, Chief Justice Burger wrote: "good intent or absence of discriminatory intent does not redeem employment procedures or testing mechanisms that operate as 'built in headwinds' for minority groups and are unrelated to measuring job capability.... More than that, the Congress has placed on the employer the burden of showing that any given requirement must have a manifest relationship to the employment in question."

The *Griggs* decision rested in large part on statistical proof that the employer's non white employees would lose chances for jobs and promotions because of its policies. Heavy reliance on statistics is typical of most disparate impact cases. Deciding what sorts of statistics justify inferences of discrimination is not always easy. Can a group of employer practices, taken as a whole, be challenged in this way? In

Wards Cove Packing Co., Inc. v. Atonio, 490 U.S. 642 (1989), the Court majority adopted an approach suggested by Justice O'Connor in an earlier plurality opinion, requiring that Title VII plaintiffs prove that a specific practice caused the disparity. This approach was partially overturned by the Civil Rights Act of 1991, which states that "if the complaining party can demonstrate to the court that the elements of a respondent's decision making process are not capable of separation for analysis, the decision making process may be analyzed as one employment practice." 42 U.S.C.A. § 2000e–2(k)(1)(B)(i).

Can subjective employment practices—as contrasted with objective requirements like education credentials or weight lifting abilities—be challenged under disparate impact theory? The Court held "yes" in *Watson v. Fort Worth Bank & Trust*, 487 U.S. 977 (1988), but the plurality opinion expressed doubt about how often a plaintiff would be able to develop adequate statistical proof, particularly in the context of a small employer.

The 1991 statute states that a plaintiff who "demonstrates that a ... practice ... causes a disparate impact" is entitled to judgment unless the employer demonstrates "that the challenged practice is job related for the position in question and consistent with business necessity." 42 U.S.C.A. § 2000e–2(k)(1)(A)(i). This was intended to end a dispute within the Court about whether the burden on an employer was a burden of production or one of persuasion. It is now clear that a burden of persuasion is involved. Just how important to the functioning of the business a practice must be to fit within the concept of "business necessity" remains elusive.

A plaintiff may also win under the 1991 statute if she "makes the demonstration described in paragraph (C) with respect to an alternative employment practice and the employer refuses to adopt such alternative employment practice." Paragraph (C) then says that the "demonstration" referred to "shall be in accordance with the law as it existed on June 4, 1989, with respect to the concept of 'alternative employment practice.'" 42 U.S.C.A. § 2000e–2(k)(1)(A)(ii), (C). This cryptic statement indicates that the Congress wished to overturn portions of the *Wards Cove* decision, since that was announced on June 5, 1989. The majority there would have required a plaintiff who wished to prove that an employer was discriminating by showing that it refused to employ a less discriminatory alternative employment practice to show also that the alternative practice would be "equally effective" in achieving the employer's goals. The statute does not, however, provide further guidance about just what the law may have been on this score on June 4, 1989. Making liability depend on whether the employer "refuses" to adopt the suggested alternative—rather than "has refused"—is also curious. Does this mean an employer could escape a judgment even after suit has been filed, by agreeing then to change its practice? Surely that seems too odd. The more sensible approach to this language would be to say that a plaintiff can establish a case by making a two part showing. (1) first, that an employer is aware that there is an alternative practice that will both (a) allow the employer to continue doing its business effectively and (b) result in less discriminatory impact on a protected group; (2) second, that the employer has nonetheless declined to adopt the alternative. If an employer agrees to the alternative after an action has been filed, that should be viewed as a settlement, in which the plaintiff has prevailed (at least in part).

E. STATUTORY BANS: DEFENSES UNDER TITLE VII AND THE ADEA

Several defense tactics have already been mentioned in discussing the proof process under Title VII. In a "mixed motive" case, for example, a defendant can lessen damages by showing that it would have fired the plaintiff anyhow. In disparate impact litigation, "business necessity" becomes a factor.

1. Bona Fide Occupational Qualification

There are some other defenses as well. At least one applies even in cases involving intentional discrimination. That is the defense provided by section 703(e), declaring that discrimination is not unlawful "in those certain instances where religion, sex, or national origin is a bona fide occupational qualification reasonably necessary to the normal operation of that particular business or enterprise." 42

U.S.C.A. § 2000e–2(e). (Note that race is not included.) The Court has repeatedly stated that this exception is a narrow one, but has allowed it in a few instances. In *Dothard v. Rawlinson*, 433 U.S. 321 (1977), the state of Alabama sought to defend a set of height and weight criteria for prison guards on business necessity grounds. The Court refused to allow this, finding that the requirements constituted improper barriers against women under disparate impact theory. The Court did not overturn the state's practice of limiting prisoner contact jobs in male maximum security prisons to men, however. The record in the case was filled with testimony about the dangerous conditions in the prisons. Many of the prisoners were sex offenders who, the Dothard majority reasoned, would be peculiarly likely to attempt assaults on women. These assaults would endanger not only any women working as guards, but also other prisoners and employees. In footnotes in his opinion for the Court Justice Stewart indicates he would have ruled differently if the prison system had been better managed, with sex offenders separated from other prisoners and better general discipline.

To what extent can the "normal operation" of a business be legitimately oriented by its owners or managers in a way that results in discrimination? It has not escaped the attention of entrepreneurs that "sex sells." When one of the country's most successful discount airlines began business, it made a heavy sales pitch toward male business travelers, in part by hiring only female cabin attendants and dressing them in "hot pants." When males charged discrimination, the company defended on the ground that this set of practices created an "image" that was part of its business. The court found for the male plaintiffs, reasoning that the essence of the airline's business was transporting passengers, and that the "love in the sky" image advertising campaign was not so central to that business that restricting cabin attendant jobs to females could be justified as a bona fide occupational qualification (bfoq). *Wilson v. Southwest Airlines*, 517 F.Supp. 292 (N.D.Tex.1981). More recently, some males protested the hiring practices of the restaurant chain Hooters. The resulting class action was settled, however, with no resolution of the legal issues.

For ADEA purposes, bfoq analysis involves a two step process. First, the employer must demonstrate that the skill or ability factor because of which it uses an age limitation is reasonably necessary to the essence of the business. Second, it must show that using age as a proxy for the job related qualification is compelled by law or circumstance. *Western Air Lines, Inc. v. Criswell*, 472 U.S. 400 (1985). Requiring airline pilots to retire at 60 would be legitimate, for example, since the FAA forbade use of pilots over 60 in commercial aviation. Refusing to employ flight engineers over that age, however, was not justified, because no FAA rule justified this, and the employer did not demonstrate that it could not identify which flight engineers over 60 would constitute a safety hazard.

2. Section 703(h)

Section 703(h) lists several practices that are not "unlawful employment practices" and most cause little controversy. They need to be read with some care, however, since they are carefully limited in scope.

- Basing earnings on quantity or quality of production is not improper, although assigning jobs with good production prospects to men and those with low production prospects to women would violate the act.

- Honoring a "bona fide seniority system" is lawful. The Act does not define "seniority system," and the Court divided closely in *California Brewers Association v. Bryant*, 444 U.S. 598 (1980) on whether "length of service" eligibility requirements for entering a permanent employee seniority system were part of the system. (The majority held "yes.") In other cases the Court has found that the fact that a system perpetuated pre-Act discrimination did not prevent it from being "bona fide." The test of bona fide status most widely used in the federal courts is a four factor test first set out in a Fifth Circuit opinion, *James v. Stockham Valves & Fittings Co.*, 559 F.2d 310 (5th Cir. 1977), cert. denied, 434 U.S. 1034 (1978):

  (1) Does the system discourage all employees equally from transferring between seniority units?

(2) Are the seniority systems in the same or separate bargaining units? (If in separate units, is that a rational structure, and one that conforms to industry practice?)

(3) Did the seniority system have its genesis in racial discrimination?

(4) Was the system negotiated (and has it been maintained) free from an illegal purpose?

- Giving or acting "upon the results of any professionally developed ability test, provided that such test" or its use is not "designed, intended or used to discriminate" is lawful. Testing is widespread in employee selection, both for physical abilities—strength tests for fire fighters who must carry heavy equipment, for example—and for intellectual skills, such as reading or math. Most of the litigation concerning tests has focused on whether the test is a valid predictor of job performance. Three validation techniques are sanctioned by EEOC regulations, which have been widely accepted by the courts. See 29 C.F.R. § 1607. "Criterion validation" requires administering the test to prospective (or possibly current) employees, and then measuring the job performance of that group. If higher scores predict better performance in a statistically significant way, the test is valid. "Content validation" requires a careful analysis of what the job requires, so that the essential skills can be identified. Then one tests those skills directly. An oft used example is analyzing a group of clerical workers and finding that half the time of workers in the group is spent in typing. Giving a test to measure typing speed and accuracy would be "content validated." "Construct validation" is the most difficult to analyze. The definition in the regulations says that construct validity is "demonstrated by data showing that the selection procedure measures the degree to which candidates have identifiable characteristics which have been determined to be important for successful job performance." This method is used, for instance, for jobs in which ability to function "as a productive member of a team" is significant. The EEOC guidelines rely heavily on standards developed by the American Psychological Association. One technique formerly sometimes used to reduce the adverse impact of a test on a gender or ethnic group is called "norming." Under that approach, two individuals who score at the 90th percentile of their gender group on a test would be treated as having equivalent credentials, even though one score was in fact higher than the other. "Norming" is forbidden by section 106 of the Civil Rights Act of 1991. 42 U.S.C.A. § 2000e–2(*l*).

- An oddly worded final sentence declares that a different wage payment is not unlawful gender discrimination "if such differential is authorized by the provisions of" the Equal Pay Act. Since that statute does not by its terms "authorize" any sort of wage differential, this language is treated as meaning that the same defenses available under the Equal Pay Act are available under Title VII. *County of Washington v. Gunther*, 452 U.S. 161 (1981).

3. Waivers

In some ADEA cases, when a plaintiff has claimed that she was wrongfully discharged, the employer has offered as a defense that the plaintiff in fact retired voluntarily and gave an explicit waiver of any discrimination claims. The frequency of this sort of dispute and the lack of agreement among the courts about how to judge the validity of a waiver led the Congress to amend the ADEA to set specific standards for waivers. An employer asserting the defense carries the burden of proving that each of the multiple factors is met. The factors include requirements that the agreement be in writing, refer to ADEA claims specifically, be limited to past claims, and involve separate consideration. There are also procedural requirements, including advice to consult an attorney, time to consider whether to agree, and at least 7 days during which to reconsider after signing. 29 U.S.C.A. § 626(f).

4. Affirmative Action Plans

For reasons of conscience, or because of a desire to improve public image, or to forestall litigation, or to improve chances for obtaining a government grant or contract, an employer may undertake an affirmative action plan. When the employer analyzes its workforce, it may well find that its employee group does not have the same diversity as the community, and decide as a result to engage in a program that will result in greater diversity. Many aspects of these plans involve little risk of legal challenge. Expanding advertising to include not just newspapers of general circulation, but also those appealing to specialized reader groups, such as a Spanish language paper, is an easy example. Sending recruiters not just to "top 25" law schools but also to schools that have been "historically" attended by members of minority groups is another. Problems arise, however, when a "protected characteristic" itself becomes a factor in employment decisions. When it is permissible to let race or gender enter into decision making, and to what extent, has been a matter of intense debate and disagreement in society generally and among the members of the Supreme Court. An oft-cited case in which a majority of the Court found an affirmative action plan justified taking gender into account is *Johnson v. Transportation Agency, Santa Clara County*, 480 U.S. 616 (1987). Both the majority opinion by Justice Brennan and the concurring opinion of Justice O'Connor emphasize that a generalized desire to achieve better conditions for minorities or women will not justify taking gender into account. Instead, the employer must engage in a careful analysis of its workforce, and that analysis must reveal a "manifest" or "conspicuous" imbalance. The imbalance in the case itself could hardly have been more clear: In the employer's skilled craft clear that this was a "traditionally segregated" set of jobs. Justice O'Connor would limit this defense to situations in which the statistical analysis undertaken by the employer would produce data that could constitute a prima facie case of violation of Title VII. The majority opinion did not. Given the increasing hostility of the Court to affirmative action concepts generally, it is difficult to know which opinion would be followed at present, if either.

5. "Reasonable factor other than age"

In *Meacham v. Knolls Atomic Power Laboratory,* 128 S.Ct. 2395 (2008), a divided Court held that the language of 29 U.S.C. § 623(f)(1), providing that an employer's action does not violate the ADEA if it is based on a "reasonable factor other than age" is not simply a clarification of the order of proof, but creates an affirmative defense. The employer therefore carries a burden of persuasion (not just a burden of production) on this issue.

F. STATUTORY BANS: PROCEDURAL REQUIREMENTS FOR TITLE VII AND ADEA CLAIMANTS

An employee who wishes to bring a claim under Title VII or the ADEA does not begin by filing suit, but must first file a charge with the Equal Employment Opportunity Commission. 42 U.S.C. § 2000e–(5)(b); 29 U.S.C. § 626(d). The statutes require that this be done promptly, within 180 days of the discrimination complained of. The charge must be

sworn, but an unsworn charge can be verified after
the 180–day period has run. *Edelman v. Lynchburg
College*, 535 U.S. 106 (2002).There is a longer period, 300 days, if the charge is filed in a state in
which there is an anti discrimination agency enforcing a statute to which the EEOC defers. In such a
deferral state, the charging party and EEOC must
give the state agency at least 60 days during which
to seek to resolve the charge. These charge filing
provisions have resulted in a fair amount of litigation.

Title VII does not define the term "charge." In
Federal Express Corp. v. Holowecki, 128 S.Ct. 1147
(2008), the Court deferred to an approach suggested
by the EEOC, saying that a document counts as a
charge if it:

- Identifies the respondent;

- Alleges the discriminatory conduct engaged in;
  and

- Includes language requesting that the EEOC
  take action.

Once a document is identifiable as a charge, other
questions arise. First, there have been questions
about when the clock starts. In termination cases,
the 180–day period begins to run when the decision
to terminate is made and communicated to the
employee, even though the decision may be the
subject of a grievance procedure that would later
reverse the discharge. *Delaware State College v.
Ricks*, 449 U.S. 250 (1980). Unlawful discrimination
in pay, however, is often characterized as a "con-

tinuing violation" so that a new charge filing period begins to run with each paycheck. *Bazemore v. Friday*, 478 U.S. 385 (1986). A 2007 decision limited the scope of *Bazemore* in wage discrimination cases, but has since been overturned by the Congress. See the Lilly Ledbetter Fair Pay Act, Pub L. 111–2, 123 Stat. 5. The language added by this statute provides that an

> unlawful employment practice occurs with respect to discrimination in compensation ... when a discriminatory compensation decision or other practice is adopted, when an individual becomes subject to a discriminatory compensation decision or practice, or when an individual is affected by application of a discriminatory compensation decision or other practice, including each time wages, benefits or other compensation is paid....

"Hostile environment" gender discrimination is treated similarly. *National Railroad Passenger Corp. v. Morgan*, 536 U.S. 101 (2002).

Seniority system cases are the subject of a provision added in 1991. If a system is "adopted for an intentionally discriminatory purpose" then a filing period begins: (a) when the system is adopted; (b) when an individual "becomes subject to the seniority system"; or (c) when the employee is "injured by the application of the seniority system or provision of the system." 42 U.S.C.A. § 2000e–5(e)(2). This is similar to the language quoted above about pay discrimination. This earlier provision was also designed to overturn a Supreme Court decision, and the pay discrimination language was modeled on it.

Second, there are questions about how the state and federal filing periods interact.

- If an individual files a charge with the EEOC even though there is a state agency to which the EEOC would defer, it is EEOC practice to relay the charge to the state agency on behalf of the individual. The EEOC will not take action itself until the period for the state to act has expired. This procedure was approved by the Supreme Court in Love v. Pullman, 404 U.S. 522 (1972).

- If the EEOC and the relevant state or local agency act entirely independently of one another, then the period for filing a charge boils down in practice to 240 days. This is because of the way the 60–day period for state action is set out in section 706(c): "[N]o charge may be filed ... by the person aggrieved before the expiration of sixty days after proceedings have been commenced under the State or local law, unless such proceedings have been earlier terminated...." *Mohasco Corp. v. Silver*, 447 U.S. 807 (1980).

- If the EEOC and the state or local agency have one of the "work sharing" arrangements that are now common, then it is likely the arrangement will include a waiver by the state agency of its right to process the charge first. This then constitutes a "termination" of the state proceedings, for the purposes of the language of section 706(c), and it is appropriate for the EEOC to begin its own investigation and conciliation attempts immediately. In *EEOC v. Commercial Office Products Co.*, 486 U.S. 107 (1988), this meant that a charge filed with the EEOC on the 289th day after an alleged unlawful firing was timely. The EEOC relayed the charge to the state agency, the state agency immediately "waived" its right to proceed, thus terminating its work. Whether a "prospective" waiver by the state agency also constitutes a blanket "termination" of proceedings begun by filing charges with the EEOC has not been settled by the Supreme Court. That result has been reached by some lower federal courts, but at least one judge has criticized the practice. See *Hong v. Children's Memorial Hospital*, 936 F.2d 967 (7th Cir.1991).

Third, there are questions about when—and whether—the filing period requirements are to be relaxed. In *Zipes v. Trans World Airlines, Inc.*, 455 U.S. 385 (1982), the Court held that the charge filing time requirement are not jurisdictional prerequisites, but are similar to a statute of limitation and thus "subject to waiver, estoppel and equitable tolling." The Court refused, however, to find that an employee's pursuit of a contract based grievance tolled the period for filing the charge of a statutory violation. International Union of Electrical Workers, Local 790 v. Robbins & Myers, Inc., 429 U.S. 229 (1976). Tolling is appropriate, however, during the period while the question of whether to certify a class that would include a particular plaintiff was being made. *Crown, Cork & Seal Co. v. Parker*, 462 U.S. 345 (1983) (tolling of period following receipt of right to sue notice).

Once a charge is in the hands of the EEOC, the charging party must give the agency at least 180 days to investigate and attempt to settle the matter. The agency's usual process is to seek enough facts to allow a "probable cause" determination to be made. If probable cause (to believe a violation has happened) is found, then conciliation efforts are appropriate. When the EEOC determines either that there is no probable cause to believe a violation has happened or that further attempts at conciliation are not feasible, it may institute a civil action on its own or issue a "right to sue" letter to the charging party. If more than 180 days have passed since a charge was filed, and the agency has not settled the case, the charging party may request the agency to issue a "right to sue letter" even though the agency process is not complete. Once the "right to sue letter" has been issued, the charging party has 90 days during which to begin a civil action. Just what other than actual receipt of the right to sue letter may start the 90–day period running is an occasional issue. So also is what constitutes adequate filing of a civil action. In *Baldwin County Welcome Center v. Brown*, 466 U.S. 147 (1984), the Court held that a worker did not start her action by mailing a copy of the right to sue letter itself to a federal district court, along with a request for the appointment of counsel.

EEOC handling of charges sometimes takes a long time. Since a charging party has the privilege of asking for a right to sue letter after 180 days, is a laches defense available to a defendant employer when several years pass before the charging party makes that request? Most courts have reasoned that giving the agency the maximum time to settle a matter out of court is a desirable result. They have therefore allowed charging parties simply to wait, although one case suggests that a "sophisticated party," like an experienced labor organization, should be expected to ask the EEOC for a right to sue letter within a reasonable time. *Cleveland Newspaper Guild, Local 1 v. Plain Dealer Publishing Co.*, 839 F.2d 1147 (6th Cir.1988) (en banc), vacating 813 F.2d 101, cert. denied, 488 U.S. 899 (1988).

The Court in 2002 overturned a Second Circuit doctrine that a complaint should be dismissed unless it stated facts sufficient to constitute a prima facie case under the *McDonnell Douglas* framework. *Swierkiewicz v. Sorema, N.A.*, 534 U.S. 506 (2002).

G.   STATUTORY BANS: REMEDIES FOR VIOLATIONS OF TITLE VII AND THE ADEA

Entire volumes have been written about the remedies available for violations of anti discrimination laws; here we treat only one or two of the most important concepts.

First, from the initial enactment of Title VII until the 1991 amendments, that statute did not provide a damages remedy. 42 U.S.C.A. § 2000e–5(g). In individual cases, the most usual remedy would be a species of cease and desist order, requiring, for example, an employer to cease refusing to hire the plaintiff and to pay that person what she would have earned but for an unlawful refusal to hire. In promotion cases, the order might well require an employer to treat a successful plaintiff as if she had received her promotion at the time she was entitled to it, requiring working out all the perquisites that would have accompanied such a promotion. Cases brought against labor organizations might well require a union to cease denying membership to a plaintiff, or to admit her to an apprenticeship program. If, in addition, a party desired general damages, then she would have to pursue that claim under one of the 19th century Civil Rights Acts. That would sometimes be possible in racial discrimination cases, but not in gender based claims. A helpful catch phrase used to characterize the remedies available during this period (as well as the content of some theories of liability) is "rightful place." A successful plaintiff should receive the equitable and restitutionary relief that would most nearly put that plaintiff in the position she would have occupied but for the defendant's wrongful discrimination.

In 1991, this changed. Section 1981A of Title 42 was added that year in an effort to expand the range of remedies that plaintiffs could recover in cases involving intentional discrimination. The provisions do not authorize these expanded remedies for cases that involve "an employment practice that is unlawful because of its disparate impact." For intentional violations of the prohibitions in Title VII, the new provision authorizes the award of compensatory and punitive damages. The latter are available against non government defendants for unlawful acts committed "with malice or with reckless indifference to the federally protected rights of an aggrieved individual." This provision includes a "cap" on the total of compensatory and punitive damages that may be awarded, the level of the cap depending on the size of the defendant's workforce. The damages remedy provided by section 1981A is in addition to, not a substitute for, the equitable relief already provided for by the original statute. Therefore a front pay remedy, since it is restitutionary, is not subject to the damages cap. *Pollard v. E.I. DuPont DeNemours & Co.*, 532 U.S. 843 (2001).

H. STATUTORY BANS: EQUAL PAY ACT

The Equal Pay Act is an addition to the Fair Labor Standards Act, the general federal wage and hour law. 29 U.S.C.A. § 206(d). The Act forbids an employer to discriminate "by paying wages to employees . . . at a rate less than the rate at which he

pays wages to employees of the opposite sex ... for
equal work on jobs the performance of which requires equal skill, effort and responsibility, and
which are performed under similar working conditions...." It is common for claims under this statute to be combined with claims under Title VII.

The plaintiff's basic burden of proof is usually
carried out by establishing that a comparator of the
opposite sex (a) performs equal work, and (b) receives higher pay. Measuring the "skill, effort and
responsibility" components of jobs can sometimes
be easy, sometimes hard. It seems clear that this is
not a "comparable worth" statute, but jobs need
not be absolutely identical to be "equal." Small
differences do not matter. See *Thompson v. Sawyer*,
678 F.2d 257 (D.C.Cir.1982) ("courts have been led
by the legislative history to a 'substantially equal'
test"). The line drawing about "effort" can get very
fine, as in *Usery v. Richman*, 558 F.2d 1318 (8th
Cir.1977), in which the court held that males who
worked the "heavy shift" did work that was not
"equal" to that of women cooks on a "light" shift.
Not just how much extra effort is used matters, but
also how often. In the case of an alleged difference
in "skill," the question is usually how essential the
skill is to the job in question. A job description
calling for a particular skill is not controlling if in
fact the skill is never used. *Brennan v. Prince
William Hosp. Corp.*, 503 F.2d 282 (4th Cir.1974),
cert. denied, 420 U.S. 972 (1975). Responsibility has
many facets. Particular weight is given to safe-

guarding employer assets and employees, and to responsibility for supervision.

The Supreme Court held in an early case interpreting the statute that "working conditions" is a term of art that refers to two factors: "surroundings" and "hazards." *Corning Glass Works v. Brennan*, 417 U.S. 188 (1974). The Court rejected an employer argument that the time of day when work was performed should be considered.

The statute lists four exceptions. These function as affirmative defenses for employers. A different payment to male and female workers is lawful if made "pursuant to

- (i) a seniority system;

- (ii) a merit system;

- (iii) a system which measures earnings by quantity or quality of production; or

- (iv) a differential based on any other factor other than sex."

The last of these is the most plastic. Since "any other factor" could include that the higher paid worker has more responsibility or greater skill, there is an overlap with the notion of what constitutes equal work to begin with. This complicates such matters as how to charge the jury on burden of proof.

I. STATUTORY BANS: THE POST–CIVIL WAR CIVIL RIGHTS ACTS

The first of the Civil Rights Acts was passed the year following the close of the Civil War. Section 1 of the Civil Rights Act of 1866, 14 Stat. 27, was reenacted in 1870 to reflect the 1868 adoption of the Fourteenth Amendment, and then split into two parts by later codifiers. The portion relevant to private sector employment law is now 42 U.S.C. § 1981(a):

> All persons ... shall have the same right in every State ... to make and enforce contracts, to sue, be parties, give evidence, and to the full and equal benefit of all laws and proceedings for the security of persons and property as is enjoyed by white citizens....

Early interpretations of the statute refused to apply it to private actors, but in 1975 the Court overturned that view (as had been expected, given the application of another section of the same statute to private actors a few years earlier). *Johnson v. Railway Express Agency, Inc.*, 421 U.S. 454 (1975). A decade and a half later, a 5–4 majority of the Court issued a restrictive interpretation of "to make and enforce contracts," but the Congress overturned this in 1991 by adding a new subsection (b) that defines the phrase to include "the making, performance, modification, and termination of contracts, and the enjoyment of all benefits ... of the contractual relationship."

The meaning of "as is enjoyed by white citizens" also required interpretation. The traditional view has been that the statute was concerned with racial discrimination, but "race" is an evolving concept. In *St. Francis College v. Al–Khazraji*, 481 U.S. 604 (1987) the Court decided that it should seek guidance from nineteenth century dictionaries about what "race" meant at the time the predecessor of section 1981 was enacted. It found that the concept of "race" at the time included ethnic groups, and decided that a plaintiff is entitled to protection against discrimination on the basis of his or her ancestry or ethnic group—but not religion or national origin. In a scattering of decisions, lower federal courts have consistently held that the statute does not address discrimination on the basis of age, gender, or sexual orientation.

J. STATUTORY BANS: AMERICANS WITH DISABILITIES ACT AND REHABILITATION ACT OF 1973

The Americans with Disabilities Act, 42 U.S.C.A. §§ 12101–12213, enacted in 1990, bans discrimination in employment (Title I), public services (Title II), and public accommodations and services operated by private entities (Title III). Employers of 15 or more persons (during 20 calendar weeks of the current or preceding year) are forbidden to:

discriminate against a qualified individual with a disability because of the disability of such individual in regard to job application procedures, the hiring, advancement or discharge of employees, employee compensation, job training, and other terms, conditions, and privileges of employment. 42 U.S.C.A. § 12112(a).

The ban bristles with terms of art, obviously, and many are further defined. "Discriminate" is given seven different meanings in 42 U.S.C. § 12112(b), for instance. As is often the case, delimiting the meaning of the basic terms is an ongoing challenge.

a. *"Qualified Individual with a Disability"*

The statute defines the phrase "qualified individual with a disability" to mean "an individual with a disability who, with or without reasonable accommodation, can perform the essential functions of the employment position that such individual holds or desires." This, in turn, leads one to wonder what may be a "disability," a "reasonable accommodation" and "essential functions." The first two of these are defined in the statute, the last is left to administrative agencies and the courts to work out. The definition of "disability" applies broadly to all the titles of the ADA:

The term "disability" means, with respect to an individual—

(A) a physical or mental impairment that substantially limits one or more of the major life activities of such an individual;

(B) a record of such an impairment; or

(C) being regarded as having such an impairment.

42 U.S.C.A. § 12102(1).

One recurrent problem in the lower courts was whether to decide the extent of a claimant's disability before or after the application of mitigating devices (such as eyeglasses). The Supreme Court decided three cases in 1999 that held the proper approach was to evaluate disability after amelioration, but the Congress recently amended the statute to overrule those decisions. The new language (effective January 1, 2009)states that whether one suffers from a disability is to be decided

> "without regard to the ameliorative effects of mitigating measures such as (I) Medication, . . . Low-vision devices (which do not include ordinary eye-glasses or contact lenses), prosthetics . . . ; (II) use of assistive technology; (III) reasonable accommodations or auxiliary aids or services; or (IV) learned behavioral or adaptive neurological modifications."

> 42 U.S.C.A. § 12102 (4)(E). (The amendment also provides, however, that the new language does not apply to "ordinary eyeglasses or contact lenses.")

The Court also intensified the burden on plaintiffs in *Toyota Motor Mfg. Co. v. Williams*, 534 U.S. 184 (2002). The plaintiff's carpal tunnel syndrome prevented her from doing a class of tasks that required gripping tools or performing repetitive work when her arms or hands were extended. She could, however, tend to a number of routine personal and household chores. The court of appeals had found for her, emphasizing the importance of employment under Title I of the ADA. The Supreme Court reversed. The Court noted that the definition of "disability" applied to all titles of the ADA, not just the employment title. It held that proving one is "substantially limited" in one or more "major life activities" requires showing he or she cannot perform activities that are of central importance to most people's daily lives. The same 2008 statute that changed the approach to persons who use mitigating devices addressed the *Toyota* opinion also, modifying it by defining "major life activities" to include "caring for oneself, performing manual tasks, seeing, hearing, eating, sleeping, walking, standing, lifting, bending, speaking, breathing, learning, reading, concentrating, thinking, communicating, and working"—as well as the "operation of a major bodily function." The amendment also added this language:

An individual meets the requirement of "being regarded as having such an impairment" if the individual establishes that he or she has been subject to ... [discrimination] because of an actual or perceived physical or mental impairment whether or not the impairment limjits or is perceived to limit a major life activity.

42 U.S.C.A. § 12102(3)(A).

This would seem effectively to sap virtually all the force from the *Toyota* decision. See, e.g., *Rohr v. Salt River Project Agricultural Imp. & Power Dist.,* 555 F.3d 850 (9th Cir. 2009).

Under an EEOC definition which the Supreme Court has approved, an individual is not "qualified" if his or her disability would pose a direct threat to the worker's health on the job. This functions as an affirmative defense for the employer, on which it carries the burden of proof. See *Chevron U.S.A., Inc. v. Echazabal*, 536 U.S. 73 (2002).

b. Reasonable Accommodation (including Undue Hardship)

The "reasonable accommodation" provision, 42 U.S.C.A. § 12111(9), is not so much a true definition as it is a list of illustrations of the kinds of accommodations the Congress had in mind. That list includes changes in physical facilities and in job structure (modified work schedules, special training programs, reassignment to vacant position), and possibly providing support personnel (such as readers) so long as such an accommodation does not impose an "undue hardship" on an employer, a term itself defined in 42 U.S.C.A. § 12111(10). Under that definition the gravity of hardship is judged in terms of the cost of the proposed accommodation, the resources of the employer, and the extent to which the accommodation would change the nature of the function being performed.

What has developed out of this open ended approach to the concept of reasonable accommodation is an interactive process, in which employer and worker swap ideas back and forth about what would make it possible for the worker to do the job in question. Generalizations are at best difficult, but employees seem to have fared reasonably well when proposing "one time" accommodations to large employers, and less well when the proposed accommodation would involve ongoing changes burdening fellow workers, particularly when those ongoing burdens are hard to predict. Consider leave requests, for example. A request for a leave extension in order to recover from a serious medical problem may well be a reasonable accommodation. See *Criado v. IBM Corp.*, 145 F.3d 437 (1st Cir.1998). Requests for repeated time off to deal with bouts of alcoholism, on the other hand, do not have much appeal. See *Evans v. Federal Express Corp.*, 133 F.3d 137 (1st Cir.1998). In *U.S. Airways, Inc. v. Barnett*, 535 U.S. 391 (2002), a closely divided Court stated that ordinarily an accommodation will not be reasonable if it requires the employer to violate the provisions of a seniority system (in this case one set up by the employer itself, not as the result of collective bargaining), but that a claimant must be given a chance to submit evidence of "special circumstances" that might make such an accommodation appropriate.

c. *Interaction with Other Statutes*

"Disability" is important in any number of statutes: workers' compensation laws, the Social Security Act, the Family and Medical Leave Act, and so on. The definition of disability, however, is not identical in each of these. The differences are significant enough so that in *Cleveland v. Policy Management Systems Corp.*, 526 U.S. 795 (1999), the Su-

preme Court held that a stroke victim who asserted
before the Social Security Administration that she
was "unable to work due to my disability" was not
barred from suing her former employer under the
ADA for terminating her because of the effects of
the stroke. In her ADA case she alleged, of course,
that she was a "qualified individual with a disability," that is, that she was a person who could
"perform the essential functions" of her job—perhaps with "reasonable accommodation"—despite
her impairment. Justice Breyer explained that:
"[T]here are too many situations in which an SSDI
claim and an ADA claim can comfortably exist side
by side." This is true both because the substantive
definition of "disability" is not identical in both
statutes, and also because of the impact of the five
step procedure by which disability determinations
are made for Social Security benefit purposes. The
opinion goes on to say, however, that it is often
appropriate for a trial court to enter summary
judgment for an employer in this kind of case.
"[W]e hold that an ADA plaintiff cannot simply
ignore the apparent contradiction that arises out of
the earlier SSDI total disability claim. Rather, she
must proffer a sufficient explanation." To be sufficient, the explanation must be one that would
"warrant a reasonable juror's concluding that, assuming the truth of, or the plaintiff's good faith
belief in, the earlier statement, the plaintiff could
nonetheless 'perform the essential functions' of her
job, with or without 'reasonable accommodation.' "

The statute that most nearly overlaps with the ADA is the earlier Rehabilitation Act of 1973, as much amended, 29 U.S.C.A. §§ 705, 791–794e. That statute applies to federal employers (sections 501, 504, 29 U.S.C.A. §§ 791, 794), federal contractors (section 503, 29 U.S.C.A. § 793), and recipients of federal grants or other assistance (section 504, 29 U.S.C.A. § 794). The substantive standards to be applied are the same as those in the ADA. 29 U.S.C.A. §§ 791(g), 793(d), 794(d). The Rehabilitation Act is significant, however, because it provides administrative remedies to employees covered by these statutes in addition to those of the ADA, which largely incorporates the enforcement scheme of Title VII, and because sections 501 and 503 require federal employers and contractors to develop affirmative action plans to benefit the disabled. A private right of action is also available to enforce sections 501 and 504; section 503 is generally thought to be enforceable solely through the procedures of the Office of Federal Contract Compliance.

d. *XIth Amendment Impact*

In *Board of Trustees of University of Alabama v. Garrett*, 531 U.S. 356 (2001) the Court held that the XIth Amendment to the Constitution bars an action brought by private individuals for money damages under the ADA against a state.

e. *Medical Examinations*

The statute imposes significant limits on medical examinations. 42 U.S.C.A. § 12112.

At the pre employment stage virtually the only sort of medical inquiry that is permitted is to ask the applicant whether he or she can perform the essential functions of the job, and to indicate how that can be done. 29 C.F.R. § 1630.13. After a job offer is made, a medical entrance examination may be administered, and the job offer can be conditioned on this, provided that certain conditions are met:

1. The examination must be administered to all employees in the same category;

2. The information obtained must be kept confidential, and released only to listed groups of persons with a need to know; and

3. Any examination results that are used to screen out examinees must be job related.

29 C.F.R. § 1630.14.

During the course of employment, medical examinations are permitted only if they are: (a) job related, or (b) voluntary tests that are part of a health program. 29 C.F.R. § 1630.14(d). In *Porter v. United States Alumoweld Co., Inc.*, 125 F.3d 243 (4th Cir.1997), the employee, a machine operator, injured his back several times. The employer told the employee that if he wanted to return to work he had to provide sufficient documentation from his doctors/therapists that he had a sustained physical ability to perform the functions necessary for his position. After it received a one sentence return to work authorization from the employee's surgeon, the employer told the employee that he would have to undergo a functional capacity evaluation for which he would have to pay. The employee never underwent the evaluation and the employer terminated him. The court concluded that the employer's required examination met the ADA's standard.

To what extent does the ADA preempt the operation of state laws with respect to medical examinations? The federal statute states that it is not to be construed "to invalidate or limit the remedies * * * of any Federal law or law of any State * * * that provides greater or equal protection for the rights of individuals with disabilities * * *." 29 U.S.C.A. § 12201(b). That language is clear enough with respect to state anti discrimination laws, but how it will play out with respect to such enactments as medical records statutes is not yet certain.

The ADA does not define the term "medical examination," except to provide that "a test to determine the illegal use of drugs shall not be considered a medical examination." Are honesty tests "medical examinations"? If so, they may be regulated not only by the Americans with Disabilities Act (ADA) and similar state statutes banning discrimination against the disabled, but also by statutes permitting access to medical records by the subjects of those records. In *Cleghorn v. Hess*, 109 Nev. 544, 853 P.2d 1260 (Nev.1993), the Nevada Supreme Court decided that employees of a firm that provides security services to a nuclear weapons facility were entitled to the results of psychological suitability tests administered to them. The court reasoned that these employees were "patients" within the meaning of the relevant state law.

K. STATUTORY BANS: TITLE IX

Section 901 of the Higher Education Amendments of 1972, 20 U.S.C. § 1681, the first section of "Title IX"—as that and the succeeding sections have come to be known—states that no person "shall on the basis of sex, be excluded from participation in, be denied the benefits of, or be subjected to any discrimination under any education program or activity receiving federal financial assistance ..." subject to several exceptions not generally relevant here. A private right of action is available to enforce Title IX. *Cannon v. University of Chicago*, 441 U.S. 677 (1979) (non-employment case). In 1982 the Supreme Court held that employment discrimination falls within Title IX, resolving a conflict in lower courts. *North Haven Board of Education v. Bell*, 456 U.S. 512 (1982). Since the statute applies to institutions that are also subject to Title VII, the Equal Pay Act, and other anti discrimination laws, there has been little litigation strictly under this provision. It remains important, however, because it provides an additional forum in which claims of gender equity may be pursued. In the *Caulfield* litigation, for instance, the Department of Health, Education and Welfare (predecessor of the Department of Education) used its Title IX power to require the board of education of New York City to make changes in the way it assigned teachers to supervisory positions. *Caulfield v. Board of Edu-*

cation of City of New York, 632 F.2d 999 (2d Cir. 1980), cert. denied, 450 U.S. 1030 (1981). A handful of women in coaching have sought to utilize Title IX as well as the Equal Pay Act in seeking to achieve salaries more nearly like those of men coaches in higher education. The attempts have generally been unsuccessful. See *Stanley v. University of Southern California*, 13 F.3d 1313 (9th Cir.1994). In two highly publicized jury trials, however, a woman softball coach at Oregon State University and a women's basketball coach at Howard University won substantial judgments.

L. GENETIC INFORMATION NONDISCRIMINATION ACT (GINA)

The employment provisions of this statute appear in Title II, codified at 42 U.S.C.A. §§ 2000ff–2000ff–11. One type of prohibited employer conduct is discriminating against an employee "because of genetic information with respect to that employee," with respect to hiring, discharge, and the like— language that is essentially the same as that in Title VII. 42 U.S.C. § 2000ff–1. The statute also forbids an employer to "request require, or purchase genetic information" about a worker except when this acquisition of information fits within specified categories. The most important of these are probably information acquired as part of a wellness program, information acquired in order to comply with the requirements of the Family and

Medical Leave Act, information acquired as part of a legally required monitoring program, or information acquired inadvertently. Similar bans on discrimination and on acquiring genetic information apply to employment agencies and labor organizations. 42 U.S.C.A. §§ 2000ff–2, 2000ff–3. The remedies provided are generally those provided by Title VII or by 42 U.S.C.A. § 1981a. For federal employees, they are the parallel remedies provided for race and gender discrimination. 42 U.S.C. 2000ff–6. One major difference between Title VII and GINA is that no disparate impact theory is available under the new statute. 42 U.S.C.A. § 2000ff–7. Regulations for administration and enforcement of GINA are still in the process of formulation as this book goes to press.

M. RETALIATION ACTIONS

Most employee protection statutes include a provision forbidding retaliation against persons who seek to enforce those laws. In recent years, the proportion of charges filed with the EEOC that are either exclusively charges of unlawful retaliation, or that combine a retaliation charge with other charges has increased substantially. This may reflect in part the impact of a series of Supreme Court decisions. In *Jackson v. Birmingham Board of Education,* 544 U.S. 167 (2005), a male coach of a girls' basketball team learned that the female teams were not receiving as much support as male teams. He protested this, and soon after the protest began to receive negative performance reviews and was relieved of his coaching duties. Title IX does not include an express retaliation provision, but a majority of the Court found that such a right of action is implied by the statute, and that it extends to those who protest against gender discrimination banned by the statute, even though they are not direct victims of that discrimination. *Burlington Northern & Santa Fe Railway Co. v. White,* 548 U.S. 53 (2006) involved retaliation claims by a woman employee whose complaints about improper job assignment and an improper suspension had ultimately been resolved in her favor, through a grievance process. She was reinstated with full back pay. She thus suffered no long-term employment harm, such as firing or demotion, or loss of pay. The lower federal courts divided sharply over whether a person so situated would have any retaliation claim under Title VII. A majority of the Supreme Court noted the language differences between the "discrimination" and the "retaliation" provisions of Title VII and concluded: "Title VII's substantive provision and its anti-retaliation provision are not coterminous. The scope of the anti-retaliation provision extends beyond workplace-related or employment-related retaliatory acts and harm. We therefore reject the standards applied in the Courts of Appeals that have treated the anti-retaliation provision as forbidding the same conduct prohibited by the anti-discrimination provision and that have limited actionable retaliation to so-called 'ultimate employment decisions.' " They concluded instead that:

"In our view, a plaintiff must show that a reasonable employee would have found the challenged action materially adverse, 'which in this context means it well might have " 'dissuaded a reasonable worker from making or supporting a charge of discrimination.' " ' " (quoting a recent District of Columbia Circuit opinion). In *Crawford v. Metropolitan Government of Nashville and Davidson County, Tennessee,* 129 S.Ct. 846 (2009), the Court held that the protection of Title VII's anti-retaliation remedy extends to those who participate in the investigation of claims of unlawful discrimination against other parties. In *CBOCS West, Inc. v. Humphries,* 128 S.Ct. 1951 (2008), the Court held that section 1981, the post-Civil War statute, provides a retaliation action. In *Gomez–Perez v. Potter,* 128 S.Ct. 1931 (2008), a federal employee was allowed to pursue a retaliation claim under the ADEA despite the fact that the statute specifically provides that protection to private sector workers, but does not mention such a remedy for federal employees. This series of Supreme Court decisions clearly makes it likely that the trend toward including retaliation claims in EEOC charges is likely to continue.

CHAPTER 5

PHYSICAL SAFETY

How much care should the law require an employer to take to protect its employees from injury and disease? How should the costs of workers' injuries and ill health be shared out among worker, employer and society at large? These questions have faced American courts and legislatures since early in our history, and continue to do so.

This chapter examines issues surrounding the prevention of accidents and disease first and then discusses some of the major systems used to determine whether an employee is entitled to compensation for an injury or disease from the employer, a third party, or a government program.

A. PREVENTION OF INJURY AND DISEASE

A host of federal and state programs regulate workplace hazards, seeking to avoid or minimize employee injury and disease. Some address relatively obvious problems, such as dangerous machinery, hazardous materials, or high noise levels. Others deal with more subtle aspects of the work environment, such as "secondary smoke" (breathing the fumes from other's cigarettes).

1. Occupational Safety and Health Act of 1970

a. Scope

The most important single program designed to prevent injury and disease among workers is the federal Occupational Safety and Health Act (OSHA) of 1970. 29 U.S.C.A. §§ 651–678 (1988). The statute applies to each private sector "employer" in the United States and principal territories. "Employer" is broadly defined to include any "person engaged in a business affecting commerce." 29 U.S.C.A. § 652(5). This broad scope of coverage contrasts sharply with the situation before 1970. Prior to the enactment of OSHA, the only federal programs dealing with occupational safety and health were those focused on federal employees, on specific industries, such as mining and railroads, and on the practices of employers with government contracts. The announced purpose of the 1970 statute is to "assure so far as possible every working man and woman * * * safe and healthful working conditions." OSHA was designed to balance the employee's need for a safe and healthy working environment against the employer's desire to function without undue interference.

The Congress has frequently restricted the power of the Department of Labor to inspect farms and some businesses employing 10 or fewer persons, in riders to appropriations bills. OSHA does not modify other federal laws prescribing safety and health standards. It does not affect any federal or state worker's compensation law or the rights, duties, or liabilities of employers or employees under any law relating to injuries, diseases or death, arising out of employment. Id. § 653(b)(4).

The Secretary of Labor is responsible for OSHA's overall administration. This includes:

- the development and promulgation of mandatory occupational safety and health standards, and

- enforcement by physical inspection and the issuance of citations requiring abatement of unsafe conditions, payment of civil penalties, or both.

Contested citations of the Secretary of Labor are heard by the Occupational Safety and Health Review Commission. This is an independent, quasi-judicial three-member board responsible for adjudicating matters associated with citations, proposed penalties, and abatement periods. If the Secretary and the Commission differ on the interpretation of one of the regulations promulgated by the Secretary, the Secretary's interpretation, if reasonable, is entitled to deference. *Martin v. OSHRC*, 499 U.S. 144 (1991).

OSHA established within the Department of Health, Education and Welfare (HEW) the National Institute for Occupational Safety and Health (NIOSH). Its primary responsibility is to carry out OSHA's research and educational functions. 29 U.S.C.A. §§ 669, 671(a) (1988).

b. Employer Duties

The statute imposes two principal substantive duties upon employers:

Each employer—

(1) shall furnish to each of his employees employment and a place of employment which are free from recognized hazards that are causing or are likely to cause death or serious physical harm to his employees;

(2) shall comply with occupational safety and health standards promulgated under this chapter.

29 U.S.C.A. § 654(a).

The statute also requires employers to report injuries and maintain fairly detailed records. These requirements have been fleshed out by extensive regulations, discussed in subsection *d* below.

c. Employee Rights and Responsibilities

OSHA grants each employee several entitlements, including the right:

1. To question unsafe conditions and request a federal inspection. Id. § 657(f).

2. To assist, on a limited basis, OSHA inspectors. Id. § 657(e).

3. To bring an action to compel the Secretary of Labor to seek injunctive relief in cases involving imminent danger to employees. Id. § 662(d).

4. To gain access to information about his or her own health records and about exposure to dangerous substances. Id. § 657(c).

Employees have the privilege to refuse to perform hazardous job activities where (1) they reasonably believe there is a real danger of death or injury and (2) there is no time to resort to administrative action to remedy the danger. 29 C.F.R. § 1977.12 (1990). However, in *Whirlpool Corp. v. Marshall*, 445 U.S. 1 (1980), the Supreme Court both upheld the validity of that regulation and also stated that employees risk termination without a remedy if they act "unreasonably or in bad faith" in refusing to work. The statute prohibits discrimination against any employee who has filed a complaint, testified in a proceeding under the Act, or otherwise exercised a right under the Act. Id. § 660(c).

The employee's duty is to comply with all OSHA standards, rules, regulations, and orders. 29 U.S.C.A. § 654(b) (1988). No legal sanctions exist, however, to penalize employees for violating OSHA standards. See *Atlantic & Gulf Stevedores, Inc. v. OSHRC*, 534 F.2d 541 (3d Cir.1976).

d. Record Keeping

Section 8(c) of OSHA, 29 U.S.C.A. § 657(c), requires employers of 11 or more employees to prepare and maintain records of occupational illnesses and injuries. The details of just what records are to be kept, what reports made, and in what form are set by regulations of the Secretary of Labor. Id. §§ 657(c)(1), 673(e). These regulations excuse an employer of fewer than 10 from most record keeping and reporting, except for job fatalities or multiple hospitalization accidents, unless that employer has been selected by the Bureau of Labor Statistics (BLS) to participate in a periodic statistical survey. 29 C.F.R. § 1904.1. A similar partial exemption applies to employers in certain industries found generally to be "low hazard," including retail, services, finance, insurance and real estate. Id. § 1904.2.

Failure to keep proper records and to report accurately on injuries and disease is treated very seriously. Penalties in the hundreds of thousands of dollars have been enforced against employers who deliberately fail to record injuries properly. See, e.g., *Kaspar Wire Works, Inc. v. Secretary of Labor*, 268 F.3d 1123 (D.C.Cir.2001).

The content of the record-keeping regulations was changed substantially under a new rule effective in January 2002. Less significant changes (mainly to forms)were made in January 2004. Under these, an employer must record any fatality, injury or illness that is: (a) work-related; (b) a "new case"; and (c) meets one of the "general recording criteria" defined in the regulations. Id. § 1904.4. These criteria, derived from language in the statute, section 8(c)(2), 29 U.S.C.A. § 657(c)(2), emphasize the seriousness of the medical situation involved. For example, an injury must be recorded if it results in death, medical treatment beyond first aid, loss of consciousness, work restrictions or transfer to another job, or days away from work. The regulations also list some specific illnesses and injuries that must be recorded, including cancer, fractures, eardrum punctures, needle sticks, and active tuberculosis.

These records must be kept in certain formats:

- OSHA 300—Log of Work–Related Injuries and Illnesses

- OSHA 300A—Summary of Work–Related Injuries and Illnesses

- OSHA 301—Injury and Incident Report

The employer may use an "equivalent" form for either OSHA 300 or OSGA 301 so long as it provides the same information in an understandable way. The records may be kept on a computer, but only if the computer program can readily produce the required forms when needed. At the end of the calendar year, the employer must prepare a summary of the OSHA 300 Log and post it by February 1. All OSHA 300 and 301 report forms must be kept for 5 years and must be available for inspection and copying by designated government agencies. 29 U.S.C.A. §§ 657(a), (c), 667, 669(b), 673 (1988). Employees, their personal representatives, and "authorized employee representatives" (generally collective bargaining agents) also have limited access rights to this information. 29 C.F.R. § 1904.35.

These regulations contemplate that the typical incident report or log entry will include the name of each affected employee, but recognize that there are situations in which privacy concerns may call for this not to be done. In such a "privacy concern case" the employer is to enter "privacy case" where the name of the employee would usually appear. The regulations list six privacy concern cases, including mental illnesses, HIV infections, some needle stick cases, injuries to the reproductive system, injuries resulting from sexual assaults, and "other illnesses if the employee independently and voluntarily requests that his or her name not be entered on the log." Id. § 1904.29(b)(7).

Section 8(c)(3), 29 U.S.C.A. § 657(c)(3), imposes an additional requirement. Under that provision, an employer is required to keep "accurate records of employee exposures to potentially toxic materials or harmful physical agents" regulated by a standard that requires monitoring or measuring. Employees or their representatives must be given an opportunity to observe the monitoring or measuring, and have rights to access to the exposure record. The records involved include:

1. Environmental monitoring data;

2. Biological monitoring results;

3. Material safety data sheets; and

4. Any other record disclosing the identity of a toxic substance or harmful physical agent.

Recognized or certified collective bargaining agents are automatically considered "designated representatives" and have an access right to employee exposure records without individual employee consent. 29 C.F.R. § 1910.1020(c)(3). OSHA also has an extensive right of access to exposure records. Id. § 1910.1020(e)(3). Access to personally identifiable employee medical records, other than exposure records, is more restricted. Each employee is entitled to see the medical record that the employer maintains with respect to that employee, regardless of how the information was generated or is maintained. "Employee medical record" is broadly defined, but there are a few exclusions, such as some records concerning health insurance claims, and those concerning voluntary employee medical assistance programs. Limited discretion is given physicians to deny access where there is a specific diagnosis of a terminal illness or psychiatric condition. Collective bargaining agents must obtain specific written consent before gaining access to these personally identifiable records. 29 C.F.R. Part 1913 (1990).

With a few exceptions, employers must preserve exposure records for at least 30 years and must preserve medical records for at least the duration of employment plus 30 years. With the exception of X-rays, employers may keep the records in any form, such as microfilm, microfiche, or computer. The employer may delete trade secret data, such as the nature of manufacturing processes or the percentage of a chemical substance in a mixture, where the employee or designated representative is notified of the deletion, although some trade secrets may have to be divulged in emergency situations at the request of a treating medical professional. Generally, access to trade secrets may be conditioned upon a written agreement not to misuse this information.

e. *Enforcement*

OSHA is enforced primarily through a system of inspections by the Department of Labor's Occupational Safety and Health Administration (often referred to as OSHA, as is the statute). Inspections are made in response to employee complaints, as a result of reported injuries or deaths, or as part of a regular program of routine inspections. If an inspector is denied access to a workplace by an employer, the Secretary of Labor may obtain a warrant to enter based either upon probable cause to believe violations of OSHA exist in that place, or upon a showing of "administrative probable cause," i.e., that the workplace has been selected for inspection on the basis of a rational, neutral scheme of selection that is justified by the statute's purposes. See *Marshall v. Barlow's, Inc.*, 436 U.S. 307 (1978).

If an inspection reveals violation(s) of OSHA, a citation will be issued, stating what the violation is, categorizing it (whether it is de minimis, non-serious, serious, or willful or repeated), and proposing a remedy. The remedy will ordinarily have two parts: a requirement to abate the violation, and a civil penalty. After receiving the citation, an employer has 15 working days to notify the Secretary it will contest the finding of violation, the proposed remedy, or both. Employees may also file a contest within that time period, protesting the time frame for abatement. 29 U.S.C.A. § 659. Contests are heard by the Occupational Safety & Health Review Commission (OSHRC), which may accept, reject or modify the Secretary's proposed finding of violation and remedy. An uncontested citation has the status of an OSHRC final order, and is not subject to judicial review. 29 U.S.C.A. § 659(a). An OSHRC order in a contested case may be challenged by "any person adversely affected or aggrieved" by filing a petition in an appropriate United States Court of Appeals within 60 days of the issuance of the order. 29 U.S.C.A. § 660(a). The Secretary of Labor may also challenge such an order or seek enforcement of it. Id. § 660(b). OSHRC findings of fact are conclusive if based on substantial evidence. Final decrees of a reviewing court may be enforced through use of the contempt powers, if necessary.

In limited instances, equitable or criminal remedies may be sought. The Secretary may seek an injunction in federal district court to restrain violations "which could reasonably be expected to cause death or serious physical harm immediately or before the imminence of such danger can be eliminated" through regular enforcement procedures. 29 U.S.C.A. § 662. Criminal penalties are available in three instances:

(1) a willful violation causing death of an employee;

(2) giving advance notice of an inspection;

(3) knowingly making false statements in reports required by the statute.

Id. § 666(e), (f), (g).

f. Proving Violations

(i) General Duty Clause

To show a violation of the "general duty clause," section 5(a)(1) of OSHA, 29 U.S.C.A. § 654(a)(1),

> the Secretary must prove: (1) that the employer failed to render its workplace "free" of a hazard which was (2) "recognized" and (3) "causing or likely to cause death or serious physical harm." *National Realty and Construction Co., Inc. v. OSHRC*, 489 F.2d 1257 (D.C.Cir.1973).

A hazard may be "recognized" in either of two senses: (1) The cited employer may know of the hazard. (2) The hazard may be one that is appreciated as a hazard in the industry in which the cited employer is operating. Whether a workplace is "free" of a hazard is usually obvious enough, but not always. In *National Realty* the hazard involved was equipment riding by employees. Employer rules forbade the practice, but a supervisor was killed as a result of breaking the rule. The court held that the Secretary must offer proof of what additional practical steps the employer could have taken, beyond what it had done, to make the site any more free of employee disregard of safety rules. In other cases, the Secretary has been required to demonstrate technical feasibility of reducing physical hazards. Thus, to the three elements listed in *National Realty* it is often fair to add a fourth: feasibility of abatement.

(ii) Violation of Standard

The Secretary's burden in cases involving alleged violations of standards always includes at least four elements:

(1) the applicability of the [cited] standard,

(2) the existence of non-complying conditions,

(3) employee exposure or access, and

(4) that the employer knew or with the exercise of reasonable diligence could have known of the violative condition. *Dun–Par Engineered Form Co.*, 12 OSHC 1962, 1965 (OSHRC 1986).

In some instances more specific, arguably additional, burdens have been imposed. In the case of generally worded standards, such as those requiring the use of "appropriate personal protective equipment," the Secretary is obliged to show what would be "appropriate," usually by resort to practices within the industry. See, e.g., *Voegele Co. v. OSHRC*, 625 F.2d 1075 (3d Cir.1980). One can view this either as an addition to the four elements listed above, or as a particularization of the first element. When a regulation uses a term of art common in the relevant industry, an employer may reasonably expect that term to reflect the usual understanding of employers in that industry until such time as the Secretary of Labor makes it clear that another meaning was intended. *Fabi Construction Co., Inc. v. Secretary of Labor*, 508 F.3d 1077 (D.C. Cir. 2007).

Applicability of Standard—Whether a standard applies may depend upon characterizing the employer's business. Standards have been grouped under four main headings: general industry (29 C.F.R. Part 1910); maritime and longshoring (Id., Parts 1915–1920); construction (Id., Part 1926); and agricultural (Id., Part 1928). Within some categories, particular standards may by their own terms apply only to specific types of businesses. See, e.g., 29 C.F.R. § 1915.2 (ship yards); 29 C.F.R. § 1910.261 (pulp and paper mills). Standards vary in their level of specificity. The standard just mentioned requires use of "appropriate personal protective equipment"; this broad language contrasts sharply with one applying to the simultaneous use of goggles and helmet filter lenses: "[T]he shade number of the lens in the helmet may be reduced so that the sum of the shade numbers of the two lenses will equal the value shown in Table I–1 in § 1915.118." 29 C.F.R. § 1915.151(c)(3). If there is a specific industry standard applicable to a work situation, may the Secretary cite the employer for violation of a general industry standard? The issue was the source of considerable difference of opinion between the Review Commission, which for a time frowned on the practice, and the Secretary. Thus far the Secretary has generally prevailed in the Court of Appeals. See the discussion in *Peterson Bros. Steel Erection Co. v. Reich,* 26 F.3d 573 (5th Cir. 1994). A similar question is whether the existence of a standard preempts application of the general duty clause. The D.C. Circuit has suggested that there should be no pre-emption if the employer knows the specific standard is not adequate protection. See *UAW v. General Dynamics*, 815 F.2d 1570 (D.C.Cir.1987), cert. denied, 484 U.S. 976 (1987), and this view has apparently prevailed. See *Safeway, Inc. v. OSHRC*, 382 F.3d 1189 (10th Cir. 2004). The validity of a standard may be challenged in enforcement proceedings, as explained below, but if not challenged a standard will be treated as validly promulgated.

Failure to Comply—Deciding whether a standard has been violated may be a fairly straightforward matter—such as determining whether the shade numbers of goggle and helmet lenses add up to the required figure—or may involve substantial issues of judgment—deciding whether the level of supervision provided in a laboratory is adequate.

Employee exposure—The Secretary need not prove that an employee has in fact been exposed to the hazard; proof that one or more employees had potential access to the violative condition is enough. See *Donovan v. Adams Steel Erection, Inc.*, 766 F.2d 804 (3d Cir.1985).

Employer awareness—The Secretary may carry her burden on this by showing either actual awareness of a violating condition or that a violation existed long enough so that an employer with a reasonable program of inspection would have known of the condition. *Kokosing Construction Co., Inc. v. OSHRC*, 232 Fed.Appx. 510 (6th Cir.2007).

The level of employer awareness is also often critical in deciding whether a violation is "willful" and therefore may merit a heavier penalty. The usual statement is that a violation is willful if there is either "intentional disregard of, or plain indifference to, the Act's requirements." See *A.E. Staley Mfg.Co. v. Secretary of Labor,* 295 F.3d 1341, 1345 (D.C.Cir. 2002).

g. *Employer Defenses*

In addition to challenging the quality of the Secretary's proof—for instance, by questioning the range of experience of an OSHA inspector who has testified about the nature of general industry practice—a cited employer may seek to establish a number of other defenses. Some are procedural: that access was gained by an invalid warrant; that "walk-around rights" were denied; that a citation was vague or referred to an incorrect standard.

Substantive defenses range widely. An employer may contest the validity of a standard during an enforcement proceeding. (The types of standards and reasons for holding them to be invalid are discussed below.)

The Commission and courts permit an employer to demonstrate that compliance with a standard may create a greater hazard than exists under the current practice; for example, that the use of safety lines by members of an off-ground painting crew may create tripping hazards more serious than the risk of falling. Some courts have denied this "greater hazard" defense to an employer that has not applied for a variance, if the violative condition is an ongoing one for which a variance application would be appropriate.

Other defenses go to feasibility. If the market does not offer the types of safety devices or monitoring equipment the standard requires, a cited employer has a good argument that compliance is not possible. Employee refusal to comply with safety standards has been submitted as a defense fairly often, but has succeeded relatively rarely. The Secretary is entitled to insist that an employer use its disciplinary powers vigorously enough to achieve compliance with its safety rules. In *Atlantic & Gulf Stevedores v. OSHRC*, 534 F.2d 541 (3d Cir.1976), the employer argued that its hands were tied because of limits on its disciplinary power negotiated by its employees' union; the Third Circuit accepted the Secretary's argument that the employer could be required to bargain for greater power to impose discipline for refusal to comply with safety rules. Totally unpredictable employee misconduct, however, may not result in a violation.

Some defenses take the shape of one employer pointing at another as the "more responsible" party, at work sites where more than one employer has workers. In such settings, an employer whose workers are exposed to a hazard may not have created the hazard nor have the power to control it; an electrical subcontractor's employees, for example, may be exposed to a fall hazard created by a carpentry subcontractor who failed to fence off an opening in the floor where an elevator is to go, and not abated by the general contractor in control of the general work site. The creating (but no longer controlling) carpentry subcontractor is liable to citation under section 5(a)(2) despite the fact that none of its employees is exposed to the hazard, provided that the hazard-creating employer could expect that persons who are "employees" under OSHA might have access to the hazard. The non-creating but controlling general contractor is subject to citation under section 5(a)(2) if it should be aware that the hazard exists and that "employees" may have access to the hazard even though none of its own employees are exposed to the hazard. An early Commission doctrine that excused an employer from liability unless its own employees were exposed was roundly rejected by the Second Circuit in 1975 in *Brennan v. OSHRC (Underhill Construction Corp.)*, 513 F.2d 1032 (2d Cir.1975), the leading case on the subject. A "non-creating," "non-controlling" subcontractor may defend on those grounds, but may nonetheless be held liable unless it has taken whatever steps it reasonably could—such as asking the controlling contractor to abate or providing personal protective equipment. See *Dun–Par Engineered Form Co. v. Marshall*, 676 F.2d 1333 (10th Cir.1982). Abandonment of the work is not required, however, in ordinary circumstances. A non-controlling employer that did not know or have reason to know of a hazard may avoid liability.

h.   *Setting and Challenging Standards*

Section 6 of OSHA, 29 U.S.C.A. § 655, empowers the Secretary to issue three types of safety and health standards: national consensus standards, regular standards, and temporary emergency standards. The substantive nature of each of the three is the same; the difference lies in the level of detail required in promulgating each. Thus all three types must fit the basic statutory definition of "standard":

> The term "occupational safety standard" means a standard which requires conditions, or the adoption or use of one or more practices, means, methods, operation, or processes, reasonably necessary or appropriate to provide safe or healthful employment and places of employment.

29 U.S.C.A. § 652(8).

In order to give OSHA some practical impact within a short time after it was passed, the statute provided for the adoption of "national consensus standards" during the first two years following the enactment of OSHA. These could be put into force without using the normal rule-making procedures of the Administrative Procedure Act, involving publication of proposed rules and the reasons for them, and allowing periods for comment and debate. The only standards eligible for this treatment were those that had already been promulgated under other federal statutes (such as those regulating workplace practices of firms supplying goods to the federal government) and those developed by a "nationally recognized standards-producing organization" whose procedures permitted input from affected groups. (The American National Standards

Institute is the principal example.) A standard promulgated as a national consensus standard could not be substantively changed in the process of rewording it into the form appropriate for a regulatory standard. See *Usery v. Kennecott Copper Corp.*, 577 F.2d 1113 (10th Cir.1977).

Regular standards, promulgated under section 6(b), 29 U.S.C.A. § 655(b), require advance publication in the Federal Register and full opportunity for comment and criticism. Objecting parties may request and get a hearing on whatever portions of the standard they attack. Standards dealing with toxic substances receive special treatment in section 6(b)(5), which requires the Secretary to:

> set the standard which most adequately assures, to the extent feasible, on the basis of the best available evidence, that no employee will suffer material impairment of health of functional capacity even if such employee has regular exposure to the hazard dealt with by such standard for the period of his working life * * * [O]ther considerations shall be the latest available scientific data * * *, the feasibility of the standards, and experience gained under this and other health and safety laws.

Emergency temporary standards do not require the full opportunity for comment that is required for "regular" 6(b) standards, but the Secretary is required to begin the procedures for adopting a regular standard on the same hazard within six months after promulgating an emergency temporary standard. In practice, the federal courts have proved extraordinarily hostile to emergency temporary standards, striking them down for a myriad of reasons so that this provision has almost become a dead letter. See *Asbestos Information Assoc. v. OSHA*, 727 F.2d 415 (5th Cir.1984).

Standards may be challenged when issued or in enforcement proceedings on both procedural and substantive grounds. Delegation of standard-setting authority to the Secretary has been found to be constitutional, over a lone dissent by former Chief Justice Rehnquist. Standards have been struck down on grounds of vagueness, internal inconsistency, and lack of need. See *Industrial Union Dept. AFL–CIO v. American Petroleum Institute*, 448 U.S. 607 (1980). A standard may be valid, however, even though it calls for employing technology not yet fully developed, on the grounds that Congress meant OSHA to be "technology forcing," but compliance must be "feasible" within a reasonable time frame. *Society of Plastics Industry, Inc. v. OSHA*, 509 F.2d 1301 (2d Cir.1975). What role economic feasibility plays has been controversial. In *American Textile Manufacturers Institute, Inc. v. Donovan*, 452 U.S. 490 (1981), the Supreme Court upheld a regulation limiting cotton dust concentrations in ambient air against a challenge that the standard could not be justified on a cost-benefit analysis. The Secretary was right, a majority held, in limiting consideration of economic feasibility to whether the proposed regulation would cause the demise of an industry. That standard was a toxic substance standard, issued under the peculiar language of § 6(b)(5). In the case of other sorts of standards, the lower federal courts have sometimes required more detailed analysis. In *Donovan v. Castle & Cooke Foods*, 692 F.2d 641 (9th Cir.1982), for example, the Ninth Circuit held that the Secretary must consider costs and benefits in deciding whether to require (very expensive) engineering controls over (arguably less reliable) personal protective devices.

Challenges by groups representing employees, arguing that a standard is inadequate, have been relatively infrequent, but have succeeded on a few occasions. One such challenge led to a ruling by the Supreme Court limiting the power of the Office of Management & Budget to object to standards. *Dole v. United Steelworkers*, 494 U.S. 26 (1990).

The Congress may, of course, determine the content of standards itself instead of delegating that authority. See, e.g., the Needlestick Safety and Prevention Act, 114 Stat. 1901 (2000). In one well-publicized instance in 2001, a newly elected Congress, with the encouragement of a new presidential administration, overturned the ergonomic injury regulation issued by OSHA the prior November after more than a decade of study. See Senate Joint Resolution 6, 115th Congress(signed March 20, 2001).

2. The Ongoing Role of State Statutes

Prior to the passage of OSHA, most workplace safety and health regulation was state law. This was largely pre-empted by the federal statute, but section 18 of OSHA, 29 U.S.C.A. § 667, provides that a state may reassume responsibility for occupational safety and health if the state's plan meets certain criteria. Some of those criteria are aimed at national uniformity; a state must require employers to make reports identical to those required by the federal plan, for example. A state's standards must be "at least as effective as" the federal standards; many states make it a routine practice to adopt each federal standard as it is issued. Some of the other criteria, such as "adequate funds," qualified staff and necessary enforcement ability, may require states to do more than simply match the federal program. *Industrial Union Department, AFL–CIO v. Marshall*, 570 F.2d 1030 (D.C.Cir. 1978). More than a score of states have adopted "section 18 plans," and in those states federal activity is limited to monitoring state efforts and continuing to enforce standards with respect to hazards a particular state may have chosen not to deal with. Federal law also does not pre-empt state regulation of risks not yet subject to a federal standard. Since 1983, when OSHA issued its Hazard Communication Standard, 29 C.F.R. § 1910.1200, several employer groups have challenged state and city "right-to-know" laws on pre-emption grounds. The results have been mixed. In *Manufacturers Ass'n of Tri–County v. Knepper*, 801 F.2d 130 (3d Cir.1986), cert. denied, 484 U.S. 815 (1987), for example, provisions of a state law requiring suppliers of chemicals to provide information to consumers and to use certain types of labels were held not pre-empted, since these provisions protected the general public; a requirement that manufacturing sector employers use certain labels to inform their employees of hazards in their work was, however, held pre-empted.

3. Other Federal Statutes

In addition to OSHA and these state laws, a number of federal statutes apply to specific industries, such as mining, transportation, and nuclear power production and manufacture. Each reflects its particular setting. Mine inspectors, for example, have the power to order the workforce out of a mine on the spot, with a judicial hearing following rather than preceding the order. 30 U.S.C.A. § 817. Section 4(b)(1) of OSHA, 29 U.S.C.A. § 653(b)(1), provides that the statute does not apply to "the working condition of employees with respect to which other Federal agencies ... exercise statutory authority to prescribe or enforce standards or regulations affecting occupational safety and health." The cited employer in *Chao v. Mallard Bay Drilling, Inc.*, 534 U.S. 235 (2002), operated an oil and gas exploration barge in territorial waters of Louisiana. An explosion on the barge killed several workers. The employer argued that OSHA lacked the authority to cite it for standards violations, because the Coast Guard had authority over the barge. The Supreme Court upheld the citations, since the Coast Guard had not in fact exercised its authority to regulate working conditions on this category of vessel. "OSHA is only preempted," Justice Stevens wrote, "if the working conditions at issue are the particular ones 'with respect to which' another federal agency has regulated." The mere existence of authority to regulate, or of minimal regulation (in this case for navigation safety purposes) is not enough.

B. COMPENSATION FOR INJURY AND DISEASE

1. Compensating Injured Workers: Historical Background

Until shortly before the First World War, the only way in which an injured worker could obtain compensation for an injury was by recovering tort damages. Recoveries were rare, in part because employees were reluctant to testify against an employer's interest, and without such testimony the injured worker could not establish employer fault. Tort recovery was also difficult because an employer could escape liability by establishing one of three defenses: (1) contributory negligence, (2) assumption of risk, and (3) the fellow-servant rule. Moreover, even if recovery of tort damages was possible, the litigation process was often an unsatisfactory way to provide compensation because it would pit employees against one another or against their employer, disquieting the ordinary operation of the workplace. In the early 1900s, therefore, attention became focused on the need for an alternative to tort litigation. British and German workers' compensation systems were often mentioned as possible models of what might be done.

Most early efforts dealing with industrial injury were enacted between 1910 and 1940 at the state rather than at the national level in the form of workers' compensation statutes. The majority of claims for compensation for job-connected injuries are still made under those state workers' compensation statutes, unless one works for the federal government (to whom the Federal Employees Compensation Act applies) or in a handful of industries subject to a special federal statute, such as the Longshore and Harbor Workers Compensation Act.

The principal federal program providing benefits to injured employees, the Disability Insurance program of the Social Security system, is limited to the severely injured and disabled. This program was added in the 1950s to the original Social Security system, which was limited to providing old-age benefits.

With respect to vocational rehabilitation, the situation is reversed. In that field the federal government has gradually assumed the leadership role. At least since 1973, the state governments have been junior partners in providing funds for this training, the vast majority of funds coming from the national government. The states remain very active partners in the operation, however, and state agencies provide the day-to-day administration of the program. 29 U.S.C.A. §§ 701–796i (1988) (Vocational Rehabilitation Act of 1973).

2. Overview of the Structure of Compensation and Benefit Regimes

Programs to provide benefits and services to disabled employees may thus be analyzed by dividing them into:

1. Actions for damages brought either against employers or against third parties. Generally, an injured worker must prove that the defendant was "at fault" in order to recover.

2. Compensation programs under which employers provide medical treatment and income replacement benefits to workers injured on the job, without regard to fault.

3. Social insurance programs providing income benefits to disabled workers from government funds, without regard to whether the injury was job-connected.

4. Vocational Rehabilitation programs.

This sub-section discusses each of these four in general terms, concluding with a brief review of some of the constitutional law opinions these programs have generated. The following sub-sections address some particular problems associated with workers compensation and with the Social Security Disability Insurance scheme.

a. Actions for Damages

Only a small number of employees obtain damages awards against their employers in the courts for the work-related injuries. This is because workers' compensation statutes always include an "exclusive remedy" provision that bars such actions unless an employer has acted intentionally to injure the worker, or (in some states) has seriously failed in its obligations under the statute (by failing to provide the required insurance to cover its workers, for example). Employees who obtain damages awards against their employers based on general personal injury tort principles are therefore those who are excluded from any workers' compensation statute coverage, such as domestic service employees, workers on small farms, and railroad workers or sailors who may pursue claims under the Federal Employers Liability Act (FELA), 45 U.S.C.A. §§ 51–60.

Allowing an injured worker to bring a damages action against her own employer for intentional injury is limited to situations in which the employer's intent to harm that worker is clear. Attempts to extend this exception to the exclusive remedy provision have increased in recent years, but with very limited success. In *Millison v. E.I. du Pont de Nemours & Co.*, 101 N.J. 161, 501 A.2d 505 (N.J. 1985), the court dismissed an action for damages brought by employees who alleged that their employer had knowingly exposed them to asbestos dust when aware of the danger involved. The court, however, permitted the plaintiffs to proceed on a claim that the employer's doctors had concealed from the workers that they were suffering from asbestos-related diseases, information obtained in annual employee physicals.

One major employers' liability statute remains in effect throughout the United States. The Federal Employers Liability Act applies to railroad workers, and has been extended by the Jones Act to be available to the members of crews of vessels. 46 U.S.C.A. § 688. This statute abolishes the fellow servant rule and the doctrine of assumption of risk, and replaces contributory negligence with a type of comparative negligence. It has been interpreted to lighten the usual plaintiff's burden of proof so that a jury may assess damages against an employer if there is proof "that employer negligence played any part, even the slightest, in producing the injury or death * * *." *Rogers v. Missouri Pac. R.R.*, 352 U.S. 500 (1957).

Members of the crews of vessels may also be eligible for two other special remedies, the ancient no-fault remedy of maintenance and cure, and the relatively recent "general maritime remedy," a claim for damages resulting from the unseaworthy condition of the vessel. The older remedy requires the vessel to provide a per diem for food and lodging (maintenance) and medical treatment (cure) until such time as maximum recovery is achieved, in the case of any injury or disease incurred by a crew member while in the service of the vessel (unless the result of the injured sailor's willful misconduct). The "unseaworthiness" remedy resembles a negligence claim in some ways, but an injured claimant is not required to show that an unseaworthy condition was caused by any employer fault, nor is proof of an act of negligence sufficient to justify recovery if that act did not produce an unseaworthy condition. See *Usner v. Luckenbach Overseas Corp.*, 400 U.S. 494 (1971). The FELA–Jones Act remedy and the general maritime remedy extend to cases of wrongful death. *Miles v. Apex Marine Corp.*, 498 U.S. 19 (1990). In *Atlantic Sounding Co. v. Townsend*, 2009 WL 1789469, a divided Court held that a seaman may recover punitive damages for an employer's willful failure to provide maintenance and cure.

Actions for damages are fairly often brought against a defendant that does not qualify for the benefit of the "exclusive remedy" provision as an "employer." Since damages awards are not limited in the same ways that workers' compensation awards are, this puts a premium on qualifying for the "employer" label. The workers' compensation statutes typically include a number of provisions dealing with this issue. For example, most statutes extend both potential liability for benefits, and also the protection of the exclusive remedy defense to a general contractor that has retained the injured worker's immediate employer as a subcontractor. Some legislatures provide the defense to all contractors "above" the immediate employer, some limit it to those contractors that do, in fact, provide benefits to the worker.

b. *Employer–Paid Workers' Compensation Benefits for On-the-Job Injury and Occupational Disease*

Although most workers' compensation statutes operate at the state rather than at the national level, it is appropriate to regard these statutes as the principal national system for compensating industrial accident and disease victims because of their ubiquity and their many common features. The majority of these statutes are very similar in overall intent. They reflect a legislative judgment to provide injured employees with a more certain remedy than that provided by tort law, but a remedy that is more limited in scope than the damages remedy tort law would provide. The greater certainty that an injured worker will receive benefits is achieved mainly by eliminating the requirement that the worker prove employer fault. In most states, the worker is also not required to go into court to seek relief, but may simply file a claim with an administrative agency if the employer fails to provide it voluntarily. Each statute sharply limits the proportion of loss that will be transferred to the employer; they all, for example, eliminate recovery for non-disabling pain and suffering. They replace only a portion of lost wages. As discussed before, each of these statutes includes an "exclusive remedy" provision, making workers' compensation benefits the employee's sole remedy against his or her employer for injury in the course of employment. The employee cannot sue for damages, even for harms that go largely uncompensated under workers' compensation statute schedules, such as pain and suffering.

The bulk of these statutes were enacted during the 1920s and 1930s. Their substance has been monitored regularly by the federal government, which reports on the content and administration of these statutes in its publications. Three decades ago the President appointed a National Commission on State Workmen's Compensation Laws, pursuant to a provision of the Occupational Safety and Health Act of 1970, to report on the performance of the workers' compensation systems. The Council of State Governments has prepared a Model Workmen's Compensation and Rehabilitation Act that incorporates many of these statutes' common features. Although it is appropriate to think of these statutes as parts of a national system, there are important differences from state to state, both in the statutes, and in how the courts interpret and apply them. These differences have grown in recent years, largely because of intense lobbying pressure on state legislatures to amend the laws in ways that will limit employer costs.

State workers' compensation statutes apply to the majority of the workforce. Other compensation statutes apply to several large specialized employee groups. Federal government civilian employees are covered by the Federal Employees Compensation Act (FECA), 5 U.S.C.A. §§ 8101–8151 (1988); workers in certain maritime shipping support occupations by the Longshoremen's and Harbor Workers' Compensation Act (LHWCA), 33 U.S.C.A. §§ 901–

950 (1988); coal miners by the Black Lung Benefits Act, but only with respect to specific lung diseases. 30 U.S.C.A. § 901 et seq. (1988).

At times, an injured employee may be eligible for benefits under more than one compensation statute, a situation that has posed difficult problems for the courts. See *Sun Ship, Inc. v. Pennsylvania*, 447 U.S. 715 (1980) (federal and state law interaction). Some states will not entertain claims for an injury for which a worker has already received benefits under the law of another jurisdiction, applying an "election of remedies" doctrine. Other states will allow a worker to pursue such a claim, but will apply a "credit rule" so that the amount of benefits already paid will be credited against any award made in the second jurisdiction.

c.   *Social Insurance Benefits for Disabled Workers*

The major program providing benefits to workers who are seriously disabled without regard to whether the cause of the disability is job-related is the Disability Insurance component of the Social Security system. Social Security Act, Publ. L. No. 271, 49 Stat. 620 (1935) (codified in scattered sections of 42 U.S.C.A. (1988)). Eligibility for these benefits is determined by whether the injured employee's Social Security account has been credited with the payment of taxes in a sufficient number of calendar quarters. The basic formulas are set out well in the second chapter of a helpful Social Security Administration publication, the *Social Security Handbook*. New editions are issued frequently, and this information is also accessible at the agency's web site: http://www.ssa.gov. A handful of states have programs of disability benefits for workers, but most provide only modest benefits.

The program extends to a large number of self-employed persons who are not eligible for workers' compensation benefits, but does not cover those employees whose employment history has been limited to work for employers not covered by the social security system, chiefly state government employees in those states that have elected not to participate in Social Security for their workforce. Benefits are paid only to those with truly severe disability that can be expected to last for more than a year.

d. *Vocational Rehabilitation*

Rehabilitation benefits may be for physical or vocational rehabilitation, or both. Physical rehabilitation benefits are provided for, at least to some extent, by all the workers' compensation statutes. An employee who has lost a limb in an industrial accident can routinely anticipate that the employer will be obligated to provide a prosthetic device, such as an artificial leg, as part of compensation benefits. The same is generally true of physical therapy to restore motion to limbs weakened by being in a cast for a long period. Vocational rehabilitation benefits are provided for by a substantial number of workers' compensation statutes. The scope of employer liability under these is usually modest, because of time or total cost limitations.

The major American program of vocational rehabilitation is a joint federal-state program established under the Vocational Rehabilitation Act of 1973, as amended, 29 U.S.C.A. §§ 701–796i. Training programs for disabled veterans and the blind were funded by the federal government as early as 1862. A number of states had already established special schools for the blind in the 1830s. It was not until 1920, however, that the Congress authorized funds for a broad program of vocational rehabilitation for civilian workers. Smith–Fess Act, 41 Stat. 735 (1920). That statute paved the way for a large number of specialized programs, such as one encouraging the blind to set up vending stands in federal buildings, and several dealing with studies of architectural barriers. The 1973 Act consolidated and rewrote most of these. That Act was modified substantially in 1998, in an attempt to coordinate this program with others aimed at getting people with a variety of problems back into the workforce. Workforce Investment Act of 1998, 112 Stat. 936 (1998).

e. Constitutionality

The statutes involved in all these programs were major departures from the past. It is little wonder, then, that they spawned a number of challenges of unconstitutionality.

Several railroads challenged the constitutionality of the Federal Employers Liability Act, claiming that its elimination of contributory negligence and the fellow servant rule offended due process, and that the statute invaded areas that should be left to the individual states. Both types of arguments were rejected in the *Second Employers Liability Cases*, 223 U.S. 1 (1912).

State workers' compensation laws were also challenged on due process and equal protection grounds soon after they were first enacted, but the Supreme Court decision approving the constitutional soundness of the general structure of such laws in *New York Central R.R. v. White*, 243 U.S. 188 (1917), eventually put an end to most of that litigation. Challenges to particular aspects of the laws continue to the present, however, under both federal and state constitutions. In one remarkable decision the Wisconsin Supreme Court held that the state legislature could not impose workers' compensation liability on golf clubs for injuries to caddies, since caddies were not "employees" of the golf club but of individual golfers. *Wendlandt v. Industrial Commission*, 256 Wis. 62, 39 N.W.2d 854 (1949). It is unlikely that would be followed elsewhere, since golf clubs clearly profit from having caddies available and have the power to control their presence on a course, connection enough to allow a legislature to impose a burden of this sort, one would think. *Wendlandt* properly reminds us, however, that due process—or some related doctrine—does require that a legislature not impose liability on a party whose connection with a loss is too remote. The Congress went too far, a majority of the Supreme Court held, in imposing liability for retired coal miner health benefits retroactively on a firm that had long since left the industry, simply because that firm had once been a signatory to collective bargaining agreements in that industry. *Eastern Enterprises v. Apfel,* 524 U.S. 498 (1998). The case generated five opinions, and there is no consensus rationale. The four-justice plurality opinion would void the statute under the "takings" clause of the Fifth Amendment, and specifically declines to apply the "due process" clause. The concurring opinion of Justice Kennedy, on the other hand, rejects the idea that takings clause jurisprudence should be used to evaluate a compensation scheme unless that scheme directly affects physical or intellectual property; his opinion supports the judgment because of a violation of due process. It seems likely that state courts and lower federal courts reading *Eastern Enterprises* may have some difficulty in deciding just how it should be followed. Another problem that has cropped up from time to time is a doctrine developed under some state constitutions that when a statute takes away a traditional common law remedy, there must be some sort of quid pro quo for the deprived party. When New Hampshire amended its workers' compensation law in 1978, it extended the exclusive remedy clause to cover employees, thus depriving an injured worker of the right to seek damages from a co-worker. No specific quid pro quo was provided. A majority of the New Hampshire Supreme Court struck this amendment down, over a dissent by Justice Souter, who argued that one should look at the adequacy of the amended statute as a whole as a replacement for common law damages actions, rather than examining the amendment by itself. *Estabrook v. American Hoist & Derrick, Inc.*, 127 N.H. 162, 498 A.2d 741 (1985).

The XIVth amendment to the federal constitution acts as a restraint on government action, not on private actors. Sometimes it is not too easy to tell one from the other. *American Manufacturers Mutual Ins. Co. v. Sullivan*, 526 U.S. 40 (1999) involved a challenge to a provision in the Pennsylvania's workers' compensation statute (since amended) that when a workers' compensation insurer was billed for medical treatment that the insurer regarded as not covered by the statute then the insurer could (a) request a "utilization review" process by an independent party (in practice, an organization of health care providers), and (b) stop paying benefits until that review process was completed. Employees would not have the opportunity to participate in the review process, and would be told only that such a process was underway. Beneficiaries under the statute urged that the suspension of benefits deprived them of property without due process of law. The Third Circuit agreed, reasoning that workers' compensation benefits are "public benefits" and that therefore an insurer that suspended benefit payments could be regarded as a "state actor" for XIVth amendment purposes. The Supreme Court reversed, reasoning that the decision to suspend benefits was simply the sort of private decision that insurers make routinely, and the fact that the decision required interpretation of statutory language was not enough to make the insurer a public actor.

The taxing provisions of the Social Security Act, known as the Federal Insurance Contribution Act, were upheld by the Supreme Court in 1937, against an argument that the national government could tax only for purposes specifically enumerated in the Constitution. A seven-justice majority approved the program under the "implied powers" doctrine. *Helvering v. Davis*, 301 U.S. 619 (1937). In *Mathews v. Eldridge*, 424 U.S. 319 (1976), the Court held that the procedure then existing for cutting off disability benefit payments before a full evidentiary hearing was held did not offend due process. (A new provision now gives a benefit recipient an option to decide whether to ask for benefits to continue during an appeal of a termination decision, taking the chance that if the decision to terminate is affirmed the worker may have to repay the money. 42 U.S.C.A. § 423(g).) In *Richardson v. Belcher*, 404 U.S. 78 (1971), the Court upheld the constitutionality of the "offset" provision in the Social Security Act under which federal disability benefit payments are reduced by the amount the worker receives under a workers' compensation law (or other public disability law) if the two combined would result in a monthly benefit that exceeds 80% of the claimant's average current earnings prior to disability.

3.   Common Issues That Arise Under Workers' Compensation Statutes

The typical statute applies to traumatic injuries and to occupational diseases. Most apply the same procedures and benefit provisions to both, although that is not always true.

a. Traumatic Injuries

A typical definition of "injury" in a workers' compensation statute is "accidental injury or death arising out of and in the course of employment." LHWCA, 33 U.S.C.A. § 902(2). The terms "accidental" or "by accident" have become less common in recent years, but this or similar language still appears in the majority of the statutes. One initial purpose of including an "accidental" component in the definition of injury was to exclude coverage of occupational diseases at a time when it was felt that this coverage would involve medical judgments too speculative. Now that virtually all states have provided for at least some occupational disease coverage, the main function of the words is to stress the requirement that an injury result from a cause that is rooted in the employment. The "by accident" requirement has caused difficulty for claimants in cases of "repeated trauma"; cases involving injury to internal organs when there has been no wounding or striking of the body; and some cases of psychological injury.

"Repeated trauma" cases involve small harms to the body that are repeated over time. For example, the injury in *Atlas Coal Corp. v. Scales*, 198 Okla. 658, 185 P.2d 177 (Okl.1947), was "miner's knee," a condition that comes from rubbing one's knee against the rough edges of pieces of coal thousands, even tens of thousands of times. Other examples are those of employees injured by dipping hands repeatedly into chemical solutions or by performing awkward motions that put unusual strain on a particular muscle or nerve. More and more states have extended workers' compensation coverage to at least some of these injuries, but they remain troublesome because it is often difficult to distinguish employment-based impairments from the non-compensable gradual deterioration associated with aging, the "wear and tear" of ordinary living. The repeated trauma injuries that have been held eligible for benefits are those that tend to be recognizably connected with a specific employment attribute, and not likely to have been the result of things one does outside the workplace.

Soft tissue injuries, including heart attacks or back strains, require careful handling because medical practitioners often cannot identify with precision just what acts and events may have led to the disabling impairment. In the case of a heart attack, for example, a physician may decide that the true operative cause was an underlying arteriosclerosis condition, and that physical activity at work can have done no more than slightly accelerate the inevitable. To the attorney, however, that accelerating, what is sometimes called "triggering," may be very significant, since it is generally held that an impairment is compensable if accelerated or aggravated by the employment. It is not essential that the employment circumstances be the sole, or even dominant, cause of the impairment for the injured employee to be entitled to benefits. See *Kostamo v.*

Marquette Iron Mining Co., 405 Mich. 105, 274 N.W.2d 411 (Mich.1979).

The "by accident" requirement has operated in soft tissue cases to make compensation available only when either the cause of or the manifestation of the impairment is relatively confined in space and time. A lower back strain that begins moments after lifting an unusually heavy load at work is more likely to qualify for benefits than a similar strain that allegedly arose out of routine bending and lifting required by the job which is similar to the bending and lifting done at home.

Many "repeated trauma" cases involve impairments of soft tissue. This combination makes it peculiarly difficult to identify causation, and American courts have differed over when compensation benefits ought to be available. A pair of cases from adjoining states demonstrate this. In each, a shoemaker sought recovery for an ulnar nerve injury, arguing that the harm was the consequence of long-term operation of an appliance in the workplace. The Tennessee court in *Brown Shoe Co. v. Reed,* 209 Tenn. 106, 350 S.W.2d 65 (Tenn.1961), allowed recovery, after a detailed review of the unusual motion required to operate the appliance. The Missouri court in *Tines v. Brown Shoe Co.*, 290 S.W.2d 200 (Mo.App.1956) denied recovery, reasoning that the activity involved in operating the appliance was intentional, albeit awkward, and the result could not occur "by accident." Recently, courts have addressed whether carpal tunnel syndrome is compensable as an injury by accident or only as an occupational disease. See, e.g., *Peoria County Belwood Nursing Home v. Industrial Comm'n*, 138 Ill.App.3d 880, 93 Ill.Dec. 689, 487 N.E.2d 356 (Ill.App.1985).

Tracing mental injuries to the workplace involves similar problems. Emotional stress is a fact of life, and the stresses resulting in a given neurosis may just as readily be domestic as occupational. There is considerable skepticism among some judges that psychiatrists and psychologists are able to make judgments about causation with the same level of confidence as orthopedists or surgeons. See *Gluck Bros. Inc. v. Pollard*, 221 Tenn. 383, 426 S.W.2d 763 (Tenn.1968) (stringent criticism of a psychiatrist's expert testimony). Recovery for mental injury has been most consistently allowed when the mental injury is associated with a physical trauma. *Casa Bonita Restaurant v. Industrial Commission*, 624 P.2d 1340 (Colo.App.1981) is a typical case of this sort. The claimant fell, injured her knee, and was unable to return to her usual work because she could not stand or walk for more than a few minutes at a time. She developed a neurosis, in large measure from worry about her injury, that made her essentially unemployable; an award of permanent total disability benefits was sustained. Many jurisdictions will award benefits when it is possible to identify a single highly stressful event at work that triggered the mental injury. In *Bailey v. American General Insurance Co.*, 154 Tex. 430, 279 S.W.2d 315 (Tex.1955), recovery was permitted where an employee could no longer go aloft to do his job on scaffolding after watching a fellow employee fall to his death. In each of those two types of cases, there is a fairly obvious way to insure that the work contributed to the mental condition in a special way. Allowing recovery when "generalized stress" at work is allegedly a cause of the mental condition is more troubling to many courts. Some jurisdictions simply deny recovery. *Lockwood v. Independent School District*, 312 N.W.2d 924 (Minn. 1981). Some, like Wisconsin, limit recovery to cases of "unusual" or "extraordinary" stress. In *Swiss Colony, Inc. v. Department of Industry, Labor and Human Relations*, 72 Wis.2d 46, 240 N.W.2d 128 (Wis.1976), the court permitted recovery because the claimant had been working extraordinarily long hours trying to meet a deadline, while being berated and harshly criticized by a bullying supervisor. Not all jurisdictions require proof of extraordinary stress, however, but allow recovery when there is satisfactory objective proof that workplace stress in fact caused the injury, whatever the level of stress. *State of Delaware v. Cephas*, 637 A.2d 20 (Del.1994).

Most statutes reinforce the "by accident" requirement with a provision that compensation is not to be awarded for self-inflicted injuries. Questions then arise about whether compensation is appropriate when the worker intentionally harms himself while suffering from a serious mental condition. Suicide is the most extreme example. It is at best difficult to reconcile the varied outcomes in suicide cases. The strongest case for compensation is one in which the work creates the mental condition that in turn leads to the suicide. See *Food Distributors v.*

Estate of Ball, 24 Va.App. 692, 485 S.E.2d 155
(Va.App.1997).

b. Occupational Diseases

Occupational disease coverage is provided in all
states. Some statutes simply omit the "by accident"
requirement from the compensable injury definition. More commonly, occupational disease is added
as a specific covered impairment.

Three different types of relationship between employment and disease are made conditions of coverage in various statutes. One increasingly rare approach is to cover only diseases listed in a schedule,
in which each category of disease is paired with an
occupation found by the legislature to be related to
the diseases. These schedules, once common, tend
to be written broadly, so that categories of diseases
rather than specific ailments are included. A second
type of statute provides coverage for all those diseases which are attributable to the employment's
"nature," or which can be said to "arise naturally
from" the type of employment in which the claimant has been engaged. These statutes often exclude
the "ordinary diseases of life" from coverage by
explicit language. The third type of statute limits
coverage to those diseases "peculiar to" the type of
employment in which the claimant has worked. See
Mutual Chemical Co. v. Thurston, 222 Md. 86, 158
A.2d 899 (Md.1960) (discussing the difference between the "nature of the occupation" and "peculiar
to the operation" standards). At times, a statute
will blend these approaches.

The underlying theme of each of these statutory types is similar. The legislature wishes to confine workers' compensation disease benefits to those cases where the disease contracted is a recognizable hazard of the work done. All statutes also provide benefits in the case of disease that is the consequence of employment trauma, under the usual "by accident" language. See *McAlister v. Methodist Hospital*, 550 S.W.2d 240 (Tenn.1977).

c. Employment Connection: The "Arising" Requirements

To be compensable under the typical workers' compensation statute, an impairment must result from an injury or disease that "arises out of and in the course of employment." This language, while generally successful in redirecting attention away from notions of fault, has been the source of a substantial number of interpretation problems concerning how close the relationship between employment and injury must be.

Injuries that occur during travel from the employee's home to the employer's premises, and during the return journey at the end of the work, are ordinarily not eligible for benefits, under a doctrine familiarly known as the "going and coming rule." See, e.g., *General Insurance Co. of America v. Workers' Compensation Appeals Board*, 16 Cal.3d 595, 128 Cal.Rptr. 417, 546 P.2d 1361 (Cal.1976). Several justifications can be given for the rule. Employers can often do little to improve the safety of this trip. Allowing recovery would create difficult problems of defining just when the "work commute" portion of the journey has begun, given the tendency to use this trip for other purposes as well, including shopping, visiting public offices, etc.

The rule appears administratively simple. It has not proved so. Four widely recognized exceptions have been developed. In *Cardillo v. Liberty Mutual Ins. Co.*, 330 U.S. 469 (1947), the Court identified at least four situations in which commuting injuries are likely to be covered:

1. The employer provides the means of transport, e.g., a company bus or van that is involved in the injury-producing accident.

2. The commuting employee is one for whom being on the road is a normal part of the work, rather than the exception, e.g., a traveling sales representative injured on the way to the employer's main office to pick up new promotional brochures the injured employee intends to use during an upcoming sales trip.

3. The injured employee is on on-call status and is injured when responding to after-hours needs of the employer.

4. The employee is hurt while performing a special errand on the employer's behalf during the commute, e.g., dropping off a package at the post office.

Commuting is only one example of employee activity that is connected with work but that is arguably outside the course of employment. Initially, some courts would not include within the course of employment activities not directly benefiting the employer, but that would now be an unusual position. Today almost all jurisdictions award benefits for injuries sustained during coffee breaks, smoke breaks, or on-premises lunch breaks. *Dukes v. Rural Metro Corp.*, 346 S.C. 369, 552 S.E.2d 39 (S.C.App.2001). Most provide benefits for injuries that occur during the sort of routine sky-larking sometimes called "horseplay," although a number of jurisdictions seek to distinguish between horseplay that amounts to "abandoning work" and that which does not. *Milligan v. Milo Gordon Chrysler Plymouth Isuzu*, 39 P.3d 164 (Okla.Civ.App.2001) (benefits denied for "popping a wheelie" while doing an employment errand); *McNamara v. Town of Hamden*, 176 Conn. 547, 398 A.2d 1161 (Conn. 1978) (benefits allowed for injury during tale tennis game on work site).

When is home itself a place of work? There have always been cases in which employers have required workers to perform tasks at home, and the hazards of those are clearly work hazards. An employee who cuts himself while repairing the employer's powered saw has clearly suffered a work injury. Less clear are injuries associated with telecommuting, a practice that has grown substantially in recent years. Whether a worker who is assaulted while in her home office has suffered a compensable injury is not an easy issue. If the motivation for the assault is connected with the work, or if the assailant is a co-worker then compensation benefits very likely should be available. If the motivation is clearly personal—an ongoing feud between neighbors, for example—then benefits ought not to be paid. When the assault is a "neutral" one, however, the question is very difficult. See *Wait v. Travelers Indem. Co. of Illinois,* 240 S.W.3d 220 (Tenn. 2007).

Injuries incurred during employer-sponsored recreation activity are compensable, but deciding how much employer sponsorship is required, or whether mere employer acquiescence is sufficient connection, remains troublesome. In *Anderson v. Employers Liability Assur. Corp.,* 498 P.2d 288 (Alaska 1972), benefits were awarded to an employee who participated in an off-duty pole-climbing contest, but the contest was unusual. The workers were in an isolated location, had set up their contest while drinking at an employer-owned bar, and did work in which climbing was a common duty. How common the activity is, and whether it takes place on employment premises are also important factors. See *Gooden v. Coors Technical Ceramic Co.,* 236 S.W.3d 151 (Tenn. 2007).

In many cases an employer has argued that recovery should not be permitted because the employee was hurt as a result of intentional misconduct. Some such injuries are excluded by specific language in virtually all statutes. Deciding whether a fight between co-employees is an act of "misconduct" or is the result of "the accumulated pressures of the environment" and not employment is not easy and must be made on a case-by-case basis. See *Hartford Accident & Indemnity Co. v. Cardillo,* 112

F.2d 11 (D.C.Cir.1940). The same is true of deciding whether a work rule infraction is mere inattention or is a major dereliction taking the wrongdoer out of the course of employment. Some statutes reduce the amount of benefits payable if employee disregard of a safety rule has caused the injury.

Should compensation benefits be paid to those hurt by "natural" forces such as lightning or a windstorm? These are hazards shared by entire communities so that the impairments brought about by them are not in one sense "employment" injuries. However, being employed often means that an injured employee's exposure to a natural hazard was quantitatively or qualitatively different from the exposure experienced by others in the community. If the temperature soars above 100 degrees Fahrenheit, for example, an employee hired to do physical labor out of doors is clearly more likely to be a heat stroke victim than is a law school professor sitting in an air-conditioned office. A windstorm may well do no harm to those working in sturdy buildings, but will cause severe harm to those whose duties are performed in flimsier structures. In *Ingram v. Bradley*, 183 Neb. 692, 163 N.W.2d 875 (Neb.1969), benefits were allowed to employees injured when a windstorm blew over a lightweight ticket booth at an outdoor theater where they worked. An increasing number of states justify compensation on the basis of the "positional risk" doctrine: If an employee is injured because of a hazard associated with the situs where the work places that worker at the time of the accident, then the injury is compensable unless it is the result of a personal hazard. *Homerding v. Industrial Commission*, 327 Ill.App.3d 1050, 262 Ill.Dec. 456, 765 N.E.2d 1064 (Ill.App.2002).

It is not necessary that an injury, to be compensable, occur in the course of employment, only that it "arise" there. If a disgruntled employee plants a bomb in his supervisor's briefcase, and the bomb does not explode until the victim is at home in his study, the injury is nonetheless clearly one that "arose in the course" of the work. The converse is also true. If an employee brings a poisoned sandwich to work, poisoned by her scheming spouse, the fact that the harm manifests itself when the victim eats the sandwich while working at her desk does not make that an employment injury. Some statutes, however, include a provision creating a presumption that if an injury arose in the course of employment it arose out of that employment if the employee is unavailable or mentally unable to testify.

The most perplexing "arise out of" problems are probably those that involve internal body processes. Whether a particular cancer was aggravated by employment-connected trauma is a matter about which medical experts may differ or express only the most tentative opinions. This is particularly true when the impairment allegedly caused by the work has not manifested itself until several years after the workplace events that arguably contributed to it. In a few instances, statutes have been amended to deal with these issues by shifting burdens of proof or by creating "irrebuttable presumptions" of causation. See *Usery v. Turner Elkhorn Mining Co.*, 428 U.S. 1 (1976) (lung disease evidentiary presumption).

d. Scope of Benefits

(i) Benefit Categories

Workers' compensation statutes typically provide that an employer is liable to provide an employee who has suffered an employment injury (or his or her dependents) with benefits in up to four categories:

- medical benefits;
- disability (often referred to as "income replacement") benefits;
- death benefits (to be paid to surviving dependents);
- some part of the costs associated with vocational rehabilitation.

The benefits for disability and death are usually to be paid on a periodic basis, weekly or monthly. A claimant with special needs may apply to have the payments commuted to a lump sum in appropriate situations. An employee who has lost legs might, for example, seek a lump sum on the grounds that this would make it possible to renovate the worker's home so it will be more accessible to a person in a wheelchair.

(ii) Medical Benefits

At one time, the obligation of the employer to provide medical treatment was typically limited either by a maximum dollar figure or by a time limitation. Most such limits have now disappeared. The employer's liability is to provide whatever medical services are required by the nature of the injury or disease involved. This does not mean that all controversy over the scope of liability for medical benefits has been eliminated.

One source of litigation is disagreement between physicians over the proper care or about whether an injured employee has achieved maximum recovery. For example, in *Atlantic & Gulf Stevedores, Inc. v. Neuman*, 440 F.2d 908 (5th Cir.1971), a dispute arose over the need for surgery. The worker's physician recommended an operation for a herniated disc. The employer contested the need for it, and on the basis of expert testimony from the employer's physicians, the tribunal denied the worker's request for this medical procedure. The worker then went ahead on his own to have the operation, which turned out to be the right choice. The employer was held liable for the cost of the surgery even though the employee did not request that treatment again after his initial request was denied.

What are "medical services"? All statutes provide for physician care, any required hospitalization or recovery center care, all needed drugs, appliances, and prosthetic devices. Home nursing service is sometimes called for, and in a few cases reimbursement has been provided to members of an injured employee's family who have stayed home to provide care. See, e.g., *Dresser Minerals v. Hunt*, 262 Ark. 280, 556 S.W.2d 138 (Ark.1977).

The method by which the employer is to provide medical services varies from state to state. In roughly half the states, the injured employee has a free hand to select the treating physician. In about a quarter of the states, the treating physician is selected by the employer, except in cases of emergency. In other states, the employee is to choose the treating physician from a panel selected by the employer or from a panel selected by the state agency administering the statutes; or the choice made by the employer is subject to modification by that agency; or the agency designates the treating physician. More and more states are providing ways of coordinating workers' compensation medical care with the care provided by a managed care organization with which the employees are already enrolled. See, e.g., Ky. Rev. Stat. § 342.352. Given the spread of managed care generally, it seems likely that states that already provide for "employer choice" plans will increasingly allow HMOs and other managed care operations to be acceptable choices.

Most jurisdictions will penalize an employee who refuses appropriate treatment by reducing or cutting off benefit rights. See 33 U.S.C.A. § 907(d)(4). This will not be done, however, if the refusal by the employee is "reasonable" or "justified" or for "good cause," under the varied wordings of these statutes. One justification would be a reasonable fear that the recommended medical procedure might result in more severe impairment or in death. *Holland v. Virginia Bridge & Structures, Inc.*, 10 Va.App. 660, 394 S.E.2d 867 (Va.App.1990).

During the past quarter century, workers' compensation medical costs have increased drastically. In many states employers are lobbying for amendments to control costs. In addition to allowing managed care organizations to provide workers' compensation care, some states have adopted fee schedules, often based on Medicare fee schedules, for what physicians or other health care providers may charge.

(iii) Disability (Income Replacement) Benefits

Workers' compensation disability benefits, payments made to compensate the injured employee for the loss of earning capacity, are commonly made in weekly increments. One measures the size of an award in terms of the number of "benefit weeks" payable. The amount of each weekly payment is a proportion (often two-thirds) of the injured employee's average weekly earnings during the period preceding the injury. Most often the preceding year is used as the computation base, but that will not be done if that year was atypical. Benefits for an employee who is injured in December after changing from a part-time to a full-time work status upon graduating from high school the prior June will be based on the full-time earnings. The weekly benefit figure is typically subject to a maximum limit, a "cap." Only a handful of states still have caps on the total number of weeks of benefits payable for permanent total disability. In some states, the weekly benefit figure will be increased by some percentage because there are persons dependent on the injured employee. Some states enhance the benefit amount if the injury arose from an employer's failure to comply with a safety law, or reduce it if the injured worker failed to comply.

Benefits are provided for four categories of disability in the most traditional statutes:

- temporary total disability;
- temporary partial disability;
- permanent total disability; and
- permanent partial disability.

33 U.S.C.A. § 908.

The term "temporary" is usually held to refer to the period during which the disabling impairment heals. See *Alaska Industrial Board v. Chugach Electric Ass'n*, 356 U.S. 320 (1958). Other statutes use only "total" and "partial" categories and deal with the time dimension in other ways.

Actual wage loss is typically used to determine the amount due for loss of earning capacity in the case of temporary injuries. See, e.g., 33 U.S.C.A. § 908(b), (e). This approach usually achieves reasonable results since the ordinary claimant would be doing the same job he or she has been doing, at the same pay rate, but for the injury. Occasionally, an individual claimant will find this measurement technique unsatisfactory because it fails to take into account a likely promotion, lost because of the injury.

Most statutes provide permanent total disability benefits in two different sorts of cases. First, there are the "presumption" cases, cases in which the legislature has determined that certain impairments are so drastic that they should be considered permanently totally disabling. The Longshore Act, for example, lists "loss of both hands, or both arms, or both feet, or both legs, or both eyes, or of any two thereof," stating that these constitute permanent total disability "in the absence of conclusive proof to the contrary . . ." 33 U.S.C.A. § 908(a). In other cases, these benefits are awarded for the inability in fact to engage on a regular basis in any occupation for which the injured employee is fitted by age, education, and experience and which is available in the relevant area's economy. See *Schnatzmeyer v. Industrial Comm'n*, 77 Ariz. 266, 270 P.2d 794 (Ariz.1954). The ability to do occasional part-time work does not disqualify one. A tougher situation arises when a truly unusual person against all odds manages to become employable again even though severely incapacitated. Should this reduce or cut off the employer's liability? See, e.g., *Taber v. Tole*, 188 Kan. 312, 362 P.2d 17 (Kan.1961), in which the court refused to allow a reduction in benefits payable to a disabled laborer who later became a teacher. (The court's approach may have been modified by the legislature. See the discussion in *Hardman v. City of Iola,* 219 Kan. 840, 549 P.2d 1013 (1976).

Measuring the economic impact of a permanent injury that is less than totally disabling may be very easy or exceedingly difficult. Suppose, for example, that the roof of a TV station caves in during the production of a variety show. An announcer, a left-handed set designer, and a pianist each lose a right index finger. Arguments could be made about the variations in impact on each person. If individualization of recovery were to be permitted in every workers' compensation case, however, the desired administrative simplicity would be lost. Prolonged litigation might become the rule rather than the exception. In order to avoid such time-consuming litigation and its attendant expense, the workers' compensation statutes measure benefits payable on the basis either of actual wage loss or of extent of physical impairment.

Permanent partial disability benefits are most often based on the scope of physical impairment. The procedure has been simplified in most states by the use of a statutory schedule under which certain levels of impairment entitle an injured employee to a specified number of weeks of benefits. Loss of a leg, for example, entitles an employee to 280 weeks of benefits under the Longshoremen's and Harbor Workers' Compensation Act. 33 U.S.C.A. §§ 901– 950 (1988). If one does not lose the limb, but loses only a portion of its function, a proportionate benefit is payable. Under the LHWCA, an employee who suffers the loss of 40 percent of the use of a leg would be entitled to 40 percent of 280 weeks of benefits; i.e., 112 weeks. See *Potomac Electric Power Co. v. Director, Office of Workers' Compensation Programs*, 449 U.S. 268 (1980).

To attempt to construct a schedule that includes all the possible impairment combinations would be a daunting challenge. Most statutes which base permanent partial disability benefits on a schedule of physical impairment list some twenty or thirty impairments, and then add a special provision that deals with the non-listed impairments. These are known as "non-schedule injury" provisions. These sometimes create an open-ended potential liability highly desirable from the injured employee's perspective but undesirable for the liable employer.

One fairly common type of non-schedule injury provision calls for the administering agency or court to determine the seriousness of the impairment by using the *AMA Guides to the Evaluation of Permanent Impairment*, developed by various panels of the American Medical Association. These guides, developed over a long period and periodically revised, attempt to analyze the importance of particular body parts relative to total body function, so that in the case of a combination of impairments not found in a statutory schedule it is possible to combine the impairment ratings for each affected part of the body to reach a total figure. Some states have found the use of these guides to be sufficiently satisfactory that they have almost eliminated the formal schedule as such, and instead rely nearly exclusively on evaluation under the *AMA Guides*. While it is clear that the use of these guides has improved the consistency of impairment evaluation, it is also clear that they have limitations and must be used with caution. One example to which critics of the *Guides* often point is contact dermatitis. A petroleum refinery worker who has become sensitive to the chemical fumes released in the refining process after working in the industry for many years may well suffer a major economic loss as a result, since it will be impossible for that worker to be employed in the occupation for which he or she is best fitted by training and experience. From a medical standpoint, however, the impairment is only slight, so that the range provided by the *AMA Guides* for this dermatitis is 0–5%, and in the hypothetical just given, in which the individual is likely to be totally functional so long as not near a refinery the most likely impairment rating is 0. The courts, recognizing that "impairment" is not the same as "disability," have usually been able to find a way to evaluate the loss of earning capacity that has been suffered. See, e.g., *Wagner v. Industrial Comm'n*, 273 Wis. 553, 80 N.W.2d 456 (Wis.1957); *Dayron Corp. v. Morehead*, 509 So.2d 930 (Fla. 1987). The usefulness of the *AMA Guides* in psychiatric cases and in evaluating the seriousness of some respiratory conditions is also a matter of controversy.

Entitlement to one or more categories of disability benefits can be lost, under many statutes, by refusing a reasonable offer of employment. Some statutes make benefit loss almost routine if one refuses an offer from one's own former employer. See *Roe v. Yarmouth Lumber, Inc.*, 785 A.2d 334 (Me.2001).

(iv) Death Benefits

Death benefits are provided by all statutes for cases in which the employee's death is the result of employment injury. The employer's liability is stated in terms of weekly benefits, as in the case of disability benefits. The entitlement is based on relationship to the deceased employee and in some instances on proof of dependency. The statutes create priority rankings so that the deceased employee's spouse and minor children living with him or her at the time of death are given preference. In *Weber v. Aetna Casualty & Surety Co.*, 406 U.S. 164 (1972), unacknowledged illegitimate children were held entitled to the same priority as legitimate children.

An employer's maximum weekly liability for death benefits is usually two-thirds of the deceased employee's average weekly wage. If the claims of spouse and children exhaust that sum, no other claimants will be eligible for benefits. Occasional problems occur with establishing paternity or with proving the existence of a marriage or of dependency.

(v) Rehabilitation Benefits

The majority of workers' compensation statutes require the employer to assist in vocational rehabilitation. The scope of liability varies. In half the states, an employer may be required to pay a portion of the rehabilitation training costs as well as disability benefits during the training period. In other states, the obligation is limited to continuing to pay disability benefits during the training period. Rehabilitation units in some state workers' compensation agencies are staffed to provide training di-

rectly. Most state agencies, however, refer rehabilitation candidates to some other agency, often the
agency administering the joint federal-state program described above.

*(vi) Successive Injuries: Second Injury Funds and
Apportionment*

A familiar workers' compensation principle is
that "the employer takes the employee as he finds
him." This principle—sometimes referred to as the
"aggravation rule"—works easily enough in the
case of relatively minor pre-existing disabilities. A
worker who has lost ten to twenty percent of the
flexion in a knee from a high school sports injury,
for example, is not likely to be hampered in performing the vast majority of jobs, and an employer
is likely to be unaware of the condition. Indeed, the
employee may well be unaware that anything is
wrong with the knee. When the worker suffers a leg
injury at work and one result is an aggravation of
the old knee injury so that now the employee has
lost fifty percent of the flexion in that knee, an
award of benefits on the basis of a fifty percent
impairment of knee function is called for in most
states.

When the pre-existing disability is more serious,
however, the impact of using the aggravation rule
can also be more serious. Suppose, to pursue the
example just used, that the employee with sharply
limited knee function goes into the job market to
seek work following the workplace injury. An employer subject to the Longshore and Harbor Workers' Compensation Act would recognize that its risk

of becoming liable to this previously injured individual for the 280 weeks of benefits for loss of use of a leg is greater than that risk would be in the case of an unimpaired job applicant. One consequence would be to prefer the job applicant with no pre-existing disability. Recognizing this, many legislatures established "second injury" funds. If an individual who already suffers from a substantial disability sustains another disabling injury in the course of employment, then the employer at the time of the second injury is liable to pay disability benefits only for the proportion of disability caused by the latter injury. The second injury fund will pay additional benefits to compensate the employee for the additional impact of, to take an extreme case, losing a second eye. See *Lawson v. Suwannee Fruit & Steamship Co.*, 336 U.S. 198 (1949). These funds are most often created by a tax on employers or on workers' compensation insurance premiums. These statutes often operate only with respect to persons whose pre-existing impairment is relatively severe, such as loss of a limb. The administration of second injury funds can become costly, since these funds are named as potential defendants in a large number of cases. As a result, some have been done away with; New York is the best known example.

A person whose prior impairment was significant but not so significant that the second injury fund is involved is dealt with in a variety of ways. One type of statute, for example, requires the employer at the time of a second injury to pay only for the portion of impairment attributable to that second injury.

These "apportionment" statutes are often applied only if the pre-existing condition could be regarded as disabling, in the sense of limiting ability to work. Sometimes this approach may be limited to cases in which compensation benefits were paid, so that the earlier payment acts as a "credit" against the later award. A statute may call for one approach in the case of traumatic injury and for another in the case of occupational disease. In Arkansas, for example, employer responsibility for an impairment is reduced in the case of occupational disease without regard to whether the non-occupational disease impairment was disabling or not, but in the case of traumatic injuries such a reduction in employer responsibility is called for only when "the prior impairment was independently causing disability prior to the second injury and continued to do so after that injury * * *." *Jenkins v. Halstead Industries*, 17 Ark.App. 197, 706 S.W.2d 191 (Ark.App. 1986).

(vii) Subrogation

An injured employee often has an enforceable claim against a person other than the employer for the same injury that is compensable under a workers' compensation statute. This has resulted in litigation on several related issues. First, there is the question of who other than the immediate employer is entitled to the "exclusive remedy" provision available to the injured employee. Most statutes give an employer's insurer the protection of the exclusive remedy provision. This is done so that an insurer whose representative conducts a negligent safety inspection of the employer's premises cannot be sued for damages as contrasted with workers' compensation benefits arising out of an unsafe condition that the representative overlooked. Fellow employees are immune to personal injury actions for workplace negligence in many states. As mentioned before, many statutes extend liability to pay workers' compensation beyond the immediate employer to a firm that has hired the immediate employer to perform some task. These provisions have the corollary effect of entitling the liable firm to the benefit of the exclusive remedy defense. These provisions are particularly important in the construction industry, in which many small firms will be hired as sub-contractors for a project by a much larger general contractor (or a property owner acting as its own general contractor). Very small firms are somewhat less likely to maintain appropriate workers' compensation insurance, and therefore making the general contractor liable is important in maintaining the desired broad sweep of workers' compensation coverage. A problem arises in interpreting these "statutory employer" provisions: If a general contractor has purchased insurance coverage for the employees of its subcontractors is that general contractor entitled to the exclusive remedy defense even if the immediate employer (the subcontractor) has also provided workers' compensation coverage (or in fact has paid compensation benefits)? The equities are evenly balanced in this situation: The general contractor has acted responsibly in providing compensation protection, but it seems harsh to require an injured worker to give up his or her claim for negligence against the general contractor when in fact that worker has not had the benefit of any payments from that general contractor or its insurer. In a well-known case involving the construction of the Washington, D.C., subway system, the Supreme Court adopted the minority position that extends the exclusive remedy defense to any statutory employer that has provided workers' compensation protection to subcontractor workers, even if it has not in fact paid benefits, but soon after the decision was announced, the Congress amended the Longshore & Harbor Workers' Compensation Act to overturn that ruling. Now the LHWCA employs the majority rule: Statutory employers have the benefit of the exclusive remedy defense only when in fact liable for benefits; potential liability if a subcontractor is uninsured or insolvent is not enough. *Washington Metropolitan Area Transit Authority v. Johnson*, 467 U.S. 925 (1984); 33 U.S.C.A. §§ 904(a), 905(a).

Second, if the injured employee seeks to collect damages from the non-employer wrongdoer, does the employee "elect" not to be entitled to compensation benefits? At one time, the so-called "election of remedies" approach had some support, but it has now largely disappeared.

Third, if the employee has been paid compensation benefits, may the employer insist that the employee pursue a claim against the non-employer? Generally the answer is yes. In many states, the employee is given a time period to decide what to do. If the employee fails to file suit, the employer may do so in the employee's name.

Fourth, once personal injury litigation has been started against the non-employer, how much control over it can be exercised by the employee, how much by the employer? The answer is often not spelled out in the workers' compensation statute. In practice, the party who has initiated the litigation will control most aspects, but is required to give due regard to the other's interest.

Fifth, if the non-employer is held liable, and is required to pay damages, to what extent is the employer entitled to recoup some of what the employer has paid or is prospectively liable to pay? Generally, the employer is given a claim against the proceeds recovered from the non-employer. This entitlement is referred to as a subrogation claim. The statutes differ on how the employer and employee share in the litigation expenses that resulted in the damage award. Probably the best approach is to share them in the proportions of net recovery.

Finally, there is the question of what should be done when a non-employer who has been required to pay damages seeks to recoup all or part of those damages from the employer because the employer was also at fault. Employers argue that to require them to contribute to the damage payment undercuts the exclusive remedy defense, which is the *quid pro quo* the employer receives in exchange for being liable where there has been no fault. The trend seems to be to allow the non-employer to recover from an at-fault employer but only up to the amount of the employer's liability for compensation benefits. See *Lambertson v. Cincinnati Welding Corp.*, 312 Minn. 114, 257 N.W.2d 679 (Minn.1977).

e. Administration and Procedure

The vast majority of statutes establish administrative agencies to operate their workers' compensation systems. The determinations made by these agencies on issues such as the existence of employer liability and the scope of impairment are reviewable in the courts, usually with a presumption of correctness as to findings of fact. One recurring problem has been how to apply that presumption of correctness when the issue involved is of the type sometimes referred to as a matter of "ultimate" rather than "evidentiary" fact, such as whether an individual is an employee or an independent contractor. Most states have attempted to keep the administration as simple as possible and to reduce the need for claimants and employers to retain lawyers. However, enough disputed cases occur to require the time of a substantial number of attorneys. Most statutes provide for agency or court review of the reasonableness of attorney fees.

Each injured employee is responsible for informing the employer that an industrial injury or disease has occurred. Failure to do so will ordinarily cut off or reduce the employee's benefit rights, particularly if the lateness in notice prejudices the employer in some way. Not giving notice, however, is excused in many circumstances. Employers who are already aware of an injury, for example, usually cannot defend because of lack of notice. *Raines v. Shelby Williams Industries, Inc.*, 814 S.W.2d 346 (Tenn. 1991). Failing to give notice is also often excused when it is the result of mental or physical disability. *Kahn v. State of Minnesota*, 289 N.W.2d 737 (Minn. 1980).

Once an employer is aware of a disabling injury or disease, and of the possibility that this is work connected, then the employer is required by the typical statute to make some sort of response. Typically, the employer must notify the state workers' compensation agency both of the injury and whether the employer intends to provide benefits. At this point, if the worker has not already done so, he or she should file a formal claim for benefits.

If there is a dispute with respect to the existence or the scope of liability, the controversy will be investigated by the agency and a hearing will be conducted. The administrative law officer who conducts the hearing will make recommended findings of fact and conclusions of law. If not contested, these ordinarily will become final. If contested, there will be one or more levels of appeal available within the agency. If the ultimate decision maker at the agency, most often a multi-member commission, rules adversely to a party, that party may then seek court review. An obvious problem exists with respect to what an injured worker is to do if the employer denies workers' compensation liability, and the employee needs prompt medical attention that goes beyond whatever is provided by the worker's usual medical insurance. The claimant in *Arnstrom v. Excalibur Cable Communication, Ltd.*, 142 Md.App. 552, 790 A.2d 764 (Md.App.2002), for example, sought vocational rehabilitation while his claim was being contested, and did not notify either the employer or the agency that he was doing so. The usual pattern for an injured worker actually receiving benefits would be to obtain approval before getting that sort of service. The employee was awarded reimbursement, but only after making a showing of need for the service, and an opportunity for the employer to contest that showing.

Statutes of limitations requiring an injured employee to assert a claim within a certain time period cause a number of problems for injuries that do not manifest themselves quickly. See *Romero v. American Furniture Co.*, 86 N.M. 661, 526 P.2d 803 (N.M.App.1974). This is primarily true in disease cases, but some accidental injuries, such as back strains, may at first seem totally insignificant but slowly worsen. The tendency of most courts has been to rule that the statute of limitations does not begin to run until a reasonable person in the claimant's position would be aware of the injury and its connection to work, and perhaps not until the employee is also reasonably aware of the condition's disabling nature. Some statutes explicitly call for that result. See 33 U.S.C.A. § 913(b); *Paducah Marine Ways v. Thompson*, 82 F.3d 130 (6th Cir.1996).

Cases involving permanent disability may typically be reopened even after benefits have been paid under a prior agency or court ruling for several years. The most usual justification for requesting reopening is a marked change of circumstance. This may arise out of an unanticipated deterioration or improvement of physical condition or mistake of fact. Under some statutes, a change in economic circumstances, such as acquiring new skills, has been held to justify reopening even in the absence of a physical change. See, e.g., *Metropolitan Stevedore Co. v. Rambo*, 515 U.S. 291 (1995).

f. Funding

Half a dozen states operate workers' compensation insurance funds and exclude private insurers from the market. Another dozen operate state funds that compete with private insurers. The great majority of states provide that employers may self-insure; the ways in which the self-insurance plan can be made effective vary.

All but the smallest employers pay insurance premiums that are adjusted by means of experience rating. The employer on whose behalf an insurer has paid out very large sums in benefits can end up paying several times as much for the same coverage as an employer with a record of little liability. This encourages safety programs. It may at times also encourage combativeness in denying liability in close cases. The base premium is ordinarily expressed in terms of a percentage of payroll, and varies by occupation, so that the rate for clerical workers might be 91 cents per hundred payroll dollars while that for underground miners would be six dollars per hundred dollars of payroll.

4. The Social Security Disability Insurance Program

a.   Brief History

As early as 1938, some reformers began to urge adding benefits for the permanently and totally disabled to the new Social Security program. Nothing was in fact done, however, until the 1950s. Monthly benefits for severely disabled persons aged 50 to 65 were established in 1956; the limit to this age bracket was dropped in 1960. The definition of disability has been amended several times, until it reached roughly its present form in 1967. Some of the changes probably reflected concerns about financing the program. A separate trust fund was established for the program early on, supported by a flat-rate payroll tax. Four successive years during which the outgo from the fund exceeded income occurred in the early 1960s, and the 1967 amendments resulted in fewer persons being eligible for benefits. The current Disability Insurance tax rate is 9/10 of one per cent each for employer and employee (1.8% for self-employed persons). In December 2007, more than seven million person received disability benefit payments; the average payment was just over $1,000 a month.

b.   "Disability" Defined

The general definition of disability used to determine eligibility for benefits under the disability portions of the Old Age, Survivors and Disability Insurance Benefits program states:

(1) The term "disability" means—

(A) inability to engage in any substantial gainful activity by reason of any medically determinable physical or mental impairment which can be expected to result in death or which has lasted or can be expected to last for a continuous period of not less than 12 months; or

(B) [a special provision for blind persons is omitted]

(2) For purposes of paragraph 1(A)

(A) an individual * * * shall be determined to be under a disability only if his physical or mental impairment or impairments are of such severity that he is not only unable to do his previous work but cannot, considering his age, education, and work experience, engage in any other kind of substantial gainful work which exists in the national economy, regardless of whether such work exists in the immediate area in which he lives, or whether a specific job vacancy exists for him, or whether he would be hired if he applied for work. For purposes of the preceding sentence (with respect to any individual) "work which exists in the national economy" means work which exists in significant numbers either in the region where such individual lives or in several regions of the country.

* * *

(3) For purposes of this subsection a "physical or mental impairment" is an impairment that results from anatomical, physiological, or psycho-

logical abnormalities which are demonstrable by medically acceptable clinical and laboratory diagnostic techniques. 42 U.S.C.A. § 423.

This language makes it clear that the Congress intended to limit benefits under this program to truly severe cases. Equally clear is the desire for simplicity and uniformity in making eligibility determinations, desires reflected in the use of as much objective measurement as possible. Subparagraph 3 emphasizes the use of objective criteria for deciding what impairment is present. Subparagraph 2(a) seeks to do the same with regard to what jobs are available in the economy. There are, nonetheless, substantial areas of potential conflict with respect to whether an impairment exists, how serious it is, and with respect to whether there are jobs in the economy appropriate for a person of the claimant's age with that impairment. See, e.g., *Broz v. Heckler*, 721 F.2d 1297 (11th Cir.1983) (on remand).

This system's coverage is thus vastly different from that of workers' compensation schemes. Those statutes provide benefits for a wide range of impairments, but only if the impairment is rooted in the claimant's work. The Social Security Disability Insurance program is limited to the most severe disability cases, but provides benefits without regard to whether the impairment stems from an employment injury or an injury suffered at home or in personal recreation.

The persons protected are those who have been paying social security taxes on their wages or self-employment earnings for a requisite number of calendar quarters during the years immediately preceding disability. Each quarter for which sufficient earnings taxes have been paid is commonly referred to as "quarter of coverage." A separate welfare program, Supplemental Security Income, exists for persons who have not worked long enough or with sufficient regularity to be eligible for OASDI disability benefits. See 42 U.S.C.A. §§ 1381–1383c. The benefit levels in that program are generally lower. Eligibility depends on being disabled under a definition essentially the same as that for Social Security Disability Insurance and on having income and assets that fall below a stated level.

Social Security Disability Insurance also provides benefits in some cases to disabled widows, widowers, divorced spouses, and children of covered employees.

An attempt has been made to integrate the disability benefits provisions of OASDI with other components of the federal social security, compensation, and welfare systems. One illustration is the "workers' compensation offset" under which the amount of the OASDI disability benefit payable is reduced because of amounts paid to the employee as workers' compensation benefits for the same time period. See *Richardson v. Belcher*, 404 U.S. 78 (1971). Other provisions of the social security statute provide for coordinating payments due to a single individual under more than one component of OASDI.

c. Benefits

Three types of benefits are available to persons who meet the Disability Insurance eligibility requirements:

- monthly cash payments,
- vocational rehabilitation services, and
- medical insurance.

The cash payments begin, provided proper application has been made, with the sixth month of disability. A constitutional challenge to the five-month waiting period was rejected by the Ninth Circuit in 1984, and the Supreme Court declined to hear the case. *Price v. Heckler*, 733 F.2d 699 (9th Cir.1984), cert. denied, 469 U.S. 1224 (1985). The amount of the monthly payment depends upon: (a) the amount of earnings on which the employee has paid social security taxes and (b) the number of eligible dependents. The "maximum family award" usually equals roughly the amount to which the disabled employee is entitled to as an individual plus allowances for two dependents.

Vocational rehabilitation services are provided through the joint federal-state program discussed in the final sub-section of this chapter. 42 U.S.C.A. § 422. Persons receiving cash payments for disability may continue to receive them for a limited time after they begin to work at or near the end of a program of vocational rehabilitation. This period is referred to as the "trial work period" and may be as long as nine months. Id. § 422(C).

Medical services are made available through the Medicare program in which a recipient of OASDI disability benefits begins to participate 25 months after the onset of disability. Id. §§ 1395–1395. This may seem a long waiting period and no doubt it is in some instances unduly long. It should be remembered, however, that persons receiving these benefits are usually persons who have been working steadily, and who are entitled to medical treatment under workers' compensation or to hospitalization and medical benefits provided under a group insurance plan. If a person becomes disabled while unemployed or uninsured, medical assistance under "Medicaid" may be available. Medicaid is another state-federal program, under which vendors of medical services are reimbursed by government for treatment provided to persons who meet certain maximum income and asset standards. 42 U.S.C.A. §§ 1396–1396i.

Medicare is a government-sponsored program of hospital and medical insurance. A beneficiary is entitled to substantial but not unlimited periods of inpatient hospitalization, nursing facility care, and to payment of or reimbursement of physician and laboratory fees, as well as other ancillary treatment costs. Each person insured under Medicare is required to pay a minimum amount, the "deductible," of these expenses personally each year before becoming eligible for reimbursement, and to pay some percentage of certain other types of medical bills, the "coinsurance" feature. Many beneficiaries take out private insurance as a means of meeting the deductible and coinsurance obligations. In some markets, a Medicare Plus Choice program may be available as an alternative to traditional fee-for-service insurance. A person who has been enrolled in Medicare because he or she receives Social Security Disability Insurance benefits may be allowed to continue in the Medicare program even after the disability ends, for as long as eight years and six months after returning to work. This benefit has been available only since October 2000, and administrative details are still being worked out.

d. Administration and Procedure

A claimant enters the program by submitting an application for benefits to a district or branch office of the Social Security Administration. This is then sent to an agency of state government with which the federal Social Security Administration has a contract for the purpose of determining whether an eligible disability exists.

The applicant must submit all medical evidence that is relevant to the application. If the medical data submitted by the applicant fails to meet the needs of the evaluating agency, the applicant may be required to submit to a consultative examination by a physical designated by the agency. The applicant will also be asked to supply information concerning education and employment experience.

The disability determination by the agency is done in a five-step process. 20 C.F.R. § 404.1520. While ordinary concepts of burden of proof do not easily fit into this determination procedure, reviewing courts sometimes say that the claimant bears the burden of proof in steps 1 through 4, the Secretary in step 5. *Tackett v. Apfel*, 180 F.3d 1094 (9th Cir.1999).

The evaluation begins with a non-medical step, determining whether the applicant is currently engaged in substantial gainful activity. If he or she is so engaged, the application is disallowed.

Next, the agency determines whether the impairment is "severe," i.e., whether it significantly affects "basic work activity."

If the impairment is found to be severe, the next determination step is comparing the data submitted by and about the claimant with a set of guidelines known as the Listings of Impairments. See 20 C.F.R. part 404, Appendix I. If a claimant is found to suffer from a condition which: (a) is included in the Listings of Impairments and (b) has the characteristics of severity required by the relevant Listing or which is the medical equivalent of that condition then the case is said to "meet" or "equal" a Listing, and the payment of benefits will be approved.

If the condition is less severe, so that it does not meet or equal a Listing, the next step is to determine whether the impairment prevents doing one's former work. If not, the application will be denied.

If the agency finds that the applicant can no longer do his or her former work, then the final step is reached, determining whether the impairment will prevent the applicant from doing other work present in the economy.

At this stage, the evaluator uses a series of guidelines that attempt to combine consideration of the applicant's residual functional capacity with the factors of age, education, and experience. The guidelines are known as "the Grids" because of their chart-like appearance. There are three principal charts. One is for persons whose residual physical capacity would enable them to perform only "sedentary" work on a sustained basis, another for those able to do "light" work and a third for those able to do "medium" work. 20 C.F.R. part 404, Appendix 2.

If the end result of the evaluation is to deny benefits to a claimant, the claimant may request a reconsideration. If the decision on reconsideration is still adverse, the claimant may ask for a hearing in which to present further evidence, including personal testimony. If the recommendation of the administrative law judge conducting the hearing is adverse, a claimant may appeal to the Social Security Administration's Appeals Council. A claimant who has exhausted all internal appeals available through the Social Security Administration may then file a civil action in federal district court seeking review of the agency's adverse determination. In *Sims v. Apfel*, 530 U.S. 103 (2000), the Supreme Court held that a claimant may raise issues during these court proceedings even though they had not been addressed in the request to the Appeals Council. The majority found that neither the statute nor the regulations called for using "issue exhaustion" principles.

A person who is found eligible for benefits will continue to receive those benefits until he or she:

- becomes eligible for regular old-age pension benefits under Social Security;
- is found to be no longer unable to engage in substantial gainful activity; or
- dies.

20 C.F.R. § 404.1587.

State disability determination agencies are required to conduct "periodic reviews" of the cases of those receiving these benefits, to determine whether the individuals are still disabled within the meaning of the statute. The requirement was first enacted in 1980 and resulted in such an aggressive removal of beneficiaries from the role that it was scaled back somewhat in 1982.

5. Vocational Rehabilitation

a. General Structure of the Traditional Federal– State Program

The present federal-state program dates back to the Vocational Rehabilitation Act of 1973. 29 U.S.C.A. §§ 701–796i. Under this program, each state government prepares a three-year plan for providing vocational rehabilitation benefits pursuant to the Secretary of Education's guidelines. Id. § 721. If the state plan meets the requirements of the federal guidelines, then the federal government will provide 80 percent of the cost of operating it. The administration of each state plan is reviewed periodically by the Rehabilitation Services Administration, a division of the Department of Education, to ensure that these programs are meeting the federal requirements, and that each state is conforming to the plan it originally submitted. Id. §§ 713, 721(d).

b. Eligibility

The test to determine eligibility for vocational rehabilitation services involves two questions:

(1) Does the applicant for services have "a physical or mental disability which for that individual constitutes or results in a substantial handicap to employment?"

(2) Can the individual "reasonably be expected to benefit in terms of employability from vocational rehabilitation services * * *?"

29 U.S.C.A. § 706(b).

If the answers to both questions are affirmative, then the individual is eligible.

The program is not limited to persons who have been injured in the course of employment, nor to persons who are eligible for disability benefits under the Social Security Act. Many individuals first enter the vocational rehabilitation program by referral from those sources. Persons who enter as the result of a referral have an added incentive to pursue vocational rehabilitation, since a refusal to accept these services may result in the termination of all or part of the benefits of those other programs. See, e.g., 42 U.S.C.A. § 422(b).

c. Services

Each state plan is required to provide for a variety of individual and group services. The individual services that must be provided for a plan to qualify for federal financial support include:

- Evaluation and diagnosis;
- Counseling, guidance, and placement assistance;
- Vocational and training services, including books and material and if not provided through some other program, medical services;
- Maintenance;
- Interpreter service for the deaf;
- Reader service for the blind;
- Necessary occupational licenses, tools, and equipment;
- Appropriate technological devices; and
- Transportation support.

29 U.S.C.A. § 723.

Group services that may be included are construction of public or nonprofit vocational rehabilitation facilities and special services to small businesses operated by severely handicapped persons. Each plan must also provide for "recruitment and training services for handicapped individuals to provide them with new opportunities in the fields of rehabilitation, health, welfare, public safety, and law enforcement, and other appropriate service employment." Id. § 723(a)(7). Some of these benefits, particularly medical services and income maintenance, will often come from workers' compensation or Social Security Disability Insurance. There are also related programs with the object of integrating handicapped persons more fully into the general community.

A state may provide these services directly through its own personnel, or by contract with private agencies or individuals. Id. §§ 721(a)(12), 721(a)(21). Medical services needed only occasionally are likely to be obtained by contract. Routine testing is more likely to be done by an agency's own workforce. The pattern varies substantially from state to state.

No two disabled individuals will have exactly the same needs and abilities. In recognition of that, the Congress has required since 1973 that each person who is eligible for these services is to participate with his or her own counselor in the joint development of an individualized written rehabilitation program for that person, the Individual Plan for Employment. Id. § 722. This written program must "set forth the terms and conditions, as well as the rights and remedies, under which goods and services will be provided to the individual * * *." The individual program must be reviewed annually.

d. *Administration and Finance*

The federal government's role in this program is to develop guidelines for providing effective programs; to approve these programs when submitted by the individual states; to monitor the performance of each state program; and to provide financing. The funds come from general revenues, not from payroll taxes, except in some cases involving persons receiving Social Security benefits. The federal government also sponsors research programs, demonstration projects, and programs involving rehabilitation efforts by private industry.

There are related federal activities. For example, the affirmative action program under which businesses awarded contracts by the federal government are required to make special efforts to identify and use the services of handicapped persons. Id. § 793. The National Council on the Handicapped, an advisory agency [Id. §§ 780–85] and the Architectural and Transportation Barriers Compliance Board [Id. § 792] also participate in related activities.

State governments develop programs of vocational rehabilitation under the guidelines described above and operate them. The states are required to include as part of their planning and review process consultation with individuals and groups concerned with rehabilitation, including providers of services and individuals who have been the recipients of these services. Id. § 721(a)(18).

e. *Individual Case Procedures*

A person who wishes to receive vocational rehabilitation services will apply to the state agency where he or she lives. (Many are referred to an agency by physicians or family members.) The first step the agency will take is to gather information enough to determine whether the individual is eligible for services, through a diagnostic study. All persons receiving disability benefits under the Social Security Disability Insurance program are automatically eligible. Once a worker is found eligible, a counselor and the worker will develop an Individual Plan for Employment that will include such items as a skills assessment, a program for training, a job search plan, and the like. Most of this is likely to be free to the applicant, but if the applicant's income exceeds a threshold amount, he or she may have to pay some portion of the cost of the training. Once an individual has found a job and held it for 90 days, the agency closes the file on that case, although an individual may re-apply if his or her circumstances change.

If the agency decides that the individual does not suffer from a disability substantially affecting employability, the applicant is entitled to an administrative review and determination, and, if still not satisfied, to a hearing. 34 C.F.R. § 361.48.

If the diagnostic study finding is that the individual suffers from a disability, but is ineligible because that individual cannot benefit from vocational rehabilitation services, then not only is that person entitled to a review of that determination, but also is entitled to have his or her case reconsidered automatically twelve months later. If an agency determines on the basis of its initial diagnostic study that an individual suffers from a disability that is a substantial handicap to employment but is unable to tell whether the individual would profit from vocational training, then a program of extended evaluation may be undertaken for up to 18 months. Whenever a person is found ineligible, for whatever cause, the state agency is to refer that person to other agencies that may be able to provide appropriate assistance and counseling.

Once a person has been accepted for services, the pivotal determinations are those involved in structuring the individual written program. This must be redone on an annual basis if the person remains a client of the agency. Id. § 361.40(c). An affected individual must be given a chance to participate in the decision. Id. § 361.40(d). Both types of decision are subject to a request for administrative review and a hearing. Appeals involving the individual written program must receive the personal attention of the director of the state agency. Id. § 361.48(b)(1).

Persons who are dissatisfied with the services they are receiving at the state level may, after exhausting all avenues of administrative review at the state level, request federal government review.

Are these determinations subject to judicial review? The federal statute does not provide for direct court review at the individual's instance. Few persons have filed civil actions seeking to persuade a court to overturn an individual adverse determination. See *Schornstein v. New Jersey Div'n of Vocational Rehabilitation Services*, 519 F.Supp. 773 (D.N.J.1981), aff'd 688 F.2d 824 (3d Cir.1982) (invalidating a regulation denying interpreter services to college students). In these few instances, claimants have achieved occasional success, but because of costs and delays it is unlikely that many persons who have been denied services will pursue this remedy.

Organizations of handicapped persons are more likely plaintiffs, in class actions challenging the structure or administration of a state plan. In *Scott v. Parham*, 422 F.Supp. 111 (N.D.Ga.1976), plaintiffs succeeded in overturning a blanket rule denying certain benefits to persons living at home. Litigation has been an effective remedy in a number of cases against employers who have violated the requirement in their federal contracts that they not discriminate against the handicapped in hiring and other employment decisions. See, e.g., *Pushkin v. Regents of University of Colorado*, 504 F.Supp. 1292 (D.Colo.1981), aff'd 658 F.2d 1372 (10th Cir.1981). Litigation is now more likely under the Americans with Disabilities Act, 42 U.S.C.A. §§ 12101–12213, enacted in 1990.

6. Ticket to Work Program

In 1999, after long wrangling over how to pay for the measure, Congress passed the Ticket to Work and Work Incentives Improvement Act of 1999, 113 Stat. 1860 (1999). President Clinton, who had backed the legislation, signed it into law on December 17 of that year. Much of the law was aimed at making a return to work more appealing to persons receiving benefits under the Social Security Disability Insurance Program or the somewhat similar Supplemental Security Income program. Allowing persons who returned to work to retain Medicare coverage for a substantially longer period was one step. Another was to institute the "ticket to work" program. A person who is receiving either SSI or Disability Insurance benefits is eligible to take the ticket to any approved employment network or vocational rehabilitation agency in order to receive training, job referrals, and other services. Also, a person who is "using a ticket" and gets work will be able to postpone medical disability reviews in many instances.

Will the program lead to more widespread use of private rehabilitation service providers? Will persons with similar disabilities tend to use their tickets to obtain services from employment networks geared specifically for those disabilities? To what extent will the work of state agencies operating under the Vocational Rehabilitation Act of 1973 be affected? It is still too early to speculate very much about these issues. The first tickets were issued in the spring of 2002 in 13 states. Nationwide coverage came slowly. Early difficulties in attracting service providers led to significant program changes in 2008. Whether the program results ultimately in major changes, or only in the extension of medical benefits for a range of beneficiaries, will take a number of years more to tell.

CHAPTER 6

WAGE AND HOUR REGULATION
A. INTRODUCTION

This and the following chapter deal with what
employees receive in exchange for their labor. The
"total compensation" package includes several
parts:

- *Wages or salaries.* These are regulated by federal and state minimum wage laws and at
  times by "prevailing wage" requirements that
  apply to government contractors.

- *Mandated benefits.* Several federal and state
  statutes require employers to provide a number
  of non wage benefits. These include workers
  compensation coverage, unemployment insurance, social security contributions, the Family
  and Medical Leave Act, and similar laws. Many
  of these programs do not apply to small employers, or in the public sector.

- *Contract benefits.* Virtually all larger employers,
  most medium size companies, and many small
  firms also provide one or more "fringe benefits" either as the result of collective or individual bargaining, or as a means of attracting a
  good workforce. Post retirement income plans
  and health benefits are the most common, but

there are many others as well: vacations, training programs, bereavement or personal leave, discounts on goods made or sold by the employer, parking, and so on. Many of these are regulated at least in part by ERISA.

Since colonial times, the direct regulation of wages and hours by governmental authorities has existed in America. The Massachusetts General Court placed a wage cap on the charges of carpenters, bricklayers, thatchers, and other craft workers, and under threat of a heavy fine, prohibited them to charge, or anyone to pay more. Virginia did much the same. The shortage of skilled workers in the colonies had resulted in high wages, with colonial crafts workers earning up to 100 percent above what their peers in England received for the same work.

Until the 1930s' Great Depression, state legislatures were more active than the federal government in regulating working conditions. They were at times frustrated in this by decisions holding these regulations unconstitutional as limits on the "freedom of contract." The decision in *Lochner v. New York*, 198 U.S. 45 (1905), striking down a law limiting bakery workers to 10 hours of work a day is a well known example. The Court also struck down a series of minimum wage laws, generally laws applicable to women and young workers only. *Adkins v. Children's Hospital*, 261 U.S. 525 (1923); *Murphy v. Sardell*, 269 U.S. 530 (1925); *Donham v. West–Nelson Mfg. Co.*, 273 U.S. 657 (1927). These decisions were finally overruled in the 1930s. *West*

Coast Hotel Co. v. Parrish, 300 U.S. 379 (1937). In the meantime, the widespread unemployment of the time cast a new perspective on wage and hour laws. Minimum wage regulation was perceived as necessary for health, efficiency, and general well being of workers and hour regulation as an important way to spread a scarce commodity: the opportunity to work. After several unsuccessful attempts to establish a comprehensive legislative scheme for wages and hours, Congress finally passed the Fair Labor Standards Act (FLSA), 29 U.S.C.A. §§ 201–219, in 1938. In passing the FLSA, however, Congress did not preempt the states' ability to regulate employment as well, and to this day state law plays an important role in protecting workers' rights. State minimum wage laws may be higher than the federal standard and may apply to workers not covered by federal law. This Chapter reviews this federal and state legislation.

B. FEDERAL REGULATION

1. Fair Labor Standards Act

a. Scope and Background

The Fair Labor Standards Act (FLSA) imposes minimum wage and overtime standards on most employers. One purpose of the minimum hourly wage standard is to insure that a full time worker can maintain "the minimum standard of living necessary for health, efficiency and general well being * * *." Designing a statute to do that is difficult, however, because workers are ordinarily members of family units. Often a worker is the only source of support for both young children and older parents; another worker may be totally free of such obligations. Many members of the "living wage" movement criticize the minimum wage levels set by the FLSA as much too low for most; others criticize the whole idea of such a law, arguing that minimum wages freeze younger workers out of the market, since their skills do not justify this level of pay, and these workers are often members of families that are well off. It takes only a moment to recognize the force of each argument, and to realize that the debate is unlikely to go away soon. The requirement that an employer pay at least "time and a half" for overtime is intended both to increase the number of people employed and to improve working conditions. As the introduction to this chapter stated, the FLSA is a non preemptive statute; none of its provisions or orders justify failure to comply with any state law or municipal ordinance establishing higher minimum wages, lower straight time hours, or stricter child labor standards. Id. § 218. Employers operating in a state or other local area having standards higher than the FLSA must abide by the higher standards.

In *United States v. Darby*, 312 U.S. 100 (1941), the FLSA was held to be a constitutional use of the commerce power. Its extension to employees of state and local governments was upheld in *Garcia v. San Antonio Metropolitan Transit Authority*, 469 U.S. 528 (1985), overruling *National League of Cities v. Usery*, 426 U.S. 833 (1976). Employees of state governments cannot enforce the statute against a state that has not waived its sovereign immunity, however, under recent decisions applying the Supreme Court's current view of federalism. *Alden v. Maine*, 527 U.S. 706 (1999). That immunity does not stretch to local government bodies. *Auer v. Robbins*, 519 U.S. 452 (1997). The Department of Labor doubtless may enforce the statute against state defendants.

Administration of the FLSA is vested in the Secretary of Labor. 29 U.S.C.A. § 204(a); Reorganization Plan 6 of 1950, 64 Stat. 1263. The Secretary is given specific rule making powers to define certain terms used in the FLSA's exemption provisions. These regulations have the force and effect of law as if they had been written into the FLSA. This is not true with respect to other administrative interpretations which are issued primarily for enforcement purposes rather than under a delegation of power. These interpretations, while not controlling, are given judicial deference and under the Portal to Portal Act may constitute a valid defense for employers who show a good faith reliance on them. See *Skidmore v. Swift & Co.*, 323 U.S. 134 (1944).

b. Coverage: The Three Coverage Formulas

To be entitled to FLSA benefits, an employee must either be:

- engaged in interstate commerce,
- engaged in the production of goods for interstate commerce, which includes work closely

related and directly essential to the production of goods for interstate commerce, or

- employed by an "enterprise engaged in commerce or in the production of goods for commerce."

The first two coverage formulas, often called the "individual employee tests," were the only bases of coverage in the original 1938 FLSA statute. The third, "enterprise coverage," was added in 1961 to eliminate anomalous situations in which one worker would be covered by the FLSA while another, performing similar duties for the same employer, would not be. These anomalies are neatly illustrated by a series of Supreme Court cases from the 1940s. In *Walling v. Jacksonville Paper Co.*, 317 U.S. 564 (1943), a dealer in paper goods would import from other states three categories of merchandise: "special order" goods that had been ordered by a customer, merchandise that the company stocked in anticipation of the known buying habits of recurring customers, and merchandise that would form part of the general inventory of such a firm, ordered without any particular customer in mind. Truck drivers, stock clerks, and others who handled goods in the first two categories were "engaged in commerce" and therefore covered by FLSA; those handling only goods in the third group were not unless actively engaged in making a delivery outside Florida, the employer's location. Three other well known FLSA cases, *Borden Co. v. Borella*, 325 U.S. 679 (1945); *10 East 40th Street Bldg. v. Callus*, 325 U.S. 578 (1945); and *Kirschbaum Co. v.*

Walling, 316 U.S. 517 (1942), involved building maintenance and service workers at three Manhattan structures. The Court found workers to be "engaged in the production of goods for commerce" and so entitled to FLSA coverage at two of the buildings: one a loft building in which items of merchandise destined for retail sale in other states were being manufactured by many of the tenants, the other a headquarters building for a company that was engaged at a number of plants located elsewhere in manufacturing food products. Workers in the third building, a locally owned structure occupied by non manufacturing tenants such as dentists and small law firms, were denied FLSA coverage. Results like these have been eliminated by the addition of "enterprise" coverage.

Enterprise coverage is determined by the nature and size of the employer's business and extends coverage to all employees of a business if that business qualifies as an enterprise engaged in commerce or in the production of goods for commerce. Coverage under the enterprise concept, like individual employee coverage, is limited by the FLSA's exemption provisions.

Enterprise coverage is governed by two statutory definitions. Section 3(r) of FLSA defines "enterprise" in terms of three elements: (1) "related activities," (2) performed under "unified operation or common control," (3) for a "common business purpose." While these three elements differ in some ways, they obviously overlap, and evidence of one may well be relevant to establishing that another

element of the definition is also satisfied. 29
U.S.C.A. § 203(r). There are several ways in which
activities may be "related." Similarity is one; a
single owner may operate two or more restaurants,
for instance. Even this simple illustration, however,
can easily be made more muddled. Suppose one of
an owner's two food service operations is Annie's
Burgers, a fast food hamburger joint; the other is
Chez Anne, an upscale continental cuisine restaurant; is there then enough similarity to find the two
related? Complementary activities may also be "related" under Section 3(r), as when a motel and an
adjoining restaurant attract much the same clientele. *Dunlop v. Ashy*, 555 F.2d 1228 (5th Cir.1977);
Usery v. Mohs Realty Corp., 424 F.Supp. 20
(W.D.Wis.1976). Common management and shared
personnel typify "unified operation," but difficult
questions often arise when similar businesses are
run by several family members, sharing some responsibilities but not all. *Brennan v. Plaza Shoe
Store, Inc.*, 522 F.2d 843 (8th Cir.1975). At some
point, parent Anne will have ceded to daughter
Annette enough of the daily responsibility for running Annie's Burgers so that there is no longer
unified operation or common control but just when
that has happened may be hard to gauge. Commonality of business purpose may be found in addressing the same clientele, as when several dealers join
forces to run what customers see as a single business. A proviso to section 3(r) sets out four types of
relationships that do not constitute enterprises, in-

cluding cooperative purchasing schemes and exclusive dealerships.

To be covered under FLSA an employer must not only be an "enterprise" but also an "enterprise engaged in commerce or in the production of goods for commerce," as defined in section 3(s). That subsection lists three categories of covered entities:

- An enterprise that has (1) "employees engaged in commerce or in the production of goods for commerce or ... employees handling, selling, or otherwise working on goods or material that have been moved in or produced for commerce," and (2) has an annual business volume of $500,000 or more;

- An enterprise that conducts one of several listed types of business (including schools and hospitals);

- An enterprise that is an "activity of a public agency."

Coverage extends to all nonexempt employees of the enterprise, not just to employees at the establishment where the interstate activities occur. Wholly exempt from enterprise coverage are "mom and pop" stores, i.e., establishments whose only regular employees are its owner or persons standing in the relationship of parent, spouse, or child of the owner. 29 U.S.C.A. § 203(s).

c. Exemptions from Coverage

Section 13 of the FLSA, 29 U.S.C. § 213, contains a long list of exemptions. Many are partial restrictions such as the twenty one categories of workers listed in subsection 13(b) who are not entitled to Section 7's overtime protection, but who are entitled to the minimum wage. The provisions of subsection 13(a), by contrast, exclude workers from both wage and overtime protection. Some exceptions reflect an allocation of power and responsibility among government agencies: control of truck drivers' hours is entrusted to the Department of Transportation, for instance, by Section 13(b)(1). Others reflect compromises between competing industry and employee groups, such as the provisions exempting lumberjacks from overtime protection, but only if they work for a firm employing eight or fewer workers.

By far the most important exemption, the one that affects the largest number of workers, is that provided by subsection 13(a)(1), familiarly known as the "white collar exemption," which removes any "administrative, executive, and professional" employee and any "outside salesman" from FLSA's wage and hour restrictions. Id. § 213(a)(1). The regulations define each of the first three categories in terms of the duties performed and also the weekly salary of the individual. Employees making less than $455 a week are not exempt under Section 13(a)(1). This relatively low figure provides a strong incentive to label as many as possible of a workforce as "managers," "night managers," "agents in charge," and so on in the hope of not having to pay overtime premiums. *Adams v. United States*, 44 Fed.Cl. 772 (Fed.Cl.1999), a case that engaged the

Court of Federal Claims for over five years, is an interesting public sector illustration, under regulations with an even lower figure. Persons exempt under section 13(a)(1) must be paid on a "salary basis," a requirement that has led to a number of cases discussing whether a complex pay plan that includes commissions and minimum guarantees might qualify. *Erichs v. Venator Group, Inc.*, 128 F.Supp.2d 1255 (N.D.Cal.2001). The regulations also limit the extent to which an employee may be subject to "docking" of pay for disciplinary or other purposes, and still be regarded as paid on a salary basis. *Auer v. Robbins*, 519 U.S. 452 (1997); *Takacs v. Hahn Automotive Corp.*, 246 F.3d 776 (6th Cir. 2001). An "executive" employee is one whose primary duty is management of the enterprise or a segment of it; who regularly directs the activities of two or more other workers; and who has authority to hire and fire workers, or to make effective recommendations about hiring and firing. An "administrative" employee is one whose primary duty is to perform non-manual work, and who exercises "discretion and independent judgment" on significant matters. A "professional" employee is one whose job involves either the use of specialized knowledge typically acquired through extensive education, or originality or talent in "a recognized field of artistic or creative endeavor." Deciding just what occupations qualify as "professional" has been a challenge. *Winkle v. Hutchinson Community College*, 28 Kan. App.2d 344, 18 P.3d 239 (Kan.App.2000) decided that a head athletic trainer qualified. Computer programmers posed so many problems that the statute now has a special provision devoted entirely to them. 29 U.S.C.A. § 213(a)(17).

There are many other exemptions, some affecting relatively few people, some applying to a great many. One increasingly common type of job is providing home care for injured and aged persons. In *Long Island Care at Home, Ltd. v. Coke,* 551 U.S. 158 (2007), the Court upheld an administrative determination that home care workers who are employed by care-providing agencies fit within the exemption provided by section 13(a)(15), 29 U.S.C. § 213(a)(15).

d. Measuring Compliance

Determining whether a worker's paycheck meets FLSA requirements is relatively easy for the "average" hourly paid Monday to Saturday employee. In an economy so large and diverse as ours, however, there are thousands of wage systems in place; many of them make FLSA calculations more complex, particularly when deciding whether the overtime premium pay requirement has been met. That is largely because the amount of the overtime premium is not a fixed dollar and cents amount, but is a proportion of the individual's own "regular rate" for the workweek in question. The four preliminary steps in analyzing compliance issues are largely the same for most pay systems:

- First, identify what the employee's workweek was.

- Next, calculate the number of hours worked during that week.

- Third, find out what "wages" were paid for that week.

- Finally, split the gross pay for the week into three parts:

  - non-wage items such as bonuses that are excluded from pay rate computations under subsections 7(e)(1)–(4);

  - premium pay, as defined in subsections 7(e)(5)–(7); and

  - basic straight time pay.

Id. § 207(e). At this point, it becomes possible to decide whether FLSA standards have been met.

(i) Determining the workweek

For the majority of workers, FLSA standards are to be applied on a workweek basis. While most employers use the calendar week as the workweek, employers that must operate around the clock often do not. An employer may begin the seven day workweek period on any day, and may change that beginning day from time to time so long as the purpose of the change is not to avoid complying with the FLSA. 29 C.F.R. § 778.105.

(ii) Determining the number of hours worked

Section 11 requires employers to maintain payroll records; most employers do so and these records constitute the principal evidence of how long an employee worked in a given week. 29 U.S.C.A.

§ 211. Some employers keep no records, however, or keep records that are shown to be untrustworthy. In these cases, an employee seeking relief under the FLSA carries the burden of proof "if he proves that he has in fact performed work for which he was improperly compensated and if he provides sufficient evidence to show the amount and extent of that work as a matter of just and reasonable inference." *Anderson v. Mt. Clemens Pottery Co.*, 328 U.S. 680 (1946). Absolute precision is not required.

Determining what hours count as working time rather than personal time involves analyzing both the benefit to the employer and the burden on the employee. In an early case, the Supreme Court held that a firefighter's time in the fire hall on call was working time, even though much of it was spent reading, playing cards or chatting. *Armour & Co. v. Wantock*, 323 U.S. 126 (1944). Both the clear value of having the employees close at hand and the limit on employee freedom of movement were emphasized. More recently,, the Court confronted the issue of how much time spent in donning and doffing protective clothing (required by the nature of the work) should be counted. *IBP, Inc. v. Alvarez*, 546 U.S. 21 (2005) In other litigation, employees required to be available by phone or pager during weekends or nights to deal with relatively infrequent calls have generally been denied pay for the on call time, because the ability to move around has not been significantly restricted. See *Martin v. Ohio Turnpike Commission*, 968 F.2d 606 (6th Cir.1992), cert. denied, 506 U.S. 1054 (1993). Short breaks during the working day are usually compensable; lunch breaks, at least those 30 minutes or longer, are usually not, unless the lunch time is also being used for the employer's benefit in some special way. Changing clothes and washing up at the end of the day are personal activities for most workers, but are part of the workday for those who are showering off toxic substances in compliance with safety laws. *Steiner v. Mitchell*, 350 U.S. 247 (1956). Meetings called by an employer to inform or inspire employees are work activities unless attendance is truly voluntary, even though no production or billable services are generated. In the case of formal apprenticeship programs that meet Department of Labor standards, however, mandatory training sessions may be treated as work time only if goods or services are produced that will be used in the employer's business. See *Merrill v. Exxon Corp.*, 387 F.Supp. 458 (S.D.Tex.1974).

(iii) Calculating what "wages" have been paid

Many workers are paid monthly or semi-monthly rather than weekly. The gross pay per week for this worker is obtained by multiplying the monthly pay by 12 (or semi monthly by 24) and dividing the result by 52.

Because state laws require virtually all wages to be paid in cash soon after the work is performed, relatively few cases have been brought under FLSA concerning non-cash credits treated by employers as part of pay. Under Section 3(m), employers may take a credit for the cost to them of food and lodging "customarily furnished" to employees. 29 U.S.C.A. § 203(m). The Secretary has persuaded some courts that the credit ought to be available only when lodging is furnished for the convenience of the employee, not when the employee is required to live on the work site by the employer. See, e.g., *Marshall v. Debord*, 23 WH Cases 1188 (E.D.Okl. 1978); *Marshall v. Intraworld Commodities Corp.*, 24 WH Cases 860 (E.D.N.Y.1980). Other courts have rejected the regulation's requirement that the employer not force unwanted meals on their workers. *Herman v. Collis Foods*, 176 F.3d 912 (6th Cir.1999). Sometimes employers also make deductions from wages for various kinds of employee errors: cash register shortages, breakage, lost items. This sort of scheme does not in itself violate the FLSA unless the result is to reduce the employee's pay for a workweek below the floor set by the statute. The same concept governs commission payment systems in which commissions earned by an employee during successful selling weeks are reduced to make up for slack weeks. Each week's paycheck must independently meet the basic FLSA minimum standard.

A special provision, 29 U.S.C. § 207(*o*), allows public sector employers to use "compensatory time" systems to compensate employees, for the overtime premium only. See *Christensen v. Harris County*, 529 U.S. 576 (2000).

The other recurring problem of deductions from pay has been the "tip credit." Section 3(m) permits an employer to pay a tipped worker as little as $2.13 in cash, if the worker has received enough money in tips so that her total hourly compensation equals the minimum wage rate. 29 U.S.C.A. § 203(m). In many restaurants and hotels, employees pool their tips, and the credit to the employer cannot exceed what the employee in question actually gets from the pool. The employer is required to inform its employees about the system, and only the employees, not the employer, may participate. See *Kilgore v. Outback Steakhouse*, 160 F.3d 294 (6th Cir.1998); *Dole v. Continental Cuisine, Inc.*, 751 F.Supp. 799 (E.D.Ark.1990).

(iv) Deciding whether the minimum wage has been paid

Once the number of hours worked and the amount to be treated as wages for the week are known, deciding whether the employer has met Section 6 minimum wage standards is simple. 29 U.S.C.A. § 206. If the employee has been paid on the basis of an hourly rate, the rate paid for each hour must at least equal the amount set by the statute,$7.25 an hour as of July 24, 2009, for the majority of workers. If the basis for pay is not an hourly rate—if, for instance, the employee is paid a commission on sales or a piece rate—then a simple "bottom line" comparison is made. Did the total of "wages" for the week equal or exceed the number of hours worked multiplied by the statutory minimum? If so, the requirements of Section 6 are met even if the total pay for the week is based on one sale made during the last hour worked.

(v) Deciding whether the overtime premium has been properly paid

Section 7 of the FLSA, 29 U.S.C.A. § 207, requires that each non exempt worker be paid a "premium" for each hour worked over 40 in a workweek; the required premium is one half the "regular rate" the worker earns. Where wages are paid on a uniform hourly basis, the "regular rate" is clearly that hourly rate. The additional amount that must be paid for hours worked in excess of 40 during the workweek is one half of this hourly rate multiplied by the number of excess hours worked. Except in this one type of case, however, deciding whether a worker's pay meets the overtime pay requirements of Section 7 can be more complex. Computing the "regular rate" when that is not an obvious single rate requires splitting the employee's gross paycheck into three parts.

(1) Section 7(e) paragraphs 1 through 4 exclude from the "regular rate" a number of items that may fairly be thought of as pay for services, but that are in some sense "extras." These include:

- Gifts, including Christmas bonuses;
- Idle time payments;
- Reimbursements for expenses;
- Discretionary bonuses;
- Profit sharing and savings plan payments;
- Radio and television talent fees;
- Welfare plan contributions; and
- Vacation and illness pay.

The sums representing items on this list are simply removed from any further consideration.

(2) The second calculation to be made in finding the "regular rate" is more critical: determining what amounts in the paycheck constitute "premium pay" under Section 7(e), paragraphs 5, 6, and 7. These amounts are both excluded from the computation of the "regular rate" and also serve as credits against the premium pay required by the statute. 29 U.S.C.A. § 207(h). The premium pay amounts identified by subsections 7(e)(6) and (7) are relatively easy to pinpoint; those are: premium pay of at least 50 per cent of the regular rate for Saturday, Sunday, holiday, days of rest, sixth or seventh day work; and premium pay of at least 50 per cent for work outside of regular 8–hour days or straight time workweeks not exceeding 40 hours. The language of subsection 7(e)(5) is broader. It treats as premium pay compensation "provided by a premium rate paid for certain hours worked * * * because" those hours exceed eight in a day, 40 in a week, or the employee's own normal or regular working hours.

(3) After these two amounts—the 7(e)(1)–(4) exclusions and the 7(e)(5)–(7) exclusions—have been deducted from gross pay, what remains represents "straight time" earnings and the

"regular rate" is found by dividing this remainder by the number of hours worked.

Any number of schemes have been tried in efforts
to stabilize labor costs for hours worked beyond
what most people would regard as the "regular"
work week. Several of these schemes involve paying
different rates at different times of day, the so
called "clock premium" system. Suppose, for instance, that an employee whose shift is from 8 a.m.
to 5 p.m. with an hour off for lunch receives what
the employer calls a "regular rate" of $7.50 an hour
for work before noon and a "premium rate" of
$10.00 an hour in the afternoon. This rate produces
a paycheck for a 40–hour week that is the same as
the earnings of a worker at a competing plant
whose all shift regular rate is $8.75 an hour. If,
however, the "clock premium" worker is called in
for an extra 8–hour shift one Saturday, the earnings
for that additional eight hours would be the same as
the earnings for the first 8 hours worked that week.
In *Walling v. Helmerich & Payne*, 323 U.S. 37
(1944), the Supreme Court held that these "clock
premiums" are not entitled to be treated as premium pay for FLSA purposes. There are, of course,
millions of workers whose regular workweeks are a
bit less than 40 hours, including clerical workers
hired for a Monday to Friday 9–to–5 workweek with
an hour off for lunch each day. Extra pay for the
36th hour worked by this employee fits neatly into
Section 7(e)(5); it is when purported premium pay
occurs after only a few hours that a subterfuge is
likely. Similarly, some employees and employers set

up schemes calling for premiums only after 47 or 52 hours. Those extra payments may well be entitled to "premium pay" treatment for the hours they cover, but the employer will remain liable under the FLSA for the required overtime due for hours over 40 prior to the hours for which the agreed premium rate has been paid. See *Brennan v. Valley Towing Co.*, 515 F.2d 100 (9th Cir.1975).

Another problem group for overtime purposes are commission paid workers. One system used by some employers involves computing pay in two ways for each worker, one using an hourly rate at or above the minimum wage plus a half time for hours over 40, the other a straight commission rate. Whichever figure turns out to be higher is the employee's gross pay for the week. If in most weeks the commission determines the take home, then the stated hourly rate is not entitled to be treated as a "regular rate." See, e.g., *Hodgson v. Baker*, 544 F.2d 429 (9th Cir.1976), cert. denied, 430 U.S. 946 (1977).

Many workers are paid on a weekly or monthly salary basis, but work varying numbers of hours. Fluctuating workweeks present a special problem and have given rise to many variations of constant wage plans. The most debated of these, and the one most frequently used as a model, is the contract rate arrangement often referred to as the "Belo" plan, named after a case in which this sort of pay scheme was involved. *Walling v. Belo Corp.*, 316 U.S. 624 (1942). Belo plans now have explicit statutory approval in subsection 7(f), provided they meet four qualifications:

1. The employee's work requires irregular hours;

2. A regular rate of pay of not less than the statutory minimum is specified;

3. Overtime at no less than 150% of the regular rate is provided for hours worked in excess of 40 during the workweek; and

4. The weekly guaranty based on these rates covers not more than 60 hours.

The requirement of irregularity is not met by fluctuations merely within the guaranty's overtime range. 29 C.F.R. § 778.406.

The "weekly guaranty," which includes both "regular rate" and "overtime" pay for the covered hours, with no additional pay contemplated unless the employee works longer than the guaranty period, is the distinguishing feature of this constant wage arrangement. It is this guaranty that makes a valid Belo plan different from other "constant wage" devices.

The other principal "fluctuating hours" overtime calculation scheme is one applied to salaried workers, who receive the same weekly pay for "straight time" no matter how many hours are worked. An employer may calculate the "regular rate" for this worker each week and satisfy the overtime obligation by adding to the fixed salary an extra "half time" for each hour worked over 40. See 29 C.F.R. § 778.114.

There are a number of other subsections that provide special treatment for several types of employers. Law enforcement personnel and firefighters may work under plans that calculate overtime pay on the basis of hours worked in a 28–day period. 29 U.S.C.A. § 207(k). Health care institutions and their employees may agree to a 14–day calculation period. Id. § 207(j). There are special provisions also for some tobacco workers (Id. § 207(m)); employees of retail and service establishments most of whose pay comes from commissions (Id. § 207(i)); and for some employees of local transit providers (Id. § 207(n)). There is also a section allowing state and local governments to compensate employees for overtime with "compensatory time," i.e., time off from work, rather than with cash. Id. § 207(*o*)).

e. Remedies

Criminal sanctions are available for willful FLSA violations, fines of up to $10,000 and (for repeat offenders) imprisonment for up to 6 months. In *United States v. Universal C.I.T. Credit Corp.*, 344 U.S. 218 (1952), the Supreme Court held that an employer who institutes and maintains an unlawful pay system commits a single offense for this "course of conduct," not a separate offense for each affected employee or workweek. In practice, few criminal prosecutions are brought, the preferred remedy being a damages action.

An action for damages may be brought either by an aggrieved employee under Section 16(b) or by the Secretary of Labor under Section 16(c). 29

U.S.C.A. § 216(b), (c). Once the Secretary brings an action, the individual employee's right to sue is suspended. Class actions are possible under Section 16(b), but only if the class member consents (sometimes this is described as an "opt in" class action). In either a Section 16(b) or a Section 16(c) action, recovery ordinarily includes both the amount of unpaid wages and also an equal amount as liquidated damages. Under the Portal-to-Portal Act, an employer who acted reasonably in good faith, believing his wage payments were in compliance with the law may avoid the liquidated damages. In a Section 16(b) action a successful plaintiff may also be awarded a reasonable attorney's fee. Whether punitive damages would ever be appropriate is a matter on which the lower federal courts are split. Contrast *Travis v. Gary Community Mental Health Center*, 921 F.2d 108 (7th Cir.1990), cert. denied, 502 U.S. 812 (1991), with *Snapp v. Unlimited Concepts*, 208 F.3d 928 (11th Cir.2000), cert. denied, 532 U.S. 975 (2001).

Section 17 authorizes the Secretary of Labor to seek injunctive relief. Id. § 217. Three sorts of injunctions are available: injunctions against unlawful withholding of wages already due; injunctions against future FLSA violations; and "hot goods" injunctions barring interstate shipment of goods made in violation of FLSA requirements. This latter remedy is sought infrequently, but it can be a powerful weapon in cases involving insolvent employers. A secured creditor can be prohibited from shipping "hot goods" produced by its debtor, even though the creditor did not know the goods were unlawfully produced. *Citicorp Industrial Credit, Inc. v. Brock*, 483 U.S. 27 (1987).

2. Federal Contractor Labor Standards

Contractors who supply goods and services to the federal government or to a variety of federally funded projects must comply with one or more other statutes in addition to the general wage and hour law:

Supply contracts, under which the government buys goods ranging from ambulances to zithers, are governed by the Walsh–Healey Act, 41 U.S.C.A. §§ 35–45.

Construction contract workers are protected by the Davis–Bacon Act, 40 U.S.C.A. §§ 3141–3148; Miller Act, 40 U.S.C.A. §§ 3131–3132; and Contract Work Hours and Safety Standards Act (CWHSSA), 40 U.S.C.A. §§ 3701–333.

Services contracts, whether for work ranging from laundries to data input, are subject to the Service Contract Labor Standards Act, 41 U.S.C.A. §§ 351–358, and CWHSSA.

Both Davis–Bacon and the Service Contract Act require each covered contract to provide that the contractor will pay its employees what the Secretary of Labor has determined to be the prevailing wages in the locality for the relevant job categories. 40 U.S.C.A. § 3142, 41 U.S.C.A. § 351(2)(*l*). These rates are typically included in invitations for bids. Construction and services contracts must also include an agreement to provide certain fringe benefits. 40 U.S.C.A. § 3141(2)(B), 41 U.S.C.A. § 351(b). The rates for many common jobs are reviewed on a routine basis for all major urban areas and the resulting "area rates" are incorporated into bid solicitations by reference. When less common jobs or less populated areas are involved a specific "project determination" is made. In the case of Walsh–Healey, the employer must agree to pay "prevailing minimum wages" and for the bulk of supply contracts, the Secretary simply uses the minimums set by the FLSA. All three sorts of contracts must forbid the work to be done in surroundings or under conditions that are "unsanitary [or] hazardous." 40 U.S.C.A. § 333(a) (construction), 41 U.S.C.A. §§ 35(e) (supply), 351(a)(3) (services). All contractors must provide premium pay for hours over 40 in a workweek.

Violation of these standards can lead to several types of sanctions. The amount of wage underpayment may be withheld from the contractor and paid over to the offended workers. If the underpayment has not been withheld, perhaps because not discovered in time, the government can bring a civil suit (for breach of contract) to recover them. Construction workers covered by Davis–Bacon have a private right of action to recover underpayments if the amounts withheld prove insufficient. 40 U.S.C.A. § 3144(a)(2). The government may by written notice cancel the contract of a non complying employer and recover from that contractor any increased cost of obtaining the goods or services. 40 U.S.C.A.

§ 3143; 41 U.S.C.A. §§ 36, 352(c). A peculiarly rigorous sanction for a firm that relies heavily on government work for its profits is to be placed on the ineligible list, since that means it is debarred, usually for three years, from bidding on federally funded work. 40 U.S.C.A. § 3144(b); 41 U.S.C.A. §§ 37, 354(a).

The courts' role in the enforcement of these laws is limited. If a labor union or prospective bidder wishes to protest that a contract letting agency has applied the wrong statute, or has used the wrong wage determination, there are administrative remedies available; most parties stop with those. On rare occasions, a district court has stepped in to enjoin further steps in the bidding process or performance on a contract. *IUOE, Local 627 v. Arthurs*, 355 F.Supp. 7 (W.D.Okla.1973), aff'd, 480 F.2d 603 (10th Cir.1973). That is usually impracticable, particularly since any money relief a party may receive is likely to be small. For that reason, most reported cases deal with "after the fact" claims: (1) by the Secretary or construction workers that a contractor underpaid those working on a covered project, or (2) by an employer that the contracting agency or the Comptroller General was wrong in withholding sums for underpayment of wages or penalties. An administrative determination that improper wages were paid is entitled to deference. *Nello L. Teer Co. v. United States*, 172 Ct.Cl. 255, 348 F.2d 533 (Ct.Cl.1965), cert. denied, 383 U.S. 934 (1966).

The Miller Act of 1935 is an important adjunct to the Davis–Bacon Act. 40 U.S.C.A. §§ 3131–3132. It requires construction contractors to execute a payment bond to protect the wages of employees providing labor before any contract covered by its provisions is awarded. The statute applies to contracts over $2,000 for the construction, alteration, or repair of any public building or public work of the United States. It does not apply to federal aid projects, but only to direct federal contracts.

3.   Portal to Portal Act

The Portal to Portal Act was enacted in 1947 to relieve employers from burdens imposed by several Supreme Court interpretations of the wage and hour laws. 29 U.S.C.A. §§ 251–262. Several provisions attempted to clarify the concept of working time, and to limit employer liability for time spent in "preliminary and postliminary" activity. Id. §§ 252, 254. A two year statute of limitations was created for actions to enforce the FLSA, the Walsh–Healey Act, and the Davis–Bacon Act. A 1966 amendment permits actions for willful violations to be brought within three years. The standard for willfulness is whether the employer knew or showed reckless disregard for whether its conduct was forbidden by the state. *McLaughlin v. Richland Shoe Co.*, 486 U.S. 128 (1988). The statute also provides employers with two "good faith" defenses. An employer is excused from any liability whatever under the FLSA, Walsh–Healey or Davis–Bacon if it can show that it paid its workers "in good faith in conformity with and in reliance on any written administrative regulation, order, ruling, approval or interpretation" of the Secretary or her delegate. Id. § 259. An employer whose wage practice fits precisely within the terms of a regulation or opinion letter is thus proof against an action for damages brought by an individual employee arguing that the regulation is in error. Having so precise a fit between practice and regulation is not required for the "Section 11" defense. Section 11 does not relieve an employer of liability for unpaid wages, but does provide a defense against a claim for the liquidated damages generally available for FLSA violations. Id. § 260. The employer must prove that its challenged wage practice was "in good faith" and that "he had reasonable grounds for believing that his act or omission was not a violation." Id. A reckless or willful violator would not qualify. See *Alvarez Perez v. Sanford–Orlando Kennel Club, Inc.*, 515 F.3d 1150 (11th Cir. 2008).

4. Garnishment Restriction

The Fair Labor Standards Act (FLSA) protects each worker's paychecks from excessive deductions by the employer, by: (1) limiting the credit available for such items as food and lodging furnished by the employer, and (2) prohibiting deductions for such items as breakage and cash register shortages that would result in a weekly paycheck that does not meet the minimum wage standard. Paychecks are protected against garnishment by third party creditors by Title III of the Consumer Credit Protection Act, 15 U.S.C.A. §§ 1671–1675. This statute defines "disposable earnings," a new term that includes both gross pay and some other compensation such as bonuses and pension payments, but excludes amounts deducted as a matter of law, such as local, state, and federal taxes. Garnishment is limited by the statute to 25 percent of "disposable earnings" or to the amount by which the worker's "disposable earnings" exceed 30 times the minimum wage, whichever is less.

An employer is forbidden to "discharge any employee by reason of the fact that his earnings have been subjected to a garnishment for any one indebtedness." 15 U.S.C.A. § 1674(a). This has been interpreted to prohibit termination until the employer is in fact required to withhold funds for a second indebtedness; mere receipt of a garnishment order is not enough if no withholding is actually required. *Donovan v. Southern California Gas Co.*, 715 F.2d 1405 (9th Cir. 1983); *Brennan v. Kroger Co.*, 513 F.2d 961 (7th Cir.1975).

C. STATE REGULATION

In addition to the wage and hour provisions of the Fair Labor Standards Act (FLSA), every state has enacted some form of wage and hour statute. These statutes vary substantially but are generally of four broad types.

First, many states have passed statutes similar to the FLSA. These statutes exist concurrently with the federal statute. State mandated minimum wages range from lower than the federal rate to higher. The state minimum controls with respect to employees not covered by the federal statute but covered by the state act, and where the state minimum wage is higher than the federal minimum. It may specify how wages are to be paid and establish timetables for payment. Some states lack general wage and hour laws, but have statutes that focus on specific issues, such as the "tip credit." See, e.g. Tenn. Code Ann. § 50–2–107.

Second, a number of states and localities have enacted "prevailing wage" programs similar to those under the Davis–Bacon and Service Contracts Act statutes at the federal level. In recent years, a significant number of municipalities have adopted some sort of "living wage" ordinance, effective with respect to municipal employees and those who deal with the city. Challenges to their constitutionality have resulted in different outcomes. Compare *New Orleans Campaign for a Living Wage v. City of New Orleans,* 825 So.2d 1098 (La. 2002) with *New Mexicans for Free Enterprise v. City of Santa Fe.,* 138 N.M. 785, 126 P.3d 1149 (2005).

Third, there are statutes that protect the integrity of paychecks by requiring payment in cash, rather than in credits at a company store, or scrip, or goods. These statutes often specify how quickly payment is to be made after the work has been done, particularly to non-executive employees. See, e.g., N.J. Stat, Ann. §§ 34:11–4.1—34:11–4.14.

Finally, many states have a wage collection statute. These statutes provide a means by which employees may recover unpaid wages, regardless of amount, from employers, by filing a claim with a state agency or going to court. See, e.g., N.J. Stat. Ann. §§ 34:11–59—34:11–67. These statutes sometimes include specific requirements for the final paycheck for a terminated employee, such as how to treat unused accrued vacation pay. See *Electronic Data Systems Corp. v. Attorney General*, 907 N.E.2d 635 (Mass.2009).

CHAPTER 7

PENSIONS AND OTHER EMPLOYEE BENEFIT PROGRAMS

A. INTRODUCTION

Many American workers enjoy a wide range of benefits for which their employer pays all or a part of the cost: employer-paid life insurance, medical care programs, education assistance, counseling, for example. Other workers, particularly part-time, non-unionized, and low-paid employees, receive very few such benefits. A small number of benefits are mandated by law. Federal statutes require employer participation in four major benefit programs for most employees:

- partial income replacement during old age, under the Old Age and Survivors Insurance program of the Social Security Act (see section D of this chapter);

- partial income replacement during periods of total disability, under the Disability Insurance provisions of the Social Security Act (see section B.4 of Chapter 5);

- unemployment compensation benefits under a joint federal-state program (see section G of Chapter 2);

- unpaid leave for absence from work caused by the birth or adoption of a child or by a serious medical condition of the employee or the employee's child or parent (see section C of this Chapter).

State laws require virtually all employers to provide:

- workers compensation protection for employees (see section B.3 of Chapter 5).

A handful of states require employers to participate in disability insurance systems. Some provide for maternity leave benefits greater than those under federal law. Hawaii requires most private employers to provide medical care for their regular work force (Hawaii Rev. Stat. ch. 393); Maryland has recently enacted a statute requiring that of large employers, although that statute was struck down under federal preemption principles. *Retail Industry Leaders Assoc. v. Fielder,* 475 F.3d 180 (4th Cir. 2007).

Many other benefits that employees enjoy, including free parking, most health insurance and discounts on employer products, are not mandated by law. They are based on the contract of employment, negotiated individually or through collective bargaining. Funding some of these benefits is made less expensive by favorable tax treatment by the Internal Revenue Code. How these voluntary plans are structured and administered is regulated by several federal statutes, including the Employee Retirement Income Security Act of 1974 (ERISA), as amended, 29 U.S.C.A. §§ 1001–1461.

B. THE EMPLOYEE RETIREMENT INCOME SECURITY ACT

1. Scope and Purpose

a. Background and Structure of the Statute

Formal fringe benefit programs were rare in the United States before the First World War. The American Express Co. established a pension plan in 1875, but it applied to only a handful of the company's employees, those with 20 years of service aged 60 or over. Over the next three to four decades, however, other large employers (particularly utilities) began to offer such benefits as a way to attract workers, and the scope of the programs broadened. The first group life insurance policy covering a group of employees was issued to an employer in 1911, and these policies soon displaced the death benefit programs provided by older "mutual benefit associations" that some employers and unions had established in the late nineteenth century. Some of those associations had also provided modest benefits for workers who suffered serious accident or disease. Group health insurance did not become available until the late 1920s, but became a common workplace benefit during and after the Second World War.

The first federal laws that responded to the development of these benefit programs were provisions in the initial corporate tax code of 1909, and in the individual income tax laws that followed the passage of the Sixteenth Amendment in 1916. These established rules for determining which expenses for employee benefits an employer could deduct from its gross income when computing taxable income, and also what portion of benefits received by workers they must count as income subject to tax. The Congress has amended these "qualification" standards many times over the years.

Traditional labor law entered the picture in 1948, when the National Labor Relations Board held pensions to be a mandatory subject of bargaining, a decision enforced the next year in the courts. *Inland Steel Co. v. N.L.R.B.*, 170 F.2d 247 (7th Cir. 1948), cert. denied, 336 U.S. 960 (1949). Later the Supreme Court would find a wide variety of benefits to be mandatory bargaining subjects, even prices in workplace vending machines. *Ford Motor Co. v. N.L.R.B.*, 441 U.S. 488 (1979), but would also hold that a union is often not entitled to insist on bargaining about benefits received by employees who have already retired. *Allied Chemical Workers Local 1 v. Pittsburgh Plate Glass Co.*, 404 U.S. 157 (1971). The union may, however, litigate on behalf of all those entitled to receive benefits under a collective agreement, including retirees. *International Union, United Automobile Workers v. Yard–Man, Inc.*, 716 F.2d 1476 (6th Cir. 1983).

In 1959, following the financial failure of a number of welfare and pension plans, the Congress passed the Welfare and Pension Plan Disclosure Act (now much amended and incorporated into ERISA). As its name indicates, the statute required plan administrators to disclose their financial data periodically to beneficiaries. This was of limited help to those who could not follow the intricacies of accounting involved, and in 1962 enforcement by participants was largely replaced by requiring disclosure to the federal Department of Labor, and adding fines and other penalties for failure to disclose to the statute.

Before the enactment of the Employee Retirement Income Security Act (ERISA) of 1974, then, employee benefit plans were subject to only a handful of federal rules. They were also subject to a wide variety of state laws, ranging from common law fiduciary principles to detailed statutory insurance regulations. Employers with multi-state operations found that state-to-state differences often made it difficult to design benefit plans that could be the same company wide. Many commentators argued that the state laws were inadequate as safeguards for the employee beneficiaries. In particular, there were charges of inadequate funding of pensions, of mishandling of trust funds set aside to provide pension and other benefits, of capricious cancellation of benefit programs, and of arbitrary treatment of those seeking benefits. Public interest in the soundness of pension plans increased when thousands of workers at a Studebaker automobile manufacturing plant in Indiana discovered that their promised retirement benefits would not be paid because of chronic underfunding. Congressional interest in these problems was coupled with a growing concern about the amount of tax revenues being lost by virtue of allowing an employer to deduct the cost of virtually any benefit as a business expense in determining its taxable income for the year.

ERISA is organized in four titles. Title I sets standards about:

- what information must be maintained and disclosed to employees and to the Secretary of Labor (29 U.S.C.A. §§ 1021–1031);

- what rules a plan may have about who is entitled to participate, and about when an employees rights to benefits vest (Id. §§ 1051–1061);

- funding of plans, particularly pension plans (Id. §§ 1081–1086);

- responsibilities of fiduciaries (Id. §§ 1101–1114);

- circumstances in which a former employee must be allowed to continue to participate in an employers group health plan, usually at the employees expense, after being fired or laid off (Id. §§ 1161–1169) (often referred to as "COBRA coverage");

- coverage and portability provisions of group health plans (Id. §§ 1181–1185b).

Title I also includes provisions for how these standards are to be administered and enforced. 29 U.S.C.A. §§ 1131–1147. Title II contains tax law provisions as amendments to the Internal Revenue Code. 26 U.S.C.A. §§ 401–418E. Title III is devoted to additional provisions related to the jurisdiction, administration, and enforcement of ERISA. 29

U.S.C.A. §§ 1201–1242. Finally, Title IV creates the Pension Benefit Guaranty Corporation and establishes a system of employee plan termination insurance, including special provisions for multiemployer plans. Id. §§ 1301–1461.

b. Tax Benefits Associated With "Qualified" ERISA Plans

The Title II tax provisions, and similar provisions affording special treatment to employee benefits that appear elsewhere in the Internal Revenue Code, lie beyond the scope of this Nutshell, not only because of their subject matter but because the complexity of some of those provisions would require a volume at least the size of this one. It is nonetheless important to have a rough notion of the general nature of those provisions to understand how some of ERISA's objectives are to be achieved. ERISA does not require that an employer offer any benefit whatever to its workers. These tax rules on employee benefits do, however, offer a "carrot" to employers to encourage them to establish certain types of plans. Take pensions, the principal subject of Title II, as an illustration. If the plan set up by an employer meets the standards of the tax code, so that it constitutes a "qualified" plan, that employer is allowed to take a deduction for any money it pays into the pension trust fund in the year in which that contribution is made. The benefited employees, however, do not report that sum as income in the year when the employer contributes, nor do they report any share of the trust fund's earnings as income until they actually receive pension payments from that fund. This deferral of taxes is a substantial benefit, and it means that the ultimate payment of pension benefits can be achieved with far fewer dollars of employer contribution than would otherwise be the case.

A similar situation exists with respect to health insurance. An individual can deduct medical expenses from taxable income only after those expenses exceed 7½ % of adjusted gross income. An employer, however, can deduct the full cost of an employee group health care plan that meets tax code standards, while none of the payments made to health care providers on behalf of the employee will be treated as taxable income. The converse of this favorable treatment of "qualified" plans is, as one would expect, a variety of tax liabilities if standards are not met. Sometimes the adverse consequence is primarily visited on the employer, through denial of a deduction; at other times an employee may also feel the pinch, by being required to pay tax on "imputed" income, including income that the employee has not yet received in cash. These tax benefits—granting deductions to employers and not treating benefits as income, or postponing taxes until a future time,—offer powerful incentives for conforming with the standards set in the tax code provisions that were so extensively amended by ERISA's Title II.

Many of the standards that must be met in order to "qualify" for favorable tax treatment have to do with Congressional judgments concerning what provisions in a plan are fair and equitable to the beneficiaries. Some of these "fairness" provisions mirror standards that appear in Title I of ERISA, codified in Title 29, the labor law title of the Code. Both 29 U.S.C.A. § 1056(d)(1) and Internal Revenue Code § 401(a)(13) require that a pension plan include a provision that "benefits under the plan may not be assigned or alienated," for example, thus protecting those benefits from most creditors. Other "fairness" provisions in the tax code are aimed at limiting the extent to which a benefit plan may be structured to favor more highly paid employees over those earning lower wages. These "anti-discrimination" requirements often require detailed calculations and can be treacherous in application. There are, however, some relatively easy-to-understand "safe harbor" provisions available to employers that are willing to contribute at least 3% of employee salaries to a 401(k) plan. Other tax code provisions are aimed not so much at notions of fairness as at limiting the amount of loss of current tax revenues. These include limits on the amounts that can be contributed to various deferred compensation plans on behalf of an individual employee, and requiring that employees begin to receive minimum pension payouts by a certain age, so that taxes can start to be assessed against the investment income that has accumulated. Other standards have to do with maintaining the integrity of trust funds used to pay benefits, by imposing fiduciary standards and limiting conflicts of interests. As in the case of many "fairness" standards, these often have parallels in the labor law title.

c. Coverage

The statute's sweep is broad. With certain exceptions, ERISA is applicable to all employee benefit plans established or maintained by:

1. Any employer engaged in commerce or in any industry or activity affecting commerce;

2. Any employee organization or organization representing employees engaged in commerce or in any industry or activity affecting commerce; or

3. Both. Id. § 1011a(c).

The coverage language is obviously similar to that used in the National Labor Relations Act (NLRA). 29 U.S.C.A. § 152(7). There are differences between the two, however; agricultural employees are excluded from the coverage of the NLRA, but included within ERISA's coverage as workers in an "industry or activity affecting commerce." *Winterrowd v. David Freedman & Co.*, 724 F.2d 823 (9th Cir. 1984).

The principal exceptions from coverage are:

● benefit plans maintained by government units,

● plans operated by religious organizations,

● any plan whose sole purpose is to comply with a state workers compensation, unemployment compensation, or disability benefits law,

● any plan administered outside the United States most of whose beneficiaries are nonresident aliens, and

- "excess benefit" plans not entitled to any of the tax breaks described above.

If a particular perquisite is not a "benefit plan," then ERISA does not apply. Two Supreme Court decisions have held specific benefit programs not to be "benefit plans." In *Fort Halifax Packing Co. v. Coyne*, 482 U.S. 1 (1987), the Court held that a one-time severance pay benefit required by a Maine statute in the case of certain plant closures did not constitute a "plan" since it required virtually no administrative machinery and would not involve advance funding. In *Massachusetts v. Morash*, 490 U.S. 107 (1989), the Court held that a company's policy of paying its terminated employees for unused vacation time did not constitute a "plan." In each case, the net result was to avoid preemption of a state statute under ERISA's preemption section.

While the statute applies to both "pension" and "welfare" plans, there are distinct differences in the scope of regulation applied to those two categories. A "welfare plan" (such as a medical insurance program) is exempt from most of the vesting and funding rules that apply to pensions and from plan termination rules. Welfare plans are also subject to tax qualification standards different from those for pension plans.

2. Administration and Enforcement

The duties imposed by ERISA fall not on the employer alone, but also on those who administer a plan. Most particularly, they fall on "fiduciaries," those who have custody of funds set aside to pay benefits. One indicator of the breadth and complexity of ERISA is the way in which the administration of the statute is distributed among departments and agencies. The four principal entities are:

1. The Department of Justice, which prosecutes criminal violations of the statute;

2. The Treasury Department, whose Tax–Exempt and Government Entities Division deals with issues of plan qualification, propriety of deductions and other Title II problems;

3. The Department of Labor, whose Employee Benefits Security Administration monitors fiduciary performance, receives most plan reports, and prosecutes civil actions for violation of many ERISA provisions, particularly those in Title I; and

4. The Pension Benefit Guaranty Corporation (PBGC) which implements the provisions of Title IV of ERISA and litigates actively to seek to have assets of failing or defaulting employers used to shore up their under-funded plans.

In addition to these principal players, a number of other agencies have a more limited role. These include:

1. The Joint Board for the Enrollment of Actuaries, which regulates persons performing ac-

tuarial services under the Act; 29 U.S.C.A. § 1241.

2. The Advisory Council on Employee Welfare and Pension Benefit Plans, which advises the Labor Department with respect to its functions under the Act; 29 U.S.C.A. § 1142.

3. The Advisory Committee to the Pension Benefit Guaranty Corporation, which advises the PBGC on policies and procedures related to its ERISA functions; 29 U.S.C.A. § 1302(h).

Finally, plan participants and beneficiaries themselves play a major role in enforcement, through civil actions for benefits and to obtain relief for a variety of breaches of Title I and of the terms of the plans themselves. 29 U.S.C.A.§ 1132(a).

Actions to protect employee rights thus take place in a wide variety of settings. In recent years, for example, much of the PBGC activity has been in bankruptcy litigation, such as the widely reported United Airlines case in which the Flight Attendants Union sought unsuccessfully to have an agreement between the airline and the PBGC, resulting in termination of a pension plan and its takeover by PBGC, set aside. In re *UAL Corp.,* 428 F.3d 677 (7th Cir. 2005). Generally speaking, retirement benefit obligations are not ended or suspended when an employer enters bankruptcy. Modification of those obligations must wait for approval by the bankruptcy court. 11 U.S.C.A. § 1114; *In re SPECO Corp.,* 195 B.R. 674 (Bankruptcy Crt. S.D. Ohio 1996).

3. Rights and Duties Under Title I

The duties imposed on an individual or entity by ERISA's Title I vary according to: (1) the nature of the benefit plan involved and (2) the role of the entity, whether employer, plan sponsor, administrator, trustee, or a combination of these.

a. *Information*

All plans, both pension plans and welfare plans, are required to furnish participants with summary plan descriptions (SPDs). Each summary plan description must contain specified information, including the administrator's name and address (and trustees and agents for process when appropriate), conditions of eligibility for benefits, circumstances that might disqualify an otherwise eligible person, how to present claims, and how to protest the denial of a claim. The summary is required to "be written in a manner calculated to be understood by the average plan participant and * * * reasonably apprise such participants and beneficiaries of their rights and obligations * * *." 29 U.S.C.A. § 1022. A copy of this is to be sent to each participant within 90 days after that worker becomes a participant, and thereafter at 5 year intervals, if modifications have been made to the plan, or ten year intervals if changes have not been made. If the SPD conflicts with the terms of the Plan, then a participant who suffers prejudice as a result of the inconsistency may insist on receiving the benefits as set out in the SPD. *Burke v. Kodak Retirement Income Plan,* 336 F.3d 103 (2d Cir. 2003).

Each plan must also file annual reports with the Department of Labor within 210 days after the close of the plan year, commonly known as "Form 5500" reports after the title of the form developed by Labor, Treasury and the PBGC to make the reports more uniform. For plan years that begin on January 1, 2008, or later, electronic filing is required; it had been an option for some time. Once the Department of Labor has received the report, it is to make it available in electronic form within 90 days. Much of the data required is financial. Some information (gross data on assets, liabilities, receipts, and disbursements) must also be furnished to participants and beneficiaries annually in Summary Annual Reports (SARs). The SAR must also tell the participant where he or she can see and copy the full Form 5500 report, and that a copy will be furnished by the administrator at a reasonable cost. If the plan is a pension plan, a participant or beneficiary may also request, no more often than once a year, a statement of the total benefits accrued for the worker, and what proportion of those accrued benefits are non-forfeitable. This information is also to be sent to the individuals. 29 U.S.C.A. §§ 1023, 1024. If an employee consents, this may be done electronically.

Some small plans are wholly or partly exempted from the Form 5500 and SAR requirements, generally plans with fewer than 100 participants that are fully insured or provide benefits only from current revenues. 29 U.S.C.A. § 1024(a)(2); 29 C.F.R.

§ 2520.104–20. In some instances, a group plan may file on behalf of individual employing units.

The statute also requires that the plan administrator must respond promptly to a written request by any participant or beneficiary for the latest updated SPD, annual report, any terminal report, or the instrument under which the plan is established or operated. 29 U.S.C. A. § 1024(b)(4).

One reporting requirement is imposed on employers without regard to their status as administrator or trustee. An employer that fails to make a payment required to meet the minimum funding standard for a pension plan within 60 days of the time that payment was due must notify each participant and beneficiary of that failure, unless excused through a waiver procedure. 29 U.S.C.A. § 1021(d).

A participant may obtain equitable relief for violation of these requirements, and may also be awarded a sum of up to $100 a day in the court's discretion. 29 U.S.C.A. § 1132(c)(1),(3). See *Otero Carrasquillo v. Pharmacia,* 382 F.Supp.2d 300 (D.P.R. 2005). The Secretary of Labor may assess a civil penalty of up to $1000 a day for failure to file the required annual report. Willful violations of the reporting requirements also carry criminal penalties, although prosecutions are rare. See *United States v. Phillips,* 19 F.3d 1565 (11th Cir. 1994), cert. denied, 514 U.S. 1003 (1995).

b.   *Pension Plan Contents and Standards*

One major set of ERISA rules limit the ways in which pension plan eligibility requirements can be structured. These rules are complex and detailed, largely because they seek to provide alternatives suitable for many different industries and occupations. In general, ERISA requires that an employee be allowed to participate in a pension plan as soon as he or she has completed one "year of service"— defined for most workers as a 12–month period during which the employee worked not less than 1,000 hours. 29 U.S.C.A. § 1052. The mode of participation will depend on what type of pension plan it is. The statute divides pension plans into two principal subdivisions:

- "Defined contribution" plans, in which employee and (usually) employer contribute a percentage of earnings into an investment fund, the earnings from which will become the basis of pension payments at the appropriate time; in these plans the employee must usually be given some options about the type of investment that will be used for his or her account. The familiar "401(k) plans" are an example.

- "Defined benefit" plans, which are, in essence, all plans other than defined contribution plans. A typical defined benefit plan is one that promises the employee a certain fraction of his or her earnings for each year of service with a given employer, but there are literally hundreds of variants on just how the payouts from these plans can be structured. Some defined benefit plans are funded entirely by the employer, others by joint contributions. The money put into the pension fund each year is invested by its trustees who seek to achieve a return that will enable the fund to provide the promised benefits when the time comes.

One variant of a defined benefit plan has been the subject of considerable comment and controversy in recent years, the "cash balance" plan. It is sometimes referred to as a "hybrid" plan, since it shares some features with defined contribution plans. Instead of being promised a monthly payment based on past earnings, the beneficiary in a cash balance plan is promised a lump sum. The amount of the payment consists of the sum of amounts credited to the individual employee's account each year (4% of that year's earnings, for example) plus an "interest credit" earned on the account balance each year (often based on an index, such as the amount paid by the 10–year Treasury note). The fund from which the benefit is to be paid need not invest in the security that is used as the basis for the "interest credit," but may diversify or invest in higher-risk instruments. The risk of poor investment performance (and also the reward for good performance) is thus borne by the employer, who must have the promised sum ready when the employee retires. Many such plans permit the retiring employee to choose whether to take the promised amount as a lump sum, or to convert it into an annuity. Establishing such a plan is itself clearly legal. Whether changing a plan from a "traditional" defined benefit structure to a cash balance plan—prior to the Pension Protection Act of 2006—violates the age discrimination bans in ERISA has divided the lower federal courts. Under the 2006 amendments to ERISA, such conversions are not a violation, provided the resulting cash balance plan meets the Act's standards.

Another major limit on plan structure is a requirement that an employee's entitlement to pension benefits based on employer contributions become non-forfeitable—"vest"—within a specified time. The usual full vesting period is three years (cut back from the original ten) if the plan uses "cliff vesting," under which an employee goes from nothing vested to fully vested in a single step. Two other options are available: A plan may postpone 100% vesting until six years of service (7 years for defined benefit plans) have elapsed by using "graduated vesting" instead of "cliff"; structuring a vesting schedule under which 20 per cent of entitlement vests after 2 years, 40% after three, etc. A multi-employer plan that has been created through collective bargaining may postpone vesting until the end of ten years of service with one or more of the participating employers. 29 U.S.C.A. § 1053. An employee's right to recover any amount she has contributed to a pension plan vests immediately.

A third set of rules govern plan provisions that set the rate at which entitlements to pension benefits accrue. The general thrust of these is to require reasonable minimum accrual of benefit rights in the earlier years of employment, so that an employee with, for example, 20 years of service will not discover that he or she has accrued only a small percentage of a full pension. 29 U.S.C.A. § 1054.

Other provisions:

- require that the rights of employee spouses be protected by making joint and survivor annuities the preferred form of pension payout, 29 U.S.C.A. § 1055;

- govern permissible starting dates for benefit payments, 29 U.S.C.A. § 1056(a);

- limit the extent to which pension benefits may be reduced by Social Security payments, 29 U.S.C.A. § 1056(b);

- prevent the erosion of benefit rights when two or more pension funds merge, 29 U.S.C.A. § 1058; and

- require the maintenance of records. 29 U.S.C.A. § 1059.

A further significant requirement is that every ERISA-controlled pension plan "shall provide that benefits under the plan may not be assigned or alienated," 29 U.S.C.A. § 1056(d), thus making pension payments proof against most creditors' claims. If an employee files a petition in bankruptcy, for example, that employee's pension right is treated much like a right under a spendthrift trust. *Patterson v. Shumate*, 504 U.S. 753 (1992). There is an exception for "qualified domestic relations orders" (QDROs) so that a court may require a pensioner to use that pension money for alimony and child support payments. A spouse may waive some of her rights in divorce proceedings in ways that do not amount to a QDRO, but only to the extent permitted by the plan documents. *Kennedy v. Plan Administrator for DuPont Savings & Investment Plan,* 129 S.Ct. 865 (2009). At least two courts have reasoned that there might also be an exception: A trustee of a pension fund who is also a beneficiary of that fund and who has misappropriated sums from the fund ought to be subject to having his or her claims against that fund charged with the amount misappropriated. See *Crawford v. La Boucherie Bernard Ltd.,* 815 F.2d 117 (D.C.Cir. 1987). In a slightly different case, the Supreme Court later held that a union could not recover the funds one of its officers had embezzled by imposing a constructive trust on his pension rights. The Court cited the *Crawford* decision, and neither approved nor disapproved its reasoning, but found it distinguishable since the union officer had not taken pension plan funds. The language of the opinion indicates, however, that the ERISA protection of pension rights is almost always to be honored. *Guidry v. Sheet Metal Workers National Pension Fund,* 493 U.S. 365 (1990).

c. *Fund Contributions*

Section 402 of ERISA requires that each employee benefit plan must "provide a procedure for establishing and carrying out a funding policy and method consistent with the objectives of the plan...." 29 U.S.C.A. § 1102(b)(1). For the most part, it is pension plans that require advance funding, and the statute includes a set of funding standards just for pension plans. 29 U.S.C.A. §§ 1081–1086. The details of these standards have been developed by the Secretary of the Treasury within a general framework set out in 29 U.S.C.A. § 1082 and related tax code provisions. In the Pension Protection Act of 2006, Stat. (2006), these standards were amended significantly, largely to require the use of more up-to-date assessments of what plan liabilities are, and also to require employers to bring under-funded plans into compliance more quickly. Some of these changes were modified again in 2008, following the sharp stock market decline in that year.

It is not just what one would ordinarily call a pension plan that involves advance funding, however. The ERISA definition of "pension plan" extends to many "deferred income" plans, including some profit-sharing plans, if the plan postpones the time when the employee receives the income until "termination of covered employment or beyond...." 29 U.S.C.A. § 1002(2). Other sorts of benefit plans may also be structured to require advance funding. There is a practical limit to how much advance funding will occur, however, because sections 419 and 419A of the Internal Revenue Code limit the amount an employer may deduct for contributions to a funded welfare plan to an amount known as the "qualified cost" for a taxable year, a sum roughly equal to the cost of benefits during that year, with some allowance for administration and amortization of certain capital expenditures. The 2006 amendments redefine these limits in order to encourage employers with under-funded plans to improve those plans into compliance quickly.

d. Fund Management and Fiduciary Responsibilities

Every funded benefit plan (all qualified pension plans, plus any welfare plans in which assets are set aside for a time to provide benefits later) must designate one or more fiduciaries to administer the plan, 29 U.S.C.A. § 1102(a), and must provide for the naming of one or more trustees to manage the fund's assets. This requirement is relaxed in the case of plan assets that consist of insurance contracts or policies and in a few other instances. 29 U.S.C.A. § 1103(a), (b). A plan may provide that a named fiduciary may delegate control of plan assets to one or more investment managers. 29 U.S.C.A. § 1102(c). If this is done with reasonable care, the investment manager is solely responsible for his or her wrongdoing. 29 U.S.C.A. § 1105(d). Similarly, the plan may name more than one fiduciary, and may allocate responsibilities among them. This relieves co-fiduciaries of personal liability for the wrongs done by their fellow fiduciary in his or her area of responsibility. 29 U.S.C.A. § 1105(c). In the absence of this delegation or sharing out of responsibility, a trustee may be liable for breaches of another either because of personal knowledge or acquiescence, or because of a failure to use reasonable diligence in looking after the affairs of the trust. Most fund-handling fiduciaries other than banks and insurers must post bonds. 29 U.S.C.A. § 1112. The statute prohibits a range of convicted felons from serving as plan fiduciaries, administrators, employees, and consultants. 29 U.S.C.A. § 1111.

The basic standards for fiduciary performance are set out in ERISA Section 404, 29 U.S.C.A. § 1104. First, the fiduciary must act "for the exclusive purpose of: (i) providing benefits to participants and their beneficiaries; and (ii) defraying reasonable expenses of administering the plan." Second, in carrying out his or her duties, the fiduciary must act "with the care, skill and diligence * * * that a prudent man acting in a like capacity * * * would use in the conduct of an enterprise of like character * * *," must diversify plan assets unless that is clearly imprudent, and must act "in accordance with the documents and instruments governing the plan * * * " unless those are inconsistent with the statute.

Application of this "prudent investor" rule can be challenging when fiduciary responsibilities are shared. Suppose, for example, that a bank serves as custodian of the securities owned by a plan, and regularly buys and sells securities so as to keep the plan's money fully invested. An investment committee, however, sets the general investment strategy for the plan. That committee requests the bank to increase its holding of the employer sponsor's stock. The bank would not ordinarily make that choice itself, because of its belief that the current price of the employer's stock is on the high side. If the plan clearly puts discretion in the investment committee, rather than the bank, to make the choice of what stocks to buy, then the bank serves as a "directed trustee," and its duty is narrowed to making sure that the direction it received is consistent with the terms of the plan, and not in violation of ERISA. 29 U.S.C.A. § 1103(a)(1). The courts have not taken fully consistent views on just how much narrowing of the duty to act as a prudent investor is appropriate and the extent to which it is appropriate to view a "directed trustee" as a fiduciary. Compare *In re WorldCom, Inc. ERISA Litigation,* 263 F.Supp.2d 745 (S.D.N.Y. 2003) (directed trustee still retains fiduciary status and duties, though limited) with *FirstTier Bank, N.A. v. Zeller,* 16 F.3d 907 (8th Cir.), cert. denied, 513 U.S. 871 (1994) (directed trustee relieved of virtually all fiduciary duty).

Those who sponsor and administer participant-directed plans, such as 401(k) defined contribution plans, act sometimes as fiduciaries and sometimes not. A "safe harbor" provision, section 404(c), provides that "if a participant ... exercises control over the assets in his account ... no person who is otherwise a fiduciary shall be liable ... for any loss ... which results from such participant's ... exercise of control." 29 U.S.C.A. § 1104(c). Therefore, so long as a trustee does no more than invest a participant's money as directed, that trustee is protected against liability. This does not, of course, insulate a trustee or sponsor from liability for choosing investment options in an improper way, or failing to tell participants about peculiar risks associated with an option. *Langbecker v. Electronic Data Systems Corp.,* 476 F.3d 299 (5th Cir. 2007); *Meinhardt v. Unisys Corp.,* 74 F.3d 420 (3d Cir. 1996). A new wrinkle to the problem developed in the 2006 amendments to the statute, amendments that permit an employer to offer a 401(k) plan with "automatic enrollment," i.e., a plan in which a worker is enrolled as soon as eligible without making an affirmative election. Since such an employee might not have chosen an investment option, someone must make a choice for her—a "default" investment. A new companion "safe harbor" provision allows an employer with an automatic enrollment plan to invest a non-electing employee's money into default options that meet regulatory standards without incurring liability for making what in hindsight proves to have been an unsuitable choice.

Other provisions place specific limits on permitted conduct. The fiduciary must not engage in most sorts of commercial dealing with a "party in interest" (usually a fund-creating employer or union, but sometimes a plan fiduciary or employee, 29 U.S.C.A. § 1002(14)). 29 U.S.C.A.§ 1106(a). Trustees must not deal with the plan on their own account, nor represent a party whose interests are adverse to the interests of the plan or its participants and beneficiaries. Receipt of "kick-backs" is specifically forbidden. 29 U.S.C.A. § 1106(b). With a few exceptions, a defined benefit plan's trust fund may not invest more than ten per cent of its assets in an employer's stock or property. 29 U.S.C.A. § 1107. This diversification requirement had not applied to the increasingly popular individual account plans, such as "401(k)" plans. After the ENRON scandals of 2001–2002, however, many proposals were made to reduce the amount of an employer's stock an employee may hold in this sort of tax-favored account. The proposal finally adopted in 2006 allows a participant to hold employer stock in his or her account, but only if the 401(k) plan provides at least three other investment options, and gives the participant a reasonable opportunity at least once a quarter to divest the employer stock and invest the proceeds in the other options. 29 U.S.C.A. § 1054(j).

Prior to the Pension Protection Act of 2006 amendments, a fiduciary could not provide investment advice to participants in a 401(k) plan. That statute now permits such advice, but implementing regulations are not yet in place. 29 U.S.C. § 1108(g).

Despite the limits on self-dealing and ownership interests in the employing enterprise, it is possible for fund trustees who are also company or union officials, as many are, to find themselves in awkward situations. The shares held by a company's pension plan may be the decisive votes in a corporate takeover battle, for instance. Should a conflict of interest situation develop, the fiduciary is expected to obtain independent counsel advice, and perhaps even to suspend his or her service as fiduciary for a time. See *Donovan v. Bierwirth*, 680 F.2d 263 (2d Cir.1982). Doing what was "good for the corporation" as corporate officers also caused trouble in *Varity Corp. v. Howe*, 516 U.S. 489 (1996). The corporate employer in *Varity* decided to spin off several divisions that were losing money into a separate new corporation. In order to induce employees to transfer their services to this new entity, corporate representatives assured workers that their benefit plans would be the same under the new corporation as under the former one. These representatives also made a number of statements about the new corporation's prospects for success, some of them misleading because they were based upon unrealistic evaluations of assets and over-optimistic projections of business growth. The benefit plans in question were administered by the employer directly. When the new corporation failed after less than two years, employees who had become employees of the new entity sought relief under ERISA on the basis of the misleading statements. The Court (6–3) concluded that the District Court was justified in holding that the benefit plan participants reasonably understood their employer to be speaking to them both as employer and also as administrator of the plans—and thus a fiduciary. It further held that making such misleading statements constitutes a violation of fiduciary duty under section 404. That the former employer could have accomplished the same thing by deciding to terminate the plan—see *Curtiss–Wright v. Schoonejongen*, 514 U.S. 73 (1995)—is not controlling. To have done that might well have caused the very difficulty in encouraging transfer that the employer was seeking to avoid by painting an artificially rosy picture.

A fiduciary who has breached his or her responsibilities is personally liable "to make good * * * any losses to the plan, * * * to restore * * * any profits * * * which have been made through use of assets of the plan and shall be subject to such other equitable or remedial relief as the court may deem appropriate, including removal * * *." 29 U.S.C.A. § 1109. The Secretary of Labor is authorized to impose a penalty of up to 20 per cent of the amount recovered in an action brought for breach of fiduciary responsibility. 29 U.S.C.A. § 1132(*l*). While participants may prosecute actions against a fiduciary for breach of responsibility, the usual resulting remedy will be for the benefit of the plan, rather than for the plaintiff, except insofar as the restoration plan assets indirectly benefits that party. *Massachusetts Mutual Life Ins. Co. v. Russell*, 473 U.S. 134 (1985). The Court held in *Varity*, however, that the district court had the power to require the reinstatement of the misled employees to the benefit plans that their former employer had continued in place. The majority rejected defendant's argument that since the Court had held in *Russell* that relief under section 502(a)(2) is limited to relief for the plan that section 502(a)(3) should also be limited in the same way. It remains "equitable" relief, in this case, since a reinstatement order to make the participants "whole" is involved. Injunctive relief against graft is available only to a limited extent under Section 302 of Taft–Hartley, 29 U.S.C.A. § 186. See *Local 144, Nursing Home Pension Fund v. Demisay*, 508 U.S. 581 (1993).

e. Benefit Claims

ERISA requires that each plan provide a participant or beneficiary written notice of why a claim has been denied, and must provide for "full and fair review by the appropriate named fiduciary" of an adverse decision. A participant or beneficiary whose claim has been denied may sue to recover benefits. 29 U.S.C.A. § 1132(a)(1). The standard to be used in reviewing the administrator's determination of ineligibility depends on the extent of discretion given to that administrator by the relevant plan document, which will usually be the document that established the plan. In *Firestone Tire & Rubber Co. v. Bruch*, 489 U.S. 101 (1989), the Supreme Court held that if the plan document entrusts the interpretation of eligibility conditions to the fiduciary's discretion then that fiduciary's interpretation of the conditions is entitled to deference unless it is an abuse of power, but if the document does not grant that level of discretionary power, then the standard of review is *de novo*.

In *Black & Decker Disability Plan v. Nord,* 538 U.S. 822 (2003), the Court rejected the position of the Ninth Circuit that in making benefit determinations, an ERISA plan administrator must give special deference to the opinion of a treating physician over other physicians, an approach borrowed from Social Security disability cases. The administrator is free to weigh the opinions of all physicians, if the plan documents do not prohibit this.

f. *Discrimination*

ERISA forbids termination by an employer, expulsion by a union, or other forms of discrimination in retaliation for exercise of any right under a covered benefit plan. It also bans acts of discrimination "for the purpose of interfering with the attainment of any right to which such participant shall become entitled under the plan * * *." 29 U.S.C.A. § 1140. Some circuits have developed a burden of proof for cases brought under this section that is analogous to that under Title VII of the Civil Rights Act of 1964. In both *Biggins v. Hazen Paper Co.*, 953 F.2d 1405 (1st Cir.1992) rev'd on different issue, 507 U.S. 604 (1993), and *Humphreys v. Bellaire Corp.*, 966 F.2d 1037 (6th Cir.1992), the court found plaintiff had made out a prima facie case by showing that he was terminated within a few weeks of the time his right to a pension would vest, and that the pension would be costly to the employer. The employer was then afforded the opportunity to show that there were legitimate nondiscriminatory reasons for the termination. The Supreme Court approved the *Biggins* holding in dicta.

The difficulty many plaintiffs face in welfare plan discrimination cases is establishing specific intent to interfere with the exercise of right to a benefit. A much publicized case, the outcome in which may have been overturned by enactment of the Americans with Disabilities Act (ADA), illustrates the nature of the inquiry. The plaintiff in *McGann v. H & H Music Co.*, 946 F.2d 401 (5th Cir.1991), was diagnosed as HIV positive and filed a claim with his workplace health care plan for treatment for his condition. Soon, the employer announced a change in that health care plan, under which benefits for treatment of AIDS would be limited to $5,000. The court held that the employer's motivation was not a specific intent to injure the plaintiff, but rather simply a desire to control escalating costs of the medical care plan.

4. Terminating and Modifying Plans

ERISA does not require that a plan have any particular duration. An employer may, however, bind itself to continue a plan by contract for a specific period, or even for the lifetime of a group of participants. *In re White Farm Equipment Co.,* 788 F.2d 1186 (6th Cir. 1986). Most employers, however, reserve the power to modify or terminate a benefit plan at their discretion. See *Sprague v. General Motors Corp.,* 133 F.3d 388 (6th Cir. 1998). In the case of collectively bargained plans, the employer must ordinarily bargain with the union before making any substantial change. If a change in retiree benefits is proposed during bankruptcy proceedings, the union that bargained for those benefits is entitled to serve as the retirees' representative. 11 U.S.C.A. § 1114. Whether the changes an employer has made in a plan are so great that a "termination" rather than an "amendment" has occurred can be a critical issue, since the steps required for a valid termination are more demanding than those for an amendment. See *Hughes Aircraft v. Jacobson,* 525 U.S. 432 (1999).

In order to terminate a pension plan, particularly a defined benefit plan, an employer must meet several conditions. The steps that an employer must take differ depending on whether the terminated plan is its own pension plan, or a multi-employer plan. 29 U.S.C.A. §§ 1341, 1341a. The principal objectives in the case of termination of an individual employer plan are to insure that adequate notice is given, both to participants and to the Pension Benefit Guaranty Corporation, and to insure that the financial obligations of the plan will be met. Only after the employer has met those conditions can it recoup any "excess" funds that may have accumulated (assets not needed to provide the promised benefits). See *Mead Corp. v. Tilley*, 490 U.S. 714 (1989), on remand, 927 F.2d 756 (4th Cir. 1991), cert. denied, 505 U.S. 1212 (1992). In *Beck v. PACE International Union*, 551 U.S. 96 (2007), the Court held that merger of a single employer plan into a union's multi-employer plan would not be a permitted method of termination. Therefore the fiduciary's decision to reject that proposal from the union would not be a violation of duty.

If an employer decides to withdraw from a multi-employer plan, ERISA imposes continuing funding obligations on that employer so that its withdrawal will not undermine the fiscal health of the plan. The Supreme Court approved a provision that gives substantial deference to the calculations of a multi-employer plan's actuary about how much a withdrawing employer is liable to pay. *Concrete Pipe and Products of California, Inc. v. Construction Laborers Pension Trust*, 508 U.S. 602 (1993).

5. Preemption

a. *Section 514: General Principles*

Section 514 of ERISA, often referred to as the "preemption" section, has three principal subsections dealing with state law: the "supersedure" clause, the "saving" clause and the "deemer" clause. The "supersedure" clause, section 514(a), is written in very broad terms:

Except as provided in subsection (b) ... the provisions of this [statute] ... shall supersede any and all State laws insofar as they may now or hereafter relate to any employee benefit plan ... not exempt under section 1003(b)....

Subsection (b)(2)(A) is the "saving" clause:

Except as provided in [the "deemer" clause] ... nothing in this [statute] ... shall be construed to exempt or relieve any person from any law of any State which regulates insurance, banking, or securities.

Subsection (b)(2)(B) is the "deemer" clause:

Neither an employee benefit plan ..., nor any trust established under such a plan, shall be deemed to be an insurance company or to be engaged in the business of insurance or banking for the purposes of any law of any State purporting to regulate insurance companies, insurance contracts, banks, trust companies, or investment companies.

29 U.S.C.A.§ 1144.

This language thus creates a three-stage analysis for deciding whether a given state law has been superseded. First, one asks whether that state law "relates to" a "plan." If the answer is "no," nothing further is required. If the answer is "yes," one then asks whether the state law "regulates insurance, banking or securities." If the answer to that is "yes," then one asks finally whether the deemer clause applies.

One must always remember also that in addition to this specific language, there is always a chance that a state law might be preempted anyhow, by application of ordinary "conflict preemption" and "field preemption" doctrines.

Does the state law "relate to" a "plan"?

In an early case, the Court gave "relate to" a broad reading: "A law 'relates to' an employee benefit plan, in the normal sense of the phrase, if it has a connection with or reference to such a plan." *Shaw v. Delta Air Lines,* 463 U.S. 85 (1983). In that case, the Court struck down portions of a New York anti-discrimination statute that would have required employers to provide disability benefits to pregnant employees as part of an ERISA-covered plan. The "reference to" language adds a concrete quality, indicating that if a state statute or common law doctrine refers explicitly to an employee benefit plan as such, it is likely preempted. In *Ingersoll–Rand Co. v. McClendon*, 498 U.S. 133 (1990), the plaintiff sought to avoid preemption by careful pleading. He alleged that he had been fired to prevent pension benefits from vesting, and that this violated public policy so that he was entitled to damages for wrongful termination; he also sought damages for mental anguish and punitive damages. He did not seek any lost pension benefits, nor did his pleading require reference to any of the details of the pension plan, only to its existence and his potential eligibility. The action was allowed by the Texas courts, but thrown out by the Supreme Court because the Texas public policy in question was one that "referred to" a pension plan—referred to it by protecting the integrity of such a plan against employer misconduct. The Court also reasoned in the alternative that the state action would be preempted by implication because of its potential conflict with the remedy provided by the ERISA's own anti-discrimination section. The Court has also found that a Washington statute providing that designation of a spouse as beneficiary of a life insurance policy was automatically revoked upon divorce was preempted. The majority emphasized the practical difficulties such a state law might cause for a plan administrator: The administrator could not act in reliance on plan documents in deciding whether to pay a claim. *Egelhoff v. Egelhoff,* 532 U.S. 141 (2001).

In some later cases involving section 514, however, the Court has seemed to back away a bit from the breadth of language in its earlier decisions. In *New York State Conference of Blue Cross & Blue Shield Plans v. Travelers Ins. Co.,* 514 U.S. 645 (1995), the Court held that ERISA did not supersede a state statute that placed a surcharge on medical care bills paid by commercial insurers, but not on those paid by Blue Cross plans. *DeBuono v. NYSA–ILA Medical and Clinical Services Fund,* 520 U.S. 806 (1997), upheld a tax on gross receipts for patient treatment at facilities operated by an ERISA plan. In each case the Court's reasoning included a "starting presumption that Congress does not mean to supplant state law." Neither statute explicitly referred to employer benefit plans, but was instead a "law of general application" that imposed a burden on a whole set of care providers. That the tax in *DeBuono* was assessed directly on a plan was not a sufficient "connection with" a plan to require supersedure, since if the plan had provided care through a contract with an HMO or similar group, the impact on plan costs would have been the same.

One implication of the "connection with" language of the *Shaw* formula, however, is that section 514 preemption applies to many "laws of general application" that may affect benefit plans. The Washington statute in *Egelhof* is one example. Earlier, the Court held that a general common law doctrine of Mississippi law requiring an insurer to handle claims in "good faith" could not be applied to an insurer administering a group disability plan covered by ERISA. *Pilot Life Ins. Co. v. Dedeaux*, 481 U.S. 41 (1987). The Court reaffirmed its commitment to *Dedeaux* in *Aetna Health, Inc. v. Davila*, 542 U.S. 200 (2004). The plaintiffs there, both covered by employer health plans, sought damages under the Texas Health Care Liability Act, which imposes a "duty to exercise ordinary care when making health care treatment decisions" on any "health insurance carrier, health maintenance organization, or other managed care entity for a health care plan." One plaintiff's provider had refused to provide a medication recommended by his physician. The claimant then took an alternative over-the-counter medication to which he had a severe reaction that required hospitalization. The second claimant's physician recommended extra time in the hospital following her surgery. The provider organization refused, and she experienced complications that required her to return to the hospital for further treatment. The Texas courts decided the state law was not superseded since it was of general application and did not alter the benefits to which the plaintiffs were entitled. The Supreme Court reversed, on the basis of *Dedeaux,* reasoning that the Texas law provided remedies that the Congress had not decided to give plan participants, and that this state law therefore conflicted with a considered Congressional judgment.

The word "plan" in section 514 has been given a functional interpretation by the Supreme Court. As mentioned earlier, the Court has refused to preempt a Maine statute requiring a one-time severance payment to workers put out of work by a plant closing, and a Massachusetts prosecution of an employer who breached its promise to make a lump sum payment of accrued vacation benefits to discharged workers. *Fort Halifax Packing Co. v. Coyne*, 482 U.S. 1 (1987); *Massachusetts v. Morash*, 490 U.S. 107 (1989). The opinions emphasize highly practical reasons to conclude that the Congress did not intend such benefits to be treated as plans, such as:

- These benefits are typically paid out of general assets, not out of funds set aside in a trust.
- Benefits such as this have long been regulated by state laws.
- To require detailed reporting and record-keeping for such one-time obligations would be highly burdensome.
- Providing a federal forum for complaints about vacation pay seems a questionable use of resources.

Does the state law "regulate insurance, banking or securities"?

The *Dedeaux* opinion also addressed the principal exception to ERISA preemption, the "saving clause." The claimant argued that "bad faith" contract law doctrine is applied so often in the insurance context that it should be thought of as part of the state's regulation of insurance. The Court rejected this argument. The principle that a party's bad faith refusal to perform contract duties is an actionable wrong extends beyond the insurance industry, the Court decided, and did not constitute part of a general scheme of regulation specifically aimed at that industry. Common law principles that apply peculiarly to insurer-insured relations can, however, be "saved" by the saving clause. In *UNUM Life Ins. Co. v. Ward,* 526 U.S. 358 (1999), the Court upheld a rule developed by the California courts to determine when an insurer could defend against a claim on the ground that the insured was too slow to notify it of a claim. This "notice-prejudice" rule was specific enough to insurance litigation, the Court reasoned, to fit within the savings provision.

More often, the saving clause is applied to statutes. In *Metropolitan Life Ins. Co. v. Massachusetts,* 471 U.S. 724 (1985), the Court upheld a Massachusetts statute that required all insurers issuing group health care policies to include benefits for mental health care. That sort of statute, the Court noted, is the very sort of enactment that has traditionally been thought of as "insurance regulation" under the McCarran–Ferguson Act, the statute that restored most insurance regulation to the states. (A mental health standard has now been added to ERISA itself; there was none in 1985. See 29 U.S.C.A. § 1185a.)

The Supreme Court clarified—and arguably expanded—the operation of the saving clause in two more recent cases, *Rush Prudential HMO, Inc. v. Moran,* 536 U.S. 355 (2002), and *Kentucky Association of Health Plans, Inc. v. Miller,* 538 U.S. 329 (2003). In *Moran,* the Court reviewed an Illinois statute requiring HMOs to provide an "independent medical review" of a denial of requested treatment. A divided Court held that HMO regulation constitutes insurance regulation, and that this procedural requirement did not constitute giving plan participants an additional remedy beyond what the Congress provided in ERISA. *Miller* found that ERISA does not supersede a Kentucky law requiring HMOs to admit to their group any health care provider willing to accept the rules and reimbursement rates of that HMO. In *Miller* the Court also announced that the courts should no longer use a three-prong test developed under the McCarran Ferguson Act, 15 U.S.C.A. § 1012, to decide whether a state law "regulates insurance" for ERISA purposes. In the place of that test, the Court substituted a new two-factor test: "First, the state law must be specifically directed toward entities engaged in insurance.... Second, ... the state law must substantially affect the risk pooling arrangement between the insurer and the insured."

Does the "deemer clause" apply?

The "savings clause" has its own limitation in ERISA, the "deemer clause" quoted above. This clause can lead to different treatment of benefit plans depending on whether they are funded or administered through insurance, or operated as self-standing plans by the employer. *FMC Corp. v. Holliday,* 498 U.S. 52 (1990), involved a welfare benefit plan, a self-funded health care plan. One provision of the plan gives the employer subrogation rights to a claim of the employee against a third-party tortfeasor whose negligence resulted in the injury for which benefits were provided. Pennsylvania's Motor Vehicle Financial Responsibility Law codifies a relatively traditional collateral source rule, under which this subrogation is not permitted. That state law is clearly directed at the practices of insurers. Because of that, the Third Circuit held that ERISA did not preempt the state law. The United States Supreme Court reversed, 7–1–1. The Court acknowledged that the Pennsylvania statute's purpose was to regulate insurer practices, but held that the ERISA "savings" clause does not apply when the entity that is in fact regulated is not an insurer but a self-funded plan, since under the "deemer" clause this plan is not to be considered an insurer. The result of the decision is that an employee of a company providing benefits through a self-funded plan does not have the benefit of the collateral source rule, while an employee of a company providing benefits through the purchase of insurance does enjoy the benefit of the collateral source rule.

b.   *Impact on Remedies*

Section 502 of ERISA, 29 U.S.C.A. § 1132, sets out the civil remedies available under the statute. Some of these are remedies available to the Secretary of Labor alone, such as collecting most civil penalties for a variety of violations of reporting and fiduciary duties. Others are available to fiduciaries, participants and beneficiaries as well. Participants, for example, may sue for benefits due them, may bring actions against fiduciaries requiring them to restore trust fund assets, and may even recover civil penalties as personal relief for an employer's failure to respond promptly to information requests. The "catchall" provision authorizes actions "to enjoin any act which violates . . . [this statute] or the terms of the plan, or . . . to obtain other appropriate equitable relief (i) to redress such violations or (ii) to enforce any provisions of this . . . [statute] or the terms of the plan." In two cases, a closely divided Court has held that "equitable relief" does not permit the recovery of damages, but only the kinds of relief that would have been awarded by a court of equity. *Mertens v. Hewitt Associates,* 508 U.S. 248 (1993); *Great–West Life & Annuity Ins. Co. v. Knudson,* 534 U.S. 204 (2002). A recent decision held that this includes claims to enforce "equitable liens," such as a plan's claim for reimbursement from a clearly identifiable fund held by a beneficiary. *Sereboff v. Mid Atlantic Medical Services, Inc.,* 126 S.Ct. 1869 (2006). How far the equitable lien concept can be extended is already being explored in the lower federal courts.

This restriction on the relief available under ERISA has led to a particularly poignant series of preemption cases involving denials of treatment to seriously ill participants. Bureaucratic delays by managed care organizations in these cases have allegedly led to making serious medical problems worse, and even to death. See, e.g., *Kuhl v. Lincoln National Health Plan of Kansas City,* 999 F.2d 298 (8th Cir. 1993), cert. denied, 510 U.S. 1045 (1994) (cardiac surgery denied; death); *Corcoran v. United HealthCare, Inc.,* 965 F.2d 1321 (5th Cir.), cert. denied, 506 U.S. 1033 (1992) (in-hospital monitoring denied during high-risk pregnancy; unborn child died); *Cannon v. Group Health Service of Oklahoma, Inc.,* 77 F.3d 1270 (10th Cir. 1996) (autologous bone marrow transplant procedure denied to cancer patient; death); *Tolton v. American Biodyne, Inc.,* 48 F.3d 937 (6th Cir. 1995) (inpatient treatment for addiction denied; death by suicide). Plaintiffs alleging this sort of maltreatment have sought to use state tort law as a basis of recovery, because under that body of law a claimant can receive general damages (for pain and suffering or the infliction of mental distress, for example) and in extreme cases even punitive damages. Under ERISA, recovery would be limited to an order that the proper benefits be provided, or some similarly restricted relief, because of the Court's reading of the phrase "other appropriate equitable relief" in the ERISA remedy provision. The state court damages actions in each of the actions listed were held to be preempted. It is unlikely that the 2006 decision in *Sereboff* can be stretched to cover the typical claim for relief for death or disability resulting from a wrongful denial of treatment.

The Illinois statute upheld in *Rush Prudential HMO Inc. v. Moran*, 536 U.S. 355 (2002) and the Texas statute held preempted in *Aetna Health v. Davila*, 542 U.S. 200 (2004) are both illustrations of attempts to address what those legislatures thought to be ERISA's inadequate remedies. The statute challenged in *Rush Prudential* withstood that challenge because a majority of the Court decided that its requirement that health care providers must establish a procedure for independent medical review of a treatment denial did not constitute a new "remedy," a decision with which the dissenters took issue. The reasoning of the Court in preempting the Texas statute requiring ordinary care by HMOs in making health care decisions is classic "field preemption" reasoning: ERISA is a comprehensive effort by the Congress to regulate welfare and pension plans. The statute includes specific remedies, carefully articulated. To allow the states to provide more would be inconsistent with this Congressional judgment. For several years there have been proposals to amend ERISA to expand its remedies for this sort of case. Thus far none has made it through the legislative process.

Damages remedies under state law are available in one sort of case. To the extent that a plaintiff can demonstrate that the denial of treatment was a medical decision, rather than simply an administrative one, the case does not involve a "breach of fiduciary duties" in the usual ERISA sense, and the federal statute does not provide a remedy. *Pegram v. Herdrich,* 530 U.S. 211 (2000). Thus the health care provider can be sued for malpractice, or something very like it. See, e.g., *Dukes v. U.S. Healthcare, Inc.,* 57 F.3d 350 (3d Cir. 1995).

Relief for fiduciary misconduct is usually to be relief for "the plan," rather than for an individual. In the case of a defined contribution plan, however, the individual may sue to have her own particular account in the plan reimbursed to make up for a fiduciary wrong. *LaRue v. DeWolff, Boberg & Associates, Inc.,* 128 S.Ct. 1020 (2008).

c. *Workers Compensation*

ERISA states that the statute does not apply to any plan that is maintained "solely for the purpose of complying with applicable workmen's compensation laws or unemployment compensation or disability insurance laws." 29 U.S.C.A. § 1003(b)(3). This does not mean, however, that the fact that a state benefit law provision happens to be located in the workers compensation code protects it absolutely from preemption. *District of Columbia v. Greater Washington Board of Trade*, 506 U.S. 125 (1992), illustrates the point. The District of Columbia amended its workers compensation statute to require that an employer that is liable to pay workers compensation benefits to an injured employee is also obligated to provide health insurance coverage to that employee equivalent to that provided for its employees in general. The Supreme Court held, 8–1, that this requirement is preempted. The requirement "relates to" a benefit plan in the *Ingersoll–Rand* sense, since for an injured worker to be entitled to employer-provided health insurance, he or she must prove that the employer has this plan in operation for other workers. That ERISA does not cover workers compensation laws is not controlling. Justice Stevens, dissenting, argued that the exclusion of workers compensation from ERISA regulation should allow the states freedom to structure benefit entitlements under workers compensation in sensible ways even though in some sense a provision like that in question may be said to "relate to" a benefit plan.

d.   *Accommodation with other Federal Laws*

Section 514(d) provides:

Nothing in this title shall be construed to alter, amend, modify, invalidate, impair, or supersede any law of the United States ... [with two specific minor exceptions] or any rule or regulation issued under any such law.

This language prevents arguments that the Congress intended "implied repeal" of other federal statutes. Two sorts of issues have arisen. One is what counts as a federal law, rule or regulation. The Second Circuit found an interstate compact does, since it had Congressional approval. *NYSA–ILA Vacation and Holiday Fund v. Waterfront Comm'n of New York Harbor,* 732 F.2d 292 (2d Cir. 1984). A provision of the Comptroller of the Currency handbook for examiners, on the other hand, is too informal a document to be a rule or regulation. *Martin v. National Bank of Alaska,* 828 F.Supp. 1427 (D. Alaska 1992).

The second type of problem is deciding what "impairs" a federal statute. In *Guidry,* discussed earlier, the Supreme Court found that ERISA's ban on attaching an embezzler's pension funds did not impair the federal statute that prohibited the embezzling. In its *NYSA–ILA Vacation Fund* decision, on the other hand, the Second Circuit held that the provisions of the Compact would be impaired if ERISA standards were applied to funding systems put in place by the Compact's administering body. The Eighth Circuit recently held that an ERISA action alleging that the employer had issued misleading SPDs could go forward without prejudicing a pending NLRB case in which the General Counsel alleged that those same SPDs were used improperly to restrain employees interested in forming a union at a Wal–Mart facility. *Lupiani v. Wal–Mart Stores, Inc.,* 435 F.3d 842 (8th Cir. 2006).

C. THE FAMILY AND MEDICAL LEAVE ACT

The Family and Medical Leave Act of 1993, 29 U.S.C.A. §§ 2601–2659, (FMLA) entitles an eligible employee of a covered employer to up to 12 weeks of unpaid leave during a 12–month period for any of four reasons:

> "(A) Because of the birth of a child of the employee and to care for this child;
>
> (B) Because of placement of a child with the employee for adoption or foster care;
>
> (C) To care for a spouse, child, or parent of the employee, if that relative has a serious health condition; and
>
> (D) Because of the employee's own serious health condition." 29 U.S.C.A. § 2612(a)(1).

Military personnel. Under a 2008 amendment a "spouse, son, daughter, parent, or next of kin" may take up to 26 workweeks of leave to care for a "member of the Armed Forces, including a member of the National Guard or Reserves, who is undergoing medical treatment, recuperation, or therapy, is otherwise in outpatient status, or is otherwise on the temporary disability retired list, for a serious injury or illness."

Covered employer. The statute applies (a) to firms that employ "50 or more employees for each working day during each of 20 or more calendar work-weeks in the current or preceding calendar year" and (b) to public agencies.

Eligible employee. Under Title I of FMLA an eligible employee is one who has worked for the employer 12 months or more, including working at least 1250 hours during the preceding 12 months, and is employed at a workplace "at which such employer employs less than 50 employees if the total number of employees employed by that employer within 75 miles of that worksite is less than 50." 29 U.S.C.A. § 2611(2).

Notice requirement. The FMLA notice provisions have generated a surprising number of cases. If the need for childbirth or adoption leave is "foreseeable" the employee is to give 30 days notice. 29 U.S.C.A. § 2612(e); see *Hendry v. GTE North, Inc.,* 896 F.Supp. 816 (N.D.Ind.1995). Thirty days notice is also required for leaves resulting from serious health conditions if this notice is "practicable," and the employee is expected to schedule treatments "so as not to disrupt unduly the operations of the employer" consistent with medical advice. 29 U.S.C.A. § 2612(e)(2). When thirty-day notice is not realistic, an employee is expected to give notice "as soon as practicable." If he does not do so, FMLA does not protect him from being fired. *Aubuchon v. Knauf Fiberglass,* 359 F.3d 950 (7th Cir. 2004). A worker who informs the employer of a medical condition that is obviously serious need not specify that she is requesting FMLA leave. *Burnett v. LFW, Inc.,* 472 F.3d 471 (7th Cir. 2006). In rare cases, bizarre employee behavior may be enough to put an employer on notice that the workers suffers from a serious medical condition. *Byrne v. Avon Products, Inc.*, 328 F.3d 379 (7th Cir. 2003).

Regulations issued under FMLA provide that employers may establish procedures for how and to whom notice is to be given, but also provide that failure to conform to such internal procedural rules should not deprive the worker of FMLA protection if the substance of the statutorily required notice is given. The circuits have divided as to the validity and application of these regulations. See *Cavin v. Honda of America Mfg., Inc.*, 346 F.3d 713 (6th Cir. 2003).

Intermittent or continuous leave. Childbirth or adoption leave is to be taken as a single continuous period unless otherwise agreed. 29 U.S.C.A. § 2612(a)(2),(b)(2). If a husband and wife both work for the same employer, they are entitled to only a twelve week leave between them for childbirth, adoption or child care. 29 U.S.C.A. § 2612(f).

Leave taken because of a serious health condition may be taken intermittently or on a reduced schedule "when medically necessary." An employer may transfer an employee on a reduced leave schedule to a different job while the treatment goes on, if the transfer job is one that more easily accommodates irregular work time. 29 U.S.C.A. § 2612(b)(2). One recurring problem has been how to calculate the amount of leave taken, when the employee is absent for only part of a workday. The statute simply says that "taking of leave intermittently ... shall not result in a reduction in the total amount of leave to which the employee is entitled...." An employee who misses an hour of work for to have a medical procedure can thus not be charged with a half-day of leave, but only the hour.

Local educational agencies may require employees whose need for intermittent leave is foreseeable either to take leave for a specified duration not to exceed the duration of the medical treatment or to accept transfer to a job with equivalent pay and benefits that can better accommodate the leave. 29 U.S.C.A. § 2618(c). A related provision permits these agencies to require an employee who takes leave near the end of a term to continue on leave until the end of that term. 29 U.S.C.A. § 2618(d).

Paid and unpaid leave. FMLA leave may be unpaid, but the employer must continue to provide benefits to an employee taking FMLA leave under the employer's group health plan, if there is one. 29 U.S.C.A. § 2614(c)(1). The cost of doing so may be recouped from an employee who does not return to work unless unable to do so for reasons beyond the employee's control. 29 U.S.C.A. § 2614(c)(2).

The employer may require or the employee may elect to substitute for all or part of the statutory 12–week unpaid leave entitlement any "accrued paid vacation leave, personal leave or family leave" provided under an employer's personnel policies. 29 U.S.C.A. § 2612(d)(2). If the employer requires the substitution, the protections of FMLA continue to apply to the paid leave. *Strickland v. Water Works and Sewer Bd.*, 239 F.3d 1199 (11th Cir. 2001). A regulation requiring that an employer make the decision to treat leave as FMLA leave and communicate that to an employee at the time the leave is taken was struck down by the Supreme Court. *Ragsdale v. Wolverine World Wide, Inc.*, 535 U.S. 81 (2002).

Serious health condition. The statute defines "serious health condition" as an illness or condition that involves either "(A) inpatient care in a ... medical care facility; or (B) continuing treatment by a health care professional." While this eliminates many ailments—the common cold, ear ache, or the like—what "continuing treatment" may mean has been a source of difficulty. While the flu would not ordinarily qualify, for instance, the severity of a particular case or the age of the patient might make it so for a particular individual. *Miller v. AT&T Corp.*, 250 F.3d 820 (4th Cir. 2001). The regulations speak of a condition that results in inability to work for at least three days and either multiple visits to a treating medical professional or a sustained treatment regimen.

Medical certification. The statute permits the employer to require that "a request for leave ... be supported by a certification issued by" the relevant health care provider. 29 U.S.C.A. § 2613(a). An employee's failure to respond to an employer request for adequate certification can result in loss of FMLA protection. *Urban v. Dolgencorp of Texas*, 393 F.3d 572 (5th Cir. 2004). An employer that finds a certification inadequate for some reason must, however, give a worker a reasonable chance to remedy the perceived deficiency. See *Sorrell v. Rinker Materials Corp.,* 395 F.3d 332 (6th Cir. 2005).

"To care for" a family member. The statutory definitions extend "parent" to include persons who stand *in loco parentis* to a worker, and also extend "son or daughter" to include a child to whom the worker stands *in loco parentis.* Deciding what activities are included within the notion of "care for" is not always simple. A district court held that an employee husband who took care of three healthy children in order that his wife could spend her time in the hospital with a sick fourth child could be protected by the statute. *Briones v. Genuine Parts Co.,* 225 F.Supp.2d 711 (E.D. La. 2002). Helping a parent pack in order to move from a two-story to a one-story home, and thus reduce the need for assistance, however, probably does not. See *Pang v. Beverly Hospital, Inc.,* 79 Cal.App.4th 986, 94 Cal. Rptr.2d 643 (2000) (state statute).

Entitlement to reinstatement. When an employee who has taken leave returns from that leave and is fit for duty, she is entitled to reinstatement either to her former position, or to an "equivalent position." 29 U.S.C.A. § 2614(a). The reinstatement should be prompt. *Hoge v. Honda of America Mfg., Inc.,* 384 F.3d 238 (6th Cir. 2004).

Reinstatement to the employee's former position may be denied if the employee is among the highest paid 10 per cent of those at the employee's work site and if this denial "is necessary to prevent substantial and grievous economic injury to the operations of the employer." 29 U.S.C.A. § 2614(b). The employer must notify the employee of the intent to deny reinstatement.

Enforcement. The FMLA provides for enforcement in the form of civil actions by employees (including class actions) or by the Secretary of Labor. 29 U.S.C.A. § 2617. Filing of an action by the Secretary terminates the right of employees to sue for the same relief. A jury trial is permitted. See *Frizzell v. Southwest Motor Freight*, 154 F.3d 641 (6th Cir.1998). However, claims relating to reinstatement or promotion are to be resolved by the court, rather than a jury. These latter remedies deal with rights traditionally granted by an equity court and not a court of law. See *Helmly v. Stone Container Corp.*, 957 F.Supp. 1274 (S.D.Ga.1997).

Employees may seek both damages and equitable relief, including reinstatement. The damages to be recovered include lost wages and benefits, or, if there has been no loss of wages or benefits, the other monetary loss suffered, such as cost of infant care during a period when leave was improperly withheld. An equal amount of liquidated damages is to be awarded unless the employer can demonstrate it acted in good faith with reasonable cause to believe it was not violating its responsibilities. 29 U.S.C.A. § 2617(a)(1)(A)(iii).

The employee plaintiff clearly must carry a substantial burden of proof, by showing: (1) she is an "employee"; (2) the defendant is an "employer": (3) she is (or was) entitled to leave for one of the four reasons set out in the statute; and (4) either (a) that she has suffered an adverse employment action because of a claim of leave (retaliation); or (b) that she was discouraged or prevented from taking leave (interference). Must she also show that she has complied with the notice requirement? At least one court has said "yes." *Bradley v. Mary Rutan Hospital Assoc.,* 322 F. Supp. 2d 926 (S.D. Ohio 2004). Litigants often seem to assume, however, that failure to give notice is an affirmative defense.

The usual statute of limitations is two years. See *Moore v. Payless Shoe Source,* 139 F.3d 1210 (8th Cir. 1998). However, for willful violations it is stretched to three years. See *Settle v. S.W. Rodgers Company,* 998 F.Supp. 657 (E.D.Va.1998).

Preemption. The statute provides that it does not supersede any state or local law that provides greater family or medical leave rights. 29 U.S.C.A. § 2652(b).

Sovereign immunity issues. In *Nevada Dep't of Human Resources v. Hibbs,* 538 U.S. 721 (2003), the Supreme Court held that the "family care" provision of FMLA (29 U.S.C.A. § 2612(C)) could be enforced against the state as an employer, on the ground that the statute serves to combat discrimination against women, who tend to be care givers more often than men. Whether the states enjoy immunity against recovery under the "self care" provision (29 U.S.C.A. § 2612(D)) is still being litigated, with the states generally winning. See, e.g., *Touvell v. Ohio Dep't of Mental Retardation,* 422 F.3d 392, cert. denied, 546 U.S. 1173 (2006).

The statute does not apply to federal employees, (29 U.S.C.A. § 2611(2)(B)) but essentially the same substantive rights are provided to them by Title II. 5 U.S.C.A. §§ 6381–6387, the major difference being that enforcement is through the Office of Personnel Management.

D. OLD AGE AND SURVIVORS INSURANCE

1. Benefits Under Social Security

The Old Age and Survivors benefits provisions of the Social Security system were enacted in 1935, and survived challenges of unconstitutionality in 1937. *Helvering v. Davis,* 301 U.S. 619 (1937). That same year, a small number of lump sum death benefits were made to survivors of covered employees. The first monthly benefits checks began to be issued in 1940.

The importance of the old age and survivors benefits provided by the Social Security system is illustrated by the sheer magnitude of the sums involved. More than 30 million retired Americans receive old age benefits each month, and those payments total more than thirty billion dollars. Another two and one-half to three million persons receive spousal or dependent children's benefits. Because of the increasing median age of the adult population, these figures are constantly increasing.

2. Eligibility

Given the scope of the old and age and survivors programs it is remarkable that they have generated so little reported litigation over the years. Probably this reflects the simplicity of the basic eligibility formula for older workers. In general, a worker is entitled to old-age retirement benefits if:

- He or she is "fully insured," because appropriate tax payments have been credited to the worker's earnings record for a sufficient number of calendar quarters; and

- Has reached the age of 62 (65 or older for full benefits); and

- Has applied for benefits. 42 U.S.C.A. § 402(a).

Beginning in the year 2003, the age at which full benefits are first payable began to increase in gradual steps, so that persons born in 1937 or earlier became eligible for full benefits at 65, while those born in 1960 or later will become eligible for full benefits at 67, in 2027.

Almost as straightforward is the eligibility formula for the benefit payable to a worker's spouse. To qualify for a monthly benefit, the spouse:

- must apply;

- must be 62 or older (or have in his or her care a child entitled to a child's benefit on the basis of the primary beneficiary's earnings record); and

- must be the present or divorced spouse of the primary beneficiary.

Two major limitations apply: (1) if a divorced spouse, the applicant must not be married; (2) the applicant must not be entitled to a benefit based on his or her own earnings record that would be equal to or greater than the amount payable as a spouse's benefit. At one time, eligibility requirements were different for widows and widowers, but those differences were struck down as unconstitutional gender discrimination. *Califano v. Goldfarb,* 430 U.S. 199 (1977).

The complexity of eligibility requirements—and thus the opportunities for litigable issues—increases in the case of other relationships between the applicant for benefits and the worker on the basis of whose earnings record benefits are sought. A worker's child, for example, may be required to demonstrate that he or she "lived with" and was "dependent on" the insured worker in order to establish entitlement. See, e.g., *Johnson v. Califano,* 656 F.2d 569 (10th Cir. 1981). Sometimes issues of state law become entangled with these problems. Some states, for instance, recognize informal "equitable" adoptions, others do not. *Blair on behalf of Brown v. Califano,* 650 F.2d 840 (6th Cir. 1981).

When a worker who is fully or currently insured dies, a lump sum payment of $255 may be made to the insured's widow or widower, or if there is none, to another eligible person. Survivors benefits may be payable to a worker's widow or widower, to a surviving child, or to a surviving parent. As with benefits payable during the worker's lifetime, the eligibility conditions for a surviving spouse are usually the simplest. See 42 U.S.C.A. § 402(d)–(h).

3. Benefit Payment and Computation

Benefit payments begin the first month an individual meets the eligibility requirements and continue through the month prior to the individual's death or, in the case of a family member, the termination of eligibility, such as passing the maximum age for a child's benefit, or marrying a person who is not also a Social Security beneficiary.

The key computation is determining the "primary insurance amount" (PIA) for the person on the basis of whose earnings record benefits will be paid. That figure is based on the individual's taxable earnings, averaged over his or her working life. For a worker who reaches the age of 62 after 1978, the PIA is usually computed by using the "average-indexed monthly earnings" method. Under that method, the worker's total earnings (as shown in the earnings record, which in many instances will be lower than actual earnings because of the "cap" on taxable wages) during the "computation years" are first "indexed" by using an adjustment formula that takes into account changes in average wages, and second divided by the number of months in those years. For most workers, the number of "computation years" used to determine retirement benefit PIA will be the number of "elapsed years" minus five. For most workers, an "elapsed year" is a calendar year after the year in which the worker reaches the age of 21, up to the year in which the worker becomes 62. For example, consider a person born in 1942. She became 21 in 1963, and turned 62 in 2004. The "elapsed years" would be each year beginning in 1964 and continuing through 2004, for a total of forty years. The computation years number would therefore be 35. Once the number of "computation years" is calculated, that number of years is selected from the earnings record (after 1950) that include the worker's highest earnings. The Average Indexed Monthly Earnings (AIME) is equal to:

$$\frac{\text{total indexed earnings for all computation years}}{\text{number of computation years [divided by] 12}}$$

Once AIME is known, the PIA is computed by using a formula that employs two "bend points." The formula calls for adding together 90% of the amount of the AIME that falls below the first bend point, 32% of the amount of the AIME that falls between the first and second bend points, and 15% of the amount of AIME that is above the second bend point. To illustrate, in 2009, the bend points were $744 and $4,483. Thus, if a worker's average indexed monthly earnings figure was $5,500, the PIA would be:

90% of $744	=	669.60
32% of $3,739	=	1,196.48
15% of $1017	=	152.55
		2,018.63

This would be rounded down. These formulas, complex as they may seem at first blush, are not the whole story: There are a number of alternative formulas for workers in special circumstances, there are provisions for recomputations (to take into account later increases in earnings) and there are cost-of-living adjustments to be made once a year. The illustration above, however, should give a sense of one significant aspect of the Social Security retirement program: It acts as an income-transfer program, so that lower-paid workers receive in benefits a higher proportion of their pre-retirement earnings than do highly-paid workers.

Once the PIA is known, adjustments are made to fit the particular circumstances of the benefit claim. For example, if a worker decides to retire at 62 instead of at the "full benefit" retirement age, that worker will receive a monthly check that is reduced by one-fifth. A worker who does not claim benefits at full benefit retirement age but continues working, on the other hand, will receive an increased monthly benefit check when she finally applies. Some particularly controversial adjustments involve reducing the amount of social security benefits payable because of other income. A worker under full retirement age who is otherwise entitled to benefits loses one dollar of retirement benefits for each $2 earned, for example. There are also offsets for pension benefits for those who worked in employment not covered by Social Security, primarily government workers.

Benefits for spouses, for children, and for survivors are, in general, computed as percentages of the PIA of the worker on the basis of whose earnings record the claim is made. There is a monthly maximum figure, recalculated each year, for the total of all such claims, known as the "family maximum."

4. The Earnings Record and Liability for Taxes

Because the earnings record is the basis on which benefits are computed, the accuracy of that record is critical to a claim for benefits. An individual may request a copy of his or her earnings record by submitting an appropriate form to the Social Security Administration. A worker who discovers that the record is incorrect may request a correction for any reason for a period of three years, three months and fifteen days after the date when the record was made. After that time, correction is allowed only for specified reasons, although the list of these reasons is fairly long, ranging from employer fraud to obvious mathematical mistakes. See 42 U.S.C.A. § 405(c)(4)–(8).

The earnings record is based upon reports filed by: (a) employers, who are required by the Federal Insurance Contributions Act both to pay the employer's social security tax and also to withhold each employee's social security tax from his or her paycheck; and (b) self-employed persons, who ordinarily pay social security taxes at the same time as income taxes. There is a cap on the amount of individual wages and self-employment income subject to the tax; in 2009, the figure was $106,800. The filing requirements for these taxes are very detailed—larger employers, for example, must provide the information on magnetic media—and the penalties for failure to file and pay on time are stiff, up to 100 per cent. Areas of controversy include determining what persons are "employees" rather than "independent contractors," and what constitute "wages" subject to the tax. The rules can be intricate. A payment by an employer into a worker's Individual Retirement Account, for instance, is included in the employee's wages, even if deductible by the employee for income tax purposes, unless the payment is made under a "simplified employee pension plan," but even then may constitute wages if the contribution is made under a salary reduction agreement. The treatment of tips has been a fertile source of disagreement. In 2002, the Supreme Court upheld as reasonable the method used by the Internal Revenue Service to estimate the amount of tax a restaurant must pay when there has been underreporting of tips by employees. *United States v. Fior d'Italia,* 536 U.S. 238 (2002).

Whether a worker is "fully insured" or "currently insured" depends upon whether the earnings record shows taxable earnings for a sufficient number of calendar quarters (periods of three calendar months ending March 31, June 30, September 30, December 31). Prior to 1978, most workers were credited with a "quarter of coverage" only if wages were actually earned in that quarter (special rules applied to workers who earned the maximum amount of wages subject to social security taxes for the year; agricultural workers; and self-employed persons). Since 1978, the number of quarters of coverage credited for a given year is determined by dividing total taxable wages for that year by an amount (in 2007, $1,000) determined by the Secretary of Health and Human Services under a formula in the statute. Thus, a worker who earns $4,000 or more of taxable wages in 2007 would be credited with four quarters for that year. The number of quarters required to be "fully insured" increases with the worker's age; 40 quarters is the maximum requirement. 42 U.S.C.A. § 414(a). To be "currently insured," a worker must have been credited with earnings in at least six quarters out of the last 13, including the current quarter. 42 U.S.C.A. § 414(b).

5. Review of Denied Claims

If a claim for benefits is denied, in whole or in part, the claimant may seek administrative reconsideration within 60 days of notice of the initial determination. Additional evidence may be submitted. If the claimant still disagrees with the determination made upon reconsideration, he or she may seek a hearing before an Administrative Law Judge of the Office of Hearings and Appeals. That decision is subject to review by the Appeals Council. Finally, a person who is still dissatisfied may file a civil action in federal district court. 42 U.S.C.A. § 405(g).

CHAPTER 8

INDIVIDUAL RIGHTS IN THE COLLECTIVE RIGHTS CONTEXT

A. INTRODUCTION

The focus of this book is the individual employee's rights, not collective action, a matter treated elsewhere in this series in Professor Leslie's excellent book. It is hardly surprising, however, to find that the rights of employees to engage in collective action have direct and significant impacts on the exercise of those individual rights. This Chapter explores some of those impacts.

B. COMMON LAW BACKGROUND

By the 1930s, the courts' inability to provide acceptable solutions to the problems of labor management relations had become obvious. The process of case by case adjudication in state and federal courts was ill suited for formulating national labor policy. Doctrines concerning union privileges and liabilities varied from state to state and were often hazy and hard to apply. Court procedures were too cumbersome and judicial remedies too inflexible.

In the early 1800s, some courts had held that any concerted employee action, even to raise wages, was a criminal conspiracy, even though the motivating purpose and the means utilized would be legal if similar actions were taken by individuals. Numerous convictions were upheld upon the conspiracy theory. Criminal conspiracy convictions became rarer, however, following the influential decision in *Commonwealth v. Hunt*, 45 Mass. (4 Met.) 111 (Mass.1842). In his opinion in *Hunt*, Chief Justice Shaw concluded that the formation of an association of workers who desire to improve their wages is not inherently unlawful. Rather, he wrote, "[t]he legality of such an association will * * * depend upon the means to be used * * * " to achieve the group objective. But even in Massachusetts and other states that largely ceased to prosecute labor unions for criminal conspiracy, their potential civil liability for damages, recoverable from individual members, remained an obstacle to the exercise of collective rights. As late as 1900, for example, the same Supreme Judicial Court of Massachusetts suggested in *Plant v. Woods*, 176 Mass. 492, 57 N.E. 1011 (Mass.1900) that a threat to strike might be coercive because it implied accompanying violence and injury "however mild the language or suave the manner in which the threat to strike is made." Many state courts held that intentional infliction of economic harm, even by means that were not illegal, was actionable unless justified by some legitimate purpose. *Vegelahn v. Guntner*, 167 Mass. 92, 44 N.E. 1077 (Mass.1896) (Holmes, J., dissenting). The first RESTATEMENT OF TORTS, issued by the American Law Institute in 1939, took that

approach. RESTATEMENT, TORTS § 775 (1939).
The courts were unable to agree as to what purposes were sufficient to justify the infliction of
harm.

The remedies courts could offer in labor disputes
also proved to be crude and unsatisfactory. Broad
use of criminal sanctions such as fines and prison
terms proved publicly unacceptable, particularly as
punishment for peaceful activity. Even when strikers engaged in violent acts, there was often a public
perception that those acts had been provoked by
employer agents, especially when the employer
hired professional strike breakers. Money damages
awards, the standard remedy in actions at law, were
unsatisfactory to both sides. The amounts of the
damages awards usually exceeded the employees'
ability to pay, so that a successful employer plaintiff
would not in fact ever get the money the court
awarded. For employees, having a huge judgment
entered against them plunged them even further
into debt, from which they could hardly ever recover. When union activity was subjected to the anti-
trust laws, a court could asses treble damages. See
Loewe v. Lawlor, 208 U.S. 274 (1908). Because of
the uncertain legality of much proposed union action, the deterrent effect of criminal penalties or
damages was the same whether the concerted action was ultimately determined to have been lawful
or not. Even more discouraging to union activity
than fines or damages was the equitable injunction
remedy. Employers turned increasingly to its use
and its enforcement through the use of the courts'

contempt power during the last two decades of the nineteenth century. See, e.g., *In re Debs*, 158 U.S. 564 (1895). The injunction was used almost exclusively by employers to prevent economic injury that might flow from picketers' appeals to workers to stop work or to delivery truck drivers to refuse to enter struck premises. It easily lent itself to this role, since it provided prompt restraint of the activity complained of, unlike criminal and common law sanctions.

During the 1920s and '30s it therefore became increasingly clear that the courts were not the appropriate institution to regulate this area. By the time a controversy reached the courts, industrial strife usually had already occurred. The remedies available limited the range of judicial decision to the question whether some form of union activity should be punished or suppressed, and, if so, by what sanction. In this legal context, most employers rebuffed union efforts and refused recognition and collective bargaining. In the alternative, employers created company unions and agreed to bargain with these unions, but with no others. In this way, an employer was able to go through the motions of recognizing and cooperating with organized labor, but was able to avoid dealing with a union that had a mind of its own. Also, while employees could lawfully organize labor unions, employers could inflict serious injury in reprisal. A pro union employee could be terminated for these activities, denied a favorable reference, or even listed by his former employer as a trouble maker. In an attempt to promote collective bargaining and to reduce the impact of labor disputes on the economy, the Congress enacted several major statutes:

- the Railway Labor Act in 1926, 44 Stat. 577, as amended, 45 U.S.C.A. §§ 151–188;

- the Norris–LaGuardia Act in 1932, 47 Stat. 70, 29 U.S.C.A. §§ 101–155; and

- the National Labor Relations Act (NLRA) in 1935, 29 U.S.C.A. §§ 151–169.

In this Nutshell's confined space, only the NLRA can be discussed in any detail.

C. PRIVATE SECTOR REGULATION

1. Federal Regulation

a. *National Labor Relations Act: Wagner Act, Taft–Hartley Act and Landrum–Griffin Act*

The original 1935 National Labor Relations Act (NLRA), often called the Wagner Act after its Senate sponsor, was enacted to provide a method of establishing employee representation for collective bargaining purposes and to eliminate coercion, restraint, or interference with employee rights to engage in concerted activity. To implement the NLRA's policies, the statute established a new agency, the National Labor Relations Board (NLRB). The Board has the power to decide whether a labor organization is entitled to represent employees in a bargaining unit, and also whether an employer or union as committed any "unfair labor practices." Id. § 153. The NLRA has twice been significantly amended, first by the Labor Management Relations Act of 1947 (LMRA), familiarly known as the Taft–Hartley Act, and later by the Labor–Management Reporting and Disclosure Act of 1959, also known as the Landrum–Griffin Act.

The NLRA applies to private sector "employees" and "employers" involved in interstate commerce. Id. § 152(6), (7). Enterprises covered by the Railway Labor Act are excluded, as are public sector employers and those engaged in agriculture. Id. § 152(2), (3).

(i) Substantive Rights and "Unfair Labor Practices"

The principal rights and obligations imposed by the statute are contained in sections seven, eight and nine.

Section 7 provides that employees have the right to "form, join or assist" labor organizations, to engage in "concerted activities" such as strikes and peaceful picketing, to bargain collectively through representatives of their own choosing, and also to refrain from these activities.

Section 8 sets out what acts constitute "unfair labor practices," a new form of statutory wrong. The original statute defined only employer unfair practices, but in 1947 section 8 was amended to define labor organization unfair labor practices as well. Section 8(a)(1), the "catchall" provision, forbids an employer to interfere with, restrain, or coerce employees in the exercise of their NLRA section 7 rights. Id. § 158(a)(1). The remaining subsections of section 8(a) prohibit specific types of employer restraint. Under those provisions, an employer cannot lawfully:

- dominate, support, or interfere with the formation or administration of a labor organization; Id. § 158(a)(2)

- discriminate in hiring, tenure of employment, or any term or condition of employment in a way that would encourage or discourage participation in a labor organization; Id. § 158(a)(3)

- retaliate against an employee for filing unfair labor practice charges and participating in their investigation; Id. § 158(a)(4)

- refuse to bargain collectively with its employees' representative. Id. § 158(a)(5) (This may occur when an employer refuses to negotiate with the employees' certified or recognized representative, refuses to arbitrate under a collective agreement, or engages in conduct to frustrate reaching an agreement.)

Section 8(b), added by Taft–Hartley in 1947, prohibits labor organization unfair labor practices. Unions are forbidden:

- to restrain or coerce employees in the exercise of their NLRA rights or employers in selection of their representatives for collective bargaining or adjustment of grievances; Id. § 158(b)(1)

- to cause or attempt to cause an employer to discriminate against an employee; Id. § 158(b)(2)

- to refuse to bargain in good faith if it is the collective bargaining agent of the employer's employees; Id. § 158(b)(3)

- to engage in "secondary boycotts"; (The term "secondary boycott" does not appear in the statute as such. A labor organization or its agents may not engage in or induce "any individual employed by any person" to engage in a strike or a refusal to perform services or threaten to coerce "any person engaged in commerce or in an industry affecting commerce" where the purpose is one of several proscribed "objects." The net result is to insulate "neutral" parties from much of the economic pressure they might otherwise experience because of being a customer or supplier of an employer with which the labor organization has a dispute (the "primary" employer).) Id. § 158(b)(4)

- to engage in organizational or recognitional picketing (a) where another labor organization is lawfully recognized as the workers' representative and cannot at the present be challenged (because under the statute it is not an appropriate time to hold an election to decide which if any union should be recognized), or (b) where an election has recently taken place, or (c) for an "unreasonable" length of time (not to exceed 30 days) without filing an election petition. Id. § 158(b)(7).

A curiously worded "free speech" provision—subsection 8(c)—states that "the expressing of any views, argument or opinion ... shall not constitute or be evidence of an unfair labor practice ... if such expression contains no threat of reprisal or force or promise of benefit." Id. § 158(c).

Section 9 focuses both on who should have the substantive rights to represent and to be represented in bargaining, and on the procedures to be used in exercising those rights. The first subsection states: "Representatives designated or selected ... by the majority of employees in a unit appropriate for such purposes shall be the exclusive representatives of all the employees in such unit for the purposes of collective bargaining...." Id. § 159(a). That language bristles with potential problems. Who can be a "representative," for instance? The statute's definition of "representative" says simply that the term "includes any individual or labor organization." "Labor organization" is then defined in an almost circular way as "any organization of any kind ... in which employees participate and which exists for the purpose, in whole or in part, or dealing with employers concerning grievances, labor disputes, wages ... or conditions of work." Id. § 152(4), (5). The Board has had to flesh this out in a variety of ways. A "company union" would, for instance, be a violation of section 8(a)(2), and therefore would not be an appropriate representative, even though it fits the definition of labor organization. The Board has also grappled with whether a labor organization that regularly engages in unlawful discrimination against women or minorities should be entitled to representative status.

Then there is the question of what is a "unit appropriate for bargaining." The statute is almost as open ended on this as on what a "labor organization" may be. Subsection (b) gives the Board full power to decide what grouping of employees is an appropriate unit with only three limits:

- The Board cannot certify a unit as appropriate if it includes both "professional" employees and non professionals unless the professionals, as a group, approve of that.

- The Board cannot refuse to certify a "craft unit" as appropriate simply because the Board had in the past decided that a broader unit was appropriate.

- The Board cannot combine in a single unit "guards" and other employees, and may not certify a union as a representative if that union admits both guards and other workers as members.

For the most part, unit determinations are made on a case by case basis. The Board applies a multi factor approach with the single most important factor being the extent to which employees in a proposed unit share a "community of interest." To make the process move a bit more easily, however, the Board has created a number of "presumptions" that certain units are likely to be appropriate. All production and maintenance employees at a single factory will usually be an appropriate unit, for example. There is a preference for system wide units for some public utilities. In one instance the

Board went beyond the "presumption" approach and adopted a formal rule governing what units are appropriate in hospitals, in the absence of unusual circumstances. The Supreme Court upheld the Board's power to do this against arguments that individual fact balancing is required in every instance. *American Hospital Ass'n v. NLRB*, 499 U.S. 606 (1991).

For the purposes of this book, however, the most interesting problems arise from the "majority rule" approach, so that once a majority of the workers in a unit select a given bargaining representative, that union represents all workers—including those who might have preferred another union, or no union at all. "Exclusive representative" status is a major asset for a labor organization, but not without its costs. In *Emporium Capwell Co. v. Western Addition Community Organization*, 420 U.S. 50 (1975), two employees were unhappy with the progress their union was making in handling grievances alleging discriminatory treatment of minority workers. These disgruntled workers sought to bargain directly with the employer, and also sought to persuade the employer to negotiate about the discrimination issues with community groups other than the union. The employer refused to do so, and urged the workers to use the union as a channel for their complaints. They refused, and engaged in a variety of public protests charging the employer with bias. The employer fired them. The two workers argued that their activity was protected "concerted activity" under the NLRA and filed a charge with the

NLRB. The Board dismissed the charge, and the Supreme Court upheld the Board. Justice Marshall's opinion offers several reasons why giving the majority union exclusive rights does not mean that individual rights go unprotected. He noted in particular that for many years the Supreme Court has imposed on exclusive representatives a "duty of fair representation" to insure that majority rule does not mean that a majority can simply disregard the interests of members of the bargaining unit who, for a variety of reasons, are not viewed as being as important or as desirable. *Steele v. Louisville & Nashville R.R.*, 323 U.S. 192 (1944) (Railway Labor Act); *Syres v. Oil Workers International Union, Local 23*, 350 U.S. 892 (1955) (NLRA). This does not mean a union may not choose bargaining objectives that are more in line with the wishes of one group of workers than another. So long as it does not act arbitrarily or capriciously in setting its priorities, the union does not violate the duty. *Air Line Pilots Association v. O'Neill*, 499 U.S. 65 (1991).

(ii) Procedures in Representation Cases and Unfair Labor Practice Cases

The NLRB conducts two main types of proceedings: (1) unfair labor practice cases involving violations of section 8 of the NLRA, and (2) representation cases to determine whether a union is entitled to be certified to represent the employer's employees. The latter are governed largely by section 9, subsections (c), (d) and (e); the former are governed by section 10.

Unfair labor practice cases begin with the filing of a charge with the Board at one of its many regional offices. The NLRB's General Counsel, who acts as the chief prosecutor of unfair practice cases, has essentially unreviewable discretion to decide whether to dismiss a charge or to issue a complaint alleging that the NLRA has been violated. *NLRB v. Sears, Roebuck & Co.*, 421 U.S. 132 (1975). Much of this authority is exercised on a day to day basis by the Regional Director in charge of each office. If a complaint is issued and the General Counsel's representative cannot reach a settlement agreement with the charged party, the issues involved will be heard by an Administrative Law Judge (ALJ), and ultimately decided by a panel of the Board. If the Board finds that an unfair labor practice has been committed, it will issue a remedial order, requiring the offender to take action such as reinstating a wrongfully terminated worker or ceasing union picketing activity. An aggrieved party may file a petition to enforce or deny any NLRB order in the federal court of appeals for the circuit within which the alleged unfair labor practice occurred, or the District of Columbia. Id. § 160(e) (f). Injunctive relief is available to the Board while an unfair labor practice complaint is pending. Id. § 160(j); 160(*l*). A closely divided Court has held that undocumented aliens, although protected "employees" under the Act, are entitled only to very limited remedies. Reinstatement and back pay are rarely available. This creates unfortunate temptations for less scrupulous employers to hire and abuse such workers.

Hoffman Plastic Compounds v. NLRB, 535 U.S. 137 (2002).

A typical representation case begins with a petition to conduct an NLRB election, which may be filed (a) by employees who wish to have a union certified to represent them or to have an incumbent union decertified, (b) by a labor organization seeking to be certified, or (c) by an employer to whom a union has addressed a claim to represent that employer's workers. Board agents determine by investigation whether there is enough support for the petition to justify an election, and whether the unit petitioned for is an "appropriate unit." Sometimes a hearing may be required to resolve some of these questions, or issues that arise with respect to the conduct of the election itself. These are sometimes decisions for the Director of the region where the election is held under power delegated by the Board, sometimes for the Board itself. NLRB decisions in representation cases generally cannot be reviewed directly by a court, but only in the context of a related unfair labor practice case, when the representation proceedings become part of the "entire record." Id. § 159(d). Suppose, for example, that the Board has certified as an appropriate unit one of five stores the employer operates, and the employer asserts that only a five store unit would be appropriate. The union wins the election in the one store unit. To get court review of the appropriate unit issue, the employer will typically refuse to bargain with the union after the results of the election have been certified, which would be a per se violation of section 8(a)(5) of the statute. When the 8(a)(5) case is heard by the Board, the employer will raise the "inappropriate unit" decision as a defense. The Board will then reaffirm its prior decision on that issue and find the employer has committed an unfair practice by refusing to bargain. Then the employer can appeal the unfair labor practice finding to the court, and will be allowed to pursue its appropriate unit argument in that context. See *NLRB v. Chicago Health & Tennis Clubs, Inc.*, 567 F.2d 331 (7th Cir.1977). Only if the Board overtly disobeys a specific prohibition in the statute—by combining professional employees with non professional against their will, for example—will a district court have power to enjoin the Board's unit determination. *Leedom v. Kyne*, 358 U.S. 184 (1958).

(iii) Preemption

In *San Diego Building Trades Council v. Garmon*, 359 U.S. 236 (1959) (*Garmon II*), the Supreme Court held that preserving the NLRB's jurisdiction over unfair labor practices is so important that state courts may not assert jurisdiction over conduct that is "arguably subject to" the NLRA's Sections 7 or 8. This broad preemption of state power, the Court said, is subject to two exceptions: The states may continue to regulate matters that are of "merely peripheral concern" to the national labor law, and also conduct that touches "interests so deeply rooted in local feeling and responsibility that, in the absence of compelling congressional direction, we could not infer that Congress had deprived the State of the power to act." Thus, states remain free to regulate violent activity that may occur during strikes. The states are not free, however, to regulate the peaceful economic tactics used by union and management against one another simply because a given tactic is not protected by the federal statute. *Lodge 76, International Ass'n of Machinists v. Wisconsin Employment Relations Commission*, 427 U.S. 132 (1976). Deciding what is "regulation" subject to preemption subject to *Lodge 76* preemption is not always simple. In *Building & Construction Trades Council v. Associated Builders and Contractors of Massachusetts/ R.I.*, 507 U.S. 218 (1993), the Court held that a state agency could require bidders on a state project to agree to abide by a collective bargaining agreement negotiated by the firm that the agency had selected to supervise the project. In *Chamber of Commerce of the United States v. Brown,* 128 S.Ct. 2408 (2008), however, a seven justice majority struck down a California statute that applied to all employers receiving state funds of $10,000 or more in a year. The statute required that no money out of those state funds be spent to "assist, promote or deter" union organizing activity.

In addition to amending the NLRA, the Labor Management Relations Act of 1947 (Taft–Hartley Act) included a provision, section 301, that states: "Suits for violations of contracts between an employer and a labor organization ... may be brought in any district court in the United States having jurisdiction of the parties...." 29 U.S.C.A.

§ 105(a). With that language on the books, federal district courts now began to wrestle with the question of what law to apply in interpreting collective bargaining agreements, assessing their validity, and deciding what remedies to grant in enforcing them. In *Textile Workers v. Lincoln Mills*, 353 U.S. 448 (1957), the Supreme Court held that the law to be applied is federal law, to be fashioned by the federal courts in an effort to promote national uniformity and to carry out the policies embodied in the national labor laws. Shortly after, the Court held in *Charles Dowd Box Co. v. Courtney*, 368 U.S. 502 (1962) that state courts also must apply this body of federal law when asked to deal with collective agreements; and in *Avco Corporation v. Machinists, Aero Lodge 735*, 390 U.S. 557 (1968), it held that suits to enforce collective agreements may be removed from state court to federal court.

(iv) Impact on Individual Rights

At this point, one can begin to assess the impact of these laws on individual employee rights. Principally, they are:

1. The NLRA provisions defining unfair labor practices protect individuals against employer and union practices that would be lawful under traditional state tort and contract law.

2. In a unionized workplace, the terms and conditions of employment for those represented by the union are set not so much by individual negotiation as by collective bargaining of the union for the group. The rights that em-

ployees acquire in collective bargaining agreements are typically enforced through arbitration. The standards to be applied in deciding what issues can be arbitrated, and what arbitration awards can be enforced, are matters of federal law.

3. Because a collective bargaining representative enjoys the exclusive right to represent a group of employees, the federal courts have imposed on that representative a duty of fair representation that prohibits arbitrary treatment of an individual employee.

The following sections explore some illustrations of these impacts.

b. *Unfair Labor Practices Affecting Individual Rights*

Three examples of employer conduct that constitutes an unfair practice are treated here: (1) surveillance, to illustrate the importance of the context in which an alleged violation occurs; (2) discrimination, to illustrate that sometimes an employer's state of mind is a significant element of an unfair practice, but not always; and (3) denying an employee the right to a union presence during investigatory interviews. The final sub section deals with union unfair practices.

(i) *Surveillance*

Elsewhere, this Nutshell makes the point that private sector employees by and large enjoy very limited protection of their right of privacy as against their employers. Labor relations law does, however, create an area into which the employer is not to intrude. NLRA section 7 protects the right of each employee to engage in concerted activity, and the right not to do so. Employer surveillance can impinge on those rights. In *Sunbelt Manufacturing, Inc.*, 308 NLRB 780 (N.L.R.B.1992), the Board held that an employer violated the NLRA by videotaping employee handbilling at the front gate of the work-place. The tapes would reveal which employees accepted the brochures offered by union supporters and which rejected them. The Board emphasized that the employer had also violated other prohibitions in the Act. An employer may also commit an unfair practice by attending or observing union meetings uninvited. Refusal to engage in unlawful surveillance is also protected. *Best Western Motor Inn*, 281 NLRB 203 (N.L.R.B.1986).

Deciding what constitutes improper surveillance involves questions not only about what the employer has done, but also about the nature of the employee or union conduct involved, and about the employer's purpose in observing. Planting a "stooge" at a union membership meeting to spy on what takes place at that meeting is clearly improper, even if no employee is aware that spying is going on. See *Bethlehem Steel Co. v. NLRB*, 120 F.2d 641 (D.C.Cir.1941). If a group of workers talk loudly about union business during a break on a factory floor, on the other hand, a visible nearby supervisor is not required to close her ears or run away. Employee awareness of being watched is often an important factor since that awareness can make employees wary of exercising rights the statute provides them. Therefore, it is an unfair practice for an employer representative to drive by or park near the site of a union meeting in order to see which employees go in and out. *Filler Products, Inc. v. NLRB*, 376 F.2d 369 (4th Cir.1967); *Custom Coating & Laminating Corp.*, 249 NLRB 765 (N.L.R.B. 1980). Lack of invitation and improper purpose are both important factors. For example, the Board has held that an employer did not engage in unlawful surveillance when its supervisor openly attended a union meeting and left when asked. *American Book Div., Litton Educational Publishing, Inc.*, 207 NLRB 1054 (N.L.R.B.1973). In *NLRB v. Computed Time Corp.*, 587 F.2d 790 (5th Cir.1979), when a supervisor arrived at a union meeting, a union official told the membership that the supervisor could be asked to leave. The membership said nothing. The union official then invited the supervisor to stay because the meeting was not secret and he knew a "stooge" would carry any desired information to the employer. The invitation was obviously grudging, but it was enough to insulate the employer from a charge of unlawful surveillance.

Surveillance options for employers may also be limited indirectly by the duty to bargain. An employer that wishes to institute a new drug testing program for current employees, for instance, is probably under a duty to bargain over the nature of that program if the collective bargaining representative asks to negotiate and has not clearly waived its bargaining rights on the subject. See *Johnson–Bateman Co.*, 295 NLRB 180 (N.L.R.B.1989). However, an employer that decided to produce a videotape as a training film to illustrate newly formulated management principles did not need to bargain with the union. *E.I. Dupont & Co.*, 301 NLRB 155 (N.L.R.B.1991). The employees gave their opinions on those principles voluntarily.

(ii) Discrimination

Section 8(a)(3) of the NLRA provides that it is an unfair labor practice for an employer "by discrimination in regard to hire or tenure of employment or any term or condition of employment to encourage or discourage membership in a labor organization. * * * " Section 8(b)(2) makes it an unfair practice for a union to cause an employer to discriminate. The forbidden "discrimination" is different treatment of one or more employees in comparison with other employees either because of status as a union member or officer, or because the disfavored (or favored) worker has engaged in activity that is protected by Section 7. Relatively few cases involve obvious status discrimination, such as overtly different treatment of union members; not many employers would be so ill advised as to advertise for non union workers only. Some collective bargaining agreements provide that union officials will be the last to be laid off and first to be rehired. These provisions violate Sections 8(a)(3) and (b)(2) unless they are confined to those union officers who are actively involved in the administration of the collective agreement, so that this "super seniority" furthers the collective bargaining process that is a core concern of the statute.

The more typical 8(a)(3) case is one in which the General Counsel alleges that an employer has acted in response to Section 7 conduct—such as a strike or picketing—in a way that is likely to encourage or discourage other Section 7 activity. Some of these cases involve employer implementation of general employment policies. In the well known *Erie Resistor* case, for example, the challenged practice was a grant of 20 years of extra seniority to employees who crossed a picket line in order to work. *NLRB v. Erie Resistor Corp.*, 373 U.S. 221 (1963). In *NLRB v. Great Dane Trailers, Inc.*, 388 U.S. 26 (1967), the Supreme Court held that employer policies that so clearly undercut the commonality of employee interests are "inherently destructive" of Section 7 rights, and thus may be held to violate the Act even though the General Counsel does not offer specific evidence of "union animus" on the employer's part. A later Railway Labor Act case, *TWA v. Independent Federation of Flight Attendants*, 489 U.S. 426 (1989), has sapped some of the force of *Erie Resistor*, but it remains the generally accepted statement of the underlying principles. Disciplining an employee who violates a rule that is unlawful under the Act is generally a violation of Section 8(a)(3). Thus an employer that disciplines employees for soliciting support for the union from other employees while on the employer's premises during non work times such as coffee breaks violates the Act, even though this conduct violates a general non solicitation rule that is applied against all solicitation, such as requests for charitable donations. Because such a rule impinges too much on the statutorily privileged right to "form, join or assist" a labor organization, it violates section 8(a)(1), and enforcing it violates Section 8(a)(3), once again without specific proof of anti union animus.

Intent does become an issue, however, in two situations. When the employer's conduct arguably lies near the core of entrepreneurial control—decisions to close a facility, for instance—then the employer's conduct is privileged unless undertaken out of hostility toward rights protected by the Act. Shutting down a plant when its employees vote to unionize and transferring that work to a non union facility elsewhere—the so called "runaway plant" case—is an archetypal example. See *Local 57, ILG-WU v. NLRB (Garwin Corp.)*, 374 F.2d 295 (D.C.Cir.1967), cert. denied, 387 U.S. 942. Closing down a newly unionized division of a multi unit enterprise to dampen the fervor of organizing activity in other divisions is another. See *Textile Workers Union of America v. Darlington Mfg. Co., Inc.*, 380 U.S. 263 (1965).

The other case in which state of mind is part of the General Counsel's burden is that of allegedly discriminatory treatment of individuals or small groups. Since terminating a single employee can be the result of many different kinds of factors—loss of business, lack of skill, and so on—and since the immediate impact of the termination is limited to the person involved, proof of the employer conduct alone is not enough. Motivation or purpose must be established. In a typical individual treatment case, the General Counsel's complaint alleges that an employee was terminated or suspended in response to that employee's exercise of Section 7 rights, such as refusing to accept unsafe work assignments that are prohibited by an applicable collective agreement. The employer defends on the ground that the termination was "for cause." The most difficult cases involve "mixed motives." Under the Board's *Wright Line* doctrine, approved by the Supreme Court in *NLRB v. Transportation Management Corp.*, 462 U.S. 393 (1983), the General Counsel makes out a prima facie case by showing by a preponderance of the evidence that a motivating factor in the treatment of the employee was the worker's Section 7 conduct. The employer can still avoid being found guilty of an unfair practice, however, by showing that the employee would have been terminated anyhow for legitimate purposes. See *ABF Freight System, Inc. v. NLRB*, 510 U.S. 317 (1994).

(iii) Investigatory Interviews

An employee who is brought into an interview that may lead to his or her being fired or disciplined is likely to be fearful and intimidated. Such a worker is also not likely to be fully conscious of rights provided by a collective agreement or by law. The worker is not in a good position to notice or to record instances of unfairness in the procedures followed at the interview. Recognizing all of this, the NLRB has developed a modest level of protection for workers in this situation. Private sector employees in unionized workplaces have had a qualified right to have a union representative present during employer initiated investigatory interviews for more than a quarter century. *NLRB v. J. Weingarten, Inc.*, 420 U.S. 251 (1975). This right arises (a) when the employee reasonably believes the investigation will result in disciplinary action, but only if (b) the employee specifically requests union representation. When an employee makes that request, the employer has two alternatives. First, the employer may pursue the investigation without an interview. Second, union representation may be allowed, but the union representative's participation may be restricted. There is no obligation to bargain with the union at the interview and the employer may insist upon hearing only the employee's version. This qualified right to union representation during investigatory interviews is justified by its elimination of the power imbalance that arises when employees confront employers without assistance. A union representative's presence shields an employee from any threat to employment while safeguarding the bargaining unit's interests. The right to representation does not arise during a routine employee employer conversation because no reason to fear disciplinary action exists in this situation.

The NLRB has changed its position from time to time on whether a similar right should be extended to include non union employees. In *Materials Research Corporation*, 262 NLRB 1010 (N.L.R.B.

1982), a majority held that non union employees were entitled to a co employee's presence because "the representative not only safeguards that particular employee's interests, but also the interests of other employees by guarding against unjust or arbitrary employer action; and, in addition, by providing assurance to other employees that, when and if they are subjected to a like interview, they too can obtain the assistance of a representative." Id. at 1011. Subsequently the Board changed its position and held that a non union employee may be terminated for refusing to participate in an investigative interview unless accompanied by a co worker. See *E.I. DuPont de Nemours & Co.*, 289 NLRB 627 (N.L.R.B.1988), petition for review denied, 876 F.2d 11 (3d Cir.1989). Then a majority of the Board returned to the earlier position that employees in non union workplaces are entitled to have someone accompany them to an investigatory interview, and the District of Columbia Circuit agreed. *Epilepsy Foundation of Northeast Ohio v. NLRB*, 268 F.3d 1095 (D.C.Cir.2001) *Epilepsy Foundation* was overturned in 2004, however, in *IBM Corp.*, 341 NLRB No. 148, 174 L.R.R.M. 1537 (2004). Some have argued that the need of non union employees to support each other through this type of conduct may well be greater than that of union represented employees. *Glomac Plastics, Inc.*, 234 NLRB 1309 (N.L.R.B.1978). Non union employees normally do not have the benefit either of a collective bargaining agreement that serves as a check or an employer's ability to act arbitrarily or the protection of a grievance arbitration procedure to challenge employer decisions.

(iv) Union Unfair Practices

Section 8(b)(1)(A), added to the statute in 1947, makes it an unfair labor practice for "a labor organization or its agent ... to restrain or coerce ... employees in the exercise of rights guaranteed in section 7: Provided, That this paragraph shall not impair the right of a labor organization to prescribe its own rules with respect to the acquisition or retention of membership therein...." Because unions do not have the same economic weapons that an employer does, it is much less frequently that a union can be said to "coerce or restrain" a worker. It does happen, however, particularly in the context of strikes or of organizing campaigns, when emotions often run high. If a union officer threatens to "keep you out of work" or makes a credible threat of physical violence, and does so with the actual or apparent authority to speak for the union, the union is subject to NLRB sanctions. *NLRB v. Laborers' International Union*, 810 F.2d 665 (7th Cir. 1987). Acts and threats of violence committed against the union's wishes, and despite its efforts to contain them are not, however, violations of 8(b)(1)(A), the Supreme Court has held, applying traditional principles of agency law. *United Mine Workers v. Gibbs*, 383 U.S. 715 (1966).

The power of a union to prescribe its own rules is not limited to rules about union membership. Like any organization, a union must be able to adopt rules that are relevant to its work. In *Scofield v. NLRB*, 394 U.S. 423 (1969), the Court upheld a Board decision that a union did not violate the statute by fining its members who exceeded production quotas that the union had set. In *NLRB v. Boeing Co.*, 412 U.S. 67 (1973) the Court found that fines imposed against members for "crossing over" a picket line during a strike did not violate section 8(b)(1)(A). Fines may not be enforced against non members, however, and in a closely divided decision the Court held that the proviso in section 8(b)(1)(A) that empowers unions to make rules concerning "retention of membership" does not permit a rule that restricts resignations from union membership during a strike. *Pattern Makers' League of North America v. NLRB*, 473 U.S. 95 (1985). The union's power to adopt rules about who may join and participate in a union is also circumscribed by other statutes, such as Title VII of the Civil Rights Act of 1964, and Title I of the Labor–Management Reporting and Disclosures Act, the "union member's bill of rights."

The other "individual rights" issues that recur with respect to unions fairly often have to do with "union security" clauses and with individual worker objections to union spending for political purposes. A proviso to section 8(a)(3) permits an employer to make "an agreement with a labor organization ... to require as a condition of employment membership therein on or after the thirtieth day following the beginning of such employment...." This would seem at first glance to authorize what is familiarly known as a "union shop." Another provision in the statute allows each state to decide to ban this form of union security if that state wishes; at any given time roughly 20 states will prohibit it, under what are known, somewhat ineptly, as "right to work" statutes. (That title can be used accurately with respect to laws banning the "closed shop," an arrangement in which an individual can get a job only if he or she is already a union member. "Closed shop" agreements are banned under the NLRA.) In practice, the Supreme Court has whittled down the "membership" that can be required of a worker to its "financial core." In *NLRB v. General Motors, Inc.*, 373 U.S. 734 (1963), the Court found that the proviso authorizes no more than a requirement that an employee pay "representation fees," and that a worker could not be required in fact to become a full fledged union member. (It is nonetheless permissible for the collective agreement to use the language of "membership" since that tracks the statute itself. *Marquez v. Screen Actors Guild*, 525 U.S. 33 (1998).) The General Motors interpretation amounts to holding that the maximum form of union security actually available in this country is not a true "union shop" but rather what is usually referred to as an "agency shop," under which the union can charge workers for its costs in acting as their agent. Employees who choose not to join unions or pay representation fees in states with "right to work" laws are generally referred to as "free riders."

Unions perform a variety of functions. Most union energy is directed to collective bargaining in one way or another, but some of the funds generated by dues also support lobbying activity, limited social programs, and organizing activity. In *Communications Workers of America v. Beck*, 487 U.S. 735 (1988), persons paying representation fees under union shop clauses because they had chosen not to join the union sought to recover from the labor organization those portions of their payments that represented expenditures on non-bargaining activity. They ultimately prevailed, in an opinion written by Justice Brennan that held that the same result should be reached under the NLRA that had been reached earlier under the RLA in *International Ass'n of Machinists v. Street*, 367 U.S. 740 (1961). The opinion in a public sector case, *Chicago Teachers Union v. Hudson*, 475 U.S. 292 (1986), requires unions to provide low cost means, such as arbitration, to settle disputes over what items should be included in "agency fees" for non members. In *Air Line Pilots Association v. Miller*, 523 U.S. 866 (1998), the Court held, however, that a union could not compel a non member to submit his claim for lower fees to arbitration unless that non member had specifically agreed to do so. That RLA decision presumably applies to NLRA unions as well. Unions may include the cost of litigation relevant to bargaining when computing the non-member fee. *Locke v. Karass*, 129 S.Ct. 798 (2009)

The term "duty of fair representation" has more than one meaning. The NLRB has held that section 8(b)(1)(A) forbids a union to discriminate unfairly in its representation of workers in a bargaining unit. *Miranda Fuel Co.*, 140 N.L.R.B. 181 (N.L.R.B. 1962), enforcement denied, 326 F.2d 172 (2d Cir. 1963); *Local No. 106, Glass Bottle Blowers Association, Local 106*, 210 N.L.R.B. 943 (N.L.R.B.1974), enforced, 520 F.2d 693 (6th Cir.1975). It is also a judicially developed doctrine of federal labor policy, for breach of which an employee can seek damages that go beyond the remedies that the NLRB can offer. Therefore, the preemption principles discussed earlier do not bar a worker from filing a duty of fair representation claim in state or federal court even though the same union conduct could be the subject of a complaint to the Board. *Breininger v. Sheet Metal Workers International Association, Local No. 6*, 493 U.S. 67 (1989).

c. Union–Management Information Exchanges

As this Nutshell explains elsewhere, an employer is not liable for defamation or for breaching an employee's right of privacy if the employer communicates information about that employee in good faith to those who have reason to need that information. This communication is privileged. To determine if a union is entitled to certain information, the union must show that it cannot fulfill its duties without the information or some alternative form of it. Individual employee rights must be balanced against those of the bargaining unit. Employer claims that the requested information should not be furnished because: (1) some employees preferred that the information remain confidential; (2) the information constituted trade secrets; and (3) disclosure might result in misuse of the information or employee harassment have rarely been found valid. See *E.W. Buschman Co. v. NLRB*, 820 F.2d 206 (6th Cir.1987).

Some types of data are so clearly relevant to a union's ability to perform its functions that failure to provide the information will routinely be held to constitute a wrongful refusal to bargain in violation of Section 8(a)(5): names, addresses, job titles and wages of all bargaining unit employees, for example. See, e.g., *U.S. Marine Corp.*, 293 NLRB 669 (N.L.R.B.1989). In other cases, the union's "need to know" may not be so immediately clear, so that the interests of union and employer must be balanced against the dignity and privacy interests of the employee. Consider, for example, names and addresses of potential managers, or of other workers the union does not represent. Ordinarily, a union would probably not be entitled to this information, since it does not represent these persons. In the case of potential managers, for instance, access to managers at work would be all the union would need to do its job. But there are times when a union will be able to carry the burden of persuading the Board and reviewing courts it really needs this sort of data to do its job. In *NLRB v. United States*

Postal Service, 841 F.2d 141 (6th Cir.1988), the union's constitution provided that union members who applied for supervisory positions were disqualified from serving as union officers. To determine if any of its members were in violation of this provision, the union requested an applicant list from the employer. The Board ordered disclosure, and its order was enforced. In analyzing the promotion process, which placed considerable emphasis on the supervisory applicants' evaluations by their immediate supervisors, a potential for divided loyalty between the union and the employer existed. A desire for supervisor approval might well affect a union official's ability to represent the employees' interests when the union's and the employer's positions were adverse. This information was therefore relevant to the union's duty to provide loyal representation and the privacy interest of individuals was not strong enough to overbalance this need. In *Blue Cross & Blue Shield*, 288 NLRB 434 (N.L.R.B. 1988), an employer refused to give a union the names of employees working overtime at home, arguing that it need not do so because the union had waived its right to bargain over implementation of the work at home program. The Board held that the union did not waive its right to verify how the program had in fact been implemented or to monitor it.

Data that otherwise would not be needed can become relevant in handling grievances. In the course of processing a grievance, a union may be able to establish a claim for information contained in personnel files, even without employee consent. The most obvious reason for this is the union's interest in the consistency of employer practice in deciding what lapses by an employee merit what discipline. See *Salt River Valley Water Users' Ass'n v. NLRB*, 769 F.2d 639 (9th Cir.1985). If that is the purpose, union access will probably be limited to records regarding disciplinary actions and performance evaluations. If it wants broader personnel file disclosure, a union must show both: (1) its need for the data and (2) that disclosure will not infringe the employee's reasonable expectation of confidentiality. In *Detroit Edison Co. v. NLRB*, 440 U.S. 301 (1979), the union sought information about the employer's testing program, including the test battery the employer used and scores achieved by individual employees. It sought this as a means to process a grievance over whether the employer was breaching a seniority clause in the collective agreement by hiring outside applicants instead of promoting from within. The employer's defense was that the in house employees had not achieved acceptable scores on these tests. A sharply divided Court struck down a Board order giving the union access to much of this data. The Court held that providing individual test score information went too far, and that such information should be made available only with the consent of the employee involved. In dicta, the Court majority indicated that a more limited access order, one that permitted assessment of the test by an independent professional under a "protective order," might have been proper.

Section 9(a) of the NLRA provides both that a majority bargaining representative is "the exclusive representative" but also that "any individual employee ... have the right to present grievances to their employer ... and to have such grievances adjusted, without the intervention of the bargaining representative...." There are two conditions that an individual "adjustment" must meet: The adjustment must not be inconsistent with any collective agreement in effect, and the bargaining representative must have been given a chance to be "present" at the adjustment. A union's right to be present at employee grievance adjustments permitted it to attend pre complaint settlement meetings under the Civil Rights Act of 1964 (Title VII) before the Equal Employment Opportunity Commission (EEOC). See *United States Postal Serv. v. American Postal Workers Union*, 281 NLRB 1015 (N.L.R.B.1986).

d. *Rights Under Collective Bargaining Agreements: Grievance Procedures, Mediation and Arbitration*

(i) *Collective Bargaining Agreements as a Source of Individual Employee Rights*

The end product of successful union management negotiations is a collective bargaining agreement. Some provisions of a typical agreement affect only the rights and duties of the employer and the signatory union—clauses recognizing the union as bargaining representative, for example. Other provisions—such as those setting wages and controlling promotion—focus primarily on the rights and duties of employees. These provisions are by implication incorporated into the individual employment contract of each member of the bargaining unit, displacing any inconsistent terms. *J.I. Case Co. v. NLRB*, 321 U.S. 332 (1944). Only in rare instances, such as professional sports, does a collective agreement function instead to set only minimum economic terms, so that the actual rate of pay is a matter of negotiation between individual employee and employer.

Whether and how much an individual employee gains from being represented by a union varies. The average employee usually obtains at least two protections he or she did not enjoy as a non represented worker:

- Instead of being subject to discharge "at will," the worker under the typical collective agreement can be fired only for "just cause."

- A range of employer decisions that the employer could have made unilaterally without being questioned will, under the collective agreement, be subject to protest through a grievance and arbitration system.

(ii) Grievance Systems and Arbitration

The vast majority of collective agreements set up a system for interpreting and applying the terms of the agreement and for resolving disputes that arise under or out of it: a "grievance procedure" that culminates in binding arbitration. This very common procedure is an attempt to provide a prompt, orderly and systematic means of challenging decisions made by the employer. Collective agreements vary with respect to what sorts of decisions may be challenged, but most allow protests about a wide range of matters: discipline and discharge, entitlement to promotion, pay rates, vacation and holidays, fringe benefits, and so on. Once an employer's decision about an issue affecting one or more employees is made, a dissatisfied member of the unit may challenge it by filing a formal "grievance." Depending on the agreement's procedure, it may be filed by an individual, by a group, or by the relevant labor organization. Some agreements also permit the employer to file grievances. A typical procedure calls for multiple "steps." The first will usually be a discussion of the grievance between a union officer and an employer representative of limited authority, such as a department supervisor. If they are unable to agree, it is possible to appeal the issues to officials at a higher level, the "second step." In a bargaining unit that includes large numbers of employees, there may well be four or five of these internal appeal "steps." The typical agreement provides that when all the internal steps have been exhausted, then an outsider will be brought in, usually an arbitrator who will act as a kind of private judge in deciding whether employee, union, or employer rights under the agreement have been violated. While parties sometimes pick arbitrators directly, most collective agreements call for selecting an arbitrator through the use of a professional service, such as the Federal Mediation and Conciliation Service or the American Arbitration Association. Most often, this outside arbitrator will decide the case as an individual; a few collective agreements still call for a three party arbitration panel, consisting of one member representing the employer, one representing the union and one neutral. In some contracts, there may be more than one "step" involving outsiders. Some agreements now call for a mediation process before bringing in an arbitrator. Even if the collective agreement does not include that sort of provision, the parties may agree to add mediation prior to taking the matter on to arbitration. Occasionally, the same individual may function in both capacities, starting out as a mediator, and then, if the parties are still unable to reach agreement, filling the role of arbitrator.

Promptness in filing grievances and appeals is often important, depending on how the parties structure the procedure. Many agreements have very short fuses indeed, requiring a grievance to be filed within three to five working days of the time when the employer's decision is disclosed. After a grievance has been filed, failure to process it promptly to the next appeal step may also bar arbitration. Arbitrators dismiss grievances because of late filing regularly. See, e.g., *In re Island County and Island County Deputy Sheriffs Guild*, 113 Lab. Arb. (BNA) 104 (Stuteville, Arb. 1999). Often, however, they also find an employer has waived this objection by failing to raise the issue promptly, or by accepting "late" grievance filings frequently. See

Internal Revenue Service and NTEU, 114 Lab.Arb. (BNA) 1169 (2000) (Abrams, Arb.); *Rainbo Baking Co. and Bakery Workers, Local 232*, 111 Lab.Arb. (BNA) 948 (1999) (Grabuskie, Arb.); *Precision Extrusions, Inc.*, 49 Lab.Arb. (BNA) 338 (1967) (Stouffer, Arb.).

Agreements vary concerning when hearings should be held at internal pre arbitration appeal steps. The higher the appeal step, the more likely a hearing is, and the more formal that hearing is likely to be.

(iii) Judicial Enforcements of Promises to Arbitrate and of Arbitration Awards Under Collective Bargaining Agreements

Once a valid agreement providing for grievance arbitration has been entered into, any controversy between the parties that is within the scope of its provisions must proceed through it to arbitration. If either the union or the employer refuses to arbitrate a grievance, the other may petition the courts for an order requiring specific performance of the promises made in the arbitration clause.

The law that a court is to apply in deciding whether a promise to arbitrate covers the dispute in question is federal law, developed under section 301 of the Taft–Hartley Act. *Textile Workers Union of America v. Lincoln Mills*, 353 U.S. 448 (1957). The Supreme Court has held that these promises are to be construed broadly in favor of sending matters to arbitration. So long as the issue is one of the agreement's construction or interpretation, it is for the arbitrator and not the court to decide. The court must order arbitration even though the claim made may seem to the court frivolous. *United Steelworkers v. American Mfg. Co.*, 363 U.S. 564 (1960). "An order to arbitrate the particular grievance should not be denied unless it may be said with positive assurance that the arbitration clause is not susceptible of an interpretation that covers the asserted dispute. Doubts should be resolved in favor of coverage." *United Steelworkers v. Warrior & Gulf Navigation Co.*, 363 U.S. 574 (1960). Questions of "procedural arbitrability," such as whether an appeal was timely filed, are for the arbitrator. *John Wiley & Sons, Inc. v. Livingston*, 376 U.S. 543 (1964).

An arbitrator's award is entitled to judicial enforcement so long as it draws its essence from the collective agreement. *United Steelworkers v. Enterprise Wheel & Car Corp.*, 363 U.S. 593 (1960). Although a court may deny enforcement of an agreement that violates public policy, "a formulation of public policy based only on 'general considerations of supposed public interests' is not the sort that permits a court to set aside an arbitration award. * * *" *United Paperworkers v. Misco, Inc.*, 484 U.S. 29 (1987). The fact that a court might disagree strongly with an arbitrator's decision about matters of fact does not justify refusing to enforce the award, so long as the arbitrator seeks to interpret and apply the agreement. *Major League Baseball Players Association v. Garvey*, 532 U.S. 504 (2001).

(iv) Applying the Duty of Fair Representation to the Handling of Grievances

Collective bargaining agreements are negotiated between employers and unions, but under some circumstances individual employees may sue to enforce them under Section 301 of Taft–Hartley. See *Smith v. Evening News Ass'n*, 371 U.S. 195 (1962). (Just what circumstances provide the individual employee with standing is an issue on which the courts have given only limited guidance to date.) This suit can be maintained in state as well as federal court. See *Charles Dowd Box Co. v. Courtney*, 368 U.S. 502 (1962). A state court, however, is required to apply federal law. *Local 174, Teamsters v. Lucas Flour Co.*, 369 U.S. 95 (1962). One major condition that an employee must satisfy before she can bring an individual suit to enforce a collective agreement is that the collectively bargained grievance and arbitration procedures be exhausted first. See *Republic Steel Corp. v. Maddox*, 379 U.S. 650 (1965); *Clayton v. Automobile Workers*, 451 U.S. 679 (1981). This does not make the individual's right to sue illusory, however, because the union owes each represented employee a "duty of fair representation." This duty obligates the union to handle individual grievances in a fair way, not arbitrarily or capriciously. If the union breaches this duty in handling a grievance, the employee is free to sue under Section 301. See *Vaca v. Sipes*, 386 U.S. 171 (1967). Under these circumstances, the court has jurisdiction to hear the breach of contract claim, either before or after arbitration. It would be pointless to require the employee to exhaust arbitral remedies when the union is not willing to be the employee's advocate. Similarly, it would be unfair to require the employee to be bound by an arbitration award tainted by union's misconduct. If a court finds that a worker's damages flow both from an employer's breach of the collective agreement and the union's breach of the duty of fair representation, liability may be shared by both. *Bowen v. United States Postal Service*, 459 U.S. 212 (1983).

A union need not pursue every grievance to arbitration, but it may not refuse to pursue a claim merely at the whim of someone exercising union authority. It may refuse to process the grievance of an uncooperative employee who steadfastly neglects, fails, or refuses to provide either the union or the employer information material to a grievance. See *Hicks v. J.H. Routh Packing Co.*, 95 L.R.R.M. 2814 (N.D.Ohio 1977). It may not, however, refuse to process a grievance because the employee who has filed the grievance is not a union member. See *Miranda Fuel Co.*, 140 NLRB 181 (N.L.R.B.1962), enforcement denied on other grounds, 326 F.2d 172 (2d Cir.1963). The union is not required to investigate exhaustively the merits of a grievance when its initial investigation shows sufficient justification for the employer's actions. A union may withdraw or refuse to arbitrate a grievance after the grievant rejects a negotiated settlement without breaching a fair representation duty. It need not process an employee's grievance if the chances for success in arbitration are minimal. A union is obligated to carry a meritorious grievance only to the point at which further action would be fruitless. See *Stanley v. General Foods Corp.*, 508 F.2d 274 (5th Cir.1975). The financial impact of the arbitration cost on the union's treasury may also be considered, although there is some doubt whether a decision not to arbitrate based solely on economic considerations would not constitute a breach. See *Curth v. Faraday, Inc.*, 401 F.Supp. 678 (E.D.Mich. 1975). As a general rule, mere errors in union judgment are insufficient to support a claim for breach of the duty, see *Ade v. Johnson Controls, Inc.*, 831 F.2d 293 (6th Cir. 1987), and a union's good faith representation at an arbitration hearing may moot an earlier alleged unfair representation in the grievance procedure. See *Crenshaw v. Allied Chemical Corp.*, 387 F.Supp. 594 (E.D.Va.1975).

(v) Effect of Enforcing Rights Under Collective Agreement on Enforcing Other Legal Claims

The preceding paragraphs emphasize some of the ways in which the rights of individual employees are enhanced by the presence of a union and the existence of a collective agreement. There is, however, a possibility that in some instances these additional rights must be balanced against a loss of state law protection. In *Allis–Chalmers Corp. v. Lueck*, 471 U.S. 202 (1985), an employee sought damages for bad faith handling of an insurance claim. The benefit program involved had been set up under the authority of a collective bargaining agreement, and that agreement required prompt fair disposition of claims. Since the court trying the bad faith claim would necessarily turn to the collective agreement in order to determine the scope of the employee's rights, the Court held that the state law cause of action was pre empted by Section 301. The employee must pursue the arbitration remedy. This restriction on court jurisdiction applies, however, only if the interpretation of a collective agreement is necessary, not if the agreement might provide a parallel remedy. In *Lingle v. Norge Div'n of Magic Chef, Inc.*, 486 U.S. 399 (1988), the Court refused to preempt an employee's action for damages for termination in retaliation for filing a workers' compensation claim. An applicable collective agreement also provided that employees could be terminated only for cause, the Court noted, but the court trying the abusive termination claim would not find it necessary to interpret the collective agreement.

A question that has troubled lower courts in recent years is whether an employee in a unionized workplace may lose the right to pursue statutory claims against an employer by seeking relief on the same facts through a grievance system. In *Alexander v. Gardner–Denver Co.*, 415 U.S. 36 (1974), a black employee filed a grievance claiming he had been wrongfully terminated. In the ensuing arbitration proceeding, the arbitrator held the grievant had been terminated for cause, poor work performance. The grievant subsequently brought an action under Title VII of the Civil Rights Act of 1964, alleging race discrimination. The lower federal courts awarded summary judgment to the employer, based on the outcome of the grievance procedure, but the Supreme Court reversed, stating:

> the federal policy favoring arbitration of labor disputes and the federal policy against discriminatory employment practices can best be accommodated by permitting an employee to pursue fully both his remedy under the grievance arbitration clause of a collective bargaining agreement and his cause of action under Title VII. The federal court should consider the employee's claim de novo. The arbitral decision may be admitted as evidence and accorded such weight as the court deems appropriate.

A similar result was reached in a case allowing employees to pursue an overtime pay claim under the Fair Labor Standards Act (FLSA) after a contract overtime claim was resolved against them in arbitration. *Barrentine v. Arkansas–Best Freight System, Inc.*, 450 U.S. 728 (1981). Seven years later, the Court held that this result still holds under the language of the arbitration clauses in the majority of collective bargaining agreements at that time. *Wright v. Universal Maritime Service Corp.*, 525 U.S. 70 (1998). The *Wright* collective bargaining agreement provided that its grievance procedure was "intended to cover all matters affecting wages, hours, and other terms and conditions of employment." This language was not sufficiently explicit to waive the individual union employee's right to litigate an Americans with Disabilities Act claim outside the grievance procedure, particularly where additional language provided that "[a]nything not contained in the Agreement shall not be construed as being part of this Agreement." In 2009, however, a five-justice majority held that language in a collective agreement so clearly called for arbitration of individual statutory claims through the grievance process, that access to the courts was foreclosed. *14 Penn Plaza LLC v. Pyett,* 129 S.Ct. 1456 (2009). How broadly that decision will affect future bargaining over grievance clauses remains to be seen.

e. Railway Labor Act

Nearly a decade before it passed the National Labor Relations Act, the Congress enacted the Railway Labor Act (RLA). 45 U.S.C.A. §§ 151–188. The federal government had been deeply involved in the regulation of railroads since the era of the Civil War. During the First World War, major railroads were put under federal control, and maintaining railroad service without major interruptions from strikes was a significant objective. After the railroads were restored to private management, a number of labor disputes arose; many resulted in significant disruptions of rail service, and this had a disturbing impact on the national economy. Both railroad management and union leaders realized that steps had to be taken. The RLA's provisions were agreed upon in advance through private negotiations between the carriers and the interested unions. Little change was made by the Congress in the version it enacted in 1926 from what the parties had agreed. The RLA's emphasis is on the peaceful settlement of labor disputes. "Major disputes" over the content of collective agreements were to be resolved by negotiation, but with the help of federal mediators. "Adjustment boards" were to be established by agreement of the carriers and employee representatives to settle "minor disputes" such as differences over contract interpretation and appropriate working conditions. The statute was upheld as constitutional in 1930. *Texas & New Orleans R.R. Co. v. Brotherhood of Railway Clerks*, 281 U.S. 548 (1930).

Section 2 of the RLA imposes a duty on both sides to exert "every reasonable effort to make and maintain agreements concerning rates of pay, rules, and working conditions * * *." Id. § 152. To assist the parties, a Board of Mediation was established. The board was empowered to use mediation to assist the unions and the carriers in the event of a breakdown in their negotiations. The mediation board was not to impose a settlement, but could encourage the parties to submit their differences to final and binding arbitration. If these techniques did not result in a settlement, the mediation board was empowered to notify the President if the dispute threatened severely to disrupt interstate commerce, and the President could then appoint an "emergency board of investigation" to consider and report on the dispute within thirty days. Neither party was allowed to change the conditions out of which the dispute arose for an additional thirty days following the making of the report. Thereafter, the parties were free to resort to economic warfare to settle their differences.

The provisions requiring that the status quo be maintained for as much as sixty days represented a substantial concession on the unions' part. In return, labor obtained a guarantee against interference by the railroads in the process of union organization. The RLA declared that the representatives of parties to railway disputes should be designated "by the respective parties in such manner as may be provided in their corporate organization or unincorporated association, or by any other means of collective action, without interference, influence or coercion exercised by either party over the self organization or designation of representatives by the other."

As time went on, certain defects in the RLA became increasingly apparent, particularly to organized labor. In 1934, substantial amendments were enacted. First, in an effort to eliminate the device of the "company union" controlled by the employer, the 1934 amendments declared it unlawful for carriers to use their funds to assist company unions or to induce their employees to join such unions. Second, to resolve employer challenges to the capacity of union representatives seeking to negotiate, the National Mediation Board (successor to the earlier Board of Mediation) was given the added task of conducting elections or using other appropriate methods to determine which union was desired by the employees. Third, both because some carriers and their unions were never able to agree on how to establish a board of adjustment for that carrier's system, and also in order to eliminate the disparities that developed among different grievance adjustment boards across the nation, Congress in 1934 created the National Railroad Adjustment Board (NRAB). 45 U.S.C.A. § 153 First. The purpose of the NRAB is to resolve grievances over the meaning of collective bargaining agreements. It is composed of representatives selected by the carriers and an equal number chosen by the employees, and is divided into four separate divisions, each having jurisdiction over different occupations. An individual as well as a union may take a "minor dispute" to the NRAB. Decisions of the board were made enforceable by the winning party in the federal district courts. Creation of the NRAB did not bring an end to system boards of adjustment, however. A carrier, or group of carriers, and one or more unions may agree voluntarily to create such a grievance handling board if they wish. 45 U.S.C.A. § 153 Second. That power was clarified and extended in 1966 to allow the parties to establish what are commonly called "public law" boards of arbitration. 45 U.S.C.A. §§ 157–159a.

The RLA was extended in 1936 to air carriers as well as railroads. There is one major difference between the treatment of railroads and airlines, however. The jurisdiction of the NRAB does not extend to airlines, which are required under section 204 to establish their own boards of adjustment. The decisions of these boards may be reviewed in federal court; the law to be applied is federal law, similar to that developed under section 301 of the

Taft–Hartley Act. *See International Association of Machinists v. Central Airlines*, 372 U.S. 682 (1963).

f. Impact of Federal Arbitration Act

The Federal Arbitration Act, 9 U.S.C.A. § 1, et. seq., is not a labor relations law as such. Arbitration under the Taft–Hartley Act is governed by principles developed under section 301 of that statute; the work of "boards of adjustment" is regulated by provisions of the Railway Labor Act. In recent years, however, cases decided outside the unionized workplace context have raised questions about how doctrines developed under the FAA might interact with those developed under these labor relations laws. In 1991, the Supreme Court decided that outside the collective bargaining context, a non-union employee can waive the right to judicial review of statutory claims. The plaintiff in *Gilmer v. Interstate/Johnson Lane Corp.*, 500 U.S. 20 (1991) was required by the defendant, his employer, to register as a stockbroker with the New York State Exchange. The registration application included an agreement to arbitrate whenever required to do so under the Exchange's rules, one of which provides for arbitration of employment disputes. The Court held that this agreement was enforceable under the Federal Arbitration Act, so that he must submit a claim under the Age Discrimination in Employment Act to binding arbitration. In *Gilmer*, the Court did not reach the question of how to interpret a provision in the FAA exempting from its scope "contracts of employment of seamen, railroad employ-

ees, or any other class of workers engaged in foreign
or interstate commerce * * *." A closely divided
Court later held in *Circuit City Stores v. Adams*,
532 U.S. 105 (2001) that this language exempts only
employment contracts of employees in transportation, doubtless including many railroad and airline
workers. (A curious footnote in *Gilmer* states that
the issue was not presented because the agreement
to arbitrate in Gilmer appeared in a stockbroker
registration form not in a "contract of employment." Any implication that a contract of employment must be a single document is clearly inadver-
tent, and obviously inconsistent with *J.I. Case Co.*)
For further discussion of mandatory arbitration of
statutory claims by nonunion employees, see Chapter 9.

2. State Regulation

Roughly a score of states have adopted private
sector labor statutes more or less similar to the
National Labor Relations Act (NLRA). Where a
state statute is patterned after the NLRA's language, decisions under the NLRA may offer guidance in interpreting it. See *Ronnie's Bar, Inc. v.
Pennsylvania Labor Relations Board*, 411 Pa. 459,
192 A.2d 664 (Pa.1963). These statutes have been
held constitutional as an exercise of the state's
police power. They do not unreasonably interfere
with property rights or freedom of contract, deprive
employees of their right to a jury trial, or constitute
special legislation regulating labor. The scope of
operation for these laws is limited, since the NLRA

preempts state laws with respect to employers over whom the National Labor Relations Board (NLRB) exercises jurisdiction. Under the Supreme Court's *Garmon* decision, states may not regulate conduct arguably protected by the NLRA's Section 7 or prohibited by Section 8. *San Diego Building Trades Council v. Garmon (Garmon II)*, 359 U.S. 236 (1959). As discussed above, the Court's decision in *Machinists Lodge 76* also forbids state regulation of conduct the Congress has chosen to leave "to be controlled by the free play of economic forces," such as peaceful partial strikes. *Machinists, Lodge 76 v. WERC*, 427 U.S. 132 (1976). Thus the range of state regulation is largely limited to employers—mostly small firms—over whom the NLRB has chosen not to exercise jurisdiction (see 29 U.S.C.A. § 164(c)) or over whom it has no power because of exclusions from the NLRA, such as agricultural labor (see *Harry Carian Sales v. Agricultural Labor Relations Board*, 39 Cal.3d 209, 216 Cal.Rptr. 688, 703 P.2d 27 (Cal.1985)).

D. PUBLIC SECTOR REGULATION

1. Federal Employees

Until the 1960s there had been little legislation affecting public employee labor relations. The National Labor Relations Act (NLRA) has always exempted federal, state, and local government employees from its provisions. State statutes did little more than prohibit strikes or collective bargaining by these persons and provide stiff penalties for violations.

The federal government itself for many years did little to encourage employees to develop a collective attitude. Enactment of the Pendleton Act of 1883, commonly known as the Civil Service Act, gave employees their first incentive for one sort of collective action. This law placed in the hands of Congress the sole authority to regulate wages, hours and other working conditions, with the result that federal workers developed the practice of Congressional lobbying.

The right of certain federal employees to join labor organizations was implicitly recognized in 1912, when Congress enacted the Lloyd–La Follette Act to allow employees of the postal service to join unions. When President John F. Kennedy took office in 1961, he appointed a six member task force to look into the question of employee-management relations. The result of the study was Executive Order 10988 issued on January 17, 1962. The order specifically recognized the right of employees of the administrative branch of the government to organize and to present their collective views on employment terms to agency management. Organization rights and the privilege of negotiating on employment terms were given added strength by the issuance of a new order by President Nixon on October 29, 1969. Under Executive Order 11491 the entire program of employee management relations was placed under the supervision of a Federal Labor Relations Council. A panel was also established to aid in the resolution of negotiation impasses and to resolve the impasse in those instances where the parties were unable to do so.

Congress passed the Federal Service Labor–Management and Employee Relations Law as part of Title VII of the Civil Service Reform Act of 1978. 5 U.S.C.A. §§ 7501–7504, 7511–7514. This Act states that unionization and collective bargaining by federal employees is in the public interest, and grants statutory protection to federal employee bargaining rights to safeguard that interest and to facilitate "amicable settlements" over conditions of employment. The Act grants rights to "employees" of the federal executive branch who are employed by an agency or who have ceased to work for any agency because of unfair labor practices and have not yet obtained substantially equivalent employment. The Act excludes non citizens who work outside the United States, armed forces personnel, supervisors, management officials, certain members of the Foreign Service, and any person who participates in an illegal strike. An agency may be excluded from the Act by Presidential order if it is determined that the agency's primary function is investigative and the provisions of the Act cannot be applied consistently with national security considerations.

The statute established several new agencies to perform both new tasks and also functions that had previously belonged to the old Civil Service Commission. The three principal new bodies are the Office of Personnel Management, the Merit Systems Protection Board, and the Federal Labor Relations Authority. The Act also created the Federal Service

Impasses Panel which may take a variety of steps to resolve an impasse in negotiations between an agency and the representative of its workers.

The Office of Personnel Management (OPM) functions essentially as the Human Resource agency of the federal government, what would once have been called a "personnel department." It performs a myriad of functions, such as administering the health benefit programs for federal workers, and advising agencies on how to implement such programs as early retirement plans, and so on.

The Merit Systems Protection Board (MSPB) performs the old "appeals" functions of the Civil Service Commission. It hears cases brought by individual employees as well as by the Special Counsel (an independent office spun off from MSPB in 1989), challenging agency actions and practices as inconsistent with the merit systems principles set out in the Act. Judicial review of MSPB decisions is limited, most often conducted under an "arbitrary and capricious" standard. See *United States Postal Service v. Gregory*, 534 U.S. 1 (2001).

The Federal Labor Relations Authority (FLRA) enforces the collective rights provisions of the Act. It determines appropriate units for union representation, conducts elections to determine exclusive representatives for appropriate units, determines whether an agency is obligated to bargain over matters which are the subject of agency rules or regulations, hears other negotiability appeals and prescribes criteria in order to resolve these and other issues relating to the duty to bargain in good faith. Resolving just how broad the duty to bargain may be has proved a challenging task. The Supreme Court has upheld FLRA determinations that an agency must engage in bargaining during the term of a collective agreement, and must at times bargain about wage structures (even though the total amount of the wages to be paid by the agency is not negotiable). See *National Federation of Federal Employees, Local 1309 v. Department of the Interior*, 526 U.S. 86 (1999) (5–4); *Fort Stewart Schools v. FLRA*, 495 U.S. 641 (1990). The Court overturned the FLRA's determination that a range of contracting out decisions were subject to bargaining. *Department of the Treasury, IRS v. FLRA*, 494 U.S. 922 (1990). It hears unfair labor practice cases prosecuted by a General Counsel whose duties are akin to those of the National Labor Relations Board's General Counsel.

A number of practices are prohibited by the Act and they generally parallel the types of prohibited activities under the NLRA. An agency must remain neutral in dealing with employees concerning their organizational activities. Agencies may not refuse to consult or negotiate in good faith with a union or refuse to cooperate in impasse decisions. Nor may an agency enforce a new regulation which conflicts with a prior bargaining contract provision or fails to comply with the Act. One provision gives federal employee unions the right to be present at investigative interviews, similar to the rights private sector employees enjoy under the *Weingarten* decision.

5 U.S.C.A. § 7114(b)(2)(B). The right extends only to interviews by a representative of the employing agency, however, not to interviews by federal law enforcement personnel. An Inspector General's office within an agency constitutes an agency representative for this purpose. *NASA v. FLRA*, 527 U.S. 229 (1999).

After the General Counsel has issued an unfair practice complaint, the FLRA may petition a U.S. district court for temporary relief. Once the Authority has established probable cause that an unfair practice is being committed, a court can grant temporary relief it considers just and proper, but cannot order relief which would interfere with the ability of an agency to carry out its essential functions. Final orders of the FLRA are subject to review in a federal court of appeals, although final orders involving bargaining unit determinations or arbitrator's awards, other than unfair practice awards, are not subject to judicial review. 5 U.S.C.A. § 7123(a).

Unions which are recognized by federal agencies must be free of corrupt influences and influences opposed to basic democratic principles. A union need not prove that it is free from this influence if it is subject to explicit and detailed governing requirements, but must prove its freedom from corrupt or antidemocratic principles when there is a reasonable cause to believe that it has been subjected to sanctions by a parent organization or federation for failing to comply with basic democratic governing requirements.

Federal sector unions must not interfere with employee rights; attempt to cause agency management to coerce an employee in the exercise of his or her rights; or refuse to consult or negotiate in good faith. Any employee who meets reasonable union eligibility requirements in the representative unit must be accorded membership in the exclusive representative if the employee seeks this membership. It is unlawful for a union to fail to cooperate in impasse procedures or to refuse to comply with the provisions of the Act. Calling, participating, or condoning a strike, work stoppage or slowdown of an agency in a labor management dispute is an unfair practice. If a union intentionally engages in this action, the FLRA must revoke its exclusive recognition status or take other appropriate disciplinary action.

Exclusive recognition may be granted only after an election in which a union has been selected by a majority of the employees in an appropriate bargaining unit. The union not only bargains for all unit employees, but also represents employees regarding their grievances and, at an employee's request, at examinations which could lead to disciplinary action against the employee. National consultation rights may be accorded to unions holding exclusive recognition for a "substantial number" of an agency's employees where no union has been designated exclusive representative on an agency wide basis. Employees are guaranteed the right to refrain from membership without fear of reprisal. Union dues deductions are allowed under the Act and may not be revoked for a period of one year except when the employee is suspended or expelled from the union or ceases to be represented under the contract.

In reaching a collective bargaining agreement, the exclusive representative of the appropriate unit and an agency have a duty to meet and negotiate in good faith. The agency is obligated to furnish the exclusive representative with any reasonably available data that it maintains in the regular course of business and which is necessary to the negotiating process and the parties must execute a written agreement reflecting the agreed to terms before implementing the contract. A bargaining agreement between an exclusive representative and an agency is binding when it has been approved by the head of the agency, or when it has not been approved or disapproved within 30 days of its execution. It must conform with applicable laws.

Bargaining agreements must provide a procedure for the consideration of grievances. The Act provides that the representative may present a grievance on behalf of an employee or group of employees, and also that any employee may present a grievance and have it adjusted without intervention by the exclusive representative, although the exclusive representative must have an opportunity to be present at the adjustment. The final step of the negotiated grievance procedure must be binding arbitration. However, arbitration may only be invoked by the exclusive representative or management. 5 U.S.C.A. § 7121.

There are critical differences between the enforcement of these awards and those in the private sector. Arbitral awards in many federal government employment cases are subject to review by the FLRA; the NLRB has no comparable power. Moreover, an objecting party may challenge the award both on grounds "similar to those applied by Federal courts in private sector" cases and also because the award "is contrary to any law, rule or regulation." 5 U.S.C.A. § 7122.

One reason for the broader scope of review of arbitration awards in the federal service is that an employee is required by the Act to choose between arbitration as a remedy and other administrative remedies established to enforce: (1) 5 U.S.C.A. § 2302(b)(1), prohibiting discrimination based on race, color, religion, sex, national origin, handicap, marital status or political activity; (2) 5 U.S.C.A. § 4303, providing for rights of appeal by a person an agency proposes to demote or fire for poor performance; and (3) 5 U.S.C.A. § 7512, requiring that adverse actions against federal employees be taken "only for such cause as will promote the efficiency of the service." Arbitral awards dealing with allegations of discrimination subject to 5 U.S.C.A. § 2302(b)(1) may be reviewed at the request of the employee either by the EEOC or the MSPB (a successor to much of the work of the former Civil Service Commission). 5 U.S.C.A. § 7121(d). Arbitral awards involving agency decisions to which 5 U.S.C.A. §§ 4303 or 7512 would apply are subject to judicial review. The reviewing court is to treat the award as if it were a final decision of the MSPB. See 5 U.S.C.A. §§ 7121(f), 7703. Clearly, the Congress is seeking substantive consistency in cases of employee challenge to agency action, no matter what remedial route has been chosen. An arbitrator may not overturn agency disciplinary action because of procedural errors unless those errors resulted in substantial prejudice to the employee. *Cornelius v. Nutt*, 472 U.S. 648 (1985).

2. State and Local Government Employees

Beginning in 1959 with a municipal employee relations law in Wisconsin, one state after another has decided that public employees should have collective bargaining rights (with limitations) and that some sort of statutory regulation of this bargaining is necessary. Currently some 25 states and the District of Columbia have collective bargaining statutes covering most, if not all, public employees. Another nine or ten states have laws granting bargaining rights to some public employees, but not to others.

State and local government employees are excluded from the National Labor Relations Act (NLRA) and there is no uniform federal policy on union management relations in the public sector. There are, however, federal constitutional limits on the content of state public sector labor relations laws. In *Abood v. Detroit Board of Education*, 431 U.S. 209 (1977), rehearing denied, 433 U.S. 915 and *Lehnert v. Ferris Faculty Association*, 500 U.S. 507 (1991), the Court upheld most provisions of a Michigan statute that awarded exclusive representation rights to a union supported by a majority of workers in a bargaining unit and permitted the union to collect agency fees from non members if represented. The Court struck down, however, provisions that would allow the union to charge non members for activities such as lobbying or the support of candidates for political office. To require these contributions would infringe first amendment rights. More recently, the Court has upheld a statute that bans a public sector union from using a payroll deduction system to collect monies the union will use for political activity. *Ysursa v. Pocatello Education Association*, 129 S.Ct. 1093 (2009).

Government workers generally still do not enjoy the same full scope of collective rights guaranteed their counterparts in the private sector. A few states permit strikes by specified occupational groups, and California has held that the state lacks the power to ban totally strikes that pose no threat to public health or safety. See *County Sanitation District No. 2 v. Los Angeles County Employees Ass'n*, 38 Cal.3d 564, 214 Cal.Rptr. 424, 699 P.2d 835 (Cal.1985). As a general rule, however, the right to strike still is prohibited. Instead of that right, state statutes usually provide for mediation, fact finding, and arbitration in various forms and combinations as the means to deal with bargaining impasses. Also, relatively few public sector unions enjoy the protection of a union security clause. Only a few states explicitly permit a union shop, and sometimes only for certain occupations, such as

firefighters (Ky.Rev.Stat. 345.050(1)(c)) or university workers (Me.Rev.Stat.Ann. §§ 1021–1035). An
additional group permit lesser forms of union security such as an agency shop clause (sometimes
called a "fair share" clause) or a maintenance of
membership clause. Pa. Stat. Ann. tit. 43,
§§ 1101.301(18), 1101.705, 1102.1–1102.9.

State representation procedures generally are
similar to those provided for the private sector by
the NLRA. Public employers may recognize unions
voluntarily or the union may petition for an election
upon a sufficient showing of interest in an appropriate bargaining unit. A state board will define the
scope of the unit, direct the election and certify the
results. Except in the case of teachers in some
states, a union will be certified as the exclusive
representative of unit employees.

Most states follow the NLRA in providing for unit
separation of professionals and nonprofessionals,
guards and workers who do not share a sufficient
community of interest. One major difference between the federal statute and many state laws is the
protection afforded to units of supervisors by the
latter. The supervisors are not included in the same
unit as rank and file personnel, but they are often
allowed to form their own unit. In Pennsylvania,
and other states, organization rights are restricted
to so called "first level supervisors" with a right to
"meet and discuss." Pa. Stat. Ann. tit. 43,
§ 1101.704.

CHAPTER 9

EMPLOYMENT LAW REMEDIES
A. INTRODUCTION

This Chapter reviews briefly the most common remedies that either an employee or an employer can obtain as a consequence of an employment dispute. It also discusses factors that may limit or affect the damages recovered or other remedies available. The chapter serves as a supplement to the discussions of specific remedy problems found in other chapters, and also as a general background for those discussions.

A successful claimant, whether suing at common law or under a statute, must consider what remedies are available, and sometimes must makes choices among them. The most common remedies are:

- damages remedies, including "compensatory" and "punitive" damages;
- restitutionary remedies;
- affirmative relief, sometimes referred to as "coercive remedies" or "equitable remedies"; and
- declaratory remedies.

The "damages" remedy is an award of money, intended usually to compensate for losses, but occasionally to punish a defendant for particularly blameworthy conduct. "Restitution" may or may not involve a money recovery. Its principal aim is usually to prevent unjust enrichment and so is concerned more with how much a wrongdoing defendant has gained than with how much a wronged defendant has lost. The most common example of "affirmative (or equitable) relief" is an injunction that is enforced by the court's contempt power. "Declaratory" remedies appear in various forms; as the name implies, these remedies are often concerned with stating what the law is, as it applies to the situation of a particular employee and employer.

Occasionally a statute will also provide for civil penalties, payable usually to a government agency, and for criminal penalties.

B. REMEDY AND DAMAGE THEORIES: THE PURPOSES OF REMEDIES

1. Common Law Tort Remedies

Tort concepts that previous chapters have discussed include such wrongs as physical injury, invasion of privacy, defamation, false imprisonment, intentional infliction of emotional distress, fraudulent misrepresentation, intentional interference with contractual relations, blacklisting, or public policy violations. Remedies for these torts are intended to "make the victim whole," and thus the most important factor to be considered is how much loss the plaintiff has suffered as the direct, natural, and proximate consequences of the defendant's wrongful act. See RESTATEMENT (SECOND) OF TORTS § 903 (1979). We generally refer to these monetary awards as "compensatory damages." Unless punitive or exemplary damages are awarded, no other recovery may generally be obtained. Such damages awards are not intended to include compensation for remote, uncertain, or speculative injuries. The damages must be the proximate consequence of the injury and not a secondary result. Proximate consequences of an act or omission are those that follow naturally without any outside or independent force intervening. They are the consequences that might reasonably have been expected. Remote damages are the unusual and unexpected result, not reasonably anticipated over which no control exists. Where malice, wantonness, or willfulness are present, however, a responsible employee or employer can be held liable for the injuries caused, even though they are beyond the natural and apprehended results. Proximate consequences for willful or malicious acts are those that might have been reasonably expected or foreseen, even though outside and independent forces intervene. It is not necessary that the activity be wanton to impose liability for all resulting injuries. Intention can be considered in assessing damages.

Measuring the loss suffered is sometimes fairly easy. A wrongfully discharged employee can show the amount of wages she has lost with fair precision in many cases, by showing what those earnings had been the last few months prior to being fired. If an

employer has harassed a worker so much that he
has sought psychiatric help, the amount of the
doctors' bills can be put into evidence. Other losses
are not so easy to quantify. What price should we
put on the humiliation associated with being wrongfully labeled a liar or a cheat or a whore in front of
other workers? How much is privacy worth? State
and federal courts alike have wrestled with these
questions long and hard, and have devised jury
instructions designed to aid triers of fact in finding
sensible answers, but inevitably there is an element
of personal judgment in all of this that simply
cannot be eliminated.

2. Other Common Law Remedies

As earlier chapters have shown, each party to an
employment relationship owes the other contract
based duties. The relationship itself is contractual
in nature, even though finding the terms of the
contract will often be a challenge. Oral promises,
written promises in documents labeled "employment contract", collective bargaining agreements,
pledges in restrictive covenants, promissory language in employment handbooks and policies are all
possible sources of claims of breach. There are a
number of "implied" promises involved in many
employment relationships also, such as an employee's duty of loyalty.

Breaches vary in importance. What remedy is
appropriate may well depend upon the extent of the
failure to perform. A breach may be minor or it may
be total. It may involve only one of several promised

performances or be a total repudiation of the entire agreement—past and future.

Traditionally, the goal in awarding contract damages is to provide an amount that will place the employee or the employer in as good a position as he would have occupied had the contract been fully performed. This gives the successful employee or employer the "benefit of the bargain" had the contract's performance occurred. Courts often speak in this connection of "expectation" damages. To the extent that anticipated gains were reasonably foreseeable and can be proven with reasonable certainty, recovery is based upon those anticipated gains. A popular news broadcast personality agrees to work for a television network; the network sells advertising based on that person appearing on its programs. The newscaster refuses to perform. The advertisers cancel. Lost advertising revenues clearly would be an appropriate item of damages. Or suppose a worker quits one job in order to take a different job he was promised by a prospective employer. The employee shows up to go to work and the new employer declines to take him on. Anticipated wages should clearly be an item of damages.

Sometimes, when the time sequence makes it feasible, it may be possible for a court to use a form of equitable remedy instead of (or in addition to) expectation damages. "Specific performance" is the traditional phrase associated with these remedies, but in a wrongful discharge or wrongful refusal to hire case it is likely to take the form of a reinstatement order, and thus is a kind of "cease and desist" injunction. When an employee refuses to perform, another sort of injunction may be used: an order preventing others from using the worker's services. Consider the television news broadcaster, for example. If she refuses to work for Channel Six as she had promised, that station may seek an order preventing her from working for Channel Seven. Injunctions are also sometimes used against former employees to enforce covenants not to compete.

Sometimes, however, affirmative relief is not possible and expectation damages are either not adequate as a measure of harm, or the benefit that can be expected is too hard to measure, too "speculative," to permit a court to use that approach. In such cases, courts may award what are sometimes called "reliance" damages, either instead of or in addition to expectation damages. Consider a worker that quits a job in one state and moves family and belongings to the location of the new job she has been promised. If the prospective employer fails to perform, then the worker may well be entitled to expenses associated with the move.

Restitution involves a benefit conferred upon (or seized by) the wrongdoer. Suppose a former employee divulges a trade secret in order to please a new employer. In a case of that sort, the profits lost by the former employer may not be adequate compensation. Suppose, for example, that the former employer was a relatively small firm, and the trade secret the formula for a new product with which the former employer hoped to enter new markets and expand. At the time the trade secret was revealed, however, that expansion had only begun, and predicting how successful the business plan would be is difficult. The new employer, however, is a dominant firm in the market the former employer wants to enter. By using the "secret formula" the new employer makes its dominant position in the market even stronger. In such a case, a court is likely to award to the former employer an amount that represents the extra profits the wrongdoing new employer has enjoyed because the former employee revealed the secret. See *Colgate–Palmolive Co. v. Carter Products, Inc.,* 230 F.2d 855, 864 (4th Cir. 1956).

Declaratory judgment actions are rare in employment law, but the remedy is available for those cases in which both parties want to continue in a contract relationship but cannot agree on the meaning of the documents they have executed, and require an outside source to tell them what the employment contract means, and how one or more common law or statutory rules may affect performance under the contract. In recent years, it has become much more common to use a form of alternative dispute resolution process for this purpose, either mediation or arbitration.

3. Statutory Remedies

Most employment law statutes provide explicitly what remedy is appropriate for that statute's violation. These remedies may include back pay, front pay, benefits, reinstatement, attorneys' fees, civil penalties, restitution, and so on. Many statutory remedies are ordinarily administrative, but like other administrative remedies they may receive judicial enforcement. The orders of the National Labor Relations Board, and the civil penalties and abatement orders authorized by OSHA fall into this category. Others, like the remedies under Title VII of the Civil Rights Act of 1964, are essentially "judicial," although at times they may be awarded in arbitration. The purposes underlying statutory remedies vary, as one would expect, according to the nature of the statute. Remedies for violations of wage and hour laws are largely "make whole" in nature, designed to put into the worker's hands the money he or she should have been paid in the first place. Those statutes will provide for interest, or in the case of private actions to enforce the federal law, a doubling of the monetary award. 29 U.S.C.A. § 216(b). A particularly important objective of discrimination law remedies is captured in the phrase "rightful place theory." The idea is to try to determine what sort of situation a worker would be in had not discrimination caused her to be denied a particular job or promotion. The purpose of abatement orders under OSHA is relatively clear: to make the work site a safer place to be. The civil penalty remedy implies that the general public good has been affected in some way by operating a business in a way that puts workers into jeopardy. A fair number of statutes also provide criminal penalties for violations that are regarded as particularly serious offenses.

C. REMEDIES AVAILABLE ONLY TO EMPLOYEES OR PROSPECTIVE EMPLOYEES

1. Back Pay

The most common remedy in cases of wrongful discharge, refusal to hire, or failure to promote is that the employee is entitled to recover back pay. This is generally the difference between the compensation the employee would have earned in the job she was denied and the amount that the employee earned, or that she reasonably could have earned in the same community. See *Frank B. Hall & Co., Inc. v. Buck*, 678 S.W.2d 612 (Tex.App.1984), cert. denied, 472 U.S. 1009 (1985).

Back pay awards generally reflect total earnings and can include overtime, shift differentials, and premium pay in addition to straight time pay. Raises and likely promotions have also been included in back pay awards where it can be inferred clearly that the employee would have received them. See, e.g., *Pecker v. Heckler*, 801 F.2d 709 (4th Cir.1986); *Saunders v. Claytor,* 629 F.2d 596 (9th Cir.1980), cert. denied, 450 U.S. 980. That the employment was "at will" is not a bar to the award of damages. *Haddle v. Garrison,* 525 U.S. 121 (1998).

2. Front Pay

Unlike back pay, which compensates the employee for prior lost earnings, front pay concerns a future earnings expectancy that has been lost or diminished. In fair employment practice litigation, front pay has been deemed particularly appropriate when no other means is available to put the employee in his or her "rightful place." It has been awarded when there was no vacancy available to which the employee could be immediately promoted, or when reinstatement was neither feasible nor advisable. *Williams v. Pharmacia, Inc.*, 137 F.3d 944 (7th Cir.1998); *Fadhl v. City & County of San Francisco*, 741 F.2d 1163 (9th Cir.1984). Front pay may be denied when the employee would no longer have been employed or if the employee is no longer seeking employment. It is most common in cases based on statutes, but may also be awarded in wrongful termination litigation. See *Kempfer v. Automated Finishing*, 211 Wis.2d 100, 564 N.W.2d 692 (Wis.1997).

3. Fringe Benefits

Fringe benefits can be recovered if the employee can establish (a) that these benefits would have been received (i.e., are not "speculative") and (b) that their loss flows naturally from the injury. See *Panhandle Eastern Pipe Line Co. v. Smith*, 637 P.2d 1020 (Wyo.1981). Fringe benefits that have been recovered include: stock options, meal allowances, severance pay, life insurance benefits, medical insurance, bonuses, commissions, sick pay, vacation pay, pension and retirement benefits, uniform cleaning allowances, travel allowances, temporary housing allowances, savings plan contributions, and job search expenses.

4. Reinstatement

Reinstatement is the employee's restoration to his or her former position after termination, layoff, leave of absence, or a strike. It offers the means to restore the status quo lost through employment loss.

Historically, courts resisted granting an employee reinstatement through a specific performance remedy against an employer unless a statute specifically permitted it. Until recently, a large number of courts have held that a reinstatement order was not a proper remedy for a "personal services" contract breach. See *Zannis v. Lake Shore Radiologists, Ltd.*, 73 Ill.App.3d 901, 29 Ill.Dec. 569, 392 N.E.2d 126 (Ill.App.1979); *Louisville & Nashville R.R. v. Bryant*, 263 Ky. 578, 92 S.W.2d 749 (Ky.1936). They indicated that the common law did not permit forcing an employee by court order to work for a particular employer or forcing an employee to continue in the employment of a particular employer. Eventually, for most courts, it has become clear that the way around this problem is to phrase the remedy as a "cease and desist" order, requiring (for example) a wrongdoing employer to refrain from refusing to employ or from refusing to promote the plaintiff for an improper reason.

Today, reinstatement is a frequently used remedy under most federal and state employment law statutes. For example, both the National Labor Relations Act [29 U.S.C.A. § 160(e)] and the Civil Rights Act of 1964 (Title VII) [42 U.S.C.A. § 2000e–

2–3] afford a strong reinstatement remedy. Likewise, under collective bargaining agreements, reinstatement has been found to be a viable remedy by arbitrators. See, e.g., *Aeroquip Corp.*, 95 Lab.Arb. (BNA) 31 (Stieber, Arb.) (1990). It may be awarded with full, partial, or no back pay.

Reinstatement and back pay together constitute a major sanction for enforcement of the federal and state employment law statutes and for violations arising under collective bargaining agreements. It can be argued that nothing is as effective as awareness of this pair of remedies to discourage an employer's arbitrary, spurious, or capricious termination of an employee. The employer is always aware that it may have to reinstate the employee and pay for lost time in addition to enduring the trouble and expense of arbitration, an administrative proceeding, or a court action unless the termination is justified. This awareness provides a substantial incentive to seeking settlement. On the worker's side, there is also awareness of the possibility that the case may be lost. If the employer does not want a plaintiff employee back under any circumstances, and the employee is interested not so much in the job itself but in a monetary award and possibly some restoration of reputation or dignity, prospects for negotiating a settlement should be good. If the employee wants reinstatement, however, and the employer is adamantly opposed to that, settlement negotiations are much more likely to fail. Sometimes, an employer decides it is willing to have the plaintiff employee as part of its workforce.

If the employer makes an unconditional offer of reinstatement to an employee and the employee rejects the offer, without a good reason, the employer's liability for back pay from the reinstatement offer's date is extinguished. See *Fair v. Red Lion Inn*, 943 P.2d 431 (Colo.1997). If the refusal is reasonable, that is not the case. *Xiao–Yue Gu v. Hughes STX Corp.*, 127 F.Supp.2d 751 (D.Md.2001).

D.   REMEDIES AVAILABLE TO BOTH EMPLOYEES AND EMPLOYERS

1.   Injunctions

An injunction is an in personam order, directing the employee or the employer to act or to refrain from acting in a specified way. It is a powerful remedy that may be enforced by a court's contempt power so that the disobedient employee or employer may be jailed, fined, or deprived of the right to litigate issues. Traditionally in some American jurisdictions an equity court had jurisdiction only to enforce or protect property rights. It did not have jurisdiction where solely personal rights were involved. See *Corliss v. E.W. Walker Co.*, 57 Fed. 434 (C.C.D.Mass.1893).

Today, it is generally accepted that equity jurisdiction may be exercised in appropriate instances for personal right protection. This has occurred when nonsmoking employees have obtained injunctions to enforce their rights to a safe and healthy workplace. See, e.g., *Smith v. Western Elec.*, 643 S.W.2d 10 (Mo.App.1982). Employers have used this remedy to enforce restrictive covenants. *Padco Advisors, Inc. v. Omdahl*, 185 F.Supp.2d 575 (D.Md. 2002).

A court will not order an employee to perform services for the firm that worker promised to work for, but will from time to time prohibit a worker from going to work for a competitor of that firm. *Boston Celtics v. Shaw*, 908 F.2d 1041 (1st Cir. 1990).

2. Punitive Damages

Punitive (sometimes termed "exemplary") damages may be recovered for employment claims in many states, despite the fact that such damages are not often allowed in breach of contract actions, and that many employee claims can be thought of as claims of breach of contract. As one court has put it, such claims are appropriate when the breach "is attended by intentional wrong, insult, abuse, or such gross negligence as to [constitute] ... an independent tort." *Willard v. Paracelsus Health Care Corp.*, 681 So.2d 539 (Miss.1996).

Good faith or its absence, mistake, evidence of consent, or of lack of consent are all matters that can be considered in assessing or withholding punitive damages. The Supreme Court has held that there are constitutional limits to the amount of punitive damages that can be assessed, and has articulated three factors that play in deciding when the constitutional limit has been exceeded: (1) the reprehensibility of the defendant's conduct; (2) the relationship between compensatory damages and punitive damages; and (3) what civil or criminal sanctions could be applied to similar misconduct. *State Farm Mut. Automobile Ins. Co. v. Campbell*, 538 U.S. 408 (2003); *BMW of North America, Inc. v. Gore*, 517 U.S. 559 (1996); *IUOE Local 150 v. Lowe Excavating Co.*, 225 Ill.2d 456, 312 Ill.Dec. 238, 870 N.E.2d 303 (2006). In a number of jurisdictions, punitive damages must bear some relation to actual damages, while in others they are recoverable even though no actual damages are awarded. See *Callantine v. Staff Builders, Inc.*, 271 F.3d 1124 (8th Cir.2001).

3. Attorneys' Fees

In the United States, the general rule is that the prevailing party in litigation is not entitled to recover attorneys' fees unless (1) a contract provides for them (See, e.g., *Leventhal v. Krinsky*, 325 Mass. 336, 90 N.E.2d 545 (Mass.1950)) or (2) a statute authorizes this recovery. Among the employment law statutes that provide for attorneys' fees are the Civil Rights Act of 1964 (Title VII), the Age Discrimination in Employment Act (ADEA), the Vocational Rehabilitation Act of 1973, and Sections 1981, 1983, 1985, and 1986. 29 U.S.C.A. §§ 626(b), 794a(b) (1994); 42 U.S.C.A. §§ 1988, 2000e–5(k). Only a party who obtains a judicial remedy that results in a change in legal rights and obligations is entitled to recover fees. *Buckhannon Board and Care Home, Inc. v. West Virginia Dep't of Health and Human Resources*, 532 U.S. 598 (2001). Attorneys' fees may also be permitted as an element of punitive damages under common law litigation theories in some states. See *Brewer v. Home–Stake Production Co.*, 200 Kan. 96, 434 P.2d 828 (Kan. 1967); contra, *International Electronics Co. v. N.S.T. Metal Products Co.*, 370 Pa. 213, 88 A.2d 40 (Pa.1952).

4. Liquidated Damages

Occasionally the parties to an employment contract will not want to leave to the courts (or an arbitrator) the question of what monetary remedy is proper in case of breach. They will insert into the contract of employment a "liquidated damages clause," spelling out what each party must pay the other in the event of failure to perform. While judges are generally not enthusiastic about such clauses, the courts will enforce them unless the amount set as damages seems so out of proportion to likely actual damages that the clause functions as a penalty. *Ashcraft & Gerel v. Coady*, 244 F.3d 948 (D.C.Cir.2001).

The term is also used from time to time in statutes, usually to indicate that a multiplier is to be applied to the "actual" damages proved. *Jarrett v. ERC Properties, Inc.*, 211 F.3d 1078 (8th Cir. 2000) (FLSA); *National Shopmen Pension Fund v. Burtman Iron Works, Inc.*, 148 F.Supp.2d 60 (D.D.C.2001) (ERISA).

E. REMEDY AWARD LIMITATIONS

1. The Duty To Mitigate Damages

An employee seeking damages for an employment claim involving back pay, front pay, and fringe benefits has an affirmative duty to mitigate damages. Although the employee need not go into another line of work, accept a demotion, or take a demeaning position, damages may be forfeited if a substantially equivalent job is refused or reinstatement is rejected. See, e.g., *Ford Motor Company v. EEOC*, 458 U.S. 219, 231–32 (1982) (offer of reinstatement without grant of seniority may cut off further liability). A court has broad discretion in determining the reasonableness of an employee's mitigation efforts when calculating damages. See *Albemarle Paper Co. v. Moody*, 422 U.S. 405 (1975).

The usual sequence in proving loss of wages damages is for the plaintiff to prove (a) the amount of time during which she received no wages or improperly low wages from the defendant, and (b) the wage rate at which she should have been compensated. This establishes the prima facie amount to which the employee is entitled for this portion of her remedy. Then it is for the employer to establish that the employee did not act reasonably to mitigate damages. See *Hanna v. American Motors Corp.*, 724 F.2d 1300 (7th Cir.1984). To satisfy its burden, the employer must show that: (1) the employee's damage could have been avoided, i.e., that there were suitable positions available that could have been discovered for which the employee was qualified;

and (2) the employee failed to use reasonable care and diligence in seeking other employment. *Sias v. City Demonstration Agency*, 588 F.2d 692 (9th Cir. 1978).

Whether an employee's efforts to mitigate are adequate involves assessing a number of factors, such as the employee's education, experience and job skills. *Yancey v. Weyerhaeuser Co.*, 277 F.3d 1021 (8th Cir.2002). Job market characteristics also matter. *Stone v. D.A. & S. Oil Well Servicing, Inc.*, 624 F.2d 142 (10th Cir.1980). The employee need not seek employment that involves conditions that are substantially more onerous than those of the previous position. See *NLRB v. Madison Courier, Inc.*, 472 F.2d 1307 (D.C.Cir.1972). Excessive commuting distances are considered an unreasonable requirement in mitigating damages. See, e.g., *Rasimas v. Michigan Dept. of Mental Health*, 714 F.2d 614, 624–26 (6th Cir.1983), cert. denied, 466 U.S. 950 (1984).

2. Limits on Availability of Equitable Remedies

Equitable remedies originated in England under the supervision of the Chancellor, and for historical reasons a number of conditions developed that a petitioner has to meet in order to be entitled to this relief. One example is the principle that an injunction will not be issued if the party seeking it has an "adequate remedy at law." In the employment context this translates into a situation in which "ordinary" workers are treated differently from exceptional ones. In a well known case from the 1960s, a judge in Ohio held that a professional athlete, at least one in the major leagues in basketball, football and baseball, is so unusually skilled that once he has agreed to play for a particular team, that team is entitled to an injunction to prevent him from playing for any other team. The court would have denied the injunction, the opinion indicates, had the employee not had such exceptional skill, since an action for damages would have been an adequate remedy. *Central New York Basketball, Inc. v. Barnett*, 181 N.E.2d 506 (Ohio Com.Pl.1961). An injunction should also be denied unless the likely harm to the petitioner seeking the order if it is not granted exceeds the likely harm to the respondent if the injunction is granted. This crops up in the context of suits to enforce covenants not to compete. Enforcement of such a covenant can, in some cases, significantly restrict a former employee's chance to make a reasonable living. There is a good chance such an agreement would be held invalid, or at least that an injunction to enforce it would be denied. Finally, there is a doctrine that states that equitable relief is available only to a party with "clean hands." Courts differ on how this is to be applied. In *New York Football Giants v. Los Angeles Chargers Football Club*, Inc., 291 F.2d 471 (5th Cir.1961), the court denied relief to a professional football team because the team seeking the injunction had signed the player while a college senior and had kept it quiet, knowing that the signing meant the player was likely to violate NCAA rules. In

Houston Oilers, Inc. v. Neely, 361 F.2d 36 (10th Cir.1966), another federal court had no problem granting an injunction, finding that the professional team owed no duty to the NCAA. Another federal court granted an injunction to a professional football team to prevent a college from hiring away its coach, disagreeing with the university's claim that it was entitled to the benefit of the Eleventh Amendment. *New England Patriots Football Club, Inc. v. University of Colorado*, 592 F.2d 1196 (1st Cir. 1979).

3. Deductions, Caps and Offsets

Whether compensation received in lieu of earnings should be treated as interim earnings and deducted from back pay awards has not been resolved uniformly in employment litigation. These deductions and offsets generally involve unemployment compensation and workers' compensation benefits.

A few statutes place "caps" on the amount that can be awarded for a particular category of damages. Probably the best known example appears in the 1991 amendments to the Civil Rights Act, limiting the amount of damages available against smaller employers. 42 U.S.C.A. § 1981a(b)(3).

Under the Civil Rights Act of 1964 (Title VII), courts disagree regarding whether unemployment compensation benefits should be deducted from back pay awards. *Bowe v. Colgate–Palmolive Co.*, 416 F.2d 711 (7th Cir.1969) (deduction allowed as within discretion of trial court); *Craig v. Y & Y*

Snacks, Inc., 721 F.2d 77 (3d Cir.1983) (deduction not allowed); *Quint v. A.E. Staley Manufacturing Co.*, 172 F.3d 1 (1st Cir.1999). The Supreme Court has held that under the National Labor Relations Act (NLRA) unemployment compensation benefits may be treated as collateral compensation and need not be deducted. *NLRB v. Gullett Gin Co.*, 340 U.S. 361 (1951). Both Title VII and the NLRA permit deduction of workers' compensation benefits that represent wage compensation. See *Canova v. N.L.R.B.*, 708 F.2d 1498 (9th Cir.1983) (NLRA); *McLean v. Runyon*, 222 F.3d 1150 (9th Cir.2000) (Title VII).

4. Tax Considerations

Employee litigation may involve claims that the employers' actions violated a statute, breached an express or implied contract, or constituted a tort. Frequently, employee litigation alleges a combination of these different recovery theories. The damages recoverable may not be similar. For example, a contractual theory may limit the employee's recovery to actual loss or back pay, while a tort theory may award punitive damages far in excess of any back pay recovery. Likewise, the tax treatment may vary.

From the employee's perspective, the general rule governing employment litigation is that amounts received as contract damages for lost wages are taxable income. See *Hodge v. Commissioner*, 64 T.C. 616 (Tax Ct.1975). This reflects a general philosophy that damage awards that are in

lieu of payments that would have been taxable—
like wages—are themselves taxable. However, until
a 1996 amendment, amounts received as tort damages for "personal injury" were excluded from taxable income under section 104(a)(2) of the Internal
Revenue Code. See *Seay v. Commissioner*, 58 T.C.
32 (Tax Ct.1972). Under that language, a good
many awards in employment cases have been
found not to be subject to tax, since they did not
represent back pay. Damages received from most
fair employment practice litigation were, however,
generally found taxable since until 1991 no "general" damages were available under Title VII, so that
the majority of these awards represented lost
wages. See *United States v. Burke*, 504 U.S. 229
(1992). Two developments have now clouded the
picture. In 1991, 42 U.S.C.A. § 1981a was enacted,
making compensatory and punitive damages available to Title VII plaintiffs who demonstrate that a
defendant acted with "malice or with reckless indifference to the federally protected rights of an individual." In 1996, the Congress amended Internal
Revenue Code § 104(a)(2) to exclude only amounts
received "on account of personal physical injuries."
A damage award for wrongful invasion of privacy is
not for physical injury; it also does not represent
lost wages that would have been taxed. What may
the successful employee claimant now exclude from
the income she reports on her 1040? The better
result would seem to be that the general "in lieu
of" philosophy was not affected by the 1996
amendment, but one can also argue that that

amendment indicated a Congressional desire that more awards be taxable. The lower federal courts have had considerable trouble applying the Supreme Court's approach to these cases, which emphasizes the "origin of the claim." *O'Gilvie v. United States,* 519 U.S. 79 (1996); see *Murphy v. Internal Revenue Service,* 493 F.3d 170 (D.C. Cir. 2007), cert. denied, 128 S.Ct. 2050 (2008).

For employers, the general rule is that payments resulting from employment litigation are deductible as ordinary and necessary business expenses, without regard to whether they were made for personal injuries. However, employers should be aware that payments made for "non personal" injuries (now perhaps non personal physical injuries) may be subject to federal income tax and social security withholding requirements for all or a portion of the recovery, if it constitutes taxable employee income.

F. ALTERNATIVE DISPUTE RESOLUTION

In 1991, the Supreme Court held in *Gilmer v. Interstate/Johnson Lane Corp.,* 500 U.S. 20 (1991) that an employee could not sue his employer for age discrimination, but must take the matter to binding arbitration. A broadly worded agreement to arbitrate disputes between the worker and his employer had been included in a registration form the employee was required to sign in order to become a broker entitled to use the New York Stock Exchange. Ever since, more and more courts and employers have supported the resolution of employment disputes through arbitration for nonunion employees. A majority of federal and state courts hold that agreements to arbitrate statutory discrimination claims and other workplace employment disputes are valid so long as the nonunion employee does not waive any rights or remedies under the statutes and the arbitral process is fair. See, e.g., *In re Prudential Insurance Co.*, 133 F.3d 225 (3d Cir. 1998) (insurance agents must submit their RICO-based dispute to arbitration); *Rojas v. TK Communications, Inc.*, 87 F.3d 745 (5th Cir.1996) (female disc jockey whose employment contract required arbitration of "any other disputes" must submit sexual harassment, retaliation, and constructive discharge claims to arbitration); *Patterson v. Tenet Healthcare*, 113 F.3d 832 (8th Cir.1997) (employee's federal and state law discrimination claims are required to be arbitrated under employment handbook's procedure). One lingering area of doubt about whether such agreements could be enforced was how the Supreme Court would treat language in the Federal Arbitration Act exempting some employment contracts from the statute's coverage. Those doubts were resolved in *Circuit City Stores, Inc. v. Adams*, 532 U.S. 105 (2001) in which a five-justice majority held that the Act applies to all categories of employment contracts except those of transportation workers.

In recent years, nonunion employers have increasingly sought the benefits of alternative dispute resolution (ADR) procedures, which contain final and binding arbitration, to resolve employment related claims. ADR offers the advantages of decreased litigation costs, minimized back pay awards due to quicker resolution of employee termination claims, removal of cases from high-risk jury trials, and a private proceeding not open to the public. An increasing number of employers have therefore required job applicants and current employees to agree to arbitrate both statutory and contract claims, rather than take the matters into court. It is important to an employer that arbitration be mandatory, and that it be final. From an employer's perspective, an arbitration agreement in the employment contract would be much less attractive if at the time the employee became upset with some employer action, the employee could opt to go to court instead of, or in addition to, using the arbitration forum. As discussed in earlier chapters, unionized employees who lost wage and hour claims and discrimination claims in collectively bargained arbitration procedures have often been able also to seek relief in court.

The Equal Employment Opportunities Commission (EEOC) for a time spearheaded a backlash against the use of mandatory arbitration of federal discrimination claims. Equal Employment Opportunities Commission, *Policy Statement on Mandatory Binding Arbitration of Employment Discrimination Disputes as a Condition of Employment* (July 10,

1997). The EEOC has taken this position despite the fact that there is substantial support in the courts for enforceability of these agreements. The agency makes the following arguments as to why arbitration agreements should not be imposed as a condition of employment:

- Courts are responsible for the development and interpretation of the law, emphasizing, e.g., the importance of precedent and the development by the courts of doctrines such as disparate impact.

- The public nature of the judicial process enables higher courts, Congress, and the public to ensure that laws are properly interpreted and applied.

- Courts play a crucial role in preventing and deterring discrimination and making discrimination victims whole.

- Mandatory binding arbitration is structurally biased against applicants and employees because:

  a. discovery is limited;

  b. arbitration is not suited to address class claims involving a pattern or practice;

  c. the employer is a repeat player; and

  d. the terms are dictated by the regulated party.

- It adversely affects the EEOC's ability to enforce employment discrimination law; i.e., it deters employees from filing charges with the EEOC.

The EEOC, however, strongly supports post-dispute agreements to mediate and/or arbitrate because it recognizes that ADR may save time and expense. In fact, a large amount of new funds granted by the EEOC in its fiscal year 1999 budget went to support ADR, specifically voluntary mediation.

In *Equal Employment Opportunity Commission v. Waffle House*, 534 U.S. 279 (2002), the Supreme Court held that an executory agreement to arbitrate future disputes, executed by an employee when he accepted employment, did not bar the EEOC from seeking to enforce the Americans with Disabilities Act on his behalf, including seeking specific relief for that particular employee. Whether an individual who seeks to intervene in a proceeding initiated by the EEOC may be required to arbitrate has been a troubling issue on which lower federal courts are not unanimous. See the discussion in *E.E.O.C. v. Woodmen of World Life Ins. Soc.*, 479 F.3d 561 (8th Cir. 2007).

Many questions remain about what standards an arbitration agreement must meet before a court should order a reluctant worker to pursue the arbitration remedy instead of going to court.

First, of course, there must be an agreement. Occasionally, a court has found an alleged agreement to arbitrate so vague or difficult to understand that it ought not to be enforced. *Prudential*

Ins. Co. v. Lai,, 42 F.3d 1299 (9th Cir.1994). Another court, however, found essentially the same language clear enough to justify ordering arbitration. *Kidd v. Equitable Life Assurance Society*, 32 F.3d 516 (11th Cir.1994). If an agreement states that the arbitrator is to decide the validity of the agreement itself, the courts must step aside and permit the arbitrator to do that. *Preston v. Ferrer,* 128 S.Ct. 978 (2008). A five-justice majority have now held that such a promise may be found in a collective bargaining agreement. See *14 Penn Plaza LLC v. Pyett,* 129 S.Ct. 1456 (2009).

There is also a question about the extent to which a worker may challenge an agreement because it is unconscionable under state law. The Ninth Circuit has held that the Federal Arbitration Act does not preempt state law doctrines on this matter. *Circuit City Stores, Inc. v. Adams*, 279 F.3d 889 (9th Cir. 2002) (on remand from Supreme Court). It refused to enforce an agreement that it found to be too much a one-way street, requiring the employee to arbitrate matters, but leaving the employer free to decide whether to arbitrate its claims or to sue the worker.

There are also basic standards that flow from the Federal Arbitration Act itself. In his opinion in *Gilmer*, Justice White listed certain features of the New York Stock Exchange rules that seemed to promise the rudiments of fair play. He pointed specifically to rules prohibiting biased panels; rules providing for at least rudimentary discovery through ''document production, information requests, depositions, and subpoenas"; and a requirement that decisions be public and written and include at the least a summary of the issues and a description of the award. Soon after that decision, several of the more important institutions concerned with arbitration formed a coalition to discuss how arbitration of public law claims by employees should be conducted. One result was a 1995 document known as the Due Process Protocol, available on the web site of the National Academy of Arbitrators and reprinted in a number of journals. It addresses such matters as the right to representation by an attorney, qualifications of arbitrators, insuring arbitrator neutrality, and procedures for discovery.

Courts have refused to enforce arbitration clauses for a variety of reasons. In *Hooters of America v. Phillips*, 173 F.3d 933 (4th Cir.1999), enforcement was denied because the worker could choose arbitrators only from a panel pre-selected by the employer. Several opinions have focused on whether the arbitration clause puts too many costs on the employee beyond what the employee would have to bear in court. *Shankle v. B–G Maintenance Management*, 74 F.E.P. Cas. (BNA) 94 (D.Colo.1997), aff'd, 163 F.3d 1230 (10th Cir.1999); *Cole v. Burns International Security Services*, 105 F.3d 1465 (D.C.Cir. 1997). Arbitration clauses that limit an employee's ability to call and examine witnesses are likely to be struck down. *Cheng–Canindin v. Renaissance Hotel Associates*, 50 Cal.App.4th 676, 57 Cal.Rptr.2d 867 (Cal.App.1996).

Each of the Supreme Court decisions from *Gilmer* on has emphasized that arbitration is a reasonable alternative to a court only if the arbitrator will apply the same substantive law and be able to grant the same remedies as would be true in court. Employer attempts to cut back on remedies will invalidate an agreement. *Trumbull v. Century Marketing Corp.*, 12 F.Supp.2d 683 (N.D.Ohio 1998). So are agreements that limit the range of what a worker may recover. *McCaskill v. SCI Management Corp.*, 285 F.3d 623, 88 F.E.P. Cases (BNA) 705 (7th Cir.2002).

The Federal Arbitration Act, 9 U.S.C.A. §§ 1–16, provides only limited grounds for judicial review. (fraud, corruption, serious arbitrator misconduct, evident prejudice, acting in excess of the powers granted to the arbitrator(s) are the principal ones). In *Hall Street Associates, LLC v. Mattel, Inc.*, 128 S.Ct. 1396 (2008), the Court held that the parties cannot by their agreement expand this scope of review. The lower federal courts are in disagreement about whether an arbitrator's award should be set aside for "manifest disregard of the law." See the review in *Citigroup Global Markets, Inc. v. Bacon*, 562 F.3d 349 (5th Cir. 2009).

INDEX

References are to Pages

561

PREGNANCY
See Discrimination in Employment

RECORDS
See also Invasion of Privacy (Privacy Act)
Medical records, 169–171
OSHA requirements, 287–292

REMEDY CONCEPTS
See also Attorneys' fees, Damages
Back pay, 539
Contract breach, 534–537
Declaratory judgments, 537
Equitable remedy conditions, 548–550
Fringe benefits, 540
Front pay, 539–540
General concepts, 531–532
Injunctions, 543–544
Punitive damages, 544–545
Reinstatement, 541–543
Statutory remedies, 537–538
Tort, 532–534

RESTRICTIVE COVENANTS and DUTIES OF LOYALTY, 88–100

RETALIATION
See Discrimination in Employment

SEXUAL ORIENTATION
See Discrimination in Employment

SMOKING, 198–203

SOCIAL SECURITY PROGRAMS
Disability benefits, 315–316, 321, 354–363, 370–371
Old age benefits, 459–467

SURVEILLANCE, 485–488

TERMINATION OF EMPLOYMENT
See also At-will Employment, Restrictive Covenants, Unemployment Compensation, Worker Adjustment and Retraining Notification Act
Constructive termination and quits, 77–78
Good cause for discharge, 71–77

TITLE VII OF THE CIVIL RIGHTS ACT OF 1964
See Discrimination in Employment

†